AURAL CULTURES

National Library of Canada Cataloguing in Publication Main entry under title:

Aural Cultures / Jim Drobnick, editor. Includes a CD of artists' sound works. Includes bibliographical references.

ISBN 0-920397-80-8
1. Sound in art. 2. Arts, Modern—20th century.
I. Drobnick, Jim
NX650.S68A97 2004   700
C2003-907041-7

Graphic Design
Associés libres
www.associeslibres.com

Printed in Canada
Kromar Printing Limited

Distribution
ABC Art Books Canada
www.ABCartbookscanada.com

Cover Image
Su-Mei Tse, *Echo*, 2003. Still from video projection. Courtesy the artist and Fondation Musée d'Art Moderne Grand-Duc Jean.

Note from the publisher: Every reasonable effort has been made to contact the holders of copyright for images, audio, and texts reproduced in this anthology. The publisher will gladly receive information that will enable errors or omissions to be rectified in subsequent editions. Permissions and credits continued on pages 286-287.

YYZ Books

Interim Managing Editor
Sally McKay

Director of Operations
Jeffrey Matt

Board Liaisons
Scott Sørli, Justin Waddell, and Si Si Peñaloza

Publishing Intern
Aubrey Reeves

Copy Editor
Lorissa Sengara

YYZ Books is an alternative press dedicated to publishing critical writings on Canadian art and culture. YYZ Books is associated with YYZ Artists' Outlet, an artist-run centre that presents challenging programs of visual art, film, video, performance, lectures, and publications.

YYZ Artists' Outlet is supported by its members, the Canada Council for the Arts, the Ontario Arts Council, and the city of Toronto through the Toronto Arts Council.

YYZ Artists' Outlet gratefully acknowledges the support of the Canada Council for the Arts for our publishing program.

YYZ Books
401 Richmond Street West
Suite 140
Toronto, Ontario M5V 3A8
www.yyzartistsoutlet.org

Walter Phillips Gallery Editions

Anthony Kiendl
Director, Walter Phillips Gallery and Visual Arts

Melanie Townsend
Curator, Walter Phillips Gallery

A collecting, commissioning, and presenting institution for contemporary art, the Walter Phillips Gallery has forged a strong record in creating professional development opportunities for cultural workers. In keeping with its mandate to provide meaningful dialogue, the Gallery publishes brochures, catalogues, and anthologies that expand its exhibition program and contribute to a larger discourse on curatorial and artistic practice.

Walter Phillips Gallery Editions
The Banff Centre
Box 1020
107 Tunnel Mountain Drive
Banff, Alberta T1L 1H5
www.banffcentre.ca/wpg

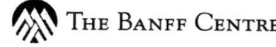

THE BANFF CENTRE

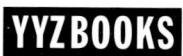

YYZBOOKS

Canada Council   Conseil des Arts
for the Arts   du Canada

AURAL CULTURES

edited by Jim Drobnick

YYZ Books | Walter Phillips Gallery Editions

TABLE OF CONTENTS

6   Acknowledgments

9   Jim Drobnick   Listening Awry

Arts of Listening

19   Richard Leppert   The Social Discipline of Listening

37   Peter L. Schmunk   What Did Van Gogh Hear?:
                                    Vibrations, Wagner, and Voices

49   Jennifer Fisher   Speeches of Display: Museum Audioguides by Artists

Artists' Pages

Santiago Sierra   62

Christian Marclay   64

Shirin Neshat   70

Su-Mei Tse   72

Martin Kersels   74

Kim Sooja   78

Bodies, Voices, Texts

83   Christof Migone   *Flatus Vocis*: Somatic Winds

96   Georgina Kleege   Voices in My Head

110   Sherry Simon   Accidental Voices: The Return of the Countertenor

120   Wes Folkerth   Tempaurality in *Twelfth Night*

127   Robert Bean   Polyphonic Aurality and John Cage

Susan Hiller with Mary Horlock   136

Raymond Gervais   146

Sound, Media, and the Environment

150   Philip Auslander   Looking at Records

157   Jodi Brooks   "Worrying the Note":
Inaudible Beats in the Gangsta Film

169   Gabor Csepregi   On Sound Atmospheres

179   Andra McCartney   Soundscape Works, Listening, and the Touch of Sound

Acoustic Hegemony and Contestation

189   Charles Hirschkind   Civic Virtue and Religious Reason:
An Islamic Counter-Public

208   Daniel Fisher   Local Sounds, Popular Technologies:
History and Historicity in Andean Radio

Ann Hamilton   218

Daniel Olson   222

Aurality and Alterity

229   Kanta Kochhar-Lindgren   Performing at the Edge of Hearing: The Third Ear

240   David Howes   Sound Thinking

253   Robert Desjarlais   Echoes of a Yolmo Buddhist's Life, in Death

271   Jim Drobnick   *Aural Cultures* Artists' Pages and CD

280   Notes on Contributors

286   Credits

ACKNOWLEDGMENTS

Aural Cultures could only materialize through a collaboration among a number of supportive individuals and institutions. At first a conference, then a publication, then an artists' residency and CD, and eventually an exhibition and performance project, it has evolved considerably over several years. I'd first like to thank all of the artists and authors for their thought-provoking and compelling contributions. Their explorations into the diverse practices of sound endow modernity's "secondary" sense with the fullest range of potentiality and significance.

It has been an honour to edit a publication under the auspices of YYZ Books and the Walter Phillips Gallery at The Banff Centre, institutions justly renowned for their innovative approach to art publishing in Canada. The efforts of the team at YYZ Artists' Outlet have been greatly appreciated. I am indebted to Jeffrey Matt, Director of Operations, Sally McKay, Interim Managing Editor, the YYZ board and publishing committee, and especially Scott Sørli, Justin Waddell, and Kym Pruesse for their devotion to professional integrity. Former directors of YYZ, Melony Ward and Dionne McAffee, embraced and ably oversaw *Aural Cultures* in its initial and middle stages. Anthony Kiendl and Melanie Townsend at the Walter Phillips Gallery added their support at a fortuitous moment so that this anthology could ultimately be realized. In 2005, the Walter Phillips Gallery will also sponsor a curatorial extension of *Aural Cultures,* an exhibition, performance event, and artist residency that will address the issues of sound, art, and society.

Five of the artists appearing on the CD participated in an audio residency sponsored by Charles Street Video, who kindly provided studio access and professional expertise. Greg Woodbury, CSV Operations Manager, served as residency director and Konrad Skrata offered technical support. Montreal-based new music composer Paul Dolden mastered the *Aural Cultures* CD and contributed invaluable acoustic advice.

All of the authors in *Aural Cultures* participated in the interdisciplinary conference "Uncommon Senses," held at Concordia University in April 2000. I'd like to thank my co-organizers of the conference, Jennifer Fisher, Constance Classen, and David Howes, as well as the presenters, attendees, and volunteers who made the conference such a success. In conjunction with the conference, DisplayCult curated an exhibition and performance series – "Vital Signs" and "Sentience" – at the Leonard and Bina Ellen Art Gallery, under the directorship of Karen Antaki. Funding for the conference was provided by the Social Sciences and Humanities Research Council of Canada through the Aid to Occasional Scholarly Conferences Programme, and by Concordia University, through Martin Singer, Dean of Arts and Science, and Frederick Lowy, Rector. Additional financial support for this publication was received from Christine Jourdan, Chair, Department of Sociology and Anthropology, and the Concordia University Part-Time Faculty Association.

I'm grateful to many individuals who gave constructive feedback, offered indispensable assistance, and graciously shared resources with me, such as Adad Hannah, Milada Kovácová, Paul Litherland, Cuauhtémoc Medina, Si Si Peñaloza, Aubrey Reeves, Kitty Scott, Brad Todd, Colette Tougas, William Wood, and Jessica Wyman, as well as the helpful staff at American Fine Arts, Peter Blum Gallery, Paula Cooper Gallery, Deitch Projects, Fondation Musée d'Art Moderne Grand-Duc Jean, Barbara Gladstone Gallery, Galeria Enrique Guerrero, Sean Kelly Gallery, Lisson Gallery, the Musée d'art contemporain de Lyon, and the Donald Young Gallery. It has been a pleasure to work again with the design team of Associés libres – Jennifer de Freitas and Rodolfo Borello – along with Oscar Varese, who have brought an inimitable sense of style and order to a disparate collection of materials.

A research fellowship at the Library of the National Gallery of Canada was invaluable during the early stages of this publication. Murray Waddington, Chief of the Library, Archives and Research Fellowship Program, Peter Trepanier, Head of Reader Services in the Library and Archives, and all of the library staff provided a welcoming and productive atmosphere. Funding by the Visual Arts Section of the Canada Council for the Arts greatly facilitated making time available for editing and administration.

Finally, I'd like to thank my partner, Jennifer Fisher. She's an everpresent inspiration in my life and work.

– JIM DROBNICK, NOVEMBER 2003

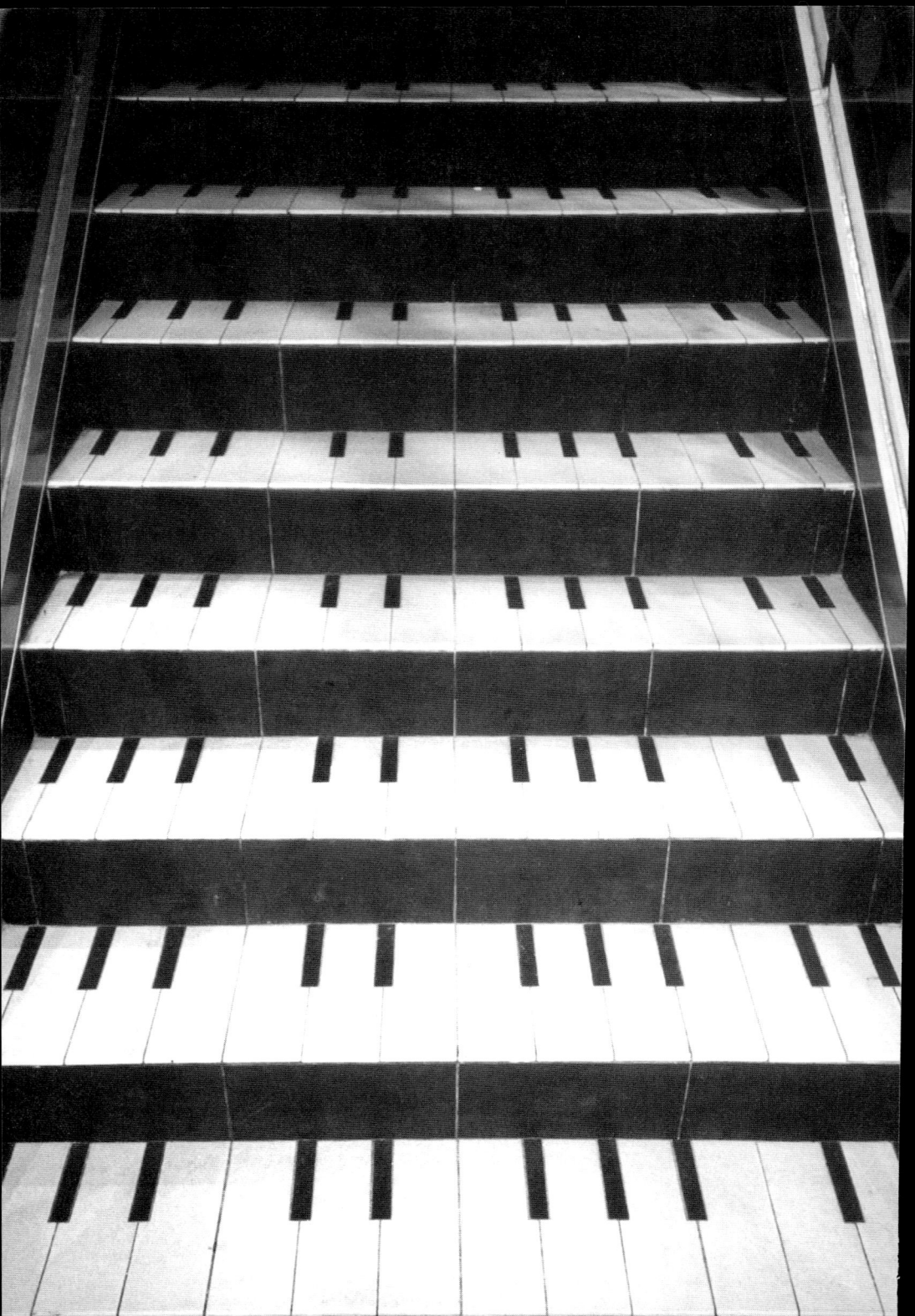

Listening Awry

Jim Drobnick

«listen»
The known world is a noisy ball.[1]
– Mystery Laboratory

In the autumn of 2003, two developments, a discovery and an invention, greatly expanded the realm of acoustic phenomena. Astronomers examining an immense black hole at the centre of the Perseus cluster of galaxies observed sound waves pulsing through its surrounding cloud of intergalactic gas – resounding a note with a ten million year period of oscillation, or a B-flat fifty-seven octaves below middle C.[2] At the opposite end of the scale, physicists at Cornell University aimed a laser at the strings of their newly created and nearly invisible nanoguitar, ten millionths of a metre in length, to play a note at forty million cycles per second, or seventeen octaves higher than the limits of human audibility.[3] Between these extremes of the nano- and cosmological levels lie about seven dozen octaves for attention and analysis, the "noisy ball" of the known world.

As the parameters of sound increase, so too does the diversity of its discourses. The last quarter century has witnessed the proliferation and maturation of sonic disciplines – from audio art and popular music studies to the philosophy of music and ethnomusicology, to name just a few – and it is quite conceivable now to assert that any discipline could profitably initiate one or more subdisciplines devoted to sound within its domain (consider Robert Desjarlais' call for an "anthropology of voice" in his text below). While this interest in sound has generated a profusion of scholarship, there nevertheless remains a tendency toward compartmentalization that separates rather than facilitates dialogue between disciplines. Such isolation was lamented by Barry Truax twenty years ago,[4] and its persistence today renews the need for more interdisciplinary efforts, like this publication, that seek to bring together disparate perspectives into the meanings and practices of sound. Because of its cultural and political complexities, "theoretical indiscipline" was the approach Jacques Attali advocated for anyone conducting research into sonic experience.[5] Such indiscipline is inevitable as sound theorists expand and rethink their disciplines' conceptual categories. Particularly symptomatic of this indiscipline is the number of neologisms reverberating within writing on sound. *Tempaurality, logic of echoes, the third ear, thunderdom* – these are only a few of the creative rhetorical strategies employed by writers in this volume to address the specificity of sound's characteristics. On a purely terminological level, these sonicisms demonstrate the generative capacity of engaging with aurality. As much as disciplines define and

Christian Marclay
Miami, 1996
From the ongoing photographic series *Snapshots*

attend to sonic phenomena, they are also liable to a reciprocal influence and to be reconfigured in the process.

Although an aural equivalent to "visual studies" has yet to become firmly established in the academy, there is nevertheless a distinct and vibrant "sonic turn" that can be discerned in the recent upsurge in sound-based scholarship and artistic work. A phrase such as "sonic turn" – referring to the increasing significance of the acoustic as simultaneously a site for analysis, a medium for aesthetic engagement, and a model for theorization – self-consciously echoes W.J.T. Mitchell's articulation of a "pictorial turn" a decade ago.[6] Making a claim for a sonic turn, like its pictorial predecessor, would depend upon several factors, not the least of which is the emergence of a critical mass of sound-inflected theory and art.[7] In just this anthology alone, authors are situated in a diversity of fields – performance studies, anthropology, art history, cinema studies, literary studies, philosophy, and cultural studies, among others – testifying to how the issue of sound resonates in cross-disciplinary analyses. As much as Mitchell asserts that *spectatorship* is as "deep a problem" as *reading*, and that pictures are not "fully explicable" within the paradigm of textuality,[8] it is equally valid to state that *listening* is as much of a problem and that sounds defy the explicatory powers of both image- and text-based theories. If the paradigm of the world-as-picture is incommensurate with the world-as-book, and demands a reconfigured set of methodologies, so too does the world-as-noisy-ball exceed these paradigms and raise its own slate of issues that require attention and theoretical analysis. Representation and interpretation, for example, are issues in which sound shares with pictures and text, yet sound reconfigures these very issues by inflecting representation with affect, and interpretation with embodiment. The act of listening is not an activity done remotely; it inevitably invokes corporeality, it envelops listeners, and, as several authors here remark, it resounds within the body. The types of "literacy" involved with listening are strikingly complex; they not only exceed but challenge the conventions of visual and textual models.

To postulate a sonic turn, however, is more than just a matter of adroitly exchanging one trope, one sense modality, for another. Sound bears a number of distinctive qualities, not only a temporal, dissipative dimension, but also an inherent performative and a social orientation. Most pertinent to this publication is the embeddedness of sound in cultural, political, and physical contexts. Contrary to the neo-modernist movement in contemporary audio art – in which soundworks foreground abstraction, perceptual effects, technological processes, and self-referentiality[9] – the essays and projects of *Aural Cultures* affirm a connectedness to the social. The nexus of sound, art, and culture is particularly rich and open to intervention, and the contributions here demonstrate sound's heterogeneous significance. Yet, however apparent sound's unique qualities may be, it is important to guard against essentializing sound as an autonomous realm. Many of the texts and artworks included here integrally link sound to the other senses, visual culture, technology, and various kinds of artifacts, and when the relation is not explicit, it often exists on an implicit level.

If what constitutes "the aural" is constantly being expanded, what constitutes "culture" is often openly contested. Given the breadth of disciplines presented here, it is not possible to work with anything but a polycentric definition of culture. Artistic, everyday, popular, and subcultural – the essays here delve into all aspects of culture, by any definition, unreservedly. Authors investigate the sound-related activities of filmmakers, concertgoers, artists, opera singers, "fartistes," radio broadcasters, and preachers. Among the subjects discussed are talking books, ambient noise, intercultural silence, deafness, abject sounds, aural obsessions, places with mystical musical powers, and the metaphysical ramifications of speech. These essays also discuss sonic contexts from around the world, including Egypt, Peru, Tibet, and Papua New Guinea. The artists in these pages and on the CD, likewise from a multitude of perspectives, have created works that deliberately contrast, confuse, or critique national geographies and high/low distinctions. Such eclecticism can hardly be considered comprehensive, yet it foregrounds the variegated ways in which sound manifests social status, corporeal affect, aesthetic experience, and political agency.

Before summarizing the texts in this anthology, as well as the artists' contributions in my concluding essay, I'd like to propose a means of sonic engagement that emphasizes dialecticalness and ethical agency – *listening awry*. My term transposes Slavoj Žižek's deft phrase, "looking awry," into the realm of hearing, yet retains the imperative to attend to things not straightforwardly, but from an angle, from an "interested" rather than objective perspective.[10] The many angles of approach in *Aural Cultures* offer the potential to find a number of reverberations between disciplines, methodologies, and sites. When hearkening to the clamour of this noisy ball, it must be remembered that listening is as much a learned behaviour as it is a perceptual function. We exist in a noisy ball, and we contribute to its racket; by listening awry we may also reflect upon the myriad meanings of murmurs and cacophony, and how the act of hearing is itself conscious, implicated, and subject to cultivation.

The first section, "Arts of Listening," examines how listening, despite its obvious physiological basis, is a practice inflected by cultural, historical, and contextual factors. The three authors here utilize the visual arts as both documentary evidence of the shifts in the etiquette of hearing and case studies in how it can be creatively reimagined or critiqued. Richard Leppert underscores that listening is a social act, one that invokes the materiality of the human body as well as the cultural and political environment. Focusing on paintings and graphic works from the eighteenth and nineteenth centuries, "The Social Discipline of Listening" elaborates on what the author considers to be a central paradox of music – the semiotic contradiction between the physical activity of its making and the abstraction and ephemerality of its experience. Through the figure and expressive freedom of the virtuosic performer, and the corresponding rapt attentiveness of the audience, Leppert inquires into the act of listening as one that combines the consumption of pleasure with a pedagogical imperative. In "What Did Van Gogh Hear?: Vibrations, Wagner, and Voices," Peter L. Schmunk teases out the relationship between music and painting, especially in the work of Van Gogh. Bearing more than just rhetorical importance, music served as a cognitive model for the painter (a Wagner enthusiast) because it indivisibly united form and content, and conveyed its affective experience without the need for representation or narrative. The paradigm of music was a conscious but subtle influence upon the artist's work, and an artistic ideal to which he aspired. Jennifer Fisher's "Speeches of Display: Museum Audioguides by Artists" investigates the discourse and function of museum audioguides. For institutions, the calm, authoritative voices featured in audioguides provide ceremonial support and confident opinions of an exhibition's artworks; when utilized by artists such as Sophie Calle, Andrea Fraser, and Janet Cardiff, however, audioguides interrogate and counter such listening presumptions. The author demonstrates how investing the audioguide with autobiographical, critical, and fictional elements foregrounds the ambivalency of interpretation, the museum's ethically conflictual power relationships, and unconventional sensory aesthetics.

"Bodies, Voices, Texts" presents essays in which vocalizations emerge from unlikely bodies and unconventional orifices, and explores how the voice resonates in literature and the act of reading. For Christof Migone the body is an irrepressible, chaotic, noise-producing entity. "*Flatus Vocis*: Somatic Winds" theorizes upon the volatile sounds emanating from the nether end of the digestive system. Impropriety and offensiveness are only the most obvious cultural registers of flatulence; through a survey of ancient and contemporary literature, anthropology, and social history, the author brings forward the relevance of farts to sex, death, entertainment, political critique, and the cycle of natural forces. Georgina Kleege's essay, "Voices in My Head," begins by questioning the assumption that listening to books on tape and reading them in print are different and incomparable. Combining recollections of being read to as a child, listening to public speakers, and interacting with voice-synthesizing technology, she details her challenges as a vision-impaired writer and teacher. Reading is often thought of as a silent escape from the clamour of the world, but her personal ruminations about interior monologues, the significance of pitch, timbre, and accent, and the voice's impact on mental imagery reveal the vibrancy and meaningfulness of spoken text. "Accidental Voices: The Return of the Countertenor," by Sherry Simon, pivots on the category-defying figure of the countertenor. The apparent mismatch between the male body and high-pitched voice caused consternation to audiences in the 1950s, who assumed a natural and fixed relationship between voice, gender, and sexuality. The countertenor's return to prominence not only sparked a revival of pre-Romantic vocal practices, such as that of the castrato, it also incited a shift in musical sensibility in which artificiality could be cultivated and the voice, regardless of its source, appreciated for its own sake. In Wes Folkerth's essay, "Tempaurality in *Twelfth Night*," literature offers compelling details about the history of acoustic experience. Shakespeare's plays, for instance, reverberate with sonic metaphors, examples, and analogies that provide clues about the meanings of sound and hearing in the Elizabethan age. Drawing out the links between music and nostalgia, and how subjective experience can be situated in time, he utilizes aural models to perceive extra layers of significance in one of the Bard's classics. The last text in this group, Robert Bean's analysis of John Cage's *Roaratorio*, is ultimately founded on another literary source, James Joyce's *Finnegans Wake*. The excessive word play and language deconstruction by Joyce is transformed by Cage's sonic exploration into dissonance and disorientation. "Polyphonic aurality" is the concept Bean develops to come to terms with this nonlinear and unconventional musical experience, recognizing that at the heart of Cage's (and Joyce's) transgressions lies a radical renewal of the act of listening.

The section "Sound, Media, and the Environment" brings forward connections and disjunctions between aurality, visuality, touch, and context. Philip Auslander's "Looking at Records" examines sound and its various forms of consumption and commodification. He senses a paradigm shift in the dematerialized way music will soon be distributed when satellite delivery systems become commercially viable, a technology that places into acute perspective the materialization of sound in objects such as LPs and CDs. Evaluating Situationist theorization of the spectacle via the specifics of sonic phenomena, the author proposes that the visual may serve as a site of resistance against alienated listening. While the soundtrack is film's most apparent aural dimension, Jodi Brooks's essay, "'Worrying the Note': Inaudible Beats in the Gangsta Film," discerns rhythmic practices in actors' gestures, editing, and pacing that significantly contribute to cinematic meaning. Singling out the genre of the gangsta film, she describes its prominent ability to summon the "spectatorial ear." The genre's use of syncopation, sampling, repetition, and suspended or elided beats has connections to jazz and African American literature, and forms a distinct means of structuring narrative time and experience. Gabor Csepregi addresses the affective qualities of sound, especially as it has become an inescapable insertion into the spaces of public and private life. His essay, "On Sound Atmospheres," analyzes contemporary "decibel culture" with its "perpetual sound-matrix" and how it exerts power over the activities and sensibilities of individuals within it. The immersive environment of sound created by background music and ambient noise makes silence a rare occurrence, and the author points out some of the psychic and cognitive effects of such continual envelopment. Andra McCartney's essay surveys the history and intentions of soundscape practitioners, especially the work of Hildegard Westerkamp. Engaging with and evoking a place's sonic qualities involve more than just documenting particular rustlings and reverberations – the technology of recording and amplification can also be utilized to intensify the awareness of touch and engage the entire body. Such works fuse tactility with sound, adding a kinaesthetic dimension as well as a sense of the soundscaper's presence for listeners to experience.

Mass technologies are often critiqued for being susceptible to propagandistic uses and serving the interests of domination. The essays in "Acoustic Hegemony and Contestation" recognize this power, yet also consider the role of recording and broadcast media to cultivate dissent and enfranchisement. In Charles Hirschkind's "Civic Virtue and Religious Reason: An Islamic Counter-Public," the production and consumption of audiocassette sermons in Egypt yield insights into the ways in which recordings can function in the public sphere. While the links between new technologies and religion have often been framed in terms of a polarity – by encouraging deliberative processes and opening discussion to individualized forms of rational piety on the one hand, or emphasizing disciplinary processes and deploying authoritative discourses on the other – the author shows how in contemporary Islamic culture technology can be simultaneously dialogic and normative. For Daniel Fisher, the sonic is a domain of social action and empowerment. In "Local Sounds, Popular Technologies: History and Historicity in Andean Radio," he charts out the history of radio in Bolivia and Peru as utilized by miners, rural peasants, resisters to military occupation, indigenous peoples, and finally, by contemporary promoters of local culture. Important as both a tool of populist political organization and a means by which cultural value is made concrete and audible, radio is an essential technology coalescing notions of place and identity.

The final section, "Aurality and Alterity," explores the ethics and responsibility of listening to Others – artistically, symbolically, theoretically, and professionally. Kanta Kochhar-Lindgren's "Performing at the Edge of Hearing: The Third Ear" discusses the problematics and politics of hearing raised by a trilogy of performances by Ping Chong. She posits the third ear as one that listens to that which cannot be literally heard and which often involves the cross-modality of synaesthesia to yield comprehension. Attending to difference in this mute but evocative way tends to operate outside of the parameters of language and to disrupt official representations and conventionalized listening habits. In contrast to the deafness afflicting cultural encounters, Chong utilizes voice, narrative, signing, and silence to revisit and rethink the legacy of colonialism. For David Howes, Western assumptions about non-European peoples is perpetuated in the theory of "aural-oral mentality" put forth by Marshall McLuhan and others. Cultures that have yet to become literate supposedly display characteristics related to their reliance on sound and speech. In "Sound Thinking," the author challenges the theory by testing it in an actual situation, the ceremony of necklace and armshell exchange in Papua New Guinea. Creating "noise" and thus fame through this circulation of goods does indeed privilege sound as the theory predicts, but not for the expected reasons. Robert Desjarlais argues for an anthropology of the voice, and his essay draws from extensive interviews with a Nepalese elder. "Echoes of a Yolmo Buddhist's Life, in Death" articulates significant aspects of this man's life, his individual sensibilities, and the culturally specific metaphysics in which he lives. Amidst this information, the author discerns a "logic of echoes" that reverberate among the ruminations about death, the afterlife, and memory. Talk, and all the discourse that circulates about a person when deceased, is believed to embody a physical and spiritual force that can influence not only one's reputation in the community, but also the ability of the soul to reincarnate and reach liberation.

If the commodification and mass distribution of music has led to a "regression of listening," as argued by Theodor Adorno,[11] the critical attention, close analyses, and inventive theorizing represented by this volume offer an effective countermeasure.

Listening awry may not only provide insights into the numerous sonic cultures inhabiting this noisy ball, it may also lead to a rethinking of listening itself as a practice.

NOTES

1. Mystery Laboratory, "Mystery Tapes," in *Sound by Artists*, eds. Dan Lander and Micah Lexier (Toronto: Art Metropole; Banff: Walter Phillips Gallery, 1990), 203.

2. Dennis Overbye, "Music of the Heavens Turns Out to Sound a Lot Like a B Flat," *New York Times* (September 16, 2003).

3. George Johnson, "Striking Notes of Progress on the World's Tiniest Guitar," *New York Times* (November 9, 2003): 12.

4. Barry Truax, *Acoustic Communication* (Norwood: Ablex, 1984).

5. Jacques Attali, *Noise: The Political Economy of Music*, trans. Brian Massumi (Minneapolis: University of Minnesota Press, 1985), 5.

6. See W.J.T. Mitchell, *Picture Theory* (Chicago: University of Chicago Press, 1994).

7. In terms of the artworld's engagement with sound, the last five years has witnessed a number of significant museum shows and catalogues: *Voices* (Rotterdam: Witte de With, 1998), *Other Rooms, Other Voices* (Zurich: Memory/Cage Editions, 1999), *Sonic Boom* (London: Hayward Gallery, 2000), *Frequencies* (Frankfurt: Kunsthalle, 2002), *Resonances* (Saarbrücken: Stadtgalerie, 2002), *Sonic Process* (Paris: Centres George Pompidou, 2003), as well as Douglas Kahn's noteworthy *Noise, Water, Meat: A History of Sound in the Arts* (Cambridge, MA and London, UK: MIT Press, 1999).

8. Mitchell, 16.

9. Christopher Cox, "Return to Form," *Artforum* (November 2003): 67.

10. Slavoj Žižek, *Looking Awry: An Introduction to Jacques Lacan through Popular Culture* (Cambridge, MA and London, UK: MIT Press, 1991), 11–12.

11. Theodor W. Adorno, "On the Fetish-Character in Music and the Regression of Listening" [1938], in *Essays on Music*, ed. Richard Leppert (Berkeley and Los Angeles: University of California Press, 2002), 288–317.

ARTS OF LISTENING

Richard Leppert

Peter L. Schmunk

Jennifer Fisher

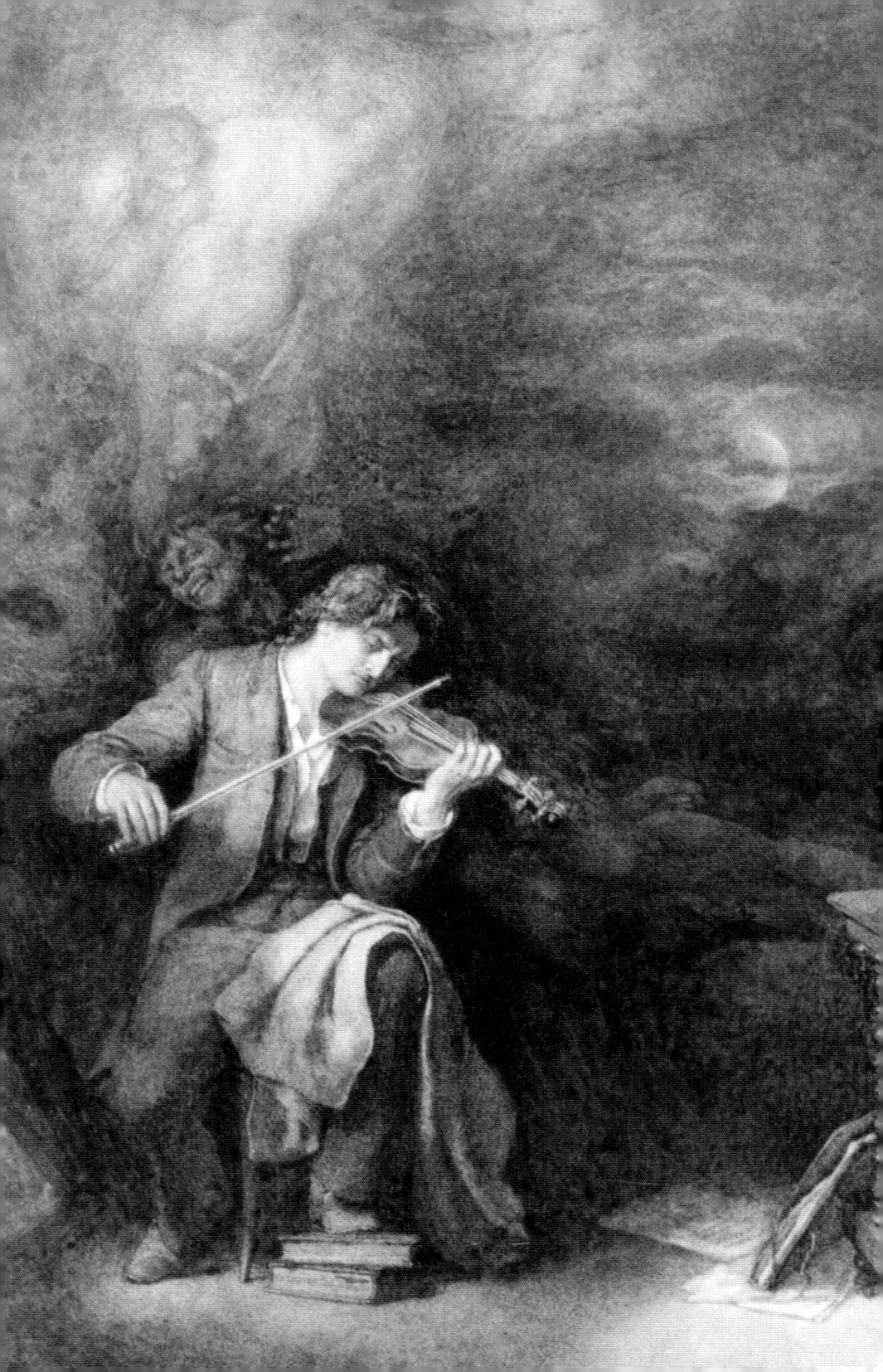

The Social Discipline of Listening

Richard Leppert

My contribution to this volume is shaped by the visual record of musical practices surrounding the phenomenon of the concert and its public. However, I should stress at the outset that my interest in the intersection of musical history with visual history has little to do with the positivistic "account" that visual evidence might provide for the study of, say, performance practice, organology, or the "listening public." Indeed, I'm highly skeptical that any one-to-one relation exists. In my view, the worth of studying visual practices relative to music history principally (though hardly exclusively) pertains to our learning more about how music was conceived in a particular historio-geographico-cultural setting by its practitioners. Conception (including visualization), after all, drives practice, though the two are hardly each other's precise mirror image.

Visual modes of perception, like aural ones, are neither simple nor "natural." As Foucault (in particular) has shown us, visibility is a matter of visuality: what is *seen* is what *can* be seen in one historical moment, yet not necessarily in another. Visuality is a matter of culture and history, not optics. "Visibilities," in other words, are not constants: "To see is always to think, since what is seeable is part of what 'structures thought in advance.' And conversely to think is always to see."[1] Beginning in the Enlightenment, and completed during the nineteenth century, an epistemological shift occurred whereby visuality and visibility became dominant means of knowing, replacing seemingly less objectively verifiable forms of knowledge, such as theology and philosophy. "Scientific verifiability" had a significant impact on musical aesthetics, criticism, performance, *and listening*, particularly to the degree to which performance concretized the semantic properties of aural experience.

Historically evident by the seventeenth century, modernity is marked and defined by an obsession with "evidence," the magical coin that has long defined most humanistic and social scientific disciplines. Evidence: from *videre*, to see – and, in the uncovering of evidence, to make visible, to make plain, to strive for the self-evident. (But in actuality, to privilege a certain way of knowing, at the expense of another.) Modernity's passion for visibility organized the myriad acts of classification that underwrite what we commonly understand as knowledge, from botany to zoology, from the *New Grove* to the *Billboard* charts. Further, the *specifically cultural* demands of visuality inform and determine the cultural necessity to render music itself legible, that is, *seeable*. This is obvious of course in narrative (whether programmatic or formalist) overlays that anchor mental images – formulated in stories of events, places, people, or structures (sonata form, etc.) – as it were, to overcome the immeasurability of absolute music, to concretize the nothingness of musical sonority. And of course the passion for visibility informs the passion

Henry J. Stock, *A Musician's Reverie*, 1888
Photo: Photographic Survey, Courtauld Institute of Art
Courtesy Harrow (Greater London), Harrow School Collection, The Keepers and Governors of Harrow School

for images that first consumed European and American inhabitants of the nineteenth century – and now threatens to capture us all in a virtual reality within the World Wide Web, a form of self-disciplining visual desire that Foucault did not live to imagine.

I wish to explore, very briefly and very provisionally, the visuality of musical listening across the historic divide separating the early modern from the modern, to suggest how music participated in the shift from aristocratic state power during the final moments of the *ancien régime* to the privatized and domesticated power of the bourgeoisie in the course of the nineteenth century with the parallel phenomenon of public listening. In the course of these remarks, I shall insist that the habits of the listening public are a matter as much of the eyes as the ears, involving sociocultural and epistemological change, as well as changes in musical style (with an implicit demand for concentrated listening). Again: the argument I shall advance builds on the premise that listening in public was a profoundly visual and aural experience.

Prior to *and* simultaneous with any musical text and/or its performance are music's various relations to lived experience. In other words, musical discourse necessarily both *precedes* and *exceeds* the immanent semantic quotient of any particular musical text and any specific instance of listening. These comments are intended to suggest that the semantic content of music – its discursive "argument," however defined – is never solely about its sound either as an abstract entity or as an isolated experience. In other words, the act of listening in public to a musical performance cannot be understood simply as phenomenological. Crucially involved are the ways of knowing (Foucault's *epistemes*) that constitute the forms of "software" unique to a time and place. For music to "occur," someone has to perform it, and someone has to hear it (even if that means only the performer him/herself, in the absence of other auditors). An *act* of hearing must occur for sonoric semantics to function. (We don't conventionally think of studying scores as making or hearing music; we clearly do not understand that the studying of scores constitutes music's performance.)

Listening, as well as performing, involves the materiality, the culture, and the politics of the human body. The semantic content of music registers through the body (and the five senses that incorporate the very foundation of embodiment), as well as the mind, its rational powers mediated by emotional reactions. The experience and meaning of music is physical, intellectual (in the broad notion of the word), and spiritual; and it is deeply and fundamentally *social*. Music's experience is especially to be understood as the result of mediations between ear and eye functioning within a "sonoric landscape" wherein music occurs as both a sound and a sight. What follows is a cursory attempt to demonstrate the working of the relationship between sight and sound in historical sociocultural efforts to establish, stabilize, and render useful music's meanings through both performing and listening.

My concern with vision focuses upon the physicality of music-making itself (the sight of the body's labours to produce sound), and on the (ironic) fact that the "product" of this activity – musical sonority – lacks all concreteness and disappears without a trace almost instantly once the musician's "physical labours" cease (what is called acoustic decay). Precisely because musical sound is abstract, intangible, and ethereal – lost as soon as it is gained – the *visual experience* of its production is crucial to both musicians and audiences alike for locating and communicating the place of music and musical sound within society and culture. (In our own visually-captivated world, I'd further suggest that the social impact of phonograph records – as we used to call them – ironically produced a pent-up demand for the re-visualization of music, the re-embodiment of music, that we witness today in the phenomena of MTV, operas on DVD, televised performances of symphony orchestra performances, and the like.)

In short, I'm suggesting that the slippage between the physical activity to producing musical sound and the abstract nature of what is produced creates a semiotic contradiction that is ultimately "resolved" to a significant degree via the agency of human sight, and that sight *and* sound *together* produce the force of sociality that music encodes. The visual code functions through the human body in its efforts to produce and receive music. When people hear a musical performance they see it as an embodied activity. While they hear they also witness: how the performers look and gesture, how they're dressed, how they interact with their instruments and with one another, how they regard the audience, how other listeners heed the performers. Thus the musical event is perceived as a socialized activity. Visual representation in effect summarizes by encapsulation more or less all of this, not as a "disinterested" record of events but as a coherent and discursive, commonly dialectical vision of the varied relations within the context of which sound occurs and hence sound means.[2]

Aural-Visual Consumption

What is it that the early-modern listener "consumed" when he or she "consumed" music? What are the relationships of this consuming to the construction of personhood; that is, to identity? What is the function of consumption, for the auditor, of the public concert? How ought this consumption be theorized? One answer to the question "What is it that one 'consumes' when one 'consumes' music?" might go something like the following: one consumes pleasure, wherein pleasure as a category of human experience is at once "disinterested" and "interested." By "disinterested" I mean that music's pleasure is produced in part by aural stimulations which in turn trigger physiological and emotional responses that result in some sense, inevitably temporary, of well-being. This pleasure is embodied; it may be simultaneously of body and mind and as such the sonoric simulacrum of an organic totality absent from an otherwise fractured reality. Nonetheless, music's organicism can only be imagined to the extent that it is lost as soon as it is gained, inevitably lost the moment sound ceases. By "interested" I mean that music's pleasures, just described, are never totally innocent, never produced or experienced solely as autonomous reaction ("disinterested"). This says no more than that any discursive practice must give meaning to, and gain meaning from, not only its own practice and result (in this case, sonority proper) but also the larger system of discursive and semantic practices of which it is never more than a part.

Pleasure by its very nature comes with a bill attached. In a culture of scarcity, even among those for whom scarcity is not more than a theoretical possibility, pleasure by definition is understood to be an unstable and exceptional category of human experience. This is because pleasure is not solely dependent upon material excess – financial means do not guarantee access to pleasure. Pleasure is an uncommodified commodity. Its materiality is only metaphoric; like music it is immaterial. Further, pleasure's consumption incorporates loss at the moment of gain. This partly accounts for the desire that pleasure produces, to the extent that we understand by desire that which we have *not* (even in the moment of having). Pleasure in bourgeois culture is always on loan, and repayment is invariably demanded. Indeed, the very identity of the bourgeois subject hinges on this somewhat pathological relation to the question of pleasure.

Even when most semantically drained, as in the abstract projection "pleasure for pleasure's sake" – as such, an ideology but not a lived reality – pleasure remains semantically rich. Pleasure is experiential; it involves consciousness and intentionality. Even when, as is often the case, it locates itself outside the mind by a nonetheless mental conception of its escape from the bounds of (instrumental) rationalization, pleasure's contingency is not only a matter of physical-emotional sensing but also the awareness of the difference it allows, momentarily, from ordinary experience where pleasure is all too often in very short supply. The desire for pleasure of whatever kind is embodied. The embodied pleasure of music to which I refer – as commonly explained by nineteenth-century aesthetics, for example – is marked by a (wished-for) totality of body and mind that hardly exists except in the imagination.

Music is a repeatedly inscribing marker. Its "repetitions," immanent to musical structure, are at once audible and visible (in the gestures of performers, for example); repetitions serve as sensory overdeterminations of every semantic value music produces. Indeed, therein lies much of music's power and pleasure: whatever it might mean, it means repeatedly – whether referring to the replaying of a piece of music over some interval of time, or referring instead to the internal repetitions found in all music but especially obvious in formal procedures like dance forms or theme and variations. Repetition inscribes reassurance and predictability. As such, it is the sonoric-visual simulacrum of contentment, the *promesse de bonheur* that Stendahl described as art, and which the Frankfurt School took up in their account of the utopian moment in culture.[3] What I mean is that music, like dance with which it is closely associated, both visually and sonorically enacts a stylized and aestheticized order that human beings valorize highly, especially in light of order's abundant opposite, chaos or disorder: noise.

Listening in Representation

I'll begin, so to speak, at the beginning, with a painting by Marcellus Laroon (1679–1774), an English "musician, singer, professional soldier and man of pleasure"[4] and a painter of what art historians call "musical conversations"; that is, depictions of musical "speakers" and listeners – producers and consumers of musical discourse produced c. 1760 (Fig. 1). Conversation – dialogic speech – is *of* the body, an abstract and ethereal breathing outward – like singing, like flute-playing – in order to connect to the body of the other so as to represent, to account for: an act of "speaking" tied to an act of "listening." There are two conversations in Laroon's picture, and their duality is made an issue.

On the left is the conversation of the (non-musical) speech-act: pairs of speaker-listeners, couples, men and women, are represented in the conventional manner as spouses or lovers, or at least intimate friends. On the right is another conversation – musical – partly texted (a man sings), but mostly not of or about words but about sounds as such. The performers in this instance do not pair off; the musicians are only men, apart from the harpsichordist. Yet their discourse defines the profoundly interactive nature of musical discourse. How do we know this? Laroon organizes his picture around a meeting, a coming-together, occurring at the centre of the painting and framed by the archway. A man and a woman meet, bow, touch; they engage. Their gestures semiotically shade into the opening moves of physical contact associated with social dancing, itself a ritual form of lovemaking, a rehearsal of bodies organizing their sensualities and desires, guided by musical sonorities which give form to their practices – expressions associated with love and lovemaking, after all, constitute the most dramatic examples of human sociality.

In the foreground is something odd – a storage case for a musical instrument, lying atop music books. There's a negative aesthetic quotient to this dark, unattractive, utilitarian object, yet its presence is asserted by the painter. Its excuse for "being" lies in its meaning. The music case, it seems to me, is like a coffin. It protects something precious, but at the same time its protection confirms loss. Both a casket and the case allude to vitality, to sound, to breath, though only by announcing death and silence. However, the music case differs from a coffin. The coffin protects the corpse from worms, if only

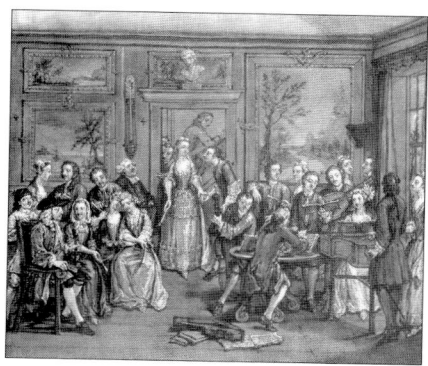

Fig. 1
Marcellus Laroon
Musical Conversation, c. 1760
Courtesy New Haven, Yale Center for
British Art, Paul Mellon Collection

figuratively, but it also shrouds the survivors from the look, and perhaps stench, of decomposition. It's a frame marking the permanent dissolution of the body it contains. The music case, on the contrary, protects something that "sleeps" and might be awakened. The awakening, as in a fairy tale, comes from the touch – of fingers, mouth, tongue – of the player who, like a lover, embraces his or her instrument and brings it to life, makes it "speak" – commonly for the "benefit" of another, the listener. (The ultimate listener in Western discursive practice is, of course, the lover, him or her to whom a serenade is addressed.) Laroon's is a painting of promise centred on people's bodies, young and old, desired and desiring. The musical conversation is ultimately one about the possibility of life itself, involving shared, embodied interiorities. In Laroon's painting, the silence encoded by the instrument case is overwhelmed by the radical, almost scandalous amount of sonority being produced: the silence it recommends is, in practice, excessively overcome. Thus, to get in on the musical act at the left, a man at the extreme right stands on a chair to reach a lute hanging on the wall: people clamour for music, and for the obvious reason that musical doing defines and indeed practices human interaction; that is, practices sociality itself.

Representing Change

I'll focus the remainder of my remarks on the last two-thirds (roughly speaking) of the nineteenth century, and address the profound changes in the habits of listening that might be described under the category of discipline. The object of my concern will be the virtuoso soloist performer, considered in light of the various sorts of visual discourses surrounding the "look" of such performers and, equally important, their being "looked at" – the fetishization of virtuosi by nineteenth-century audiences most dramatically marks the issues I'm attempting to raise and clarify. But I'll begin with a little background relative to the bourgeois listener, seen through the lens of Theodor Adorno.

Throughout his writing, Adorno laboured to understand the sociocultural import of Western individuality in both its philosophical and practical functions. This individuality dates as far back as Homer's Odysseus and culminates in what Adorno would surely recognize today in human types as diverse as media stars, sports tycoons (both owners and players), and celeb-status musicians, whether Toscanini-type classical-orchestral titans, Spandex-clad 1980s rockers, or Madonna-types. Adorno – typical for a high modernist – saw individuality as the very basis of history, as the defining principle of the West. But he viewed it dialectically, as something both paradoxical and contradictory, at once liberating and enslaving. Individuality constituted the basis of social organization, yet individuality in its competitive, appetitive, ultimately solipsistic drive was ironically anti-social, anti-communal, and fundamentally private. And Adorno brilliantly – and to be sure scandalously – linked individuality in its most radical phase – the modernity first defined by the nineteenth-century triumph of the bourgeoisie, economic capitalism, and the Industrial Revolution – to music itself: opera, symphony, concerto, and chamber music.

For example, to Adorno, chamber music, both as sound *and* as a social phenomenon, constituted a place of momentary refuge, a *place* of promise, a place of imagination, perhaps of memory, where an atypical kind of individuality might be thought, seen, and indeed heard. In chamber music he located a space for a lost sociability, where each musical voice was heard by mutual consent, and where being heard was not defined by the competitive survival of the fittest, the loudest, the most clever. In chamber music, as a principle of musical organization, Adorno *heard and saw* what Laroon drew: namely, *musical conversation*, musical give-and-take, musical sharing, the musical support of intertwining voices – in sum, mutual respect and, in fact, an acoustic and physical-visual manifestation of "friendship." In chamber music, Adorno could imagine the possibility of what otherwise seemed unavailable: a society that was in fact actually social (or sociable).

The utopian element of chamber music, for Adorno, wasn't defined simply by what went on among the few players; the effects he projected likewise involved chamber music's audience. Adorno clearly understood that the audience for chamber music was largely privileged. It was small, typically an economic and educational elite; its audience was *comfortable*. Paradoxically, the audience for chamber music constituted the embodied reminder of the profoundly *unequal* society that Adorno saw chamber music itself sonically imagining in more democratic form. Adorno was neither romantic nor cynic, about either music or political sociology. As he put it, "Chamber music is specific to an epoch in which the private sphere, as one of leisure, has vigorously parted from the public-professional sphere."[5] How was or is the chamber music audience different from, say, the audience for the London Symphony or the Berlin Philharmonic? What was Adorno getting at? He's not entirely clear about this, but I think that his understanding goes something like the following. Chamber music does *not* in fact eschew the competition inherent in, say, the concerto: the four string parts of the quartet *do* after all interrupt one another, one part struggling against the momentary hegemony of another, for example. Further, the audience *sees* this in the physical gestures necessary to make one instrument heard with or against or above another – the biting attack of bow against string, maybe of *pizzicato*, or *col legno* use of the bow, introducing a new sonority like an exclamation or an insistence against the prevailing discourse. We can see all this: the players do things with their bodies that have visual and aural consequences. Piano trios and string quartets, in other words, are not necessarily the musical equivalents of love feasts. But neither is chamber music merely a reduced-in-size analogue to large orchestral compositions.

So far as I can hear – and see – the nineteenth-century piano concerto fast movements commonly depend for their impact on the thrall within which the audience is held on account of the soloist's ability to hold our attention as the one and only. That is, the concerto's success is defined by the soloist in opposition to the orchestra. It's not the orchestra that thrills us, no matter how well it plays; it's the soloist. Indeed, if the soloist is sufficiently commanding, the orchestra increasingly serves to underscore the soloist.

With the symphony orchestra, the audience's visual attention is centred on the conductor who commands attention, who for that matter commonly promotes attention to himself via his gestures, his body language. Thus the plethora of nineteenth-century cartoons that at once make light of the phenomenon and acknowledge the audience's appetite for it (Fig. 2). From our own time, Leonard Bernstein comes immediately to mind. Recall the endless television footage of Bernstein from the 1950s to the 1980s, the degree to which the camera "looked" at him, giving to *his body* the authority to "read" the music's meaning for us. In the 1950s, one New York City FM DJ, I forget who it was, but not a devotee of Bernstein in any event, referred to Bernstein, in light of his famous gestural carryings-on, as a *con*-ductor, as in con-man. I mention this not to defame one of the genuinely great American musicians of this century, but to reiterate the fact that the issues Adorno wrote about were based on quite ordinary experiences of how music, functioning as a sound and a sight, firmly anchors itself in the social-political, even as it commonly claims to be a refuge from such mundane, usually unpleasant realities. As many orchestral musicians have experienced, the conductor's literal power over the orchestral musicians, at times tyrannical, can engender fear and loathing, and reflects what Adorno once sarcastically referred to as conductors' "Führer-complex."

Focused Listening as a Decentring Experience: The Virtuosi

The archetypal musicians in nineteenth-century mythology were the virtuosi – Paganini, Liszt – simultaneously virtual factories of sound, limitless output, the embodiment of the Superman, and the supersexed (Fig. 3). (Filmmaker Ken Russell, rather more than merely perverse, got that much "right" in his outrageous filmic "account" of Liszt, *Lisztomania* [1975], fittingly enough with Roger Daltrey of The Who in the title role.) In the film, as in an 1886 magazine illustration published in Paris, Liszt's musical prowess is directly and unambiguously linked to sexual prowess, rather vulgarly evident in the hyper-phallic sword slung from his waist. Liszt's eight arms and multiple long fingers only reinforce the phallocentrism of the image (and not coincidentally equate him with the insect world), arms and fingers in abundance resonating with another popular image of the

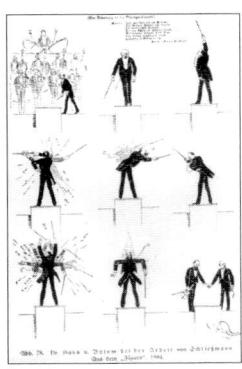

Fig. 2
Schliessmann
Hans von Bülow Conducting, 1884
Published in *Figaro*

time, that of the Medusa. Such performers served as the ultimate realization of a socially impossible unity of the public with the private, of power and desire realized and linked – and projected onto men who were bracketed off from quotidian life by nature of their status as entertainers and as artistic freaks. (And as is well known, virtuosi *self-consciously* acted out – literally made visible for spectators – in physical form the sonoric pyrotechnics. In every sense of the word they were performers.)

Listening, to belabour the obvious, demands a listener. But listen*ing* is not properly understood as a biological phenomenon, rather a historico-sociocultural one: the listener is framed by history, society, and culture. The nineteenth-century bourgeois, living a life of sharp division between the private sphere and the public – the man of the world, so to speak – took his identity in no small portion from a code of rigid self-discipline that staged human emotion in the being of his wife rather than himself. But the greater the degree to which the bourgeois male's self-domination excised his emotional life (the better to be fit for the rigours of intense economic competition), the higher the demand for emotion's reappearance elsewhere – and not only in the person of his wife. Emotional life

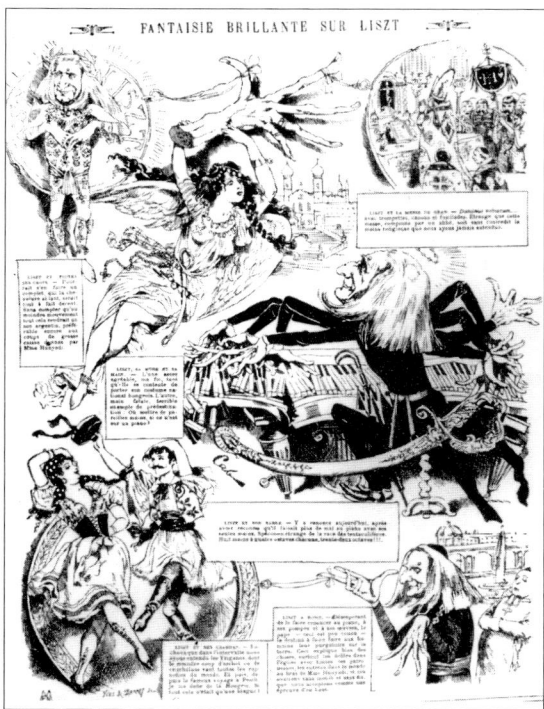

Fig. 3
Anonymous
Liszt-Fantasy (detail), 1886
Published in *La vie parisienne*, April 3

was made explicitly *visible and audible* through musical art, but experienced collectively in the concert hall as a phenomenon of transference. The physical rigidity of the audience (often seated on backless benches, discomfort raised to a principle of metaphoric honour) precisely mirrored the physical heroics on the raised platform: spectacle. The virtuoso is born of *visual and aural* genetic stock. The effects of sound, the plethora of Paganini's notes, is matched by the violence of his bodily movements, via effects of visibility of which he was conscious, and whose impact he carefully exploited. Performances are described as being "watched," and not simply heard (Figs. 4–6).[6] Similarly, the silence of the audience, purportedly listening ever more intently, is precisely mirrored in the form of the orchestra, whose size gradually increases until it reaches the literal breaking point with Bruckner and Mahler. The "stakes" of sound, more and more sound, are the perfect reflectors of the increased discipline of silence required of the audience: the bourgeoisie's silence is paid for by an "assault" on the ears. Whereas early in the nineteenth century audiences called out during orchestral concerts, not only between movements but during the playing, by the century's end audiences had recessed into tight-lipped quiet and bodily immobility. And just as this happened, the histrionics of sound and sight proceed upscale: violinists, pianists, singers, and of course conductors. As Richard Sennett points out: "The artist is forced ever more into a compensatory role in the eyes of his audience, as a person who really can express himself and be free. Spontaneous expression is idealized in ordinary life but realized in the domain of art."[7]

The virtuoso constitutes the wish fulfilment, the desires hidden within repressed identity:

> For the spectator [the virtuoso] creates feelings which are both abnormal and safe. He appears to feel spontaneously in public, and that is abnormal; through his shock tactics, he makes others feel. But momentary shock is safe because of his very isolation. Here is no emotional experience the audience must measure against their own powers; after all, he is an extraordinary man. Thus appear both the public identities produced by personality in public: on one side, an extraordinary actor, on the other, spectators who can be comfortable in their passivity.[8]

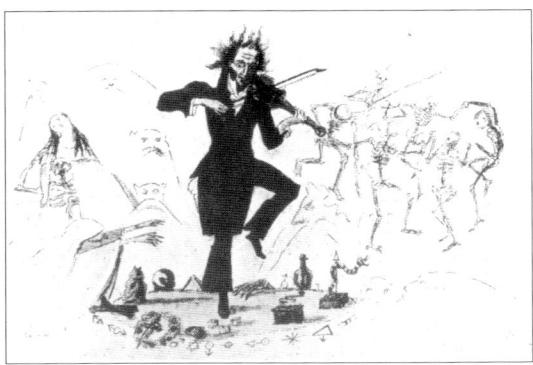

Fig. 4
J.P. Lyser
Paganini as Sorcerer, n.d.

Composer Robert Schumann understood this implicitly, per remarks on the Liszt *Études*: "One ought also to see the composer play them, for just as the sight of any virtuosity elevates and strengthens, so much more does the immediate sight of the composer himself, *struggling with his instrument, taming it, making it obey*."[9] Schumann smartly defines musical virtuosity opposite to what we might expect. Critics of virtuoso visual display and critics of virtuoso sonoric display both commonly allude to tastelessness, as though the letting go, so to speak, was a manifestation of the hysterical (oddly, at once the stuff of manly superheroes and womanly weakness: analogous to Hercules, powerful, super-developed yet feminized by his hyper-curvaceous body). But Schumann recognized the other side of this coin: the virtuoso's virtuosity is a hyperbolic form of self-disciplining bourgeois who himself disciplines, who wrests the chaos of infinite sonoric possibility into the shape he demands – and who turns it into *work*. Not for nothing is the étude the perfect metaphor for the complicated links between nineteenth-century Romanticism and the dearest-held precepts of industrial capitalism and the Protestant work ethic.

Henry Stock's *A Musician's Reverie* (Fig. 7) attempts to connect an impassioned music with an imagination giving vent to distinctly male fantasies conventionally suppressed by bourgeois ideology. That is, Stock's image valorizes the unrepresentable, in essence the libidinal sublime. Music serves as a cultural transfer point between daily life and the locked closet containing self-discipline and self-repression. The male sitter's position is frontal, and his dream is dark, swirling, and conflicted, potentially frightening and unpredictable: in a word, exciting for its possibilities. Yet the dreamer is not the bourgeois everyman, but the (anti-bourgeois) artist-musician. That is, at the moment the repressed returns, it is nonetheless located at a "safe" distance from the likely bourgeois viewer (the men who bought such pictures, of which many similar examples survive). The artist is isolated, conjuring a masturbatory fantasy (in the picture's background) of Watteauesque nudes and Goyaesque demons in an experience that brings on night. Here there is no concern with domestic completeness, but with a yearning for unremitting solitary passion. Woman and devil float together in the dreamer's psyche, pushing reason aside (this man's use for books is as a footrest). However, this is not merely an image about music as such; it is about improvisatory music; notated music lies abandoned on

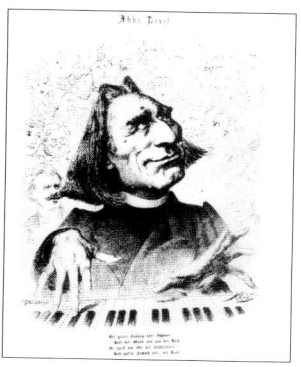

Fig. 5
Klie
Abbé Liszt, 1873
Published in *Humoristichen Blättern*, Vienna

the floor, in the lowest space available in the image. The dreamer's is an art – a false art – produced by abandoning the text; his music moves into *unscripted*, hence socially dangerous, space. The price of liberation, sexually charged, is the loss of reason – marked in the painting's murky background by a bastardized recollection of Goya's famous etching *The Sleep of Reason Produces Monsters*, which opens his series *Los Caprichos*.

On the one hand, the absolutes of gender difference are obvious. The man's playing is interactive with his instrument, impassioned, and deeply soulful, as his furled brow encodes. It is hot, threatening, and stimulating, and it is ultimately contemporary, not classical; thus it preserves Victorian male prerogatives over time and history, as opposed to then-common images of prim women sitting stiffly at their pianos. On the other hand, the singularity of Stock's subject removes it from the more measurable reality of contemporaneous imagery. Its singularity is principally embedded in the openly acknowledged connection between male desire and music. Yet the sexual desire is nonetheless unrealized; it fails. As a fantasy – a dream and not a "reality" – it marks its own inadequacy in precisely the one domain where successful performance codifies masculine identity. The image transfers lack, though a dynamic lack, to a man. Physical sexuality is transformed into musical improvisation. By this means, the putative social dangers immanent in the dreamer's abandonment of the musical text – his refusal to follow the notation, the sonoric simulacrum of the social script – are rendered harmful to him alone, and not to other men. Still, it is not that simple; the message is mixed. The improvising musician in effect "refuses" to read a musical text, which both social convention and cultural practice mark as feminine. By refusing to follow a notated "code" – his determination to improvise – he lays claim to his masculinity at another level. Yet in the very act of performing he re-establishes the link between music and feminine identity – endlessly articulated from the eighteenth century onwards – that he sought to break. He acknowledges that music is the displacement of his true object of desire: music is woman; woman is evil; both are captivating, castrating.[10] The pleasures afforded by both ironically conflate with evil and terror. Take your pleasure; pay the price.

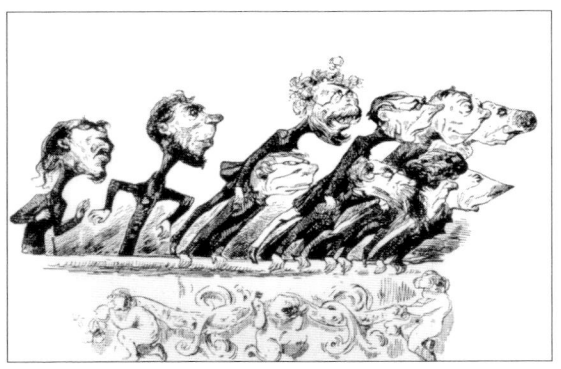

Fig. 6
Gustave Doré
Those Who are Carried Away, 1849
From *Grotesques*

What does this suggest about music? The socio-erotics of music established by these private-public dichotomies, wherein the visual inscription of music serves as a substitute for both emotion and sensuality, operate also as momentary compensations and consolations for social fracturing within the increasingly competitive, class- and gender-separated world of nineteenth-century capitalist industrialism. (To say this does no more than acknowledge the ideological thrust of most nineteenth-century aesthetics.) Imagery preserves the sedimented memory of what has been lost in the process, even as memory is continually mediated by the fast-changing present.

Sites for Looking: Space and Desire

Social space is commonly a musical terrain; indeed, the terrain of music sometimes provides the opportunity to make visual an aestheticized schema of social classification. Concert halls and opera houses were at once public spaces and, paradoxically, privileged ones. In the eighteenth-century opera theatre – to cite but one example (representing a situation that changed in the course of the nineteenth century to some degree) – cheap seats existed, but what might be *seen* from such quasi-public space was all that space to which the public was denied access. The opera fan (Fig. 8), printed on paper, or sometimes silk, and revised each season, provided the more elite participants with a spatial diagram of the social register: who was who depended on and helped determine where one sat, and *knowing* that order was crucial to the rhetorical function of claiming one's identity within the circle of theatrical spectacle, part of which involved the performance onstage, part of which involved the performance by the audience of its claim to privileged identity. The musical experience of the opera was a matter not just of hearing (and seeing) what was being sung, it was also a matter of seeing the social order enacted within an architectural, sonoric, and aesthetic frame, one guaranteed to be kept in place for an entire season. That is, the spatial order inscribed within the printed seating chart possessed as well a temporal dimension that added to the total power of the experience that the audience at once witnessed and helped to enact. The lorgnette (opera glasses) was a standard accoutrement of dress, used as much to surveil fellow spectators as to

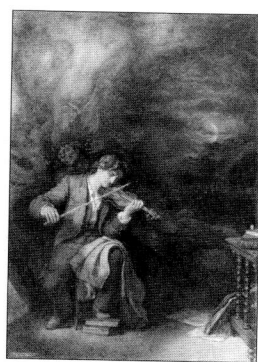

Fig. 7
Henry J. Stock
A Musician's Reverie, 1888
Photo: Photographic Survey,
Courtauld Institute of Art
Courtesy Harrow (Greater London),
Harrow School Collection, The Keepers
and Governors of Harrow School

watch the action on the stage.[11] Social order was not a matter of the moment; it repeated itself night after night via spatial, temporal, spectacular, and sonoric paradigms all acting in consort – especially via staged narratives organized around sexual conflict, which by the second half of the nineteenth century almost totally defined opera.

As virtuoso display (aural and visual) increased, there should be no surprise that listening became even more its opposite, namely, quiescent: listening increasingly occurred under self-imposed conditions that discouraged any visible or audible reaction to the music (Fig. 9), *provided one had claims to being a bourgeois*:

> To sneer at people who showed their emotions at a play or concert became *de rigueur* by the mid-19th Century. Restraint of emotion in the theater became a way for middle-class audiences to mark the line between themselves and the working class. A "respectable" audience by the 1850s was an audience that could control its feelings through silence; the old spontaneity was called "primitive."[12]

According to Sennett, disciplined silence was foremost a phenomenon of urban centres, less so provincial outposts. As he further notes, the dimming of house lights, which began in the 1850s and was virtually universal by the 1890s, contributed to audience self-restraint.[13]

James Johnson reiterates the point: "Policing manners...became an act of self-reassurance. It confirmed one's social identity by noticing those who didn't measure up, whether through (choose your label) ignorance, laziness, bad upbringing, insensitivity, or overall dullness."[14] Not the least contributor to the discipline of quiescent listening was fear: "To not show any reaction, to cover up your feelings, means you are invulnerable, immune to being gauche. In its dark aspect, as a mark of self-doubt, silence was a correlative of 19th Century ethology."[15]

Still, compensation came in other forms. It became scored, literally texted, and hence not "merely" the result of supposedly spontaneous lettings-go by odd men behaving oddly (Paganini, Liszt). Virtuosity became codified in (some) notation. Not surprisingly, it is in the concerto, which is nothing if not the metaphor of the isolated and indi-

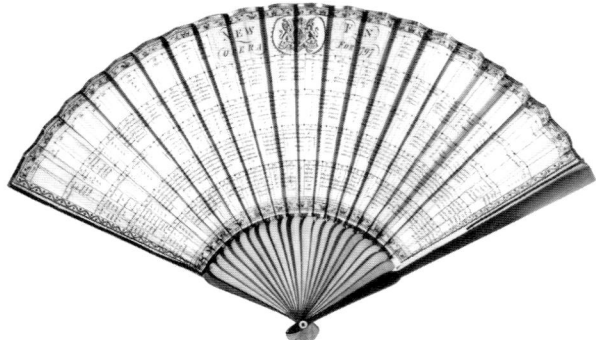

Fig. 8
New Opera Fan for 1797, 1797
Photo: London, British Museum, Department of Prints and Drawings © The British Museum

vidualized hero pitted against the collective identity of the orchestra (itself led by a titan with whom one sometimes worked in concert, at others times seemingly against), that the soloist momentarily and triumphantly breaks free, especially in the cadenza. This moment metaphorically acknowledges the victory of steady hard work: while the hero marches on, his energies at full force, the exhausted (orchestral) masses/minions catch their breath.

Close

> The inexpressible inner essence of all music, by virtue of which it flows past us so utterly comprehensible and yet so inexplicable, like a familiar but eternally distant paradise, is rooted in the fact that it reproduces all the movements of our innermost being but quite divorced from phenomenal life *and remote from its misery.*[16]
> – Arthur Schopenhauer

Schopenhauer, addressing the question of musical affect, acknowledges that the "condition" of music is less an aspiration of art and more a desire for an embodied happiness that does not exist in material life, but resides buried in the imagination. In the aesthetics of autonomy, in other words, the social enters surreptitiously via the back door, its presence denied yet named. Schopenhauer's notion of "the inexpressible inner essence of all music" involves the decentring of the self, a letting go of mind (balanced in social practice by a disciplined and publicly immobilized body), a cultivation of desire, and a simultaneous transference of desire onto the Other, a projection of the self into and onto the sight and sound of the performer, especially the virtuoso, who as it were enacts the desires imagined – and stage-manages them as well. Thus marks the discourse network within which the aural spectator is invited to experience concert music.

This discourse network likewise manifests itself in the work of many Victorian artists who took directly to heart Pater's assertion that "All art constantly aspires to the condition of music." Invariably the art that aspired to music, in representing music,

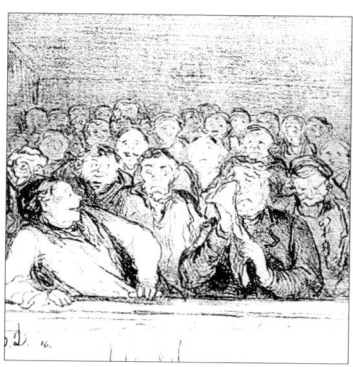

Fig. 9
Honoré Daumier
The Public Gallery, n.d.

rendered it feminine: Music = Woman, and not coincidentally Woman = (object of) Desire. Specifically, the aesthetic image commonly envisioned the focus of male emotional decentring in the form of female personifications of music, the female subjects provided names like "The Prelude," "A Symphony," or even *Lieder ohne Worte* ("songs without words").[17] In these images, the musical female subject is *labelled* musical, pre-texted. And never in the history of painting did so many artists supply their own titles to the images they produced.[18] Ironically, in other words, the visual personification of *Lieder* was seldom left *ohne Worte*. The music defined in these pictures is one of societal remove: it has no place in the world. It is perfectly mental, ethereal, disembodied, ahistorical, or of another place – or all of these at once. Yet the music depends for its effects on physical desire, perhaps, more accurately, on an erotics often quite blunt and sometimes illicit.

Meanwhile, the listener sat silent and immobile, the body still and the imagination adrift. (How we might account for the differences in listening experience across the gender boundary, in different geographies, and among different races and ethnicities has to date hardly been defined, let alone researched. Indeed, the listener which I myself imagine in the foregoing remarks is male and bourgeois, the obvious character with which to start, but no more than that.) In the course of the nineteenth century, the sociality of active music-making evident in Laroon's late eighteenth century, with which I began, reforms itself into the sociality of the musically passive self, attentively listening. The public concert experienced in the ideologically correct manner *was* a social event, but one organized around highly dynamic but absolutely interiorized emotions, ideally rendered invisible to others, a matter of soul, not body – a psychic projection onto the musical body of the performing Other that was openly acknowledged only by massed applause – applause sometimes less a spontaneous reaction than an arranged demonstration (claques), an early manifestation of what Adorno and Horkheimer termed the "culture industry" at work to manipulate "consumer" response.[19]

Arguably, public music under the conditions of modernity was less a manifestation of sociality than a simulacrum of a lost but imagined one. The participatory musical spontaneity evident in Laroon was replaced by ritual, manifesting the aesthetics of a sonoric secular religion, organized around musical bodies meant to be looked at as much as heard. Public listening was a pedagogical event through which identity could be learned and projected through codes of etiquette that were specifically visual but notable as visual absences: stasis instead of movement, hidden emotions, not feelings on public display. Not least, the visual presences of the same code, in mirror image, were enacted in musical sound in performance as spectacle. Moreover, these conduct codes were overdetermined by their relation to the large sociocultural and socioeconomic realm from which the public concert itself stemmed. The look of frenetic performers, and equally frenetic conductors and their disciplined orchestras, constituted in sight the aesthetic transformation of human mass labour, and in sound the aesthetic manifestation of the results of work: namely, artistic production. Not for nothing does the cartoon of von Bülow (Fig. 2) remind us of things to come, the high-speed motion of modernity captured in early industrial films celebrating ever-more-efficient Taylorist technologies of material manufacture. The comedy of the cartoon reflects not just derision but, in equal measure, the disquieting awe demanded by Superman, where actions speak much louder than words. Indeed, the viewer-listener's thrall is evident in the faces of "those who are carried away" (Figs. 5–6), whose attention manifests the look of the star-struck.

NOTES

1. John Rajchman, "Foucault's Art of Seeing," *October* 44 (1988): 93.

2. See Norman Bryson, *Vision and Painting: The Logic of the Gaze* (New Haven: Yale University Press, 1983); Richard Leppert, *Music and Image: Domesticity, Ideology, and Socio-Cultural Formation in Eighteenth-Century England* (Cambridge: Cambridge University Press, 1988).

3. Fredric Jameson, *Late Marxism: Adorno, or, the Persistence of the Dialectic* (London: Verso, 1990), 146–147; Herbert Marcuse, "The Affirmative Character of Culture" [1937], in *Negations: Essays in Critical Theory*, trans. Jeremy J. Shapiro (Boston: Beacon Press, 1968), 115.

4. Robert Raines, *Marcellus Laroon* (London: Routledge & Kegan Paul, 1966), 2.

5. Theodor W. Adorno, *Introduction to the Sociology of Music* (New York: Continuum, 1976), 86.

6. James H. Johnson, *Listening in Paris: A Cultural History* (Berkeley and Los Angeles: University of California Press, 1995), 232.

7. Richard Sennett, *The Fall of Public Man: On the Social Psychology of Capitalism* (New York: Vintage Books, 1978), 191.

8. Sennett, 202.

9. Robert Schumann, *On Music and Musicians*, ed. Konrad Wolff, trans. Paul Rosenfeld (New York: Pantheon, 1946), 150; Sennett, 203 (emphasis added).

10. See Richard Leppert, *The Sight of Sound: Music, Representation and the History of the Body* (Berkeley and Los Angeles: University of California Press, 1993).

11. Johnson, 29.

12. Sennett, 206.

13. Sennett, 207.

14. Johnson, 232.

15. Sennett, 210.

16. Arthur Schopenhauer, *Die Welt als Wille und Vorstellung* [1819], excerpted and reprinted in *Music and Aesthetics in the Eighteenth and Nineteenth Centuries*, eds. Peter le Hurray and James Day (Cambridge, UK: Cambridge University Press, 1981), 300, emphasis added.

17. Leppert, *The Sight of Sound*, 217–227.

18. Allen Staley, "The Condition of Music," *Art News Annual* 33 (1967): 81–87.

19. See Theodor W. Adorno and Max Horkheimer, *Dialectic of Enlightenment*, trans. John Cumming (New York: Continuum, 1972).

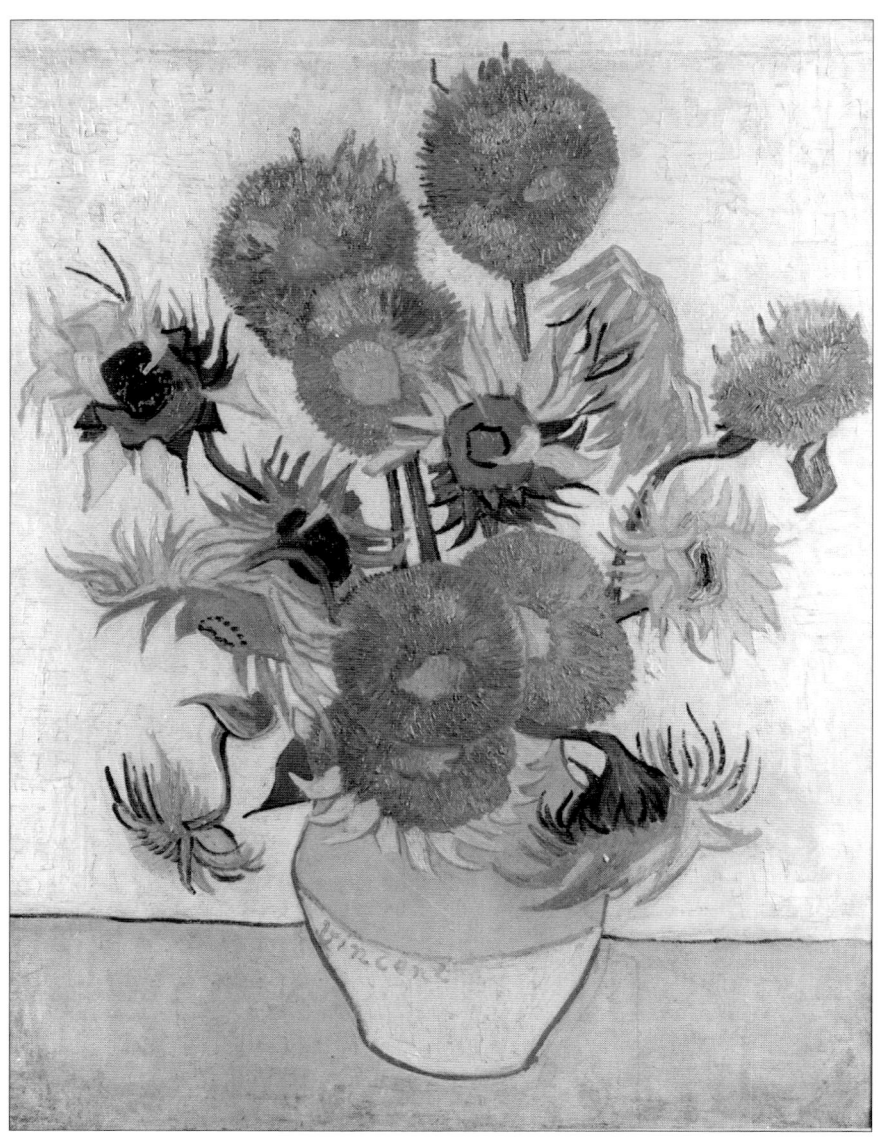

Fig. 1
Vincent van Gogh
Vase with Fourteen Sunflowers, 1889
Oil on canvas, 95 x 73 cm
Courtesy Rijksmuseum Vincent van Gogh,
Amsterdam

What Did Van Gogh Hear?:
Vibrations, Wagner, and Voices

Peter L. Schmunk

In April of 1888, Vincent van Gogh was newly settled in Arles in the south of France and was producing the brilliantly coloured canvases that constitute his most character-istic and enduring works of art. A letter written at this time to his sister Wilhelmina pro-vides important documentation of his artistic aims and the diverse sources he drew upon as formal and expressive models. Van Gogh wrote:

> [Y]ou will observe when you read Zola and Guy de Maupassant – what they absolutely insist on is a great richness and a great gaiety in art – even though this same Zola and Guy de Maupassant have said perhaps the most poignantly tragic things that have ever been said – this same tendency is beginning to be the rule in the art of painting too....
>
> You will understand that nature in the South cannot be painted with the palette of Mauve, for instance, who belongs to the North, and who is, and will remain, a master of the grey. But at present the palette is distinctly colorful, sky blue, orange, pink, vermillion, bright yellow, bright green, bright wine-red, violet.
>
> But by intensifying all the colors one arrives once again at quietude and harmony. There occurs in nature something similar to what happens in Wagner's music, which, though played by a big orchestra, is nonetheless inti-mate.... You will be able to get an idea of the revolution in painting when you think, for instance, of the brightly colored Japanese pictures that one sees everywhere....[1]

In three short paragraphs, which testify to the artist's breadth of cultural awareness as well as his considerable powers of assimilation, Van Gogh's thought ranges from French naturalist literature to the music of Wagner and Japanese prints. In all three media – visual, musical, and literary – he finds an exemplary richness of form that func-tions to convey a wide range of meaning, from the "poignantly tragic" content of Zola's novels to the consoling "quietude and harmony" of Wagner's music. Two of these mod-els, the literary and the visual, have been the subject of considerable study in the schol-arship on Van Gogh, while the musical has received little attention, as if Van Gogh's read-ing and looking were the only experiences truly significant to the formation of his art.[2] And yet the letter to Wilhelmina quoted above is far from the only indication of Van Gogh's interest in aural experience, in the formal elements of music and their effect on the listener. A letter to his brother Theo in September of the same year, written about the time Vincent painted the well-known *Night Café* and the series of *Sunflowers* (Fig. 1), offers this prediction: "Painting as it is now promises to become more subtle – more like music and less like sculpture – and above all it promises *color*. If only it keeps this promise."[3] Writing again a few days later, Van Gogh returned to the subject of music, stating: "in a painting I want to say something comforting, as music is comforting. I want to paint men and women with that something of the eternal which the halo used to symbolize, and which we seek to convey by the actual radiance and vibration of our coloring."[4] These and other statements, coinciding with the production of some of Van Gogh's most important works, indicate the artist's reliance on a musical paradigm and prompt one to consider: what did Van Gogh hear? What kinds of music did he actually listen to and with what frequency? Were other aural experiences significant to the formation of his art? Or was his awareness of music and its value as a model for painting a matter of reading about hearing, that is, an intellectual construct grounded in reading and discourse with other artists rather than actual sense experience?

Though talk of "musicality" was becoming commonplace among progressive artists in France in the mid-1880s, Van Gogh's discovery of the relevance of music to painting was apparently independently made and privately pursued in the beginning. This interest stems from the middle of 1884, when Van Gogh was still residing in The Netherlands. At that time he read two texts by Charles Blanc: the first an article on Delacroix published within a collection of biographical essays entitled *Les Artistes de mon temps*, and the second Blanc's textbook on the visual arts, the *Grammaire des Arts du Dessin*.[5] Van Gogh studied these texts closely prior to painting his first major work, *The Potato Eaters*, at a time when he was struggling to gain some confidence and control in the handling of colour. In both writings Blanc makes extensive use of musical metaphor, comparing, for example, Delacroix to a singer endowed with the whole register of the human voice or likening the effect of white in a dark painting to the sound of a gong within the full orchestra.[6] Van Gogh, in turn, began to use musical metaphors in his discussion of painters and painting, whereas before reading Blanc, such language had been nonexistent in his correspondence. A new frame of reference thus entered his thinking about art, one he employed on occasion to conceptualize, describe, and evaluate paintings. He writes, for example: "Suppose I have to paint an autumn landscape, trees with yellow. All right – when I conceive it as a symphony in yellow, what does it matter if the fundamental of yellow is the same as that of the leaves or not?"[7]

Of particular importance for Van Gogh was Blanc's insistence that there exists a phenomenological correspondence between sound and colour. Both stimuli come to the sense organs in the form of vibrations, he says, and through incremental modifications both phenomena may be almost infinitely varied. Blanc asserts further, here citing the Swiss mathematician and physicist Leonhard Euler, that "the parallel between sound and light is so perfect it is sustained even in the least particulars."[8]

That Van Gogh took this discussion very seriously, apparently regarding it as a potentially pivotal discovery in his efforts to gain a mastery of colour, is evident in his decision to undertake the study of music. We know of this endeavour through the reminiscences of two acquaintances from the artist's Nuenen period. Anton Kerssemakers, a tanner in nearby Eindhoven who befriended Van Gogh in November of 1884, remembered:

> He was always drawing comparisons between the art of painting and music, and in order to get an even better understanding of the values and the various nuances of the tones, he started taking piano lessons with an old music teacher who was at the same time an organist in Eindhoven. This, however, did not last long, for seeing that during the lessons Van Gogh was continually comparing the notes of the piano with Prussian blue and dark green and dark ocher, and so on, all the way to bright cadmium-yellow, the good man thought that he had to do with a madman, in consequence of which he became so afraid of him that he discontinued the lessons.[9]

Kerssemakers' account seems to indicate that these were not piano lessons in the conventional sense, for Van Gogh's interest lay in theoretical rather than performative aspects of music. His aim was not to learn to play the piano but to understand how sounds are related to one another in a musical composition and how such concepts of musical form might guide the selection and placement of colours in a painting. In the other reminiscence, Eindhoven resident D. Gestel, who, as a young art student, met Van Gogh and painted with him on at least one occasion, recalled that "Vincent studied the theory of colors in books [about] Delacroix and others, who also tried to demonstrate a connection between colors and music."[10] Gestel identified Van Gogh's music teacher as Van der Sande, the organist of St. Catherine's Church in Eindhoven.

Attempting to ascertain through his own concrete sense experience the parallels that Blanc and Euler had claimed to exist between sound and colour, "even in the least particulars," Van Gogh's project was cut short by an uncomprehending teacher. Predictably, the comparison of a particular sonority to cadmium yellow or Prussian blue would have seemed peculiar, if not ludicrous, to one of conventional musical training and outlook. Kerssemakers' reminiscence also suggests that Van Gogh's attempt to learn music may have foundered upon an overly literal search for equivalents between music and painting, an effort that has been attempted again and again without ever yielding definitive results. Ultimately, the association of particular sonorities and colours is a subjective determination. For example, there are no primary harmonies in music as there are colours in painting, only sonorities that provisionally hold primacy within the harmonic structure of a particular composition. Some comparisons between formal elements seem natural and have been the subject of general agreement (for example, between pitch and luminosity, with high pitch being comparable to lightness in value). Yet in every such case contrary views may invariably be found.[11] Van Gogh may also have felt defeated by the difficulty of isolating the harmonic and timbre-related qualities of sound – i.e., those elements of music he seems to have regarded as analogous to colour in painting – from the temporal elements of music (rhythm, metre, tempo) that govern their unfolding in time.

The only reference in Van Gogh's vast correspondence to this brief study of music dates from about two and a half years later, when he wrote to Theo from Arles that "I have got back to where I was in Nuenen, when I made a vain attempt to learn music, so much did I already feel the relation between our color and Wagner's music."[12] Thus, Van Gogh confirmed the experience of having studied music, but labelled it in retrospect a failure, perhaps because he recognized it was simply too big a challenge to take on, aside from the matter of needing a sympathetic teacher. However, while this experience produced no immediate result, it did prepare him to be receptive, and possibly even modestly knowledgable, when he came to Paris and encountered there a milieu in which music held a central place in social life and in critical discourse.

Our knowledge of Van Gogh's activities during a two-year stay in Paris is extremely sketchy because his cohabitation with Theo obviated the need for the frequent and detailed correspondence that took place between the two brothers at other times. We do have reliable documentation, however, locating the artist at concerts of Wagner's music. In March of 1888, about three weeks after Vincent left Paris for the south of France, Theo remarked in a letter to his sister that "before he left, I went to listen to a Wagner concert with him a few times. We both thought it was very beautiful."[13] These concerts would not have been fully-staged productions of Wagner's operas – or music dramas, as the composer called them – because those did not occur in Paris on any regular basis until the 1890s. Though Wagner's dramatic works were being performed by the 1880s everywhere from Prague to Philadelphia, his music and ideas were so highly politicized in France that attempts to mount fully-staged productions inevitably led to verbal warfare in the press, fisticuffs, and even death threats, and eventual cancellation. However, orchestral excerpts such as the Funeral March from *Götterdämmerung*, the March from *Tannhäuser*, and the Idyll from *Siegfried* were presented almost weekly to enthusiastic audiences by several conductors who championed Wagner's music. Typically, such concerts took place on Sunday afternoons during the concert season and included a selection of works by a variety of composers with the relatively short orchestral pieces by Wagner comprising only a small part of the program's total time.[14] Theo's label, "a Wagner concert," suggests that the Van Gogh brothers thought of these musical experiences primarily as opportunities to hear the exciting and much-talked-about music of Wagner. If Van Gogh attended such concerts only a few times, then he could have heard little more than about half an hour of Wagner's music. From this time on, however, he acclaims Wagner in his correspondence as a model artist, a hero figure, for the creation of a profoundly expressive and consoling art.

Van Gogh's enthusiastic response to the example of Wagner and to modern concert music in general, though his own actual experience of this music was apparently very limited, suggests that his thinking was significantly influenced by the aesthetic discourse, then current in Paris, which held music to be the ideal art for its indivisible union of form and content, its expressive force without reliance on imitation or narrative. It is impossible to know what Van Gogh may have read while in Paris; however, the absence of any mention in his correspondence of the mythic narrative content of Wagner's works suggests that he was not familiar with the *Revue wagneriénne, Le Symboliste,* or other periodicals that contained translations and analyses of Wagnerian libretti. One may presume, though, that some discussion of music and its paradigmatic value for the visual arts occurred between Van Gogh and some of the artists and critics with whom he formed friendships while in Paris. Among these, Gauguin, Bernard, and Signac, along with the critics Félix Fénéon and Gustave Kahn, stand out as the most likely contributors to his development of a musical approach to painting. Gauguin, for example, had begun thinking by the mid-1880s about the relative strengths and weaknesses of the different arts and the correspondences between them. In the manuscript entitled "Notes Synthétiques," he asserts that "harmonious colors correspond to the harmonies of sounds" and then briefly describes the analogous means by which both sounds and colours are derived from basic units.[15] Seurat was embarking at the time of Van Gogh's final months in Paris on a series of paintings of entertainment subjects, which include musicians and which thematize music as the embodiment of, and means of access to, a higher reality. In an 1891 obituary article on Seurat, Kahn noted that the artist "spoke...in a very literary and articulate fashion, seeking to compare the progress of his art with the evolution of the arts of sound, very preoccupied with finding a unity at the heart of his efforts and those of poets and musicians."[16]

The artists mentioned here have long been cited as significant influences on Van Gogh's rapid development as a painter while in Paris. What has not been recognized is that his contact with members of the Parisian avant-garde almost certainly reawakened Van Gogh's earlier belief in the relevance of music to painting. That Van Gogh sought to attend concerts of Wagner's music during this same period of time lends support to the conclusion that his relationships with Signac, Gauguin, Bernard, and perhaps other artists included some discussion of music and its paradigmatic value for painting.

What Van Gogh thought of the music he had heard before leaving Paris and what lessons he might have drawn from his own aural experience and the aesthetic discourse linked to it is most clearly indicated by scattered statements in his subsequent correspondence from Arles. These statements may be grouped under three different themes, the first of which is music's value as a formal model for painting.

"Why am I so little an artist," Van Gogh wrote in the summer of 1888, "that I always regret that the statue and the picture are not alive? Why do I understand the musician better, why do I see the raison d'etre of his abstractions better?"[17] A week or so later he penned a related statement reflecting on the future of art: "Painting as it is now promises to become more subtle – more like music and less like sculpture – and above all it promises *color.* If only it keeps this promise."[18] Conscious of the expressive inadequacies of imitation, Van Gogh sought an abstracted harmony that gave primacy to the element of colour. How the example of music might actually function as a model for his own painting practice he articulated most clearly in the letter to Wilhelmina cited above. "But by intensifying all the colors," Van Gogh wrote, "one arrives once again at quietude and harmony. There occurs in nature something similar to what happens in Wagner's music, which, though played by a big orchestra, is nonetheless intimate."[19] In other words, just as Wagner had scored his music for a large orchestra of diverse instrumental timbres and yet achieved effects of great beauty, even serenity and calm, so Van Gogh might intensify his palette of colours to create harmonious images that would convey, as he variously put it, calm, rest, reassurance, the grandeur of nature, and his love for his fellow human being. Significantly, the artist's thinking has moved beyond an effort to identify simple correspondences between the elements of music and painting to a general principle transferable from one art to the other. Whether this principle was a conclusion drawn from Van Gogh's few listening experiences or was adopted from things he read and heard said by others in Paris is impossible to determine, though the latter is more likely. However, it served him profitably in Arles and afterwards in his efforts "to express [himself] forcibly," to express even calm and rest with vehemence.[20] The *Sunflower* series (Fig. 1), for example, painted six months after his move from Paris to Arles, was conceived as a "symphony in blue and yellow," in Van Gogh's words, with the golden flowers placed against a brilliant yellow background in one variation and before a complementary blue background in another.[21] In painting *Vincent's Bedroom in Arles* (Fig. 2) a few weeks later, Van Gogh included all three complementary colour pairs – violet walls against yellow chairs and bed, red coverlet and green window, orange table and blue basin – but sought to balance these vivid hues to express, as he wrote to Bernard and Gauguin, "absolute restfulness" or "sleep in general."[22]

The second theme related to music that emerges in his correspondence from Arles is the example of music as a powerfully expressive art, comforting and consoling, the means to a better life which Van Gogh described metaphorically as "musical." Van Gogh believed that the purpose of art was to offer hope and reassurance in a world full of despair and heartbreak. Modern concert music, he thought, had fulfilled this goal in an exemplary fashion that painters should seek to emulate. "Ah! My dear friend," Van Gogh wrote to Gauguin, "to achieve in painting what the music of Berlioz and Wagner has already done...an art that offers consolation for the broken-hearted!"[23] In the summer of 1888 Van Gogh began a series of symbolic portraits in which individual figures were por-

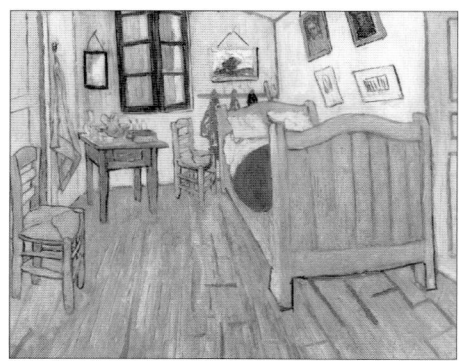

Fig. 2
Vincent van Gogh
Vincent's Bedroom in Arles, 1888
Oil on canvas, 72 x 90 cm
Courtesy Rijksmuseum Vincent van Gogh, Amsterdam

trayed as human types: the poet, "a man who dreams great dreams," the peasant, "a man with a hoe...terrible in the furnace of the height of harvest time," and the woman, who rocks the cradle.[24] He explained his aims to Theo with reference to the expressive effects of music: "In a painting I want to say something comforting," he wrote, "as music is comforting. I want to paint men and women with that something of the eternal which the halo used to symbolize, and which we seek to convey by the actual radiance and vibration of our coloring."[25]

Thirdly, Van Gogh's post-Paris letters compare the act of painting to a musical performance. He writes, for example, of the difficulty when the mistral is blowing of getting "one's brushwork firm and interwoven with feeling, like a piece of music played with emotion."[26] He wondered whether he had "really sang a lullaby in colors" in the painting of *La Berceuse* and, on another occasion, likened his interpretive copying of the works of Millet and other painters to what a musician does in performing the work of a composer.[27] The trope of painter as musician is a recurrent motif in the writings of Van Gogh, employed in a variety of contexts to signify the artist's own identify, the manual practice of his art, and his expressive aims.

In Arles, where he suffered his first mental breakdown in December 1888, Van Gogh began to report hearing voices and to describe specific aural experiences as having affected him deeply. Having mutilated his ear, the instrument of his hearing, Van Gogh seems to have suddenly become more aware of voices within and more sensitive to the expressive implications of the sounds he heard around him. Recounting the parting of the postmaster Roulin from his family due to a reassignment in Marseilles, Van Gogh wrote: "Now I myself was also witness...of other heart-breaking things. When he sang to his child, his voice took on a strange timbre in which one could hear the voice of a woman rocking a cradle or of a sorrowing wet-nurse, and then another trumpet sound like a clarion call to France."[28] In a letter from the end of January 1889, Van Gogh describes his experience of a theatrical performance by a Provincial literary society:

> They were giving what they called a *Noel* or *Pastorale*, reminiscent of the
> Christian theater of the Middle Ages.... But the amazing thing about it...was

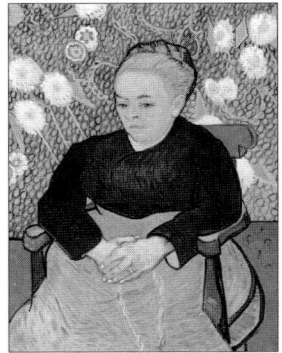

Fig. 3
Vincent van Gogh
Lullaby: Madame Augustine Roulin Rocking a Cradle (La Berceuse), 1889
Oil on canvas, 92 x 72 cm
Courtesy Museum of Fine Arts, Boston

Fig. 4 (far right)
Edgar Degas
Singer with a Glove, c. 1878
Pastel on canvas, 63 x 50.4 cm
Courtesy the Fogg Art Museum, Harvard University Art Museums
Bequest from the collection of Maurice Wertheim, class of 1906

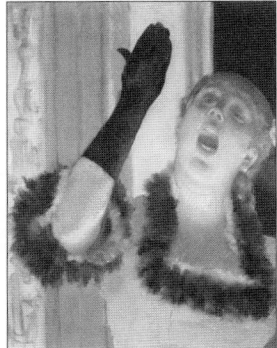

the old peasant woman...with a head of silex or flint, dishonest, treacherous, silly.... [I]n the play that woman, led before the mystic crib, began to sing in her quavering voice, and then the voice changed, changed from the voice of a witch to that of an angel, and from an angel's voice to a child's.[29]

These statements indicate an extraordinary sensitivity to the expressive nuances of sound, but also a tendency on the artist's part to interpret aural experience in terms of pre-existent beliefs and ideas. Van Gogh had earlier described the postman as "a terrible Republican" and thus, in saying that his singing was "a kind of faraway echo of the trumpet of revolutionary France," Van Gogh was hearing in Roulin's voice a quality he had formerly observed in Roulin's character.[30] The reference to a "sweet and mournful lullaby" comes from Van Gogh's conception of his portrait of the postman's wife, a project with which he was then deeply involved.[31]

After invoking the example of music as a formal and expressive model for his own efforts in painting for almost a year, Van Gogh attempted to paint the sound of singing. This effort began in December of 1888 and was sustained over the following several months as he completed five versions of *La Berceuse* (Fig. 3), a portrait image of Augustine Roulin, the postman's wife.[32] She is portrayed as a solid maternal figure seated in a simple armchair while holding onto a curl of rope that implies the presence of an infant's cradle at her feet. Because Van Gogh worked on this subject over such a long period of time, his letters contain numerous passages of reflection on the construction and meaning of the image as it was rethought and reworked again and again. In writing to the Dutch painter A.H. Koning, he identified a literary source for the work's subject and style in a novel by Van Eeden: "I call it *La Berceuse*, or as we say in Dutch...or in Van Eeden's Dutch quite simply 'our lullaby or the woman rocking the cradle.'"[33] Van Gogh goes on to describe the painting's arrangement of colours, concluding that "in this I think I have run pretty well parallel with Van Eeden and his style of writing, which consequently can be considered analogous to my style of painting in the matter of colors. Whether I really sang a lullaby in colors is something I leave to the critics...."[34] In a letter to Theo written a few days later, Van Gogh described the design in musical terms: "A woman in green with orange hair standing out against a background of green with pink flowers. Now these discordant sharps of crude pink, crude orange, and crude green are softened by flats of red and green."[35] This use of a musical terminology is revealing because, while it may function effectively as metaphor, it indicates a misunderstanding of basic concepts of music theory. Sharps are not balanced against flats in a musical composition, nor are sharps inherently "crude" in contrast to the "softness" of flats. As at the beginning of the Arles period, Van Gogh's "orchestration" of colours was guided not by a genuine understanding of musical composition, but by general concepts of musical form so highly abstracted as to be applicable to any art.

To Gauguin, Van Gogh wrote of becoming the woman who rocks the cradle and of assuming her voice during the disorientation of his mental breakdown:

In my mental or nervous fever, or madness...my thoughts sailed over many seas...and it seems that, while thinking what the woman rocking the cradle sang to rock the sailors to sleep, I, who on other occasions cannot even sing a note, came out with an old nursery tune, something I had tried to express in an arrangement of colours before falling ill...."[36]

Van Gogh's prolonged engagement with the image of *La Berceuse* was, no doubt, due in part to his own need for reassurance and consolation at a time when his psychological well-being, his capacity to continue an independent existence, was in serious jeopardy. Needing comfort at a time of personal crisis, he created a personification of reassurance in an image of one who sings comforting songs. He then imagined himself singing those very songs. Throughout his career as a painter, Van Gogh sought to make images that would offer hope and consolation. That aim was specifically and consciously his intent in *La Berceuse*, with which he sought to attain a synaesthetic response by arousing the memory of the viewer's own cradle song.

Van Gogh's representational approach in *La Berceuse* may be understood more clearly through comparison with Degas' *Singer with a Glove* of 1878 (Fig. 4). In the latter an elegantly attired figure is portrayed as if glimpsed summarily in the act of a musical performance, her gloved hand gesturing emphatically and her open mouth a blur of movement. In Van Gogh's symbolic portrait, the act of singing is not literally portrayed but nonetheless integral to Madame Roulin's identity as "the woman rocking the cradle." Avoiding the explicit representation of music-making, Van Gogh relied instead on the abstract means of colour to convey the feeling of the work, to evoke the song of the nursemaid's lullaby. The green of her skirt and the orange of her face are modulated within themselves, while, throughout the painting, complementary green and red hues heighten one another through juxtaposition – two kinds of colour relationships identified by Blanc. The formal character of the image embodies Van Gogh's understanding of Wagnerian orchestration, with intense hues applied to simplified shapes but carefully balanced to achieve a richly sonorous harmony. Perhaps thinking these formal signs were insufficient for a painting so heavily freighted with intended meaning, Van Gogh took the extraordinary step of inscribing the words "*La Berceuse*" in the area of the floor to the right of the figure, giving the viewer three visual indicators – the image of one who sings, sonorous colour, and the written words – of the musical response, the memory of song, that he sought to arouse.[37]

Would we be aware of the influence of music on the making of this work had Van Gogh not provided written explanations of such? Probably not. And this is perhaps most surprising, even ironic, in the case of a painting that thematizes the consoling affect of music. Unlike contemporary French painters such as Degas, Renoir, Fantin-Latour, Seurat, and Toulouse-Lautrec, Van Gogh almost never chose to portray the making or experience of music.[38] This may be explained, at least in part, by his frequent social isolation and by his preoccupation with landscape and portrait subjects. And yet, as indicated by the general remarks he made to his sister Wilhelmina implicating music in the "revolution in painting" and by the many statements particular to the *Berceuse* project, Van Gogh consciously drew on a musical paradigm, assimilating it with visual and literary models, in developing the formal and expressive dimensions of his art.

The terms "vibrations, Wagner, and voices" thus encapsulate some of the significant ways that the sense of sound contributed to the formation of Van Gogh's art. He discovered the connection between music and colour in the writings of Blanc and then sought, earnestly if briefly, to experience and comprehend the vibrational parallels between aural and visual phenomena. In Paris, he came under the influence of the music of Wagner, who became for Van Gogh an exemplary figure invoked again and again in his letters. "What an artist," he wrote of Wagner in one letter, "one like that in painting would be something."[39] Van Gogh's actual experience of sound as a concertgoer or a student of music seems to have been minimal, and yet those episodes of aural experience were sufficiently magnified by verbal discourse – in the things that he said and read and in the conversations that likely took place with fellow artists – to acquire an important place in his thinking about art. Working in Arles at the height of his career, Van Gogh then invoked a musical model for the future of painting and for the consoling art he sought to create, an art that in one pivotal project joined sight to sound in an attempt to evoke the singing of a nursemaid's voice.

NOTES

1. *The Complete Letters of Vincent van Gogh*, 2nd ed., 3 vols. (Greenwich, CT: New York Graphic Society, 1959), Letter W3, III, 431–32; hereafter cited by letter, volume, and page number only.

2. My own essay, "Van Gogh in Nuenen and Paris: The Origins of a Musical Paradigm for Painting," in *The Arts Entwined: Music and Painting in the Nineteenth Century*, eds. Marsha M. Morton and Peter L. Schmunk (New York: Garland, 2000), 177–207, charts Van Gogh's discovery of music as a model for painting and the experiences – literary, auditory, pedagogical, and social – that contributed to his formulation of a musical paradigm. Two other studies, both more narrowly focused, concerning music as an influence on Van Gogh's art are Roland Dorn, "Van Gogh, Gauguin und Richard Wagner, eine Etude auf das Jahr 1888," in *Symbolistes et Richard Wagner/Die Symbolisten und Richard Wagner*, ed. Wolfgang Storch (Berlin: Edition Hentrich, 1991), 67–75, and Kermit S. Champa, "*La Berceuse* – Authored by Music?" in "*Masterpiece*" *Studies: Manet, Zola, Van Gogh, and Monet* (University Park, PA: Pennsylvania State University Press, 1994), 91–118.

3. L528, III, 21.

4. L531, III, 25.

5. Blanc's essay on Delacroix was first published in 1864, a year after the artist's death, as an article in two parts in the January and February issues of the *Gazette des Beaux-Arts*, and then reprinted within *Les Artistes de mon temps* (Paris: Librairie de Firmin-Didot, 1876), 23–88. Published in 1867, the *Grammaire des Arts du Dessin* (known in English as *The Grammar of Painting and Engraving*) had a significant influence on many artists of the late nineteenth century, including Seurat, Signac, and Gauguin.

6. Charles Blanc, *The Grammar of Painting and Engraving*, trans. Kate Newell Doggett (New York: Hurd & Houghton, 1874), 157.

7. L429, II, 427.

8. Leonhard Euler, *Briefe an eine deutsche Prinzessinn über verschiederne Gegenstünd aus der Physik und Philosophie*, Leipzig, 1773–74, cited in Blanc, *The Grammar of Painting and Engraving*, 164.

9. *Complete Letters*, II, 447.

10. *Complete Letters*, II, 442.

11. See Philippe Junot, "The New *Paragone*: Paradoxes and Contradictions of Pictorial Musicalism," in Morton and Schmunk, 28–29.

12. L539, III, 44.

13. Letter from Theo to Wilhelmina van Gogh, March 14, 1888; cited in Dorn, 211.

14. The most comprehensive account of performances of Wagner's music in Paris is found in *Le Ménestrel* (Paris, 1833–1940), which contains both reviews of recent concerts and announcements of upcoming performances. The specific works Van Gogh may have heard performed in the weeks preceding his departure from Paris are identified by Schmunk, "Van Gogh in Nuenen and Paris," 191.

15. This text is reprinted in Hershel B. Chipp, ed., *Theories of Modern Art* (Berkeley: University of California Press, 1968), 60–64, where a date of c. 1888 is given.

16. Gustave Kahn, "Seurat," *L'Art moderne* (April 5, 1891): 107–10, cited in Paul Smith, *Seurat and the Avant-Garde* (New Haven: Yale University Press, 1997), 155.

17. L522, III, 10.

18. L528, III, 21.

19. W3, III, 431.

20. L520, III, 6.

21. L526, III, 19.

22. B22, III, 527; L554, III, 86.

23. This letter to Gauguin was first published in its original French in Douglas Cooper, *Paul Gauguin: 45 Lettres à Vincent, Théo et Jo van Gogh* ('s Gravenhage: Staatsuitgeverij, 1983), 264–71, and is translated in *The Letters of Vincent van Gogh*, ed. Ronald de Leeuw (London: Penguin, 1996), 430.

24. L520, III, 6.

25. L531, III, 25.

26. L543, III, 57.

27. L571a, III, 124; L607, III, 216.

28. De Leeuw, 428–29.

29. L574, III, 131.

30. While engaged in the painting of Roulin's portrait in August 1888, presumably shortly after they had become acquainted, Van Gogh first commented on the postman's ardent Republican views, L516, II, 623. Writing in January 1889, Van Gogh interpreted Roulin's singing as an expression of his deeply held Republican sentiments, L573, III, 126.

31. L573, III, 126.

32. The five versions of *La Berceuse*, virtually identical in size and all mentioned in the artist's correspondence, are now located at the Kröller-Müller Museum in Otterlo, the Annenberg Collection, Rancho Mirage, California, the Art Institute of Chicago, the Stedelijk Museum, Amsterdam, and in the Museum of Fine Arts, Boston.

33. L571a, III, 123.

34. L571a, III, 123–24.

35. L574, III, 129.

36. De Leeuw, 430.

37. See Champa, 113–14, on the inscription as a substitute for the artist's signature.

38. Within Van Gogh's large body of work, images with musical subjects are limited to approximately a dozen small sketches, mostly of individual musicians in a dance-hall setting, probably produced during the latter half of 1886 in Paris, and a single painting of *Marguerite Gachet at the Piano*, dating from June 1890. See Jan Hulsker, *The Complete Van Gogh: Paintings, Drawing, Sketches* (New York: Abrams, 1980), 252–53, 469.

39. L494, II, 578.

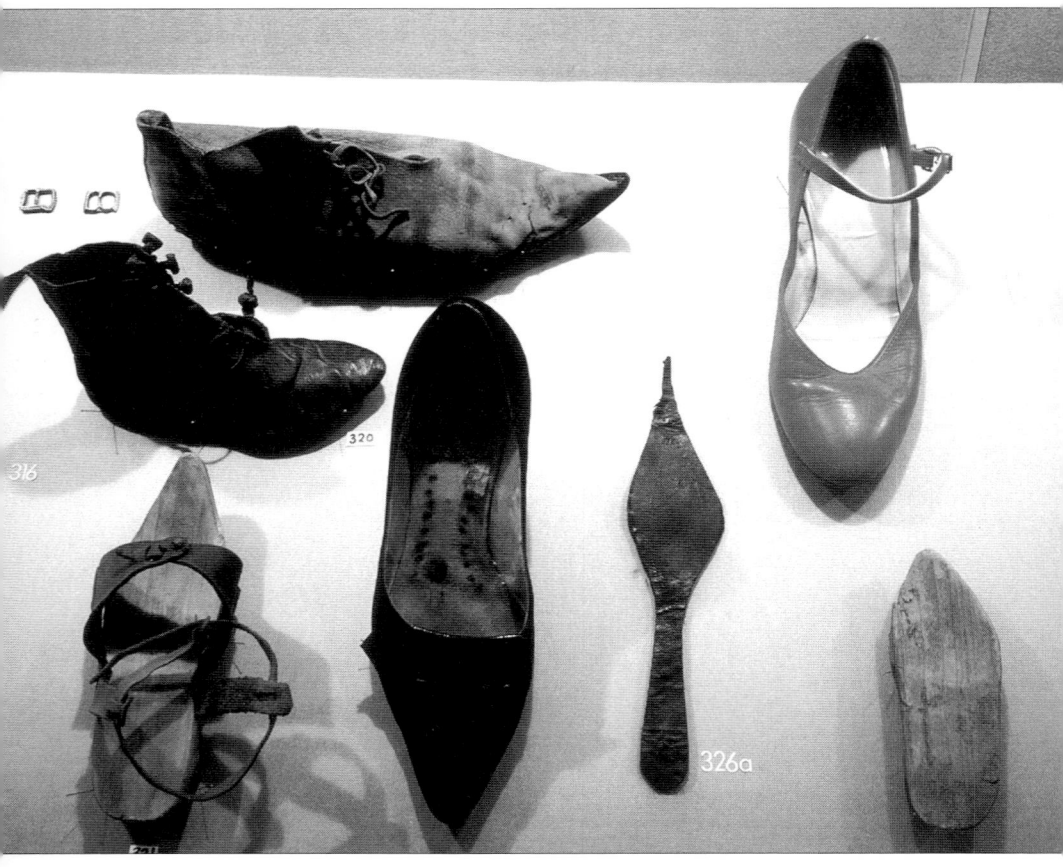

Sophie Calle
La Visite guidée, 1994
Installation view, The Red Shoe
Courtesy the artist and Donald Young Gallery, Chicago

Speeches of Display:
Museum Audioguides by Artists

Jennifer Fisher

During a typical blockbuster exhibition at a major museum of art, the galleries are crowded with people. Those wearing audioguides resemble little cocktail parties grouped around specific works of art. Their behaviour seems formal; newcomers are politely accommodated. If words are exchanged, they are quietly spoken. To observe this phenomenon is to watch individuals within a processional enactment of space, punctuated by "toasts" along the way.

As a form of exhibition rhetoric, audioguides – along with labels, catalogues, signage, and guided tours – support the performative present of an exhibition experience. As such, they constitute a form of *epideictic* or ceremonial rhetoric.[1] Epideictic discourse is used with regard to conditions in the present tense. It takes the form of toasts, congratulations, dedications, praise, or religious invocation; conversely, it can assume the form of declamation or blame. Its purpose is traditionally to "honour" or "dishonour." When oriented to a person, it qualifies character or accomplishments. When oriented to a work of art, it plays a role in legitimizing or otherwise contextualizing the work at the very moment it is being experienced. According to Aristotle, epideictic rhetoric is a "speech of display":

> In epideictic speaking, where the main thing is to show that a man's deeds were noble and of service, your chief means will be *amplification*.... [T]he facts themselves must be taken on trust; proof of them is given but rarely – when a deed seems incredible, or when it has been ascribed to some other man.[2]

A key technique of epideictic rhetoric, then, is amplification. A traditional toast may honour the presence of someone by expanding their good qualities, or by augmenting the importance or significance of their actions. In turn, written forms of museum discourse – such as labels and signage – provide details on works of art that are read in the presence of the work. The catalogue essay, likewise, generally supports an exhibition or artist. It would be unusual for an author to severely critique a work of art in a catalogue essay: its function is more epideictic – to provide an insightful salute. Moored to a museum bench, the catalogue is presented at the same time and in the same context as the exhibition itself.

In the same way, audioguides are conventionally provided to supplement an exhibition, giving background on the works and their contexts. But unlike textual forms, the audioguide moves beyond the primacy of visual engagement to stage sound inside the beholder's body. The use of sound expands the resonance of the exhibition and gives intensity to inert objects. An audioguide tour involves the viewer in the affective climate generated by the sound script: involving music, emotional sensibility, and the timbre of the spoken voices. The soundtracks of audioguides not only compel particular reasoning, emotions, and identifications, but also have the physical effect of putting beholders into action, drawing them through a series of suggestions and mood states. In many instances scripted movement engages the proprioceptive sense – the felt dimensionality of the exhibition – which unfolds through a series of perambulatory transits and stops. The audioguide tours in use by art museums for their permanent collections, such as Ottawa's National Gallery and New York's Museum of Modern Art, or those of more temporary blockbusters, typically underscore the curatorial intent of the exhibition and amplify its effect.

However, the artists' audioguides discussed here, I will suggest, work in counterpoint to the conventional audioguide. Rather than serving as exhibition support, Sophie Calle, Andrea Fraser, and Janet Cardiff nuance the dynamics of the relationship between audiotour, art, and beholder in distinct ways that move beyond the ceremonial epideictic toast to the invocation of other realms of presence. I will first describe the sensory aesthetics of conventional audioguides, then turn to examine how artists engage this technology for altered effects.

Perambulatory Aesthetics

The "acoustiguide" – the foundational audioguide – was invented in 1957 by Valentine Burton, a Hollywood actor and composer. Inspired by his walk through an exhibition with its curator, Burton returned with sound equipment and repeated the experience, producing the first mobile audioguide in the form of a reel-to-reel tape recorder that weighed between fifteen and twenty pounds. An easily portable audioguide was facilitated by the invention of audiocassettes in the 1960s, and the watershed museum blockbuster – the 1976 touring exhibition "Treasures of Tutankhamen" – marked its acceptance by major art institutions.

Early versions of the audioguide featured non-rewindable audiocassettes, which resulted in a unidirectional enactment of the exhibition script. During the seventies, a technology of radio wand audioguides evolved that received commentary broadcast from each exhibit zone. While radio wands enabled free movement through the exhibition, they had other, unforeseen effects. Quick perambulation produced a cacophony of truncated – if earnest – commentary, or, conversely, repetitions of narrative fragments that effected a robotic insincerity. Before long, radio wands became obsolete in major urban centres because of the interference caused by cellular phones.[3] A more recent innovation, Inform, logs soundtracks on CDs, and users access different entries as they punch numbers coded to specific exhibits. In contrast to the linearity of cassette tours, Inform audioguides permit beholders to invent their own path through an exhibition.[4] Since the arrival of the blockbuster exhibition, audioguides have been widely used by museums to achieve educational objectives, bring celebrity cachet to the institution, and encourage traffic flow.

According to Mary Enright, marketing director of Acoustiguide Corporation, the goal of the audiotrack is "to record the curator's vision." Acoustiguide employs its own writers, who research the exhibition and prepare a text in an amazingly brief time. Once the show is installed and as close to the opening as possible – usually just two days beforehand – the writer tapes a walk-through of the exhibition with the curator.[5] Then the tour is written and sent to the curator involved for approval. Finally, commentary is scripted and re-recorded in a studio.

Audioguides ostensibly give scholarly background to exhibitions, anticipating the questions of beholders and providing answers. But this technology has aesthetic significance as well, specifically, in how relationships and the senses are structured in the audioguide experience. The voice on the soundtrack is characteristically an entertaining authority: an art expert, creator, or celebrity. Commentary by museum directors, curators, or educators often provides the frame. Artists' narrations of their exhibitions offer a level of connection akin to a personal interview, a primary – if monologic – source not otherwise available. The recorded voice substitutes for the presence of an actual tour guide.

Conventionally, the audioguide's mode of address is the first person, speaking to an implied "you" *about* the display. This relational aspect of the voice of the audioguide effects a feeling of intimacy. Reesa Greenberg has likened the audioguide dyad to the one-to-one physical relationship of mother and child. Yet, in this instance, she notes, it is the listener who is affectively the child, carrying the technological mother who enchants with her stories.[6] Indeed, the aural affect of audioguides can be profoundly determining, even to the extent of displacing the viewer's own inner dialogue and intuitive responses.

On another level, audioguides involve the senses in ways distinct from the labels or didactic panels found in exhibitions. The sonic choreographies of audioguides engage the audio, tactile, and haptic senses in a performative mediation. Whereas textual forms enable spectators to "keep their distance," audioguides demand participation and interaction with both the technology and the proximal space of other beholders (i.e., the "cocktail party" manners at each listening station mentioned earlier). The audioguide machine involves the sense of weight as it is carried and the pressure of earphones clamped to the head. Whether the user is standing still before a work of art or moving between works, the proprioceptive sense is engaged in specific ways. Typically, the audiocassette script alternates between speaking and the transitional signal. As we hear the voice, our attention is directed. Then the music fades and a beep or other signal indicates that it is time to move to the next point of focus. These perambulatory transitions suggest what Gilles Deleuze and Félix Guattari have described as "smooth" space. They argue that "smooth" space is directional and transitional, in contrast to "striated" space, which – because it centres on analytical foci – tends to closure. Enactments of smooth space privilege the haptic-proprioceptive functions; that is, the faculties of touch and movement as they are sensed both inside and outside the body. The beholder moves at varying paces, stops, accelerates, or changes spatial orientation within a continuous process.[7] Exhibition scripts are conventionally enacted according to the preferences and proclivities of the viewer, effecting a smooth space of individual enactment. But with the linearity of audio-guides, the transitions – those spaces of possibility – are also prescribed.

Significantly, the confluence of sight, hearing, and movement affects memory as well. Chris Tellis, head of the San Francisco-based company Antenna – Acoustiguide's main competitor – describes how audioguides impact the recollection of an exhibition:

> [The voice] directs your attention and provides immediate educational mate-rial. There's no secondary shift in focus, no video screen or wall label on the side. If you're looking at the real thing and you're hearing about it, there's a magic moment that allows you to remember the fact better. The machine is simply the vehicle.[8]

The "magic" of this moment has to do precisely with how the means of per-ception impinge on the creation of memory in the viewer. The engagement of visual, auditory, and proprioceptive faculties scripts sensorial experience, creating what is, in effect, pre-recorded memory.

The cognitive aspects of audiotours involve a similar sensorial dynamic as an ancient mnemonic technique, the Greco-Roman "art of memory." This practice was based on the contention that the process of memory interconnects with that of move-ment. The art of memory was used by orators to recall long speeches without the aid of written notes. It consisted of imagining oneself walking though a series of rooms filled with remarkable objects. Each room – loci or place – corresponded with a part of the speech, and each object would relate to a particular point. The exaggeration of the affec-tive qualities of these objects – as beautiful or hideous, comic or obscene – was found to give additional acuity in remembering.[9]

Audioguide narratives substitute for the oratorical component in this mnemonic practice. Whereas the art of memory involves visualized proprioception in order to recall a speech as it is being performed, an audioguide involves actual proprioception accom-panied by a soundtrack that substitutes for memory. While the art of memory enables an orator to contain a speech, the acoustic and proprioceptive space of the audioguide in effect contain the beholder.

The three artists that I will discuss here challenge the hegemonic use of the audioguide to interpret and elucidate an exhibition. Sophie Calle's La Visite guidée (1994) describes the significance of objects belonging to the artist, each placed in arrangement with the museum's collection. Andrea Fraser's audioguide "Untitled" (An Introduction to the 1993 Whitney Biennial) (1993) is a non-narrative sound work that not only reveals the behind-the-scenes humanity of the museum staff, but turns curatorial authority inside out. And Janet Cardiff's museum tour Chiaroscuro (1997) draws the beholder through real and virtual atmospheres with an overlay of relational, auditory, and sensorial elements that impact on the beholder's awareness in specific ways. In each instance, the artist works in strategic relationship to the exhibiting institution through political and personal intervention. These audiotours provide instances of sensorial experience that exceed the boundaries of representation or meaning, and provide moments that interrupt the closures of fixed discursive frameworks.

La Visite guidée

Sophie Calle's audioguide focuses on a series of personal objects inserted into the permanent exhibitions of the Museum Boymans-van Beuningen in Rotterdam. Corresponding to each tableau, Calle's recorded voice relates a story and amplifies the significance of a seemingly benign object. Calle gives presence to these objects by relating intimate details about the roles they have played in her life. She "tells the objects" in much the same way that relics are handled as touchstones for stories. Inverting the *Kunstskammer*'s centrifugal logic that draws worldly objects into the hands of the collector, the logic of Calle's recollections is centripetal; that is, she uses objects to project the personal into the public sphere. Each object becomes a souvenir of a moment in her life. In the manner that Michel de Certeau has described the capacity of memory to interrupt space, each station on Calle's guided tour fractures the museum's public exhibitions with private and autobiographical assertions.[10]

Calle's audiotour is consistent with her other works that foreground what is conventionally "unseen" in the relationships between individuals, objects, and spaces. The expanses of the unseen, where the object becomes a focus for feelings, sensibilities, longings, and imaginings, act as apt metaphors for the relational aspects of aesthetic experience. Just as Calle's sensorial aesthetic blasts open the seriality of the museum, her audiotrack interrogates the gaps that occur between cultural and individual memory, museum label and personal memoir.

Often the object is a referent of a sensory mode, contextualized by narratives that describe a bathrobe touched by a lover or a cup summoning the smell of coffee. This is a novelistic litany of revelations through objects – a telephone, a bucket, a razor blade – that reveal details of what is supposedly Calle's personal history. The stories often

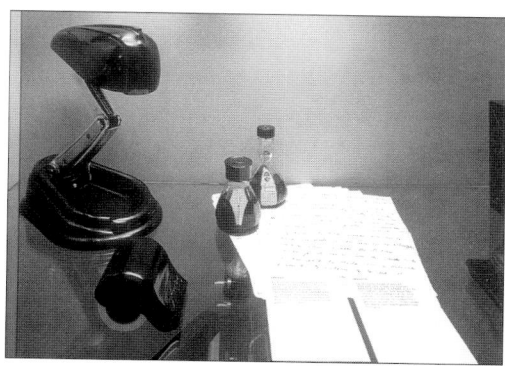

Sophie Calle
La Visite guidée, 1994
Installation view, The Letter (2)
Courtesy the artist and
Donald Young Gallery, Chicago

detail some significant exchange. Like tabloid television, the disclosures carry a *frisson* of illicitness: confessions that she hired a public notary to write her a love letter, or stole a pair of red shoes as a pubescent girl. The soundscript for a white terrycloth bathrobe displayed in a vitrine tells of how it became a relic:

> *The bathrobe*: I was eighteen years old. I rang the bell. He opened the door. He was wearing the same bathrobe as my father. A long white terrycloth robe. He became my first love. For an entire year, he obeyed my request, and never let me see him naked from the front. Only from the back. And so, in the morning light, he would get up carefully, turning himself away, and gently hiding inside the white bathrobe. When it was all over he left the bathrobe behind with me.[11]

The souvenir bathrobe carries the index of her lover's presence. The story relates a pact between intimates that permitted touch but prohibited sight. This is heard by the beholder in the context of museum conventions that effect the opposite – encouraging sight but prohibiting touch.

Calle's audioguide reconstitutes the sensorial and sensational affect of objects. These souvenirs sustain the relational charge between artist and object within the cultural narratives of museum display. Where the beholder is ultimately guided in this visit is to the interiority of a confidential telling, which – like an oral graffiti tag – inscribes personal signature in the perambulatory domain of public culture.

Calle's object-centred memoirs work serially as closed tableaux. The viewer-object-audioguide relationship occurs as the listening beholder stands still before the object. In contrast, audiotours by Fraser and Cardiff are directional and transitional, moving the beholder through space.

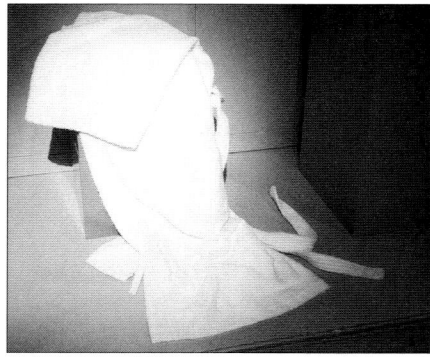

Sophie Calle
La Visite guidée, 1994
Installation view, The Bathrobe
Courtesy the artist and Donald Young Gallery, Chicago

"Untitled" (An Introduction to the 1993 Whitney Biennial)

Like Calle's work, Andrea Fraser's audiotour for the Whitney Biennial interrogates official museal discourse and territorializes its spaces. But while Calle's interventions reconstitute the presence of objects, Fraser's audioguide reveals the institutionally produced "voice" of the museum. In her tour, Fraser rescripts excerpts of interviews with the museum's staff. The focus of this tour, then, is not objects – as it is with Calle – but people. Conventionally, the "voice" of the museum is a discourse managed from behind the scenes: filtered through memos, meetings, discussions, and statements which are, in turn, reformulated and refined before reaching the public. Fraser's audiotrack is constructed from interviews undertaken by the artist with museum personnel, including the director, curators, and education staff. Where conventional audioguides aim to reveal the curator's vision, Fraser's interview questions ask museum staff about the audience; she asks them, "Who do you think your audience is?" or "What do you want that audience to get out of their experience with a particular piece?" But Fraser's questions are edited out of the tape, dislocating the answers from the context of the conversation. They become speech fragments or even outtakes. In contrast to Calle's first-person narrative to a beholder about an object, Fraser's audience in effect overhears a discussion about itself.

In other sections, phatic exclamations such as "That's great!" "Very effective" or "Fabulous" punctuate the perambulatory route. Fraser's instructions to beholders move them through an abstracted soundscape. Her voice – seemingly continuous with the patrician docent Jane Castleton (the persona Fraser adopted for several gallery-talk performances) – instructs: "Let's view the exhibition together." "Take the elevator." "Go to the fourth floor and turn right." "Proceed to the next gallery." "Please proceed to the next gallery to the reading room on the right."[12] The sequence of spaces is vague and attention is dissociated from the artworks. The works are neither addressed directly nor referred to specifically due to the concerns of museum curators, who felt that it would not be appropriate for an exhibiting artist to produce commentary on the works of other artists in the same exhibition. Fraser edited out of the tape any direct references to works of art. This audioguide diverges from other tours because it does not hinge on objects. The movement through abstracted museum spaces has no mnemonic hooks to ground it.

In this tour, the "voice" of the museum is revealed to be neither singular nor absolute in its authority. What is brutally interesting is how Fraser teases out uncomfortable moments where speakers pause midway through a thought; she foregrounds instances of aphasia where speakers lose their concentration, say something, and then declare that they want it edited out, or give up seemingly in frustration. What becomes evident in the spaces between their inflections of warmth, intimacy, and controlled humour are the unspoken appeals to Fraser to be fair with their representations. Some voices assume a tenor of familiarity that cajoles, while others implore with a formality that sounds either rigid or too eager.

The artist moves us into a dangerous terrain where "connoisseurship" – that state of knowing – gives way to evidence of "not knowing," through voices utterly

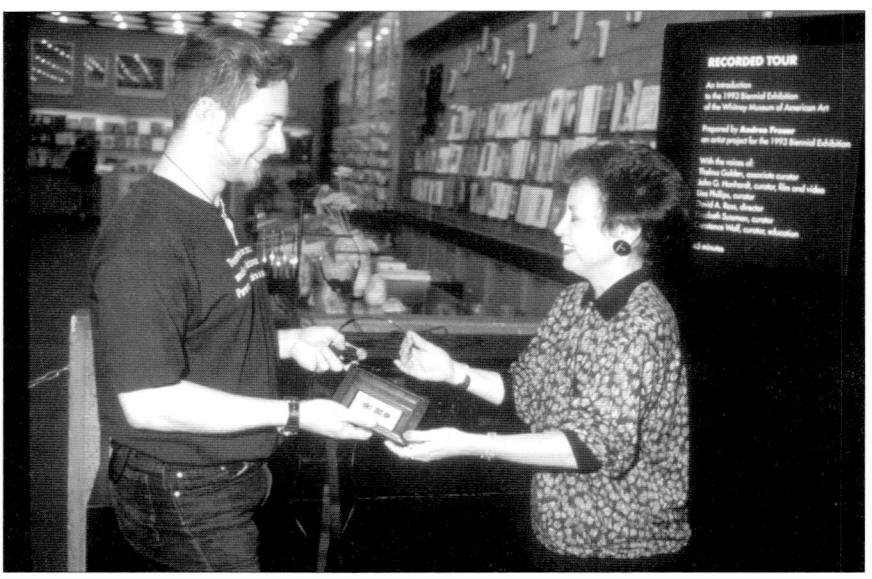

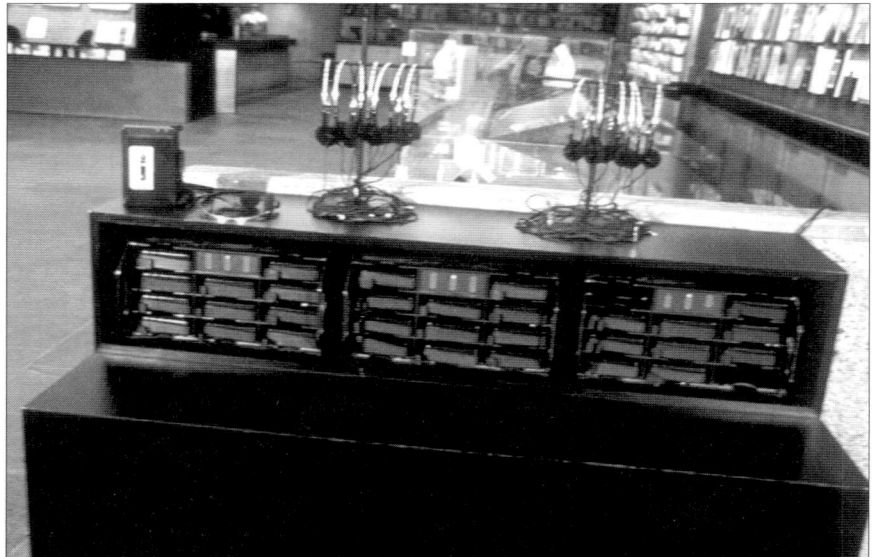

Andrea Fraser
*"Untitled" (An Introduction to the 1993
Whitney Biennial)*, 1992-3
Installation views
Photos: George Hirose
Courtesy American Fine Arts, New York

stripped of the veneer of authority. It was Fraser's intention to "not only represent the speaker's anxiety but to confront the viewers with their anxiety."[13] While Fraser claims that she did not intend to misrepresent the Whitney administration, it is understandable that they were made very uncomfortable by this piece. What is at issue is that the requisite authority required of the "museum voice" simply cannot tolerate what Trinh T. Minh-ha has termed "critical not-knowingness" as part of the curatorial process.[14] In the shadow of the anxiety revealed by the interviewees lurks the spectre of the consummate connoisseur, the one "who always knows." But more to the point perhaps is the notion that whereas the connoisseur's position is historically assured by wealth, the station of the contemporary museum curator is assured by a more vulnerable currency: the cultural capital of "reputation." As Fraser admits, this deconstruction of the institution through the fallibility of human beings who are its actual agents was perhaps asking too much.[15] But despite the conflicts raised, Fraser's audiotour, precisely by revealing manners of both "knowing" and "not knowing," provides a remarkable instance of the audioguide as exhibitionary countertext.

Chiaroscuro

Like Fraser's guide, Janet Cardiff's audiotours use sound to impel the proprioceptive sense: the feeling of moving through the exhibition and encountering various presences. The focus of this piece is not objects or people, but the affective significance of spatial practices. To participate in Cardiff's audiotour is to merge with an archaeology of fictional and actual place.

     Chiaroscuro is the title of Cardiff's eleven-minute audiowalk through the San Francisco Museum of Modern Art. It is the sole audioguide of the three discussed here that involves the actual acoustic atmosphere of the museum. As the work progresses, the museum's quotidian spaces give way to other moods woven into the soundtrack, like being drawn into a *film noir*, or whodunit.

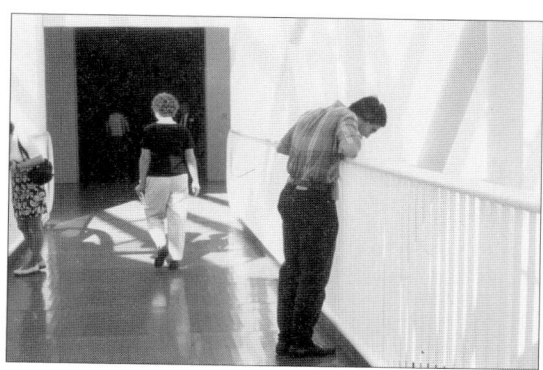

Janet Cardiff
Chiaroscuro, 1997
Installation view of audio walk
Courtesy the artist

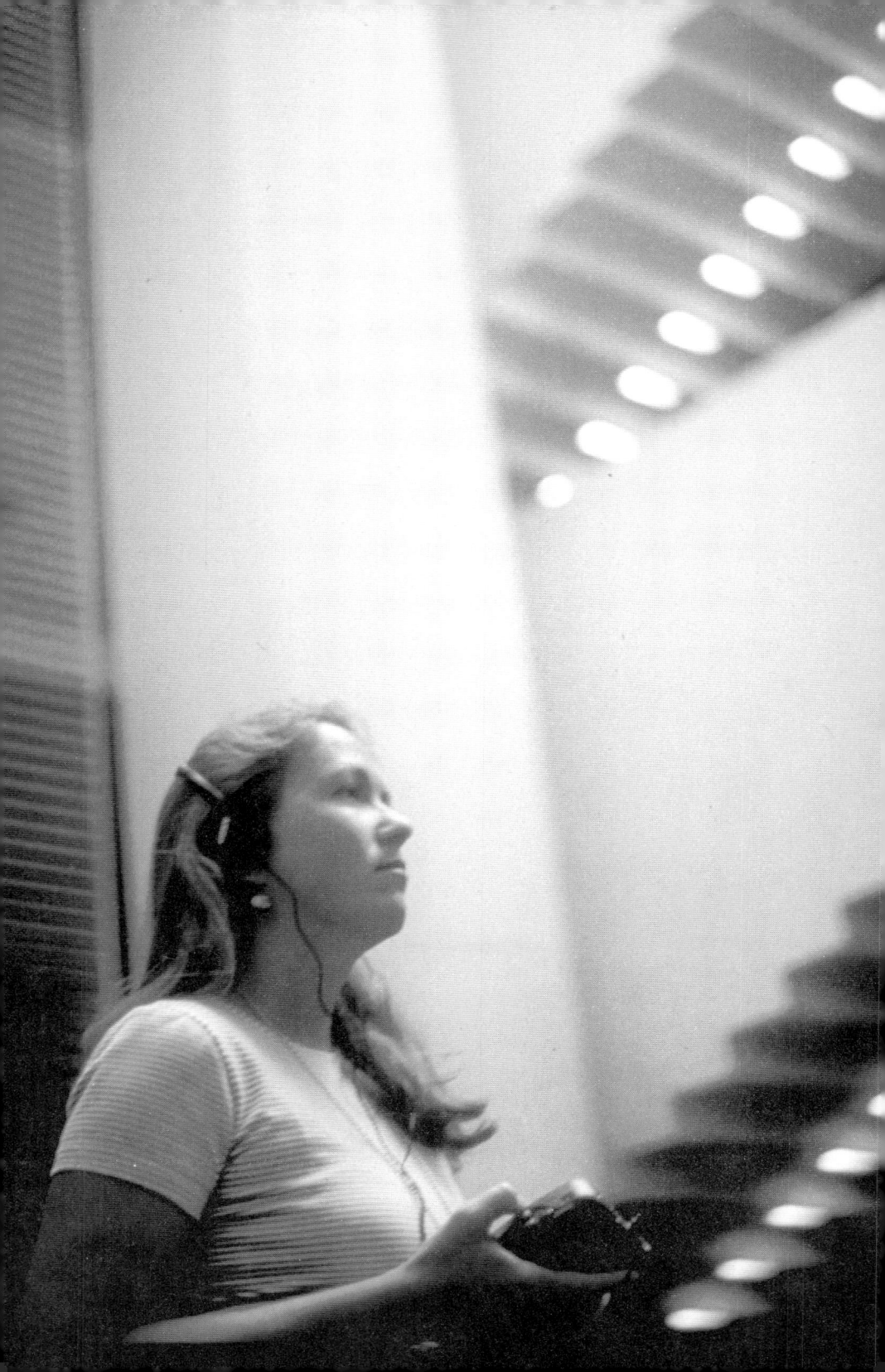

At the beginning of this tour, like Cardiff's other tours, the participant is asked: "Try to walk with the sound of my footsteps, so we can stay together." The sense of proprioception is central to this piece in that the motion of the speaker directly parallels that of the listener. As Cardiff's footsteps mark time for the participant, they trace a route through the virtual soundscape that blends with the actual proximate space of the museum.[16] The binaural recording technique gives a three-dimensional sonic presence and the sense that the recorded sound is inside you, sharing your own interoceptive processes. As Cardiff inhales deeply in the elevator, you are inevitably reminded of your own breathing.

Cardiff addresses the beholder as a "known" companion, as distinct from Calle's "passive listener" or Fraser's "eavesdropper." Cardiff seems to chat with the beholder, asking questions and leaving spaces for response. The effect is one of conversant space. The museum's economy of connoisseurship – being "in the know" – gives way to the sense of "being known" by the artist.

The sound collage weaves together a variety of narratives and sound effects so direct and timed to the beholder's actions that it mimics intuitive processes. Cardiff is well aware of the link between movement and memory. This becomes evident in her explanation of how the museum reminds her of Greek architecture for the "art of memory." But she extends this mnemonic technique beyond intellectual recollection alone to invoke sensorial memory and engage diverse climates of feeling:

> I remember the feel of walking barefoot on gravel.
> I remember the smell of old straw in the barn.
> I remember wading into the river, mud squishing through my toes.
> I remember running through the house in fear.[17]

Multiple narratives weave through the soundtrack. The dominant "present" is that of Cardiff and the beholder as companions walking through museum space. Other voices elicit more seductive or conspiratorial relations. A man's whispers direct a woman how to dress. Cardiff relates details of being stalked, of a dream of transgression and

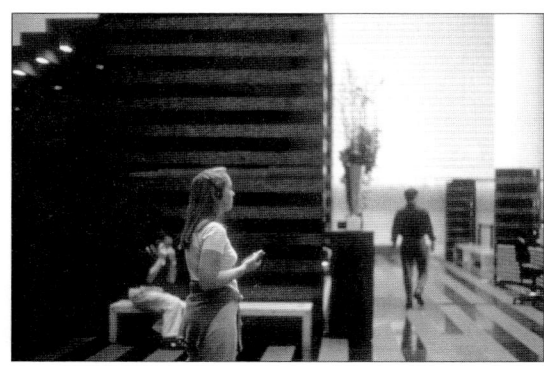

Janet Cardiff
Chiaroscuro, 1997
Installation views of audio walk
Courtesy the artist

revenge, of being mistaken for someone else. In the echoing resonances of the museum we overhear a phone conversation; another visitor enthusiastically exclaims, "I can't wait to see the Rothko!"; we pass a docent lecturing on the museum as a temple. Additional layers of sound punctuate the narrative: film music, opera, a Catholic mass, elevator beeps.

Cardiff interrupts the movement flow with a pause to look over the museum's balcony. Coming to stillness amplifies the significance of these places as sites of vertigo, dizziness, loss of balance. Cardiff's vestibular disturbance encompasses the felt dimensionality of space: "I like the strange feeling I get when I look over a railing like this. My body tingles all over. I imagine myself jumping. Do you do that? I don't completely trust myself not to." A film soundtrack symphonically swells with a blood-curdling scream.[18]

Cardiff's tour invokes ghostly presences in the museum, overlaying the listener's "present" with her observations of the same place at a previous time. In this way, the space between two temporalities – like the space between two thoughts – becomes at once a practiced and revelatory space.

The museum audiotours I've described all work beyond the boundaries of vision. They function as artworks that can be neither seen nor touched, but impel the beholder to see and move in particular ways. Each audioguide provides a distinct atmosphere that frames the experience of viewing with the sense of sound and felt space.

The tensions between the visual, aural, and proprioceptive senses are vital to understanding how exhibition scripts pertain to the body in space, and thus how exhibition codes are incorporated (or resisted) by beholders. Specifically, tactile and aural resonances have the potential to challenge the hegemony of visuality in exhibition aesthetics and politics. This has important implications for renegotiating notions of a passive viewer (conventionalized according to patriarchal notions of the feminine and archaic notions of "being acted upon") by shifting strategic relationships in experiences of beholding.

Significantly, none of these artists deals with the actual exhibitions within which the audiotour takes place. Instead, ambience and atmosphere are treated as an aesthetic support for particular interrogations of artist, audience, objects of attention, and transitions through the museum. While these artists' audioguides differ conceptually, each functions as a relational form merging sound and proprioception to link the viewer with particular continuums of experience. These audioguides are not educational or interpretative but rather, in themselves, generative.

NOTES

1. Aristotle, *The Rhetoric of Aristotle*, trans. Lane Cooper (New York: Appleton-Century-Crofts, 1932), xxxvii. Epideictic rhetoric is one of three kinds – deliberative (political, advisory), forensic (legal), and epideictic (ceremonial) – each of which is distinguished by its modality of address, its temporal orientation, and anticipated result.

2. Aristotle, 233 (emphasis mine).

3. Mary Enright, interview with the author, March 6, 1997.

4. Rene Chun, "Voices at an Exhibition," *New York Times* (March 5, 1995).

5. Enright, interview with the author. Recent digital technology has permitted more complex audio-guide scripts, evidenced in the general trend towards multiple voice tracks.

6. Reesa Greenberg, "The Acoustic Eye," *Parachute* 46 (spring 1987): 108.

7. Gilles Deleuze and Félix Guattari, *A Thousand Plateaus: Capitalism and Schizophrenia*, trans. Brian Massumi (Minneapolis: University of Minnesota Press, 1987), 479, 482, 494.

8. Judd Tully, "In Your Ear: The Audio-Tour Industry," *The Journal of Art* (January 1991): 35.

9. Frances Yates, *The Art of Memory* (Chicago and London: University of Chicago Press, 1966), 1–26.

10. Michel de Certeau, *The Practice of Everyday Life*, trans. Stephen Rendall (Berkeley: University of California Press, 1984), 82–90.

11. Sophie Calle, *La Visite guidée*, artist book including CD of audiotour with music by Laurie Anderson (Rotterdam: Museum Boymans-van Beuningen, 1994), n.p.

12. Fraser has tactically usurped the "official" speaking position of the museal in several works. In 1986 she developed the character of Jane Castleton, who gave museum "tours" during the "Damaged Goods" show at the New Museum, New York, and later at the Philadelphia Museum of Fine Art. As the tour proceeded, the well-groomed, civilized, bourgeois docent would progressively "lose her grip" in her interpretations of artworks, revealing instead more personally nuanced stream-of-consciousness projections.

13. Andrea Fraser, interview with the author, New York, February 24, 1997.

14. Trinh T. Minh-ha, *When the Moon Waxes Red: Representation, Gender and Cultural Politics* (London and New York: Routledge, 1991), 234.

15. Fraser, interview with the author.

16. Thomas Heyd, "Touching Us Softly," *Border Crossings* (April 1994): 62.

17. Janet Cardiff, *Chiaroscuro*, videotape soundtrack, 1997.

18. Among the cinematic references of this piece is Alfred Hitchcock's *Vertigo*.

SANTIAGO SIERRA

Space Closed by Corrugated Metal, 2002
Installation view

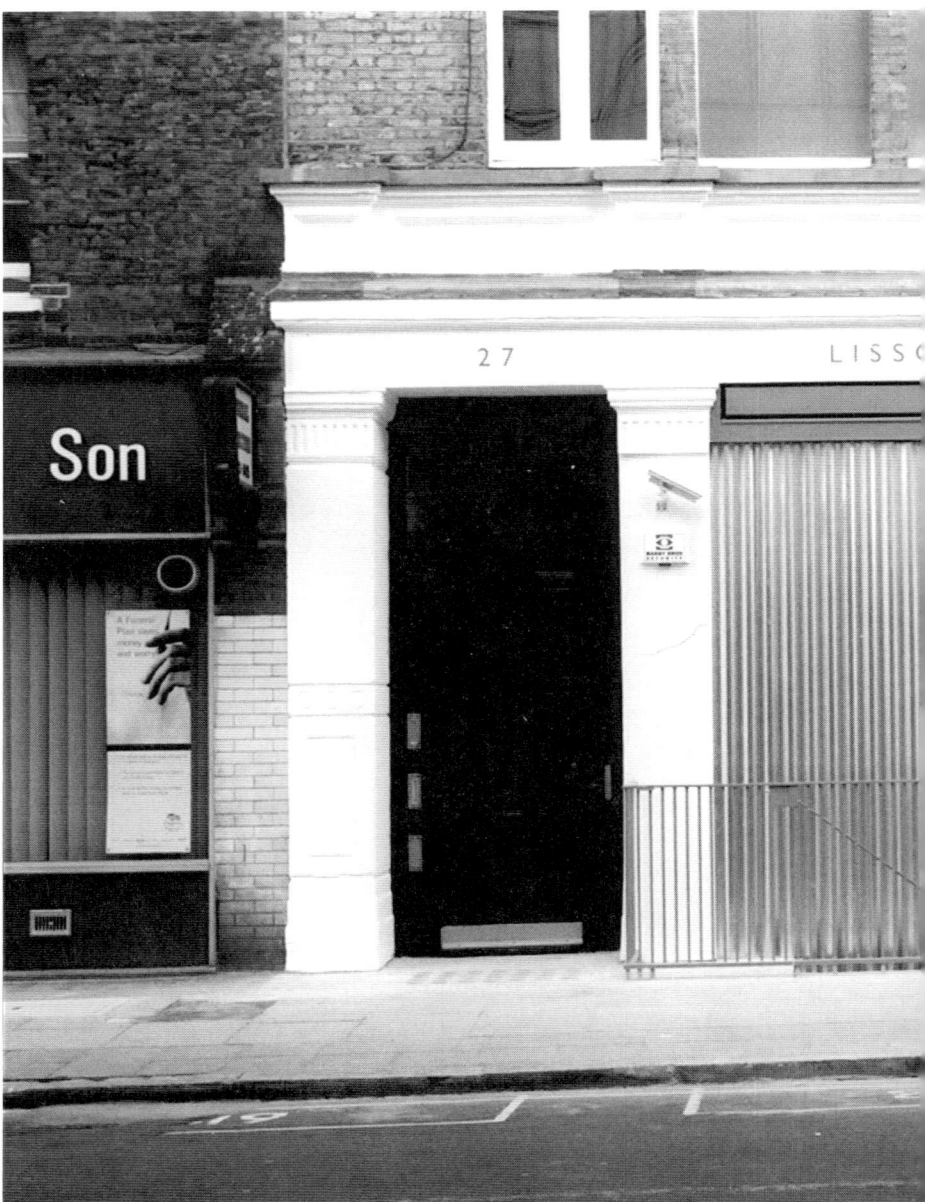

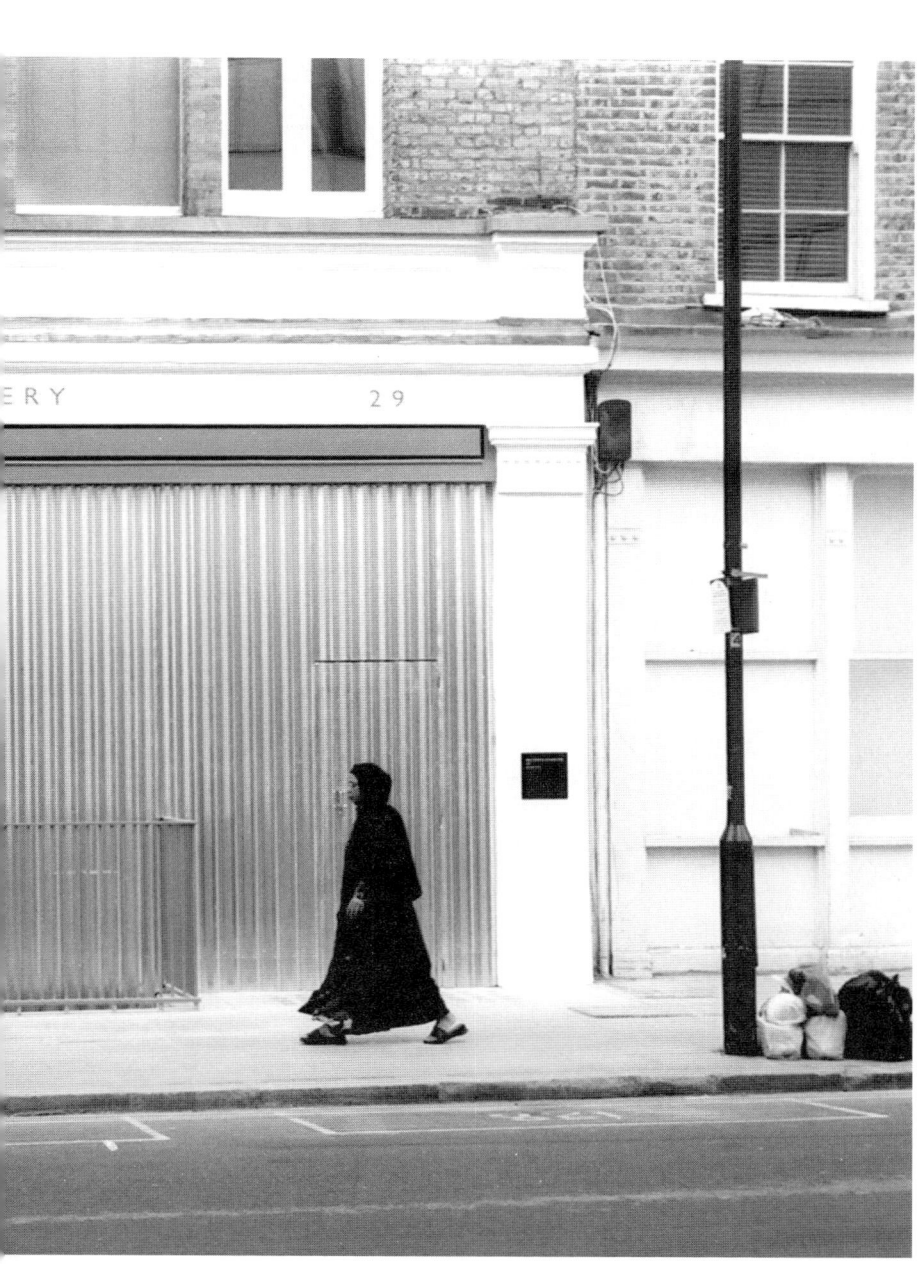

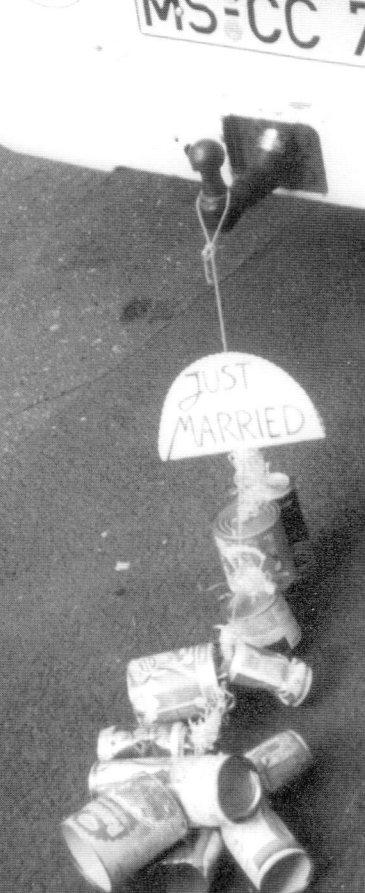

CHRISTIAN MARCLAY

Snapshots

Frankfurt, 1992

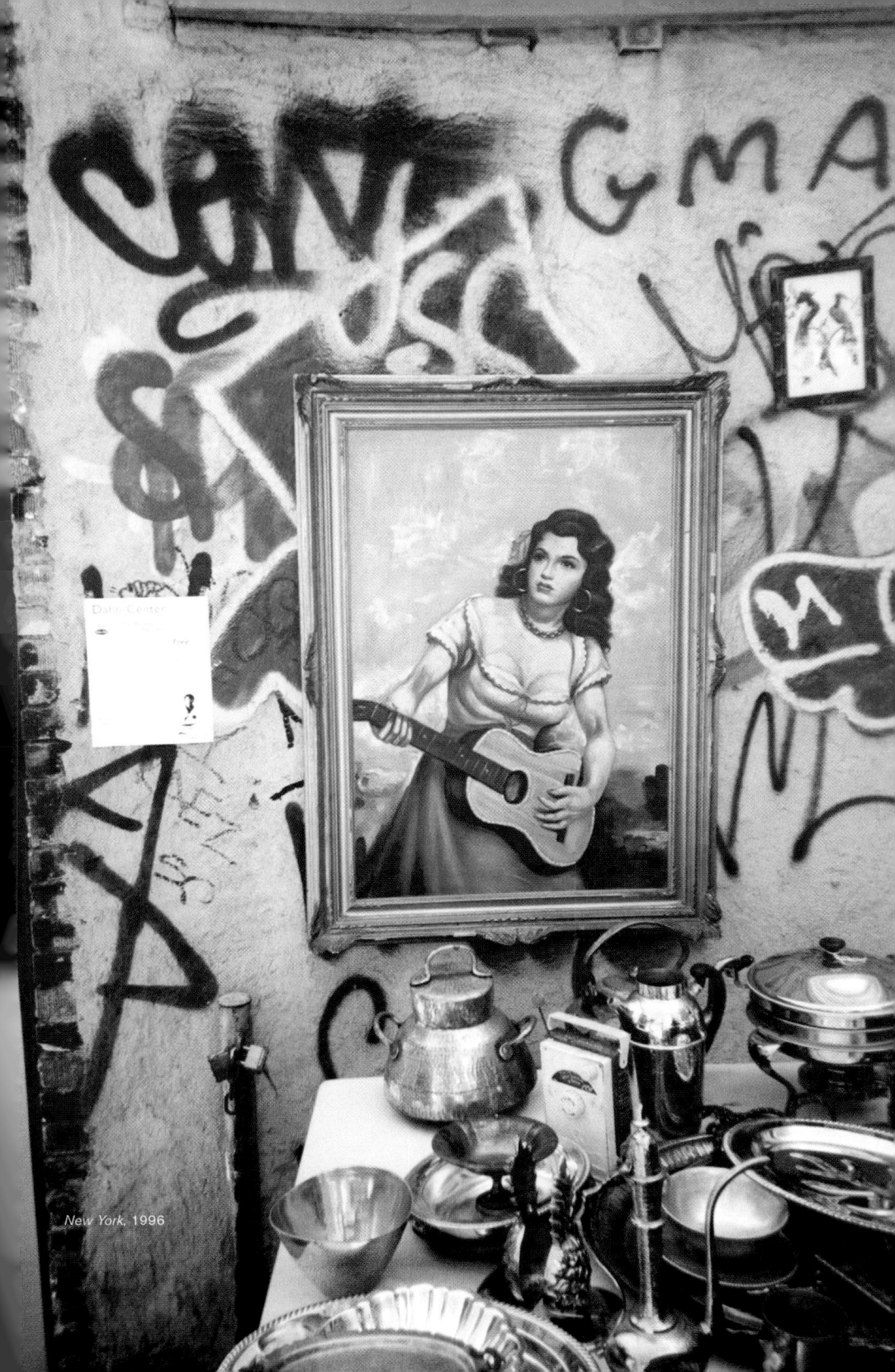

New York, 1996

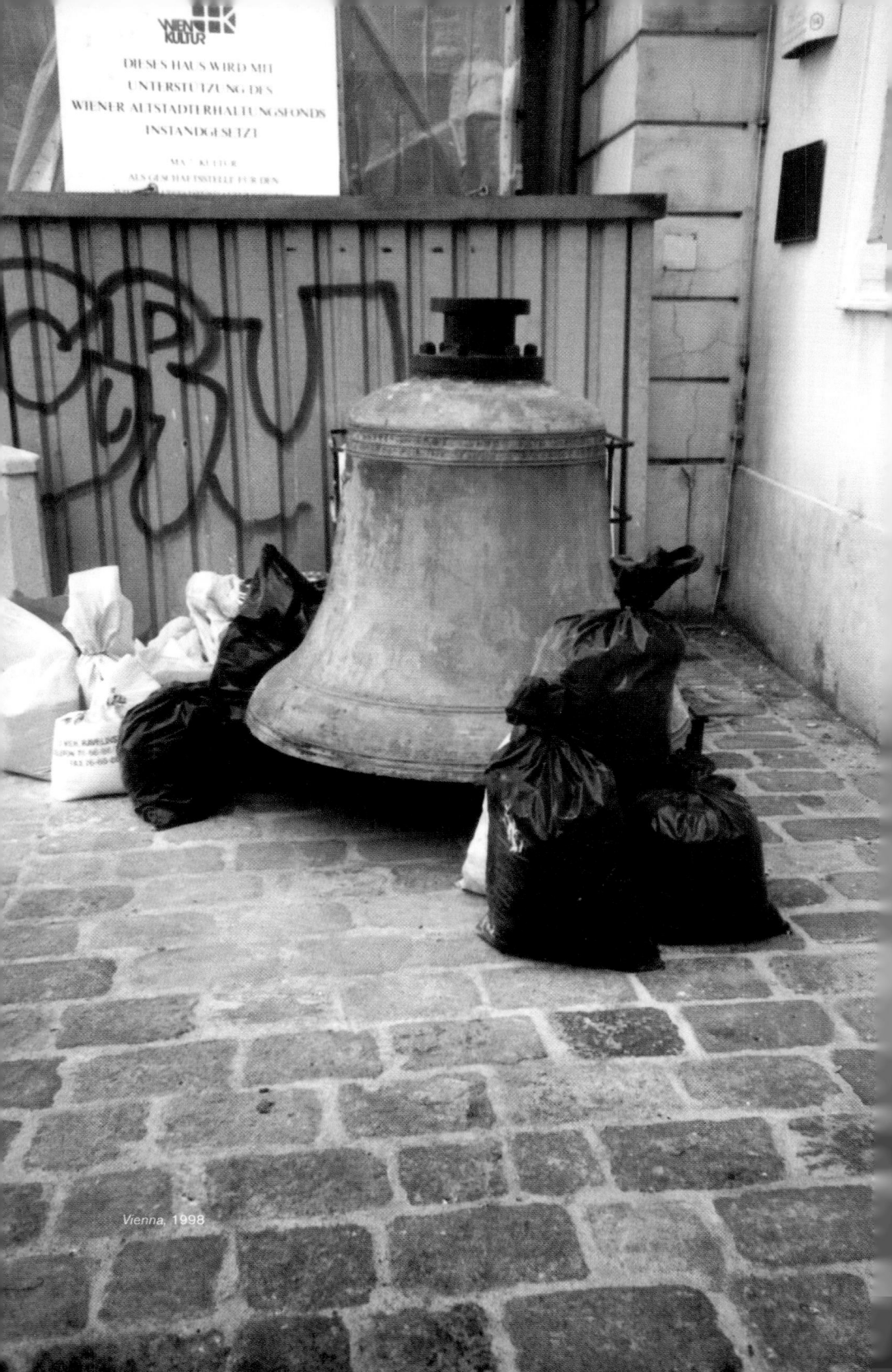

Vienna, 1998

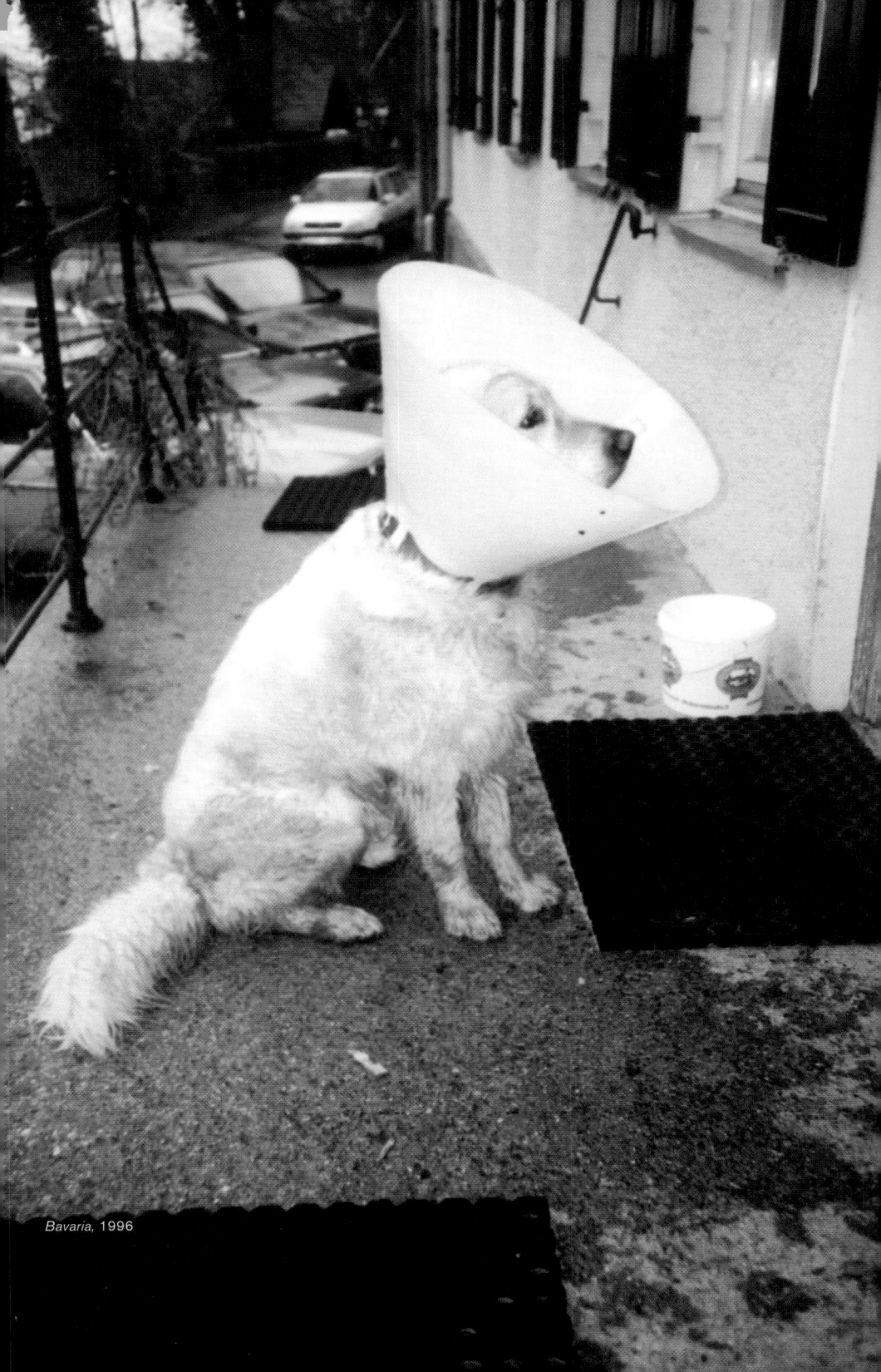

Bavaria, 1996

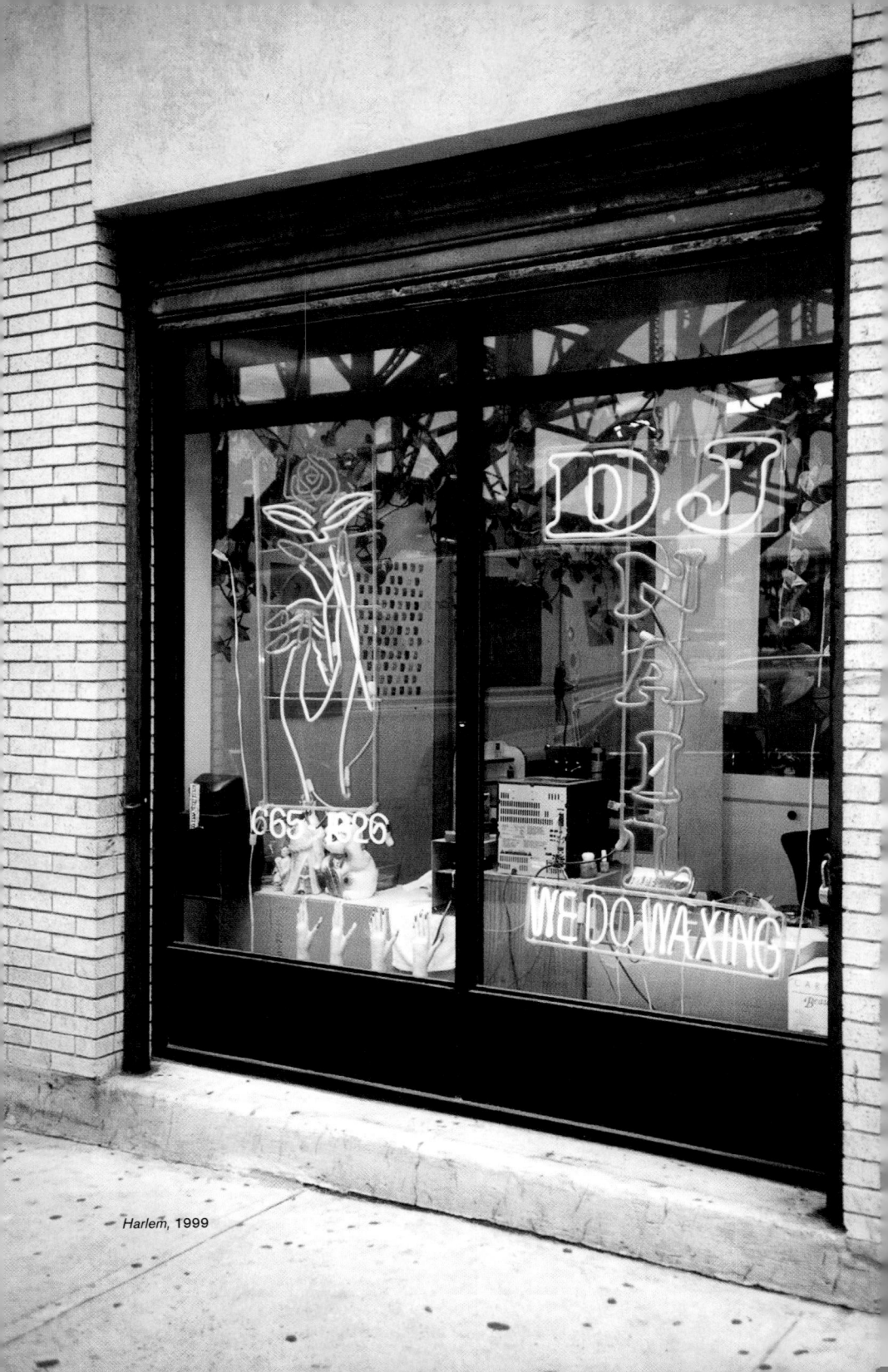

Harlem, 1999

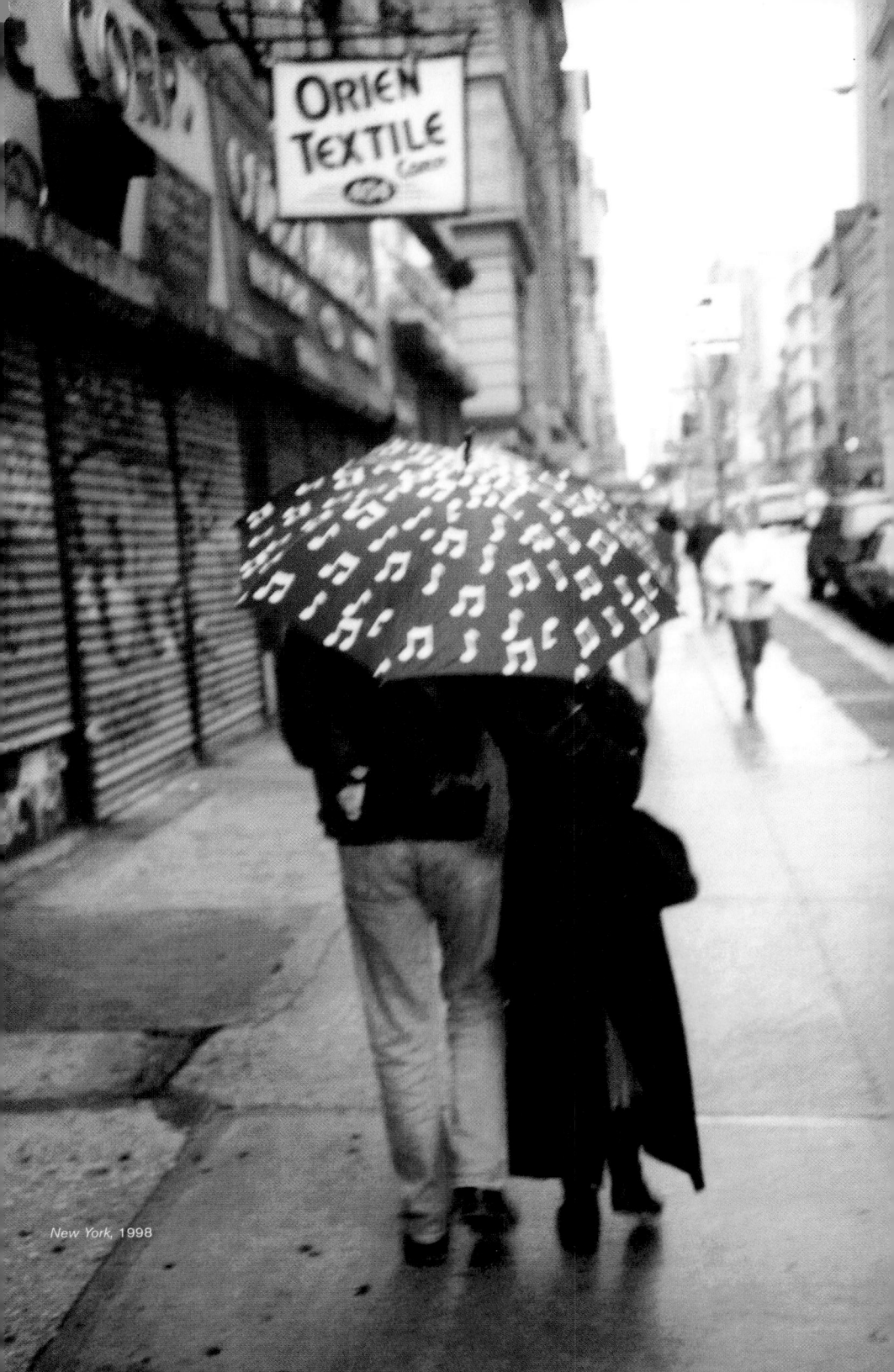

New York, 1998

SHIRIN NESHAT

Soliloquy, 1999
Production stills

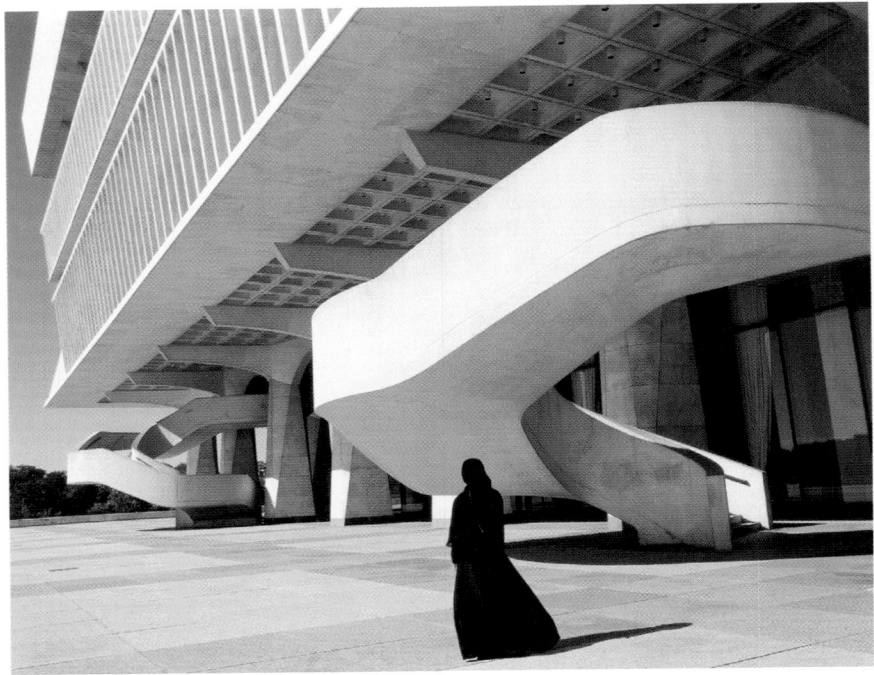

SU-MEI TSE

Echo, 2003
Still from video projection

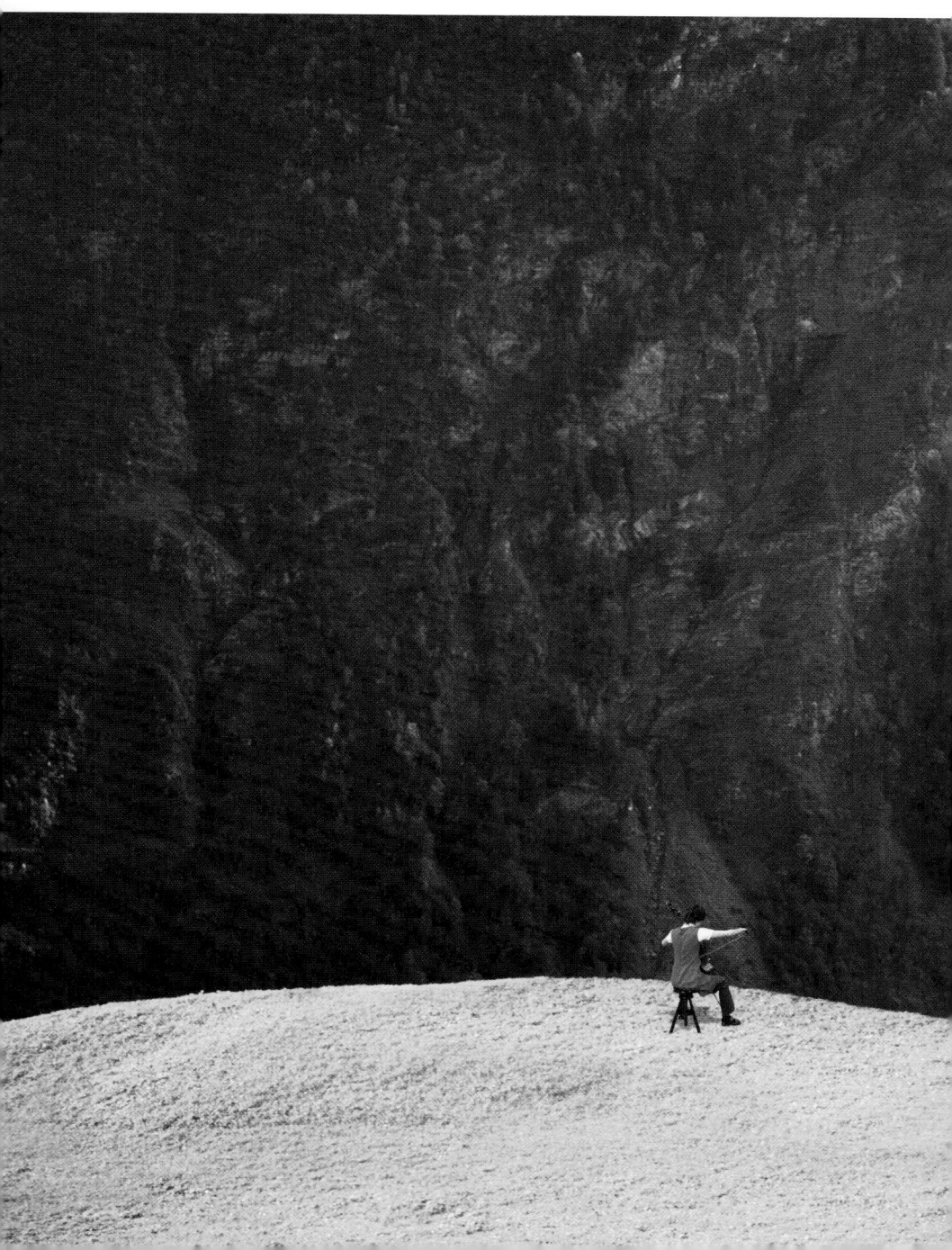

MARTIN KERSELS

Loud House, 1998
Sheet metal, bottles, wood, monitor, VCR, bass shakers, vib isolators, amps, and other media

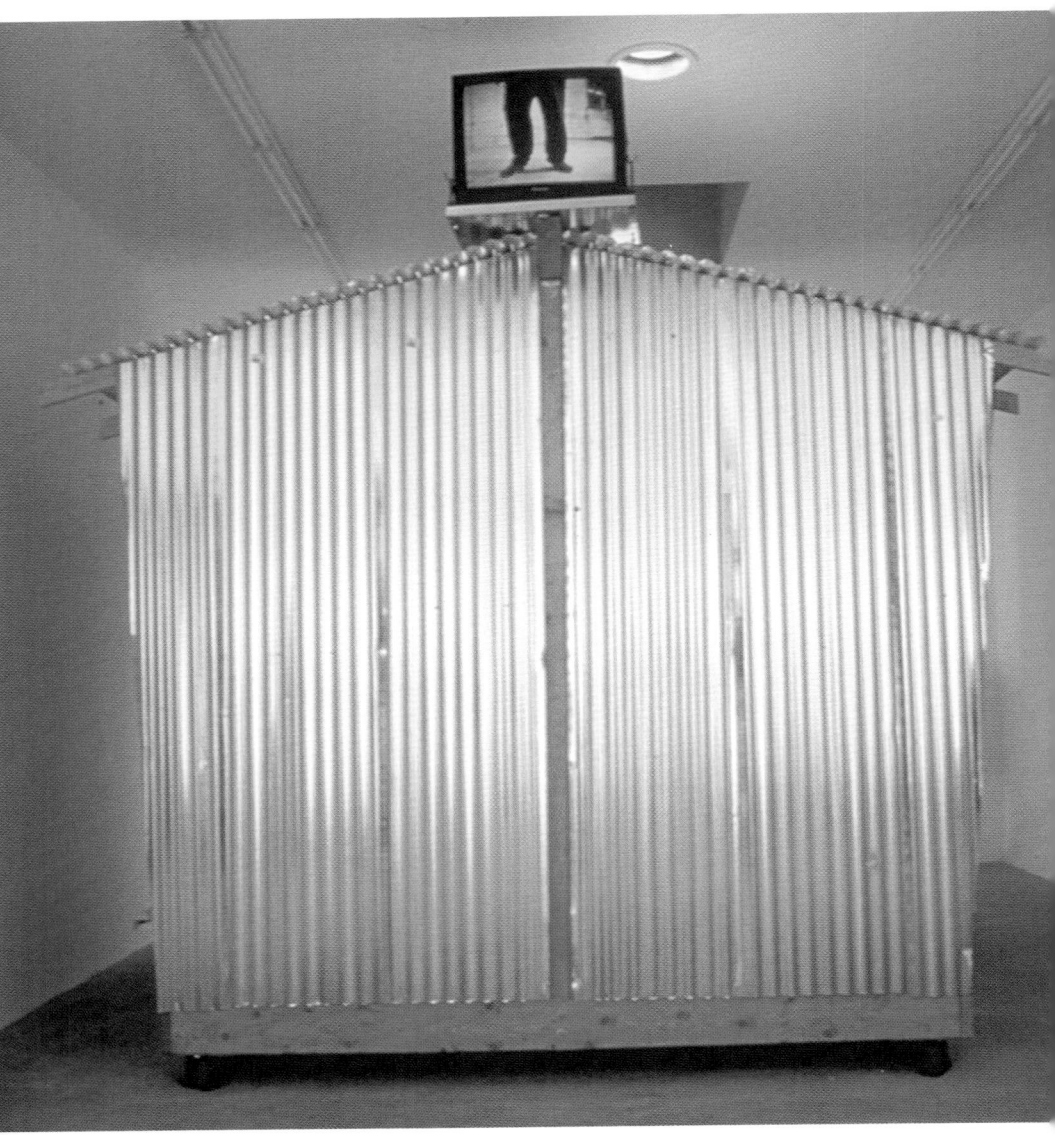

Objects of the Dealer, 1995
Mixed media with soundtracks

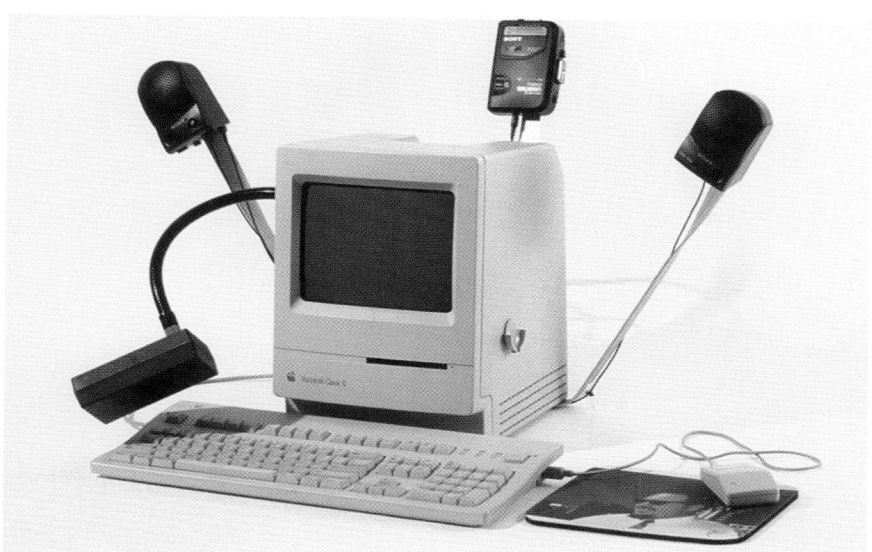

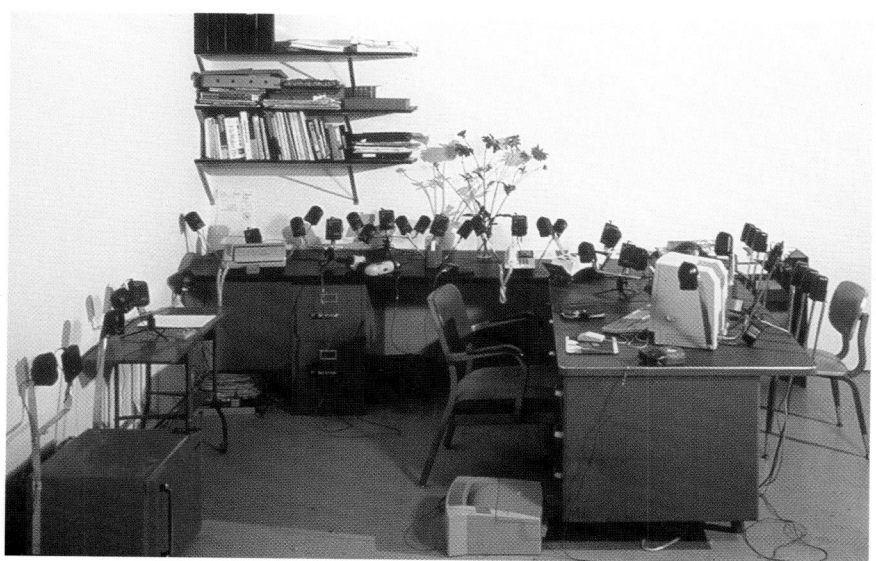

Brown Sound Kit, 1994
Speaker, amplifier, equalizer, oscillator, carrying case

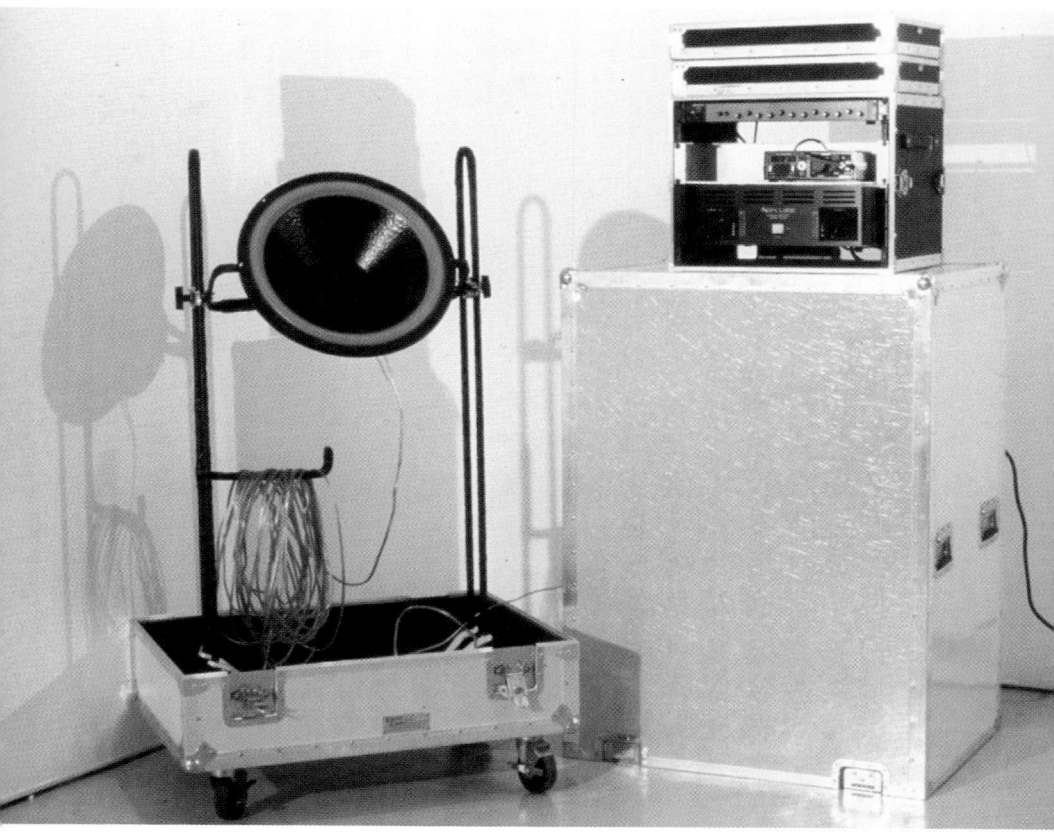

Tumble Room, 2000
Mixed media

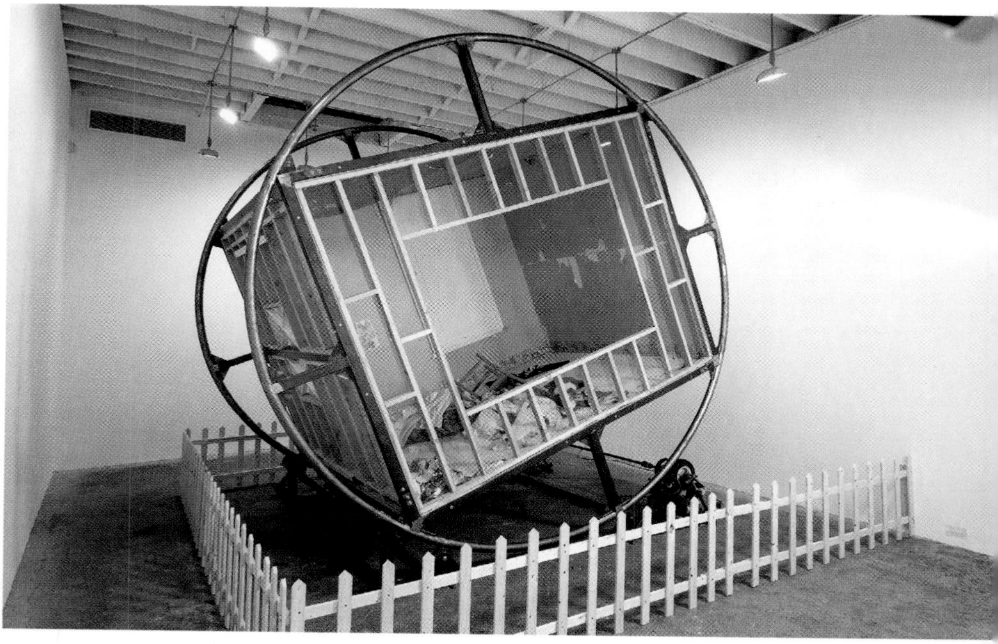

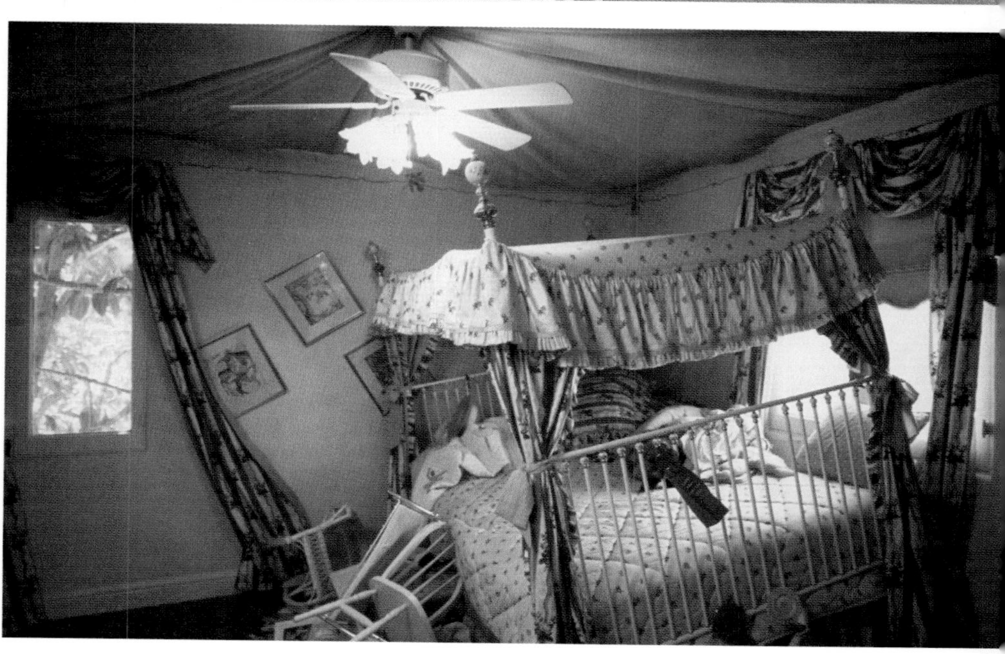

KIM SOOJA

A Mirror Woman, 2002
Used Korean bedcovers, fans, mirrored walls, Tibetan Monk chant

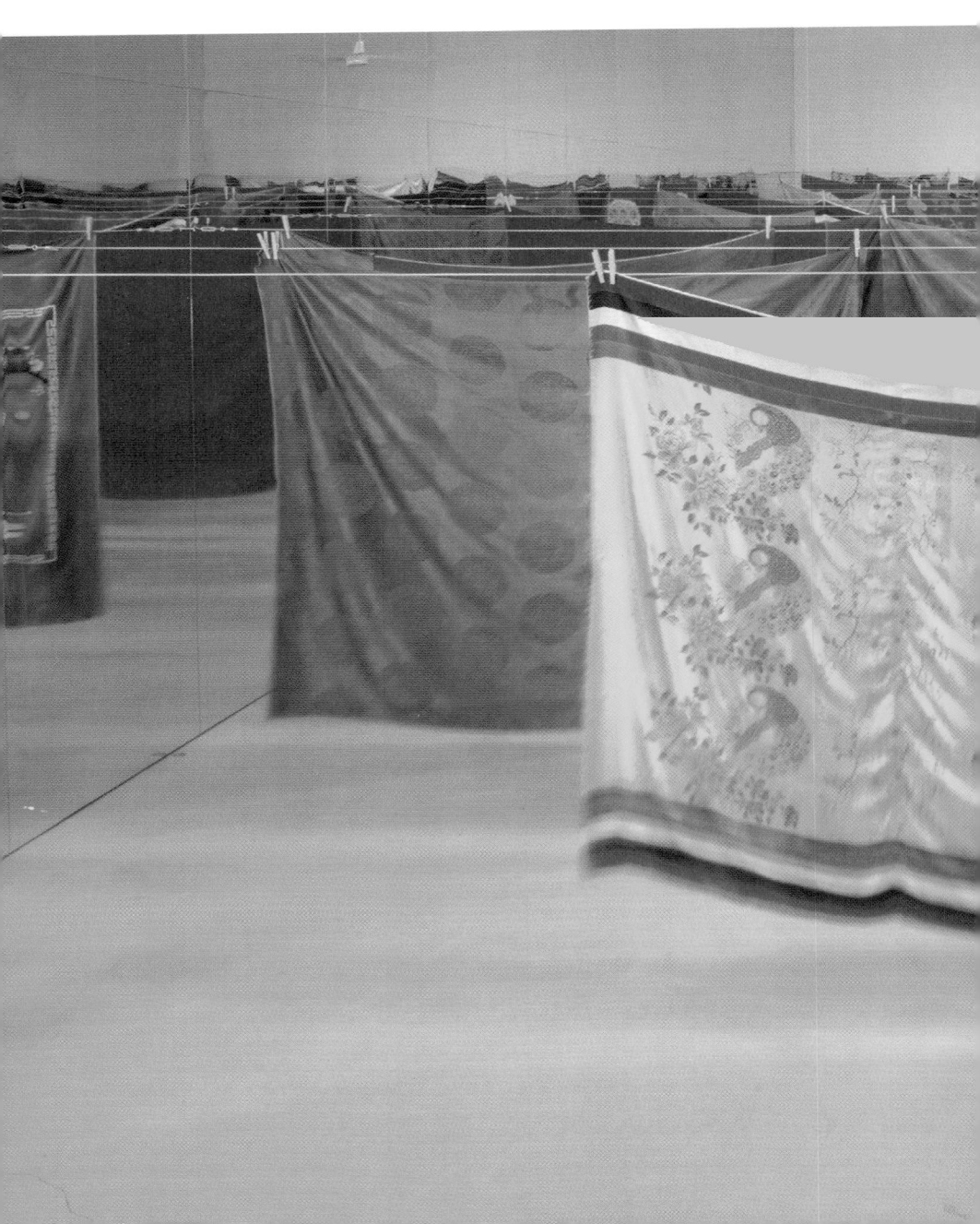

Mandala, 2002
Jukebox speaker, Mandala chant

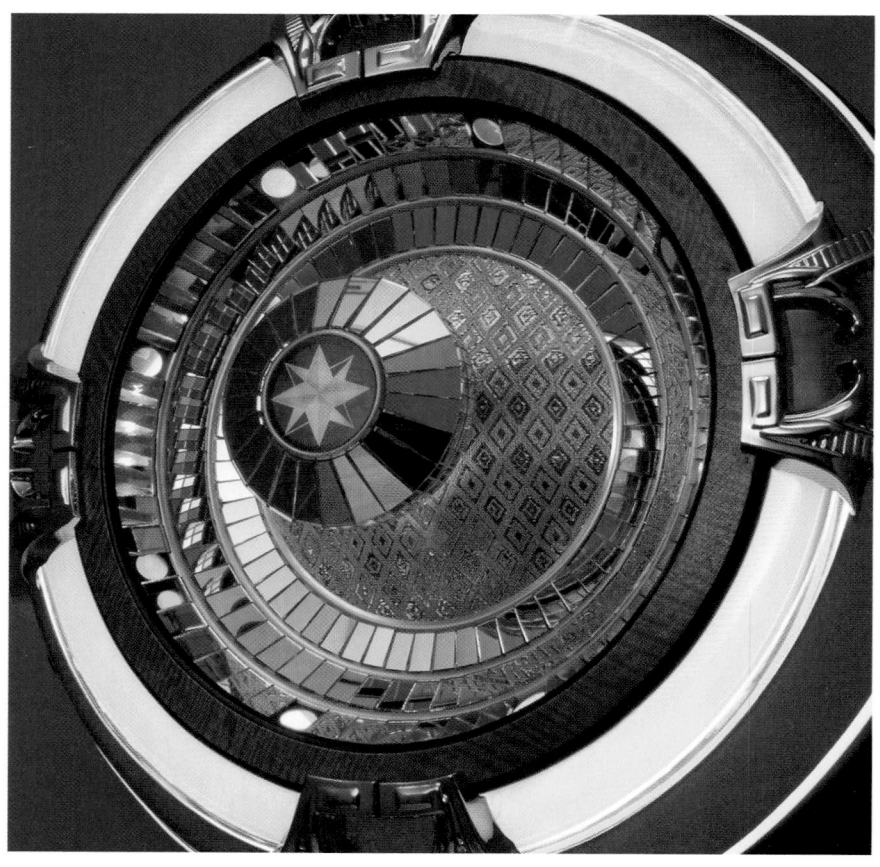

BODIES, VOICES, TEXTS

Christof Migone

Georgina Kleege

Sherry Simon

Wes Folkerth

Robert Bean

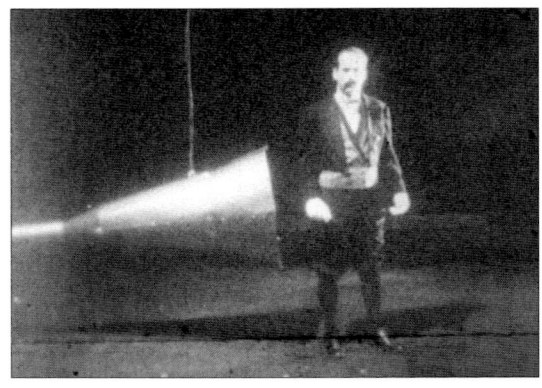

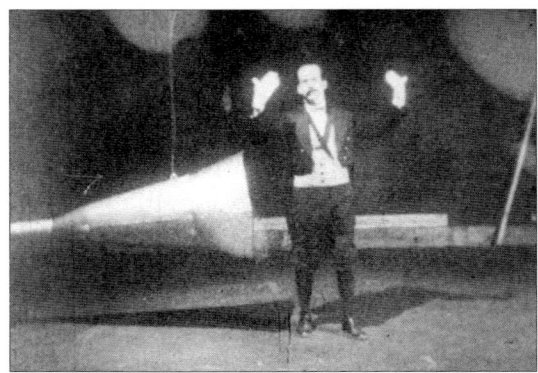

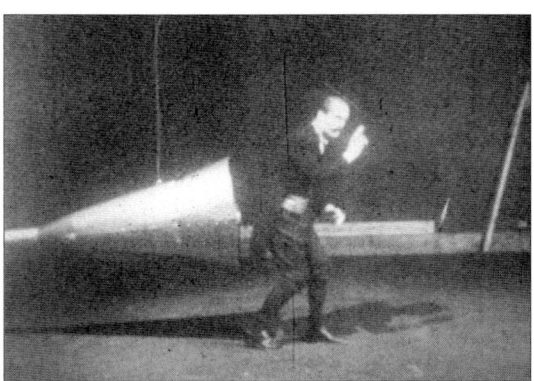

Joseph Pujol performing for Edison's "kinetophonolfactograph"
during the 1900 Paris World Fair
From Igor Vamos' documentary film
Le Petomane: Fin-de-siècle Fartiste, 1998
Courtesy The Cinema Guild, New York

Flatus Vocis: Somatic Winds

Christof Migone

Pa Pa Pax Pa Pa Pa Pax Pa Pa Pa Pa Pax![1]
– Anonymous, *L'Art de péter*

[P]et, *a-mor mor, oc-cu-pet, cu, pet, a-mor oc-cu, semper nos amor occupet.*[2]
– Alfred Jarry

to petar
e tanta fetura
ta fetura
e fula fetra
ra ta
petra
bari
re de pina
ta petar
ta feta
tralicha[3]
– Antonin Artaud

The onomatopoetic farts in Jarry and in *L'Art de péter* meet the glossolalic *pet* in Artaud at that "other" end of the mouth-anus axis and give the flatus its voice on the page. Amplified, it mows down the page like a machine gun, it rips the pages, it breaks open the book with a somatic wind. Flatulence rarely enters discourse; scatology, its cohabitant, offers more substance, more disgust, more metaphors. Flatulence is insubstantial, it does not produce an object, it assaults the ears, it offends the nose, and then dissipates. It is a safer excretion – there are no fart sewers. Yet flatulence contains properties and particularities of interest. As with any undertheorized subject, its delimitations are unfocused, it permeates into disparate territories. This text will reflect this effusiveness.

The anus enters social discourse via two principal routes: humour and insult. It is a difficult subject to discuss with sobriety; perhaps this is precisely its forte. Freud, in his foreword to John Bourke's infamous *Scatalogical Rites of All Nations*, remarked that "anyone who studies such things is regarded as scarcely less 'improper' than someone who actually *does* improper things."[4] In the case of flatulence, the situation is puzzling. Everyone actually *does* it, but the one who studies it potentially faces the tag of impropriety. This text will not eschew the comic; there will be nudging and winking, but it will also attempt to coalesce this material into a base from which to draw critical observations of how the social body prescribes the flesh body – with Antonin Artaud as lightning rod.

The Fanfaron

The body is a noisy place. It emits and transmits, it cannot contain itself, it has no built-in muffler. Its only silencer is willed, and, as we shall see later on, to retain a fart is sometimes just as ill-advised as to expel it. The orchestral renderings of our innards are rarely appreciated for their musicality. Rather, they are consistently considered as an affront or offense in Western mores. In particular, anything related to the anus brings embarrassment and is frowned upon. Yet Peter Ostwald, a clinician, has found the analogy of the orchestra to be a useful way to account for the body's sound emissions:

> Among the internal organs of the body which make noises, the digestive tract is probably the most musical, a sort of miniature band. The mouth, a kind of trumpet, can hiss, blare, and chomp. The esophagus, like a bassoon, produces gulps, burps, and belches, which, when properly timed, can produce considerable hilarity. The stomach, akin to a French horn, gurgles, growls, and groans. The intestines, resembling nothing so much as a glockenspiel, tinkle during peristalsis. The trombone-like colon zooms as it leisurely churns away at semisolid gruel. Now and then its noises, especially the sudden high-pitched beeps and bloops, embarrass the band director. Tuba-like "brummps" indicate the deposit of feces in the rectum in anticipation of the final discharge to the accompaniment of a fanfare of noises.[5]

A similar but more vindicative formulation is offered by Julia Loktev in her permutation of the famed "Body without Organs." With Loktev, the BwO becomes "The Body as Organ" and it "is neither a conquest nor a transcendence of the body. It is the pleasure of it. The freeplay of the flesh.... An ever-mutating improvisational instrument, the Body as Organ is entirely corporeal, finite, and musical."[6] This body is filled by Loktev to counter the truism found in the audio arts of the voice being disembodied. It would also seem to contradict the Artaudian BwO and, more directly, Gilles Deleuze and Félix Guattari's interpretation and extrapolation of Artaud's BwO. The concepts, however, concur, for they all posit the body as non-organism – that is, the body without organization, without rigidity, without arborescent structure. Deleuze and Guattari depict the full BwO as "the unproductive, the sterile, the unengendered, the unconsumable"[7]; Loktev describes the body as "chaotic and volatile."[8] Both versions conceive of the body as potential, as flux, as unbridled, primed for flow, in a state "which hesitates between gas and water."[9]

According to these concepts the body would seem to be indigestible to itself, or perhaps this is precisely the only function it can fulfil. It can digest, but otherwise it remains fully incomprehensible. It can digest, only because in that migration south it accumulates chaos, it amplifies its affective powers, it intoxicates itself – for our discharges are toxic gifts. Joseph Pujol, the legendary Petomane, called his gift "the principle of intoxication."[10] We shall pay attention to Le Petomane in a short while, but of interest here is the correlation between flatulence and intoxication, for the latter is concomitant with madness. Issues of control, and particularly self-control, accompany discussions of flatulence, and also permeate Artaud's writings. As a prelude, Diderot in *Rameau's Nephew* offers a salient example that precedes Artaud and amplifies the Ostwald digestive-tract orchestra sounded earlier. This is an encore where the whole body tunes up. Or perhaps *detunes* would be more fitting, for this orchestra is delirious. Rameau's nephew is the prototype of a jukebox that has derailed; he is a DJ with innumerable turntables and as many arms:

> And off he went, walking up and down and humming some of the tunes from *L'Île des Fous*...and now and again he raised his hands and eyes to heaven and exclaimed: "Isn't that beautiful! God, isn't it beautiful! How can anyone wear a pair of ears on his head and question it?" He began to warm up and sang, at first softly, then, as he grew more impassioned, he raised his voice and there followed gestures, grimaces and bodily contortions.... He sang thirty tunes on top of each other and mixed up: Italian, French, tragic, comic, of all sorts and descriptions, sometimes in a bass voice going down to the infernal regions, and sometimes bursting himself in a falsetto voice he would split the heavens asunder, taking off the walks, deportment and gestures of the different singing parts: in turn raging, pacified, imperious, scornful.... He relents, wails, complains, laughs, never losing sight of tone, proportion, meaning of words and character of music.... Everything was there: the delicacy of the air and expressive power as well as grief. [S]ometimes leaving the vocal line to take up the instrumental parts, which he would suddenly abandon to return to the voice part, intertwining them so as to preserve the connecting link and unity of the whole.... With cheeks puffed out and a hoarse, dark tone he did the horns and bassoons, a bright, nasal tone for the oboes, quickening his voice with incredible agility for the stringed instruments to which he tried to get the closest approximation; he whistled the recorders and cooed the flutes, shouting, singing and throwing himself about like a mad thing: a one-man show featuring dancers, male and female, singers of both sexes, a whole orchestra, a complete opera-house, dividing himself into twenty stage parts, tearing up and down, stopping, like one possessed, with flashing eyes and foaming mouth.... What didn't he do? He wept, laughed, sighed, his gaze was tender, soft or furious: a woman swooning with grief, a poor wretch abandoned in the depth of his despair, a temple rising into view, birds falling silent at eventide, waters murmuring in a cool, solitary place or tumbling in torrents down the mountain-side, a thunderstorm,

a hurricane, the shrieks of the dying mingled with the howling of the tempest and the crash of thunder; night with its shadows, darkness and silence, for even silence itself can be depicted into sound. By now he was quite beside himself. Knocked up with fatigue, like a man coming out of a deep sleep or long trance, he stood there motionless, dazed, astonished, looking about him and trying to recognize his surroundings…. "Well, gentlemen, what's up? What are you laughing at?"…"Now that's what you call music and a musician."[11]

The scene deserves to be quoted extensively – delirium is diarrhetic. It overflows, it runs amok and renders every dry space leaky like a sieve. One might qualify the nephew's madness as orchestral. He is the prototypical "one-man band." For our purpose, however, this one-man band has not yet tapped into the potential of the body as instrument to add to his array of available sonorities. Towards this, I would like to introduce a renegade instrument to this mad orchestra, one suggested by Loktev and Ostwald: the rectum. As the flute emerging out of the anus of a body in Hieronymus Bosch's *The Garden of Earthly Delights* suggests, this organ is both instrument and instrumentalist.[12] It plays itself. Artaud succinctly confirms the musicality of that end of the digestive apparatus: "We fart, madmen, have you smelled the p of fa" (*O.C.* XXII, 283).

South Winds

The euphemism "to break wind," once reversed, alludes to the power of wind; its invisibility does not portend its all-too-visible ravages. Yet the devastation a high wind can reap on objects may be negligible compared to the damage it can cause to our psyche. South winds reference not only the nether region of the body that is the focus here, but also the south end of France – more precisely, Marseilles. Birthplace of both Antonin Artaud (1896–1948) and Joseph Pujol (1857–1945), Marseilles is in the path of the infamous Mistral, a wind which "has the ill-natured habit of scattering roof tiles about, knocking down chimneys, blowing small children into canals, [and] tumbling walls onto the unsuspecting natives."[13] Greek geographer Strabo describes the Mistral with similar awe, as "an impetuous and terrible wind which displaces rocks, hurls men from their chariots, breaks their limbs and strips them of their clothes and weapons."[14] This brutal wind funnels through the valley of the Rhône bordered by the Alps to then do its damage on the French Riviera.

Lyall Watson concisely states "we are air conditioned."[15] In other words, we are at the mercy of air's whims. We are under atmospheric pressure. Winds, integral to climate, colour the temperament alongside the myriad exterior forces that condition us: topography, architecture, family, neighbours, schools, economies, and so on. Gertrude Stein expresses this in her inimitable manner:

[A]nybody is as their land and air is. Anybody is as the sky is low or high, the air heavy or clear, and anybody is as there is wind or no wind there. It is that which makes them and the arts they make and the work they do and the way they eat and the way they drink and the way they learn and everything.[16]

Wind can have soothing properties, even apotropaic effects, but as Robert Burton expounds, the air conditioning must fit certain criteria:

> [T]o this cure of melancholy, amongst other things, the rectification of Air is necessarily required...the medium must needs be good, where the air is temperate, serene, quiet, free from bogs, fens, mists, all manner of putrefaction, contagious and filthy noisome smells.[17]

Under the right conditions air can rectify, but it can also unhinge. An Englishman, Patrick Brydone, in *A Tour Through Sicily and Malta* (1776), writes of being under the effects of the sirocco:

> [T]he spring and elasticity of the air seems to be lost; and that active principle which animates all nature appears to be dead. This principle we have sometimes supposed to be nothing else than the subtle electric fluid that the air usually contains; and indeed we have found, that during this wind, it appears to be almost annihilated.[18]

Here the author is prescient in his allusion to electromagnetic fields, for recent studies confirm that ionization and sferics have physiological consequences. It is tempting to correlate the electrical charges diffusing at a global level with Artaud's submission to electroshock therapy. Electroshock as a high dosage of windy ions, a highly concentrated spurt of wind.

The wind by itself is the disembodied epitomized; it necessitates the body of the earth to incorporate, like a voice awaiting its speaker – be it human or electromagnetic. Wind is 5,600 million million tons of air in motion, it is the earth's breath. The cover of Christian Marclay's fart audio piece, *Untitled* (1996), materializes the somatic wind at this scale: one side a cloudy sky, the other a field with furrows and agricultural workers.[19] Marclay's metaphor is explicit: the wind of the fart is fertile, it is earthed air, soiled sky. Evidently, air circulates through every register but the heavenly. In several languages, the words for breath and wind are the same; it is the same air in motion, in constant circulative corporeality. Breath or wind, a mere difference of scale. As Aristophanes states in *The Clouds*, "Thunder is nothing more than a fart."[20] Madness is perhaps also a question of scale; it is as if Artaud inhaled the Mistral whole. *Le Mômo marseillais*. His fury is fuelled by the Mistral – a force that evacuates all in its path and in its past:

> I have no father, no mother, the real and nature are definitions, concepts, which I will no longer enter. I come from the total and absolute NOTHINGNESS of myself (*O.C.* XV, 338).

This absolute is the swallowed infinity of the wind, constantly blowing up the insides. His insides; Artaud's carnality is measurable only in terms of infinity. André Roumieux followed up his first book, *Je travaille à l'asile d'aliénés*, with a study on Artaud. In it he notes how, even in his teens, Artaud seemed to breathe the unconditional:

> My dear mommy,
> Pardon, pardon, I beg of you a guilty son, a repentant heart. Oh! Mommy, I love you more than anything, I love you and I am tortured by the remorse at my wrongdoing, I am crazy. I am a monster, but forgive me. What fury compels me to perpetrate such acts.[21]

Pujol, Le Petomane, also ingested an entire geophysics – in his case it was the Mediterranean. He discovered his gift (*of intoxication*, as described earlier) following an experience he had when bathing – "the sea had come in through his anus."[22] Once he substituted water with air, and learned to control his "gift," his career was born:

> When the gas comes out with enough force and with a certain degree of tension from the sphincter, noises are produced of intensity, timbre and of great variety. At times these are genuinely musical sounds. Although, as it is almost impossible to obtain given notes, these turn out to be common chords or, what is more extraordinary, recognizable tunes.[23]

The Body with Organ, indeed. Pujol embodies a particularly interesting reversal of the ingestion to digestion to excretion path. In him "the intestine plays the role of the chest in storing air and the anal sphincter that of the vocal chords, the throat and the mouth."[24] The body turned upside down. If the anus can sing, then how much closer is it to the sacred and pure? Or is it voice and song that are now sullied? Artaud's answer to that question elevates flatulence to a science, and with it he posits an alternate consciousness:

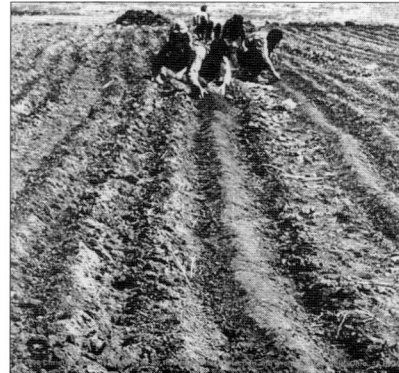

There is a science of mephitic gases, more commonly known as farts. And a consciousness is based on this science, that is, it is born from it. The mephitic gas is a spirit, cultivated by very fine initiates, and it is one of the ways which is learnt by which the most harm is done to life. The madmen ignore this, but in them are some very high (and very perfect) spirits which take advantage of their madness, but what psychiatrist has understood this? (*O.C.* XXII, 305)

Le Petomane was doubtlessly unaware of the loftiness his gift could have aspired to. He was of a lineage that confined itself mostly to the frivolous. But it is a lineage that works to undermine the predominance of the mouth as sole site of expression. Here are references to several Petomanes *avant la lettre*: In 430 AD St. Augustine wrote, in *The City of God*, "There are those that can break wind backward so artfully you would think they sang"; Edward I in 1331 granted land to "Roland le Fartere" for "making a leap, a whistle and a fart"; a German at the court of Maximilian (c. 1500) "could rehearse any song whatsoever with his tail."[25]

Retention

An arsehole who breathes is one by which the animus can pass. Breath, wind, animal, spirit, life, air – all circulate in this passage. The inclusion of such essential elements alongside, and inside, the anus might be difficult to reconcile with "civilized" mores. Yet the etymology, mythology, and history of farts might help one reconsider this difficulty. As Beckett said, "[W]e underestimate this little hole, it seems to me, we call it the arsehole and affect to despise it. But is it not rather the true portal of our being and the celebrated mouth no more than the kitchen-door."[26]

Flatulence features predominantly in the context of self-control issues. Both Cicero and Plutarch deplored the restraining order that admonished the flatulent. Plutarch asks, "Why was it ordained that they who were to live chaste should abstain from pulse? Or rather was it because they should bring empty and slender bodies to their

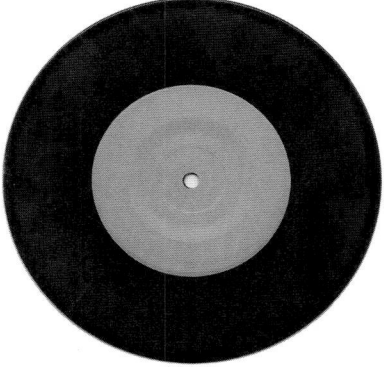

Christian Marclay
Untitled, 1996
45-rpm record cover (front and back) and record
Robert Shiffler Collection and Archive
Courtesy the artist

purifications and expiations? For pulse are windy and cause a great deal of excrement that require purging off. Or is it because they excite lechery by reason of their flatulent and windy nature?"[27] Thus flatulence here performs a role in sexual mechanics. There is abundant literature that links flatus with erection and ejaculation. Artaud, for example, exclaims: "I ejaculate this good-for-nothing fart" (*O.C.* XX, 172). In terms of diet, the equation was: foods that cause flatulence aid in the production of semen. At the other end of the spectrum, "anaphrodisiacs are foodstuffs that do not engender semen, but dry it and dissolve flatulence."[28] Flatulence here functions as an engine translating aphrodisiacs (beans figure prominently) into sexual fuel. Of note, this abetment is gender-specific for, as Clement of Alexandria comments, the eating of beans was outlawed because it was purported to make women sterile.[29]

On the other hand, the literature of manners removes explicit references to sex from the equation, and merely seeks to regulate a proper way to digest. It accepts the inevitability of farts, but seeks means to hide their occurrence – striving for the inaudible and innocuous fart. Erasmus referred to ancient proverbs to make his point: "Let a cough hide the sound" and again "Listen to the old maxim about the sound of the wind. If it can be purged without a noise that is best. But it is better that it be emitted with a noise than that it be held back."[30] The general edict these formulations attempt to frame is one where certain forms of behaviour and bodily activities are acceptable in public and certain others should be relegated to the private realm. When bodily functions such as flatulence arise so do the difficulties, for one is not always in command of their flatus. What our bodies do despite ourselves has always been a source of anxiety and fascination. Incontinence is a fear on par with madness, in fact often a synonymous fear. We are attracted by these fears as spectacle when exhibited in others and compelled by them when they overcome us. As Guy Scarpetta states, "Nothing is more erotically charged than bringing one's partner to overcome his or her distaste."[31] One would imagine (and hope) that a statement from the perspective of the subject overcoming this barrier would be even more erotically heightened.

The last paragraph began negating sex and ended permeated by it. Despite the earlier correlation made between flatulence and arousal, an erotics of farts seems to be absent from the common repertoire. Flatulence does not appear in the vocabulary of seduction, as, say, oysters might. It is only through a discussion of incontinence and its opposition to retention that flatulence attains a level of discourse beyond the jocular. Flatulence by itself principally appeals to the puerile imagination. There are several examples, from Benjamin Franklin's excursions in scurrilous texts, to Howard Stern's radio fart contests, to the video *American Flatulators*, a horrendous spoof of *American Gladiators* (horrendous enough on its own), to *Austin Powers* and *South Park*. Farts as gags are by no means undeserving of critical attention; they illustrate a desire to debase, even deprave. The only risk is that this line of indulgences tends to supersede and thus obscure other threads where the desire might be the same but the tack differs. Pujol's career is not dissimilar to the above examples; his was not an avant-garde project.

Aristocrats and celebrities who attended his show were slumming, and often went incognito. Nevertheless, Pujol's stint at the Moulin Rouge in the midst of turn-of-the-century Parisian cabaret life made for interesting cross-pollinations. The most unusual to mention here is that in the assemblage of curios one finds in Freud's consulting room is none other than a picture portrait of Le Petomane.[32]

Incontinence

In *La Potière Jalouse*, Claude Lévi-Strauss traces an Amerindian creation myth featuring flatulence as protagonist. In the tale's climax, a nightjar blows up a giant rock by the violence of its farts. The rock is shattered into many pieces, and this is said to be the origin of all the stones one now sees in the world.[33] Lévi-Strauss contrasts this with the role of the sloth in Central and South American native cosmologies. In the myth, the sloth has never been observed eating. It is thus speculated that the sloth takes its nourishment solely from the air, as it is often seen with mouth agape in the direction of the wind. The corollary of this perceived idleness is that the sloth is reputed to have no anus (the sloth excretes just once every six to eight days).[34] There are all sorts of variants of these myths, but suffice it to say that these are two examples that lead Lévi-Strauss to propose a schema depicting mythology and its relationship to the oral/anal opposition:

> [Orifices] can be open or closed, and whether they are in either position they can fulfill three different functions: closed it retains, open it absorbs or evacuates. Thus, six options are possible: oral retention, oral avidity, oral incontinence; and anal retention, anal avidity, anal incontinence.[35]

The schema does complicate the oral/anal binary, but it remains reductive in comparison with the Body without Organs, which is the formulation of the infinite multiple. If one were to retain the Lévi-Strauss structure for a moment, one would note a progression from full control to full lack of control, from retention to avidity to incontinence.

Flatulence consistently figures under the rubric of incontinence. However, the expulsive force of flatulence also translates into instances where flatulence is wielded. The nightjar, for example, exercised its power. French playwright Valère Novarina also uses flatulence as sign of will: "The gas God produced in farting the world when he produced it – I wonder if he himself heard it?"[36] Presumably this points to a form of incontinence, which is particularized by a willingness to be unable to restrain oneself; in other words, a disdain for self-restraint, and a relish for lack thereof. Louis Althusser, in his memoir, narrates such an episode:

> All of a sudden, I noticed my great-grandmother...standing bolt upright and did not say a word as a loud spurting noise issued from beneath her long black skirt.

A clear stream ran past her feet. It took me a while to "realize" that she was peeing standing up…. I was astounded to discover there were women-men, unashamed of their sexuality, who went ahead and pissed in front of everybody, without shame or modesty, and without giving any warning whatsoever![37]

Without restraint, with abandon, the incontinent one functions in an economy of excess. Releasing unabashedly, unconcerned with social context, and wantonly letting desire go, the incontinent one composes with blurts and spurts.

Alienated Gas

Artaud, in the passage espousing the powers of the mephitic gas quoted earlier, also attributed a will to incontinence. In his case he pointed to nefarious spirits as the scientists in control of this new science. The science of incontinence; a science with a learning curve: "To have slept 9 years amongst the noise and smell of the farts of madmen is a unique learning experience that no doctor has ever known" (O.C. XXII, 101). Artaud was immersed in this greenhouse environment; his body was no barrier to the onslaught. But the greenhouse was already rampant inside Artaud before the asylums: the swallowed Mistral, the suspected hereditary syphilis,[38] the neurasthenic adolescence, the addiction to opiates. He was persecuted on all fronts, from the inside out to the outside in: "I have never ceased to think that *more* and *more* I could silence enemy and foreign thinking and swallow it in my interior fire…. Why are beings which are not in me moving inside of me?" (O.C. XXII, 105). A science of possession where the possessor is possessed, where there is infinite retention alongside infinite incontinence, desire and repulsion fluxing between the two. Artaud's possession takes the form of an impossibility: he is a bloated body sieve, infinity infinitely passing through. Passing through a negation, or a negation containing all possible negations, "no anatomy, no physiology, no psychology, no physics, no cosmic law, des gris-gris. I am the earth and of the earth…. I love neither the air nor the light, but the infernal night of my ass and of all asses for I am the voluminous assassin, the depth of my being is the volume of my body"(O.C. XXII, 308).

One of the concrete manifestations of the voluminous was Artaud's abundant fecal production (O.C. XXVI, 58). Conversely, Artaud's passages pertaining to flatulence are not of his own production but are attributed to the generic plural "des aliénés" and the lowercase "dieu." These passages take the form of invectives tempered with awe: "there is nothing like madmen for farting, I have heard the peyote sorcerers fart but I must say that in this domain they are no match for even the least of the madmen" (O.C. XXII, 304) and "While you, god, fart in your clouds, incapable spirits sprung from the tomb of my ass, I flip over the angels' box in my double cracking grave" (O.C. XX, 170–71). Thus, Artaud was more affected by consistency, by the soil and soiled, by what festered and not by what dissipated. Therefore, he might have concurred with Merleau-Ponty's line of questioning: "Where to assign the limit of the body and the world, since the world is flesh? Where in the body can one place seeing, since, by all evidence, our body is no more than a 'darkness stuffed with organs'?"[39]

Again here the extremes of infinitude coincide. The body is synonymous with the world: open, open wide; and the body is also opaque, sealed, and stuffed: closed, closed shut. Monique Wintz sets a scene in which these two states enact their paradox: "In his tomb, Antonin grinds his teeth and pierces through earthworms with jabs of his jaw. He is beside himself."[40] Artaud, posthumously vehement and vociferous. He is beside himself, he is forever. Beside himself, as in sublimated, not in the psychoanalytical sense but in the alchemical sense. His solids have become vapour. He is gas. He is spirit and its negation.

Exit Wound

A first breath is the condition of possibility of a last breath. The anus as exit figures prominently in death. In a fourteenth-century farce by Le Muynier, a dying man is convinced that the soul leaves the body via the anus at the moment of death. A priest and his wife are at his side, waiting as he approaches death:

> [They] place him in such a position that if the doctrine of the soul-departure via the anus be true, they may witness the man's final performance. The phenomenon of rectal flatulence is now observed, when suddenly, to the consternation of the wife and priest, a demon appears and, placing a sack over the dying man's anus, catches the rectal gas and flies off in sulphurous vapor.[41]

In Marco Ferreri's 1973 film *La Grande Bouffe*, Michel (Michel Piccoli) is a TV personality who suffers from a tenesmus of gas. He does manage to expulse a couple of times but he is engaged (with three companions) in a suicide pact by way of gastronomical and sexual excess, which for him culminates in one long final double breath – one from the mouth, the other from the anus. In Rabelais' *Pantagruel*, we witness another scenario adjoining flatus and death: inhabitants of the "Isle of Winds" die while emitting gases, and their souls leave the body via the rectum.[42] Death by way of the anus is the great leveller, debaser. A folk legend recounted by Rabelais and Molière, amongst others, starts with: "This is the court of King Petot, where all are equal."[43] All equal in the face of finitude, the last incontinence.

The death fart is a clear example of how this alternate breathing circuit plays its role as universal leveller. It clears the field, much like a gale sweeping all in its path. Césaire has wind hissing through every nook of his *Cahier d'un retour au pays natal*, the wind of a return, of change, of leakage, of the night, of the apocalypse... Winds here cause anaphoric phrases that are endless from the start. The body facing the wind is either obstacle or accomplice. A body incontinent is complicit, it gives in, "and it is not only the mouths who sing, but the hands, the feets, the asses, the sexes, and the creature entire which liquifies [again, alchemical sublimation] in sounds, voice and rhythm."[44]

Somatic winds are also endless from the start. For they are not all the same; they differ not only according to physiognomy and diet but also in terms of causality. A taxonomy of farts could begin thus: slowpoke, cauliflower farts; thermodynamic and nuclear farts; wakeup farts, chocolate farts, elevators of shame farts, open-air diffused farts; the rectal cancer farts of Artaud; deathbed spirit farts, blushing farts, the cow farts of planet methane; hardcore farts, loitering farts; tiny skinny fart series that fall out like dominoes; vociferous extroverted farts, nefarious silent farts; neverending air-sucking farts, minuscule prelude farts preceding an onslaught; *non sequitur* farts, surprise party farts, the you-might-try-to-hold-me-in-but-I-am-coming-out-anyway farts; prank mouth farts, armpit farts, blame-the-neighbour farts, nasty revenge farts, almost angelic farts, innocent farts, cute farts, *petite mort* farts...

Rameau's nephew, after his stint as embodied jukebox, advocates for the stage a frenzy to better reflect reality: "[W]e need exclamations, interjections, suspensions, interruptions, affirmations, negations; we call on, we invoke, we shout, we emit, we cry, we laugh heartily."[45]

To this call I would add: We need incontinence; we fart.

Suddenly the toad's descending colon thundered, and the nonalimentary bolus of pure fire took its usual path once more toward the pole of the devil Plural.[46]
– Alfred Jarry

NOTES

1. *L'Art de péter*, 1776, cited in Orlando de Rudder, *Ces mots qui font du bruit: dictionnaire des onomatopées, interjections et autres vocables d'origine onomatopeique ou expressive de la langue française* (Paris: J.C. Lattès, 1998), 253.

2. Alfred Jarry, "Exploits and Opinions of Doctor Faustroll: A Neo Scientific Novel" [1898], in *Selected Works of Alfred Jarry*, eds. Roger Shattuck and Simon Watson Taylor, trans. Simon Watson Taylor (New York: Grove, 1965), 217. The onomatopoeia is followed by: "The white-bearded energumen concluded the coprolalic phrase with a throat cry and an obscene contortion."

3. Antonin Artaud, *Oeuvres Complètes* XXII (Paris: Gallimard, 1986), 54. All further quotes from Artaud will be referenced in parentheses in the text. The dates of the other volumes are: XV (1981), XX (1985), XXVI (1994). All translations mine.

4. John G. Bourke, *The Portable Scatalog*, ed. Louis K. Kaplan (New York: William Morrow, 1994 [1891]), 6. Original title: *Scatological Rites of All Nations: A Dissertation upon the Employment of Excrementitious Remedial Agents in Religion, Therapeutics, Divination, Witchcraft, Love-Philters, etc., in all Parts of the Globe Based upon Original Notes and Personal Observation and upon Compilation from over One Thousand Authorities.*

5. Peter Ostwald, *The Semiotics of Human Sound* (The Hague: Mouton, 1973), 28.

6. Julia Loktev, "The Body as Organ," *Musicworks* 53 (1992): 42.

7. Gilles Deleuze and Félix Guattari, *Anti-Oedipus, Capitalism and Schizophrenia*, vol. 1, trans. Mark Hurley, Mark Seem, and Helen R. Lane (Minneapolis: University of Minnesota Press, 1983), 8.

8. Loktev, 40.

9. Artaud in Gilles Deleuze, *The Logic of Sense*, ed. Constantin V. Boundas, trans. Mark Lester with Charles Stivale (New York: Columbia University Press, 1990), 89.

10. Joseph Pujol in Jean Nohain and F. Caradec, *Le Petomane 1857–1945*, trans. Warren Tute (Los Angeles: Sherbourne Press, 1968), 10.

11. Denis Diderot, *Rameau's Nephew*, trans. Leonard Tancock (New York: Penguin, 1966), 102–104.

12. For a study of sound in this work by Bosch, see Sharon Brooks, "Silent Machines and Tortured Voices: Bosch's *The Garden of Earthly Delights*," *Public* 4/5 (1990/91): 151–159.

13. S. Brown in Lyall Watson, *Heaven's Breath: A Natural History of the Wind* (New York: William Morrow, 1984), 36.

14. Strabo in Watson, 36.

15. Watson, 205.

16. Gertrude Stein in Watson, 45.

17. Robert Burton, *The Anatomy of Melancholy*, Second Partition, Sect. II, Mem. III (New York: Frederick Ungar, 1979), 90.

18. Patrick Brydone in Watson, 278–9.

19. Christian Marclay, *Untitled* (Greenville, OH: Robert Shiffler Collection and Archive, 1996).

20. Aristophanes in Bourke, 91.

21. Artaud in André Roumieux, *Artaud et l'asile 1.: Au-delà des murs, la mémoire* (Paris: Séguier, 1996), 16–17 (translation mine).

22. Nohain and Caradec, 21.

23. Nohain and Caradec, 62.

24. Nohain and Caradec, 63.

25. The first and third examples are from Joseph T. Shipley, *The Origin of English Words: A Discursive Dictionary of Indo-European Roots* (Baltimore: Johns Hopkins University Press, 1984), 310–11. The second example is from Suzanne R. Westfall, *Patrons and Performance: Early Tudor Revels* (Oxford: Clarendon Press, 1990), 91.

26. Samuel Beckett, *Molloy* in *Three Novels: Molloy, Malone Dies, The Unnamable*, trans. Patrick Bowles with the author (New York: Grove Press, 1991), 80.

27. Plutarch in Bourke, 90–1.

28. Constantine the African in the entry under "flatulence" in Gordon Williams, *A Dictionary of Sexual Language and Imagery in Shakespearean and Stuart Literature* (London: Athlone Press, 1994).

29. Williams, "flatulence."

30. Both quotes by Erasmus in Norbert Elias, *The Civilization Process: The History of Manners and State Formation and Civilization* (Oxford: Blackwell, 1994 [1939]), 106.

31. Guy Scarpetta, "Variations," *Traverses* 37 (April 1986): 27.

32. From a video documentary by Igor Vamos, *Le Petomane: Fin-de-siècle Fartiste* (1998).

33. Claude Lévi-Strauss, *La Potière Jalouse* (Paris: Plon, 1985), 89. A nightjar is a grayish-brown bird also known as a goatsucker.

34. Lévi-Strauss, 123–4.

35. Lévi-Strauss, 96.

36. Valère Novarina, *L'Inquiétude: adaptation pour la scène du Discours aux animaux* (Paris: P.O.L., 1993), 8 (translation mine).

37. Louis Althusser, *The Future Lasts Forever*, eds. Olivier Corpet and Yann Moulier Boutang, trans. Richard Veasy (New York: The New Press, 1992), 74.

38. Roumieux, 18–19. The author here does leave this open for speculation as he acknowledges that this diagnosis appears all too frequently in the period. In this early case, as in subsequent diagnoses, the treatment that Artaud was prescribed had no curative effect and often caused more damage. In this particular case, the mercury iodine injections he was given permanently damaged his dentition.

39. Maurice Merleau-Ponty in Jacques Garelli, *Artaud et la question du lieu: Essai sur le théâtre et la poésie d'Artaud* (Paris: Librairie José Corti, 1982), 128.

40. Monique Wintz, "Antonin le sublimé," *Recherches* 36 (1979): 136.

41. Bourke, 151.

42. Mikhail Bakhtin, *Rabelais and His World*, trans. Hélène Iswolsky (Bloomington: Indiana University Press, 1984), 151, n. 6.

43. Bakhtin, 264, n. 41.

44. Aimé Césaire, *Cahier d'un retour au pays natal* (Paris and Dakar: Présence Africaine, 1983 [1939]), 14.

45. Diderot, 109.

46. Jarry, 219.

Voices in My Head

Georgina Kleege

At a dinner party recently, I heard a woman talking about her long commute to work. She estimated that she spent close to fifteen hours a week driving to and from work, not to mention regular road trips required by her job. She listed the little comforts that make her commute bearable – the optimum temperature setting, the necessary adjustment to the seat back, the best way to minimize road glare. She listened to music sometimes, but said it's often too soothing. Music made it too easy to doze off. Besides, no matter what tapes she brought with her, they were never quite the ones she wanted. And she couldn't count on the radio to meet her moods. She listened to talk radio, but only in small doses; the opinions of hosts and callers could enrage her. And the all-day murder news stations were even worse. So she started to listen to books on tape and found them a pleasing solution. She evaluated the various companies that produce them, favouring those who do not try to glitz up the text with mood music or sound effects. She refuted the assumption that all books on tape are always abridged, listing the titles of numerous nineteenth-century classics she'd heard in their entirety. She said that when she was in the middle of a big novel she would actually look forward to getting into the car. Sometimes she even sat in the parking lot for a few extra minutes, eagerly listening to the end of a chapter. She knew people, she said, who listened to books on tape while they jogged or exercised or did housework. Increased demand, she predicted, would continue to improve the product, making a wider range of titles available.

Then she said, "But of course, it's not really reading."

She probably said this because there were English professors present, and she feared they would dismiss the practice as lamentably middlebrow, if not philistine. I doubt she knew that I am legally blind, or that my primary method of reading is on tape.

I know more and more sighted people who admit to reading recorded books. Books-on-tape sections in bookstores and libraries proliferate, and publishers simultaneously release recorded and print versions of the same books. Celebrities record themselves reading their own tell-all memoirs – O.J. Simpson, to name only one. Big-name actors record readings of everything from classic poetry to self-help manuals. Obviously none of this would happen if there were not a growing market for it. But when people admit that they have listened to a book on tape, there is always some degree of shame, or at least sheepishness, always a disclaimer, "Well, I listened to it. I wouldn't say I really read it."

Why the shame? I need to know. Reading is fundamental to who I am and what I do. I seem to be reading something every hour of the day – my own work, research materials, student papers, letters, and recipes. Most of the time, I do this reading aurally. Reading books on tape is not merely a pastime for me. When I teach literature and writing courses, I read recordings of both the required texts and the students' work. I am supposed to be teaching students something about reading and writing. But if I am not really reading, what can I hope to impart to them?

When I read visually, my retention is better than when I listen to a taped text. For me, reading visually means deciphering every word syllable by syllable. So any text I manage to get through I have essentially memorized. It is impossible for me to do a cursory visual reading. Reading a recorded book can make cursory reading all too easy – in one ear, out the other. But I head off the risk by listening to things two or three times. I find I can rarely listen to a book while doing something else. To walk around outside with earphones on would be dangerous. And if I am doing exercises or cooking dinner, the mental instructions I occasionally give myself make me lose track of the text. To get the most out of a taped book, I must sit upright with my eyes open. When I prepare to teach a text, I follow along in the print version as I listen, marking passages I will want to discuss in class. Actually, to say I follow along is something of an overstatement. Even with magnification, my eyes cannot move fast enough. I tag along, recognizing new paragraphs from pauses, turning the pages when I'm told. When I read student papers, I listen to them once, then again, moving through the magnified text with a pen in my hand, stopping the tape to write comments and corrections as I go. Naturally, all this takes time. But is my experience of these texts still inferior? Should my students feel shortchanged? Should I feel ashamed of myself for calling this reading?

It's not as if it's such an alien experience. Many of us were read to as children, by parents, babysitters, or teachers. For most, it was a happy experience, combining the pleasures of brightly coloured storybook pictures, the warm proximity and undivided attention of a beloved grown-up, and the drowsy comfort of bedtime. But reading aloud to children is more than simply a safe soporific. It is also how most of us began to learn to read. Even infants, who cannot understand the words read to them, start to internalize the sounds and rhythms of spoken language. As they mature, they acquire firsthand knowledge of written language as well. They absorb the fact that sounds are represented by letters, and letters cluster together to form words, which can be strung together with spaces between them to form sentences. They learn that reading is done in a particular direction, and pages are turned when the words run out.

So when adults admit to enjoying listening to recorded reading, it seems a form of regression. It's something they should have outgrown. The child learns early that reading, real reading, adult reading, is done silently and alone. My husband Nick recalls when his sister, fifteen months his senior, first learned to read to herself. She sat in an armchair, the book in her lap. Her eyes moved systematically, her gaze absorbing the words off the page. She turned pages. But she made no sound. It was clear to him that she was reading; he'd seen his parents read this way. But she no longer had to do it aloud. He wanted her to read it to him, but suddenly she had the power to refuse. Nick recalls this as his first experience of jealousy. He was equating the ability to read silently with maturity and autonomy, and felt betrayed that his sister had received this extraordinary gift while he was left out. It was then that Nick understood that reading to oneself was not merely a trick to please teachers and parents, but also a vital necessity in a world where adult readers might be too busy or tired to read aloud.

Books on tape perhaps satisfy an impossible longing. With them you can have storytime any time, wherever you please. You can fill the intimate space of your car with it. You can carry it around with you, your Walkman stereo earphones whispering to you, while you walk, jog, do the ironing, ride the train. Tune the earphones carefully enough, and you will "feel" the voice not so much in your ears as up there in the crown of your head, a constantly chattering companion to your every activity. You can wrap yourself in a comforting cocoon of narrative, which provides continuity to your disjointed day.

But is it really reading? Reading is a private, silent, almost secret act. A large part of the pleasure of curling up with a good book comes from the fact that reading offers a refuge of silence and solitude from the noise of the world. The reader encounters the text alone. The printed symbols on the page enter the eyes and are translated by the vision and language centres in the brain into something meaningful. When a text is read aloud, it is essentially a theatrical performance. The audience absorbs the text through the mediation of the voice reading it. Intonation, inflection, phrasing all contribute. The voice interprets the written text in ways the audience cannot help being conscious of. Even the most neutral, unpolished reading adds a third dimension to the encounter between reader and text.

Once Nick was reading a storybook to the three-year-old daughter of a friend. After only a few pages she stopped him, eyeing him suspiciously, as though he were perpetrating some fraud. "You're reading it wrong," she said, though she acknowledged that he had not left anything out and was turning the pages at the right points in the story. The problem was that in Nick's rendition the bear-hero spoke with a southern drawl, while when her mother read it (the right way) the bear had no such affectation. Nick's reading was "wrong" because it was at odds with the reading she was used to.

That's what people object to about books on tape. No matter how well-spoken or polished the readers are, they can still add something to the text that is not supposed to be there. But when you read to yourself, don't you sometimes hear a voice? It probably doesn't happen all the time. You probably need to be reading something that gives you pleasure, or else something that gives you trouble, forcing you to slow down your reading to a pace closer to speech. But isn't there, at those moments, something like a voice in your head? Whose voice is it – yours, a parent's, your first-grade teacher's, a favourite actor's? Are there different voices for different texts, different voices for different characters? There's no reason you shouldn't hear voices when you read to yourself. You learned to read aloud first, sounding out the words or playing "see and say." You know too that language was oral before it was written, and that writers, good writers anyway, are conscious of the rhythm and texture of spoken language. When you close your eyes and make a mental image of something, blood flow increases to the vision centres of your brain in much the same way as when you open your eyes and look at something. Similarly, when you imagine a sound – a voice reciting a line of verse, a phrase of music, a jackhammer pulverizing pavement – blood rushes to the auditory centres of your brain, as if the sound were outside rather than inside your head. When you read, perhaps this is what's going on. Neurons fire. Juices flow. Electrochemical changes occur. You begin to "hear" something, not quite a voice, but a shadow of a voice. You might even feel something, a tickle in your throat, a twitching in your tongue and jaw muscles, as if that interior voice were really on the verge of pressing outward, down through larynx and lips, to make itself heard.

But these voices are essentially in your control. You can decide if a certain character should have a gruff or mellow voice. And you can tune down or turn off the voice altogether if you choose. This is what you prefer about reading to yourself, or, if you are a closet listener to books on tape, think you should prefer.

Is it a question of control then? I have an advantage in this regard. Though I am dependent on others to read to me, I have a wider range of voices to choose from than people who get only those books on tape that are commercially available. I rely on two free services for the blind – the National Library Service for the Blind and Physically Handicapped, and Recordings for the Blind. The NLS employs professional readers and has extremely high production values, but it is sometimes difficult to order exactly what you want. RFB readers are all volunteers, and the sound is slightly less polished, but ordering is easier. Sometimes the same texts are available from both services, so theoretically I should choose the voice that sounds best to me. I also hire readers to record student papers and exams, as well as books and periodicals not available from the services. In this too, I could exercise more control than I do. I could audition voices for specific qualities of pitch and timbre. I could also supply readers with lists of preferred pronunciations – *sk*edule not *sh*edule, to-*may*-to not to-*mot*-o. When they are recording student work, I may tell them to announce paragraph breaks and punctuation, since I may have to correct this. But otherwise, I generally tell my readers to "read it straight," to make no special effort to add emphasis through intonation, pacing, or inflection. No need to "do the police in different voices." This is not theatre, only reading.

I also have readers tape my own writing, as a part of my editing process. Like a lot of writers, I hear a voice or voices when I write. Or at least I have an idea of how my prose is supposed to sound. I may want the stress to fall on a particular word in a sentence, and could put it in italics. But a copy editor might find this obtrusive, or a reader could ignore it. I do what I can with sentence structure and punctuation. Listening to a tape of my work in progress I hear flaws – unintentional repetitions, awkward constructions, clumsy phrasing, graceless syntax. Did that last sentence have one too many beats? Does that parenthetical phrase disrupt the rhythm? I also listen for larger, more global aspects. Do I dwell too long on a certain section or scene? Does the pace bog down in the middle? Does it screech to a too-abrupt halt at the end? When the voices of my readers are in sync, or at least in harmony, with the voices in my head, I feel I have succeeded. If not, I revise. But for this method to work, I must not over-prime my readers to the idiosyncrasies of my style, or the special requirements of a particular piece of work, just as I cannot publish work with instructions. So I don't say, "Read the first four pages in a near-neutral monotone. Pick up the pace on page six. Watch out for hissing sibilants on page seven, but make those plosives really pop. Hit the last two pages at a breathless gallop. Then pause before the final paragraph and take it slow, allowing a subtle throb of emotion to come into your voice on all highlighted words."

Every writer knows you have very little sway over the voices in your readers' heads. Those voices have accents, tonalities, tendencies different from yours. For all you know, they may lisp or stutter. And because of these flawed interior voices, your readers may miss something or hear more than you intended. You can only do so much. And besides, anyone who has ever studied, taught, or thought about literature, or attended a production of a play, knows that numerous interpretations of any text are possible. I know plenty of literature professors who routinely read and reread passages aloud to their students, as a way to make a point plain. They raise and lower the volume on certain words, or quicken and slow the pace, adding nuances of interpretation that would require elaborate underlining, italics, and other font changes in print. "Hear that?" they say in effect, rather than "See what I mean?" But this doesn't prevent a student from reading back the same passage, adding different vocal highlights to make a contradictory point.

I won't deny that listening to texts can be frustrating. The professional voices at the NLS or the commercial publishers are sometimes too good. Their well-rounded tones are polished to such a rich lustre, I find myself listening to nothing but their voices and lose track of what I'm reading. The volunteer readers at RFB and my students and assistants have other vocal foibles. Some voices are hard on the ears. They are too shrill, or too gruff. They may slur sounds or mispronounce things. Some impose quirky cadences on everything they read. Others crack or quaver, inserting high emotion where it may not belong. They get head colds, sore throats, dry mouth, tongue-tied, sleepy, bored. Once I listened to a tape of Conrad's *Heart of Darkness* where the reader's habit of reading to small children was audible in his phrasing. There was a certain disingenuous "And then guess what happened" quality. When we got to "the horror, the horror," I almost couldn't go on.

Sometimes one text may be read by two or more readers. It can take a few seconds, even minutes, to adjust to the new voice. Also, it means that the new readers may be obliged to pick up a book they have never read and start in the middle. On a tape of Margaret Atwood's *The Edible Woman*, a new reader assumed a slightly ironic tone, which was not quite appropriate. The suggestion of a smirk in his intonation distorted the sound slightly and distracted me. A voice in my head piped up, "You've got it wrong. This is a serious part."

Eventually, however, the reader's voice lost its curled-lip tightness. His pace quickened. Words slipped from his lips without any self-conscious pre-processing. He sounded intrigued. This kind of tone shift happens often, and it always pleases me. I hear the voices becoming interested, engaged, engrossed. They want to know what happens, how the story plays out. A woman reading Sherwood Anderson's "The Egg" got a girlish giggle in her throat. Her mirth made it hard to get her words out, but it was also contagious. Sometimes a healthy skepticism tightens readers' tones. Sometimes wonder or fear makes them breathy. They let out little snorts of indignation, or small coughs of triumph. Sadness drags down the corners of their mouths and deepens their pitch.

There are a few universal responses. I've noticed that all readers reading for the blind, both professionals and volunteers, have trouble with the word "blind" when it's used in its pejorative figurative sense. Their voices put it in quotation marks, then in italics, distancing themselves from the usage. I was reading a work of sociology where the author relied heavily on such phrases as "blind to the needs," "blind to the concerns," "blind to the obvious solutions." The woman reading, a pro, became increasingly tense with each repetition. The word stuck in her throat. She might have been distressed simply by bad writing. Didn't the editor see the needless repetition? But other flaws in the prose did not affect her voice in the same way. It was as if having to pronounce the word "blind" made her conscious that her audience might prefer to have the word replaced by adjectives that don't equate stupidity with sight loss.

Am I projecting? Do I hear only what I want to hear, only what coincides with my own emotional response? The last time I visited the unicorn tapestries at the Cluny Museum in Paris, a group of schoolchildren came in as I was leaving. A girl let out an "Ooh!" of delight, and it brought a tear to my eye, because it seemed the most appropriate response to seeing those tapestries for the first or even fiftieth time. But she might have made the sound to impress her teacher, or in response to a secret her friend was telling her. I have to be careful not to make too much of voices. I try not to make the types of assumptions about the voices I hear that sighted people make about people's facial expressions. Does a downcast gaze mean someone is shy, respectful, or devious? Does a hushed tone mean the reader is awed, aroused, or annoyed? When words catch in a reader's throat it may only mean she needs a drink of water.

I also try to avoid making a mental image of the strangers who read books on tape. Though in daily life I often rely on the sound of a voice to recognize someone, it is not a sure-fire method. When an acquaintance approaches me at a party, my brain will register the presence of a shadowy body of a certain size and shape. When she speaks, other details of her physiognomy will seem to emerge from the cloudy form before my eyes. Just as I will not recognize an unfamiliar object on my desk until I can touch it, I need to hear a voice before a person's indistinct image resolves into someone recognizable. But voices can be deceiving. I used to be acquainted with a man; we encountered each other about twice a year at parties. Whenever we met, I had to resist the urge to compliment him on his weight loss. In fact he had not lost weight. He was thin and had always been thin. But he had a fat voice. It was the voice of a man who was not only overweight, but oversized. It was a thick voice which seemed to boom out of a cavernous chest, resonating through a thick coating of flesh. But when I looked at him, I saw a thin man, or rather, an elongated shadowy man-shape. When he spoke, the uncertain, smudgy outlines of his body seemed to swell. Before my eyes, he ballooned outward in every direction. Even his head got larger. Only when he stopped speaking could I force his image to deflate to something approximating his actual size.

I've noticed that listeners to National Public Radio frequently write in to comment on the shock of seeing a photograph or television image of one of the network's familiar voices. They seem not only surprised but indignant to discover how Bob Edwards or Cokie Roberts or Nina Totenberg actually look. I sense that sighted people are much quicker to create mental images from voices, because images matter so much more to them. What assumptions I make about the people whose voices I hear are rather rudimentary and general. Older voices, both male and female, tend to be deeper than young voices. The sounds acquire a grainy texture. But I know many older people with very youthful voices, and vice versa. So when I start listening to a tape, I may think, "Female over fifty from the Midwest." But I'm conscious I may be wrong on all counts. And I usually won't hazard a guess about hair, eye, or skin colour, educational level, marital status, or socioeconomic background.

There is a voice who reads for the New York unit of RFB who sounds to me like Lauren Bacall. The voice has overtones of what a friend calls "Park Avenue lockjaw" combined with a rough-and-ready huskiness. I have no idea if it is Bacall – RFB readers do not identify themselves by name. And I make no mental image of Bacall bent over a book in a recording studio. But I enjoy the voice anyway. She lends glamour to whatever she reads.

Besides these passing fancies about possible identities, personalities, or emotions, I hear more substantial things as well. I've heard Faulkner read by Southerners who readily take on all the dialects. But I've also heard him read by Yankees. After a few awkward pages, their voices seem to slip effortlessly into Mississippi cadences. Their inflections lilt a little, even in parts not written in dialect. They pause to breathe, breaking blocks of unpunctuated prose into comprehensible conversational units. I doubt they are entirely conscious of this. They read the words as written and it comes out that way. Faulkner's prose seems to fall naturally into a certain rhythm and roll. I am awed by the power of writing that can mold a voice in this way. I'm not sure I would know this about Faulkner if I were not accustomed to hearing his work read aloud.

Reading an edition of Stendhal's *Le Rouge et le Noir* intended for English-speaking students, the native French reader reads a footnote in English, "Here the author is being somewhat ironic," and emits an involuntary "Humph." She is responding, I suppose, to the obviousness of the irony – who could miss it? – or else disagreeing with the editor's assertion. I wish she would say more. Her voice and the certainty in the "Humph" suggest she's someone worth listening to. I rewind. I hear the irony in the passage, or is irony the right word? Isn't it something more subtle than that? The reader reads the footnote and humphs again. I echo the sentiment.

I listen to F. Scott Fitzgerald's "Winter Dreams" read by a woman with a southern accent, which seems a bit at odds with the Minnesota setting of the story. In the final scene, the protagonist, Dexter Green, a poor boy who made a fortune with a chain of specialty laundries, converses with an acquaintance, Devlin. Devlin brings news of the marriage of Judy Jones, the wealthy beauty who tormented Dexter's youth:

> "Awfully nice girl," brooded Devlin meaninglessly, "I'm sort of sorry for her."
> "Why?" Something in Dexter was alert, receptive, at once.
> "Oh, Lud Simms has gone to pieces in a way. I don't mean he ill-uses her, but he drinks and runs around –"
> "Doesn't she run around?"
> "No. Stays at home with the kids."[1]

The reader pronounces the phrase "run around" as "run 'round." This startles me. I check the print text and see it's a mistake. But it makes me think. The phrase, as this reader speaks it, has an old-fashioned coyness, a discreet but knowing unwillingness to specify particular acts. The phrase winks, at once disapproving and condoning. And it seems exactly right for Judy Jones and the society she inhabits, which tolerates a certain degree of sexual misconduct, even from unmarried females, as long as marriage is the outcome and social hierarchies are rigidly preserved. The Judy Jones whom Dexter remembers did "run 'round," with every boy in town. But part of her appeal for him was her poignant awareness that her "runnin' 'round" was tolerated only because her social status was so lofty. Girls who were less beautiful, less rich, less socially prominent (girls from Dexter's background) could not "run 'round" without risk. I try not to make too much of this minor slip of the tongue. Another reader might not even hear it. When I teach the story I may not even discuss this passage, except to remark on the perfect aptness of the name Lud Simms, or the way Fitzgerald reveals Dexter's uncharacteristic agitation through his testy repetition of other phrases in the dialogue that follows. But still, this momentary halt in my reading helps me rearticulate something in a new way, with a new accent.

For better or for worse, reading this way almost always feels like a shared experience. I feel myself not merely a passive audience but engaged in a kind of exchange. Readers are not reading to me; we are reading together. I have a sense of a continuous back-and-forth commentary, where I bounce my own ideas off the readers' ideas, or what I perceive of their ideas from their intonations, mistakes, involuntary grunts, and sighs. This is precisely what confounds the sighted reader who thinks of reading as a private and intensely personal act, a solo flight with no copilot to look over your shoulder, make snide comments, or gush about the view. But I can't help myself. This way of thinking about reading comes from the habit of listening to people I know read aloud to me. My mother read to me throughout her life, before and after I lost my sight. She loved to read aloud and had an extraordinary ability to read for prolonged periods at a startling speed. Hers was the first voice I ever heard and I must have imbibed some of her pleasure for reading long before I knew what reading was. Also, I inherited her voice; there were many people who could never tell us apart on the phone. So when she read aloud to me it was akin to hearing my own voice reading. She read the newspaper to me, selecting the articles she knew would interest us both. Or perhaps it's more accurate to say that she shaped my interest through the articles she chose to read. She preferred to read me long novels or massive biographies of writers and artists. We seldom talked about these books during or after the reading, but part of the powerful connection between us came from our shared experience of them.

From my mother I learned that knowing what someone is reading at a particular moment can give you access to that person's thoughts and state of mind. When the reading is shared and simultaneous, that access feels all the more immediate. One of my college roommates read me several novels by Henry James. Perhaps she was just being nice, but she claimed she would have done this even if I were not there because reading James' prose aloud made it easier to comprehend. Breaking his long sentences into manageable units of speech, holding his words in her mouth and then giving them voice, gave her mind the necessary breathing room to absorb his meaning. Reading these books together also allowed us to share observations and interpretations as we went along, almost paragraph by paragraph. When Nick reads to me, usually a big novel or epic, the text becomes a topic of conversation throughout the day. The initial impressions one has during the course of reading, the ideas one revises or rejects as reading continues, become mutual property between us. We share the process of reading, a real-time event in the intimate space where ideas first take shape.

I require my writing students to turn in taped readings of their own work. This is partly a convenience that allows me to return their work in approximately the same amount of time a sighted teacher takes. Also, reading their work aloud is supposed to make them more conscious of flaws in their prose. I notice that frequently, particularly after reading a longer piece of work, they feel compelled to speak to me at the end of the tape. They find they have something to explain or disclaim. "I tried to do it another way first, but I think this works better," they say. "Reading it over I see the ending is kind of abrupt." I don't discount the possibility that these outpourings are staged pleas for me to go easy on them. But I also think there is something about having just read aloud, for an extended period of time, that makes them unguarded. I sense they are not so much speaking to me as thinking aloud. I feel myself invited briefly into the mysterious space between the writer and the text. It always sounds like it's late at night when this happens. Their voices are soft, muted. Roommates and pets are all sleeping. Street noise is reduced to the infrequent shush of a passing car. I imagine them sitting alone, in the circle of light from a solitary reading lamp. The text lies in their laps, or else they read it off the computer screen, the reading punctuated by an occasional tap-tap-tap of the scroll command. Outside the circle of light, in the general darkness, I hover, a receiving presence.

I describe this to one of my reading assistants and he is not surprised. He says that when he finishes taping something for me he often feels compelled to speak to me, to express an opinion, or elicit mine. He goes on to say that if I were to give him the same text to read to himself and tell me what he thought, it would be different somehow.

Reading something aloud makes him notice different things. But also, the responses he has feel raw, unembellished, connected somehow to the realm of spontaneous utterance rather than considered contemplation. It's as if the act of reading aloud seems to open a more immediate line of communication. From his lips to my ear.

Of course, everything I describe only illustrates that reading books on tape is fundamentally different in every way from reading to oneself. So perhaps people who read this way are right to offer disclaimers. Our brains process aural and visual information differently, so the reading medium can affect the message. Public speakers know that what you can expect a reader to follow may leave an audience in the dark. Speechwriters adhere to rules and guidelines with an ear to future sound bites, while a political position paper can deliver the same idea in a greater number of syllables. I am listening to texts that were written to be read silently. I interpret the text, the voice reading the text, the experience of the person reading the text, piling layer upon layer over and around the text like so many scarves and sweaters. Can I really claim to experience the text at all?

And then there's the whole problem of reading illustrations, diagrams, charts, tables, photographs, reproductions, maps, and other visual aids that may be a part of the text. Some standard math and science textbooks are available with raised diagrams so sight-impaired students can trace graphs and figures with their fingertips. But for the vast majority of books using illustrations, readers must provide a verbal description. A reader says, "On the facing page there's a portrait of René Descartes. His face is very intelligent and sensitive." This comes as no surprise. Everything I know about Descartes would lead me to believe he was intelligent and sensitive. But what aspects of his face these adjectives are meant to designate, I do not know. I am glad to know there's this image in the book, that Descartes rates a portrait, but beyond this, I'm unimpressed.

In a textbook on visual perception, the reader says, "There's a simple line drawing, a cartoon really, of a rabbit. And apparently, if you look at it the right way, some people see a duck." Since I am reading a chapter on optical illusions, I know what's going on. I may even develop a theory about why this reader sees the rabbit first while another would see the duck, and how the image could be altered to change each reader's experience of the illusion. If I had the print version in front of me and I could magnify it sufficiently, I could experience the illusion for myself. But I might miss the graphic illustration of how it works on someone else.

If you listen to enough books recorded specifically for the blind, you sense which readers are accustomed to describing things to the blind and which are not. Some describe images in a systematic, supposedly neutral way, with so much specific detail, it becomes difficult to imagine what is represented. Others skip to the chase and explain what point the image is meant to illustrate. A reader says, "There's a bar graph on the bottom of the page which shows...." She pauses to assess the diagram, then concludes, with some annoyance in her tone, "exactly what the author said in the last paragraph." This reader was beginning to get impatient with the author's reliance on graphs, charts, and figures, and was ready to drop all pretense that there was something in these images a blind reader could not gather from words alone. Granted, writers in certain fields must conform to convention in their use of images. A pie chart is worth a thousand words. But when all these images must be translated into words for a blind reader, the authors' insecurities begin to show around the edges. It's as if they assume readers will only skim unless the bribe of a three-colour image is offered to make them linger.

Some books offer particular challenges in this regard. John Berger's *Ways of Seeing* has a vast number of images – reproductions of paintings, photographs, advertisements.[2] In some cases, the images are presented without text as pictorial essays. The sequence and juxtaposition of the images is supposed to create a nonverbal argument, leading the reader to an inevitable conclusion. The RFB readers on the taped version I listen to are up to the task. One in particular seems very well versed in the terminology of traditional art history. She's able not only to pronounce artists' names correctly but also to identify works of art even when the painters and titles are not given in the caption or text. She describes one image as "thickly painted" and another as "a fresco" when it would be impossible to tell this from the reproductions in the book, suggesting she's already familiar with the works. And she seems to enjoy describing the images. She revels in it. Her voice becomes excited, even agitated. At points she speaks so rapidly I have to slow down the tape to understand her. Her language is lush with adjectives. I'm a bit startled at first. Her enthusiasm is such a switch from the usual "nothing but the text ma'am" neutrality I'm used to. But then I start to enjoy it. Why should she repress her pleasure? It's infectious. I'd love to visit the Louvre with this woman. I picture her stopping for long moments before each painting, pointing out details here and there, making broad sweeping gestures in the air. A small crowd would gather, attracted by her enthusiasm. A tour given by Berger would presumably be more laconic. "Look at that," he would say. "Now, look at that. See what I see?"

At times the reader's interpretations are somewhat at odds with Berger's. In the third chapter, Berger presents a detail from Ingres' *La Grande Odalisque* next to a photograph from a girlie magazine, then suggests that the expressions of the two women are "remarkably similar."[3] The reader describes Ingres' model as looking "alluring, seductive, and knowing," while the woman in the photograph is "merely pornographic." When she reads Berger's assertion she pauses for a second, perhaps to look back at the images, but does not revise her own interpretation. What am I to make of this? Should I denounce the reader for her elitist assumption that because Ingres' painting hangs in the Louvre the nudity depicted has redeeming social value? Should I applaud Berger for revealing the shared intention to titillate of both works? Neither the reader nor Berger tells me what I really want to know about the two facial expressions. Could the resemblance be merely coincidental, due to the fact that there are a finite number of possible expressions facial features can assume? I wish I could bring in a third party to settle the matter. Then I find myself wondering about the photographer and his model. Is it possible that the photographer purposefully posed the model in this way, so his photo would prompt this comparison? Did the model assume this expression because she'd seen it once on a painting in a museum and wished to give her occupation dignity by conforming to conventions of the Western artistic tradition? All this speculation is beside Berger's point. But I get Berger's point, I follow his argument, I know what he means even though I can't see it. And I enjoy the book immensely, though at least part of my pleasure comes from the sometimes ludicrous disjunction between reader and author.

But did I really read this book? Or did I get only a secondhand hybrid version from someone who did not always see eye-to-eye with the author? It could be said that there are books that are simply not appropriate for blind readers. *Ways of Seeing* and similarly image-heavy works are required reading in courses in art history, sociology, psychology, cultural studies, film theory, and other disciplines. RFB records books according to the requests that come in from student subscribers, so I imagine there are other blind readers with similar questions about this text. For us to get closer to a definitive reading of Berger's book, perhaps we should watch and listen to the BBC television production and hear what role the soundtrack plays in shaping viewers' responses.

But despite all these potential problems, limitations, and distortions, books on tape are here to stay, for both blind and sighted readers. More and more people adopt this form of reading all the time, for a variety of reasons. The two free book services have long recognized that sighted people could also benefit from books on tape; people with physical disabilities are also eligible. In 1995 Recordings for the Blind added the words "and Dyslexic" to its title because almost sixty percent of the borrowers are dyslexic or have some other type of learning disability that prevents them from reading print. Even sighted people without any print disabilities may resort to books on tape occasionally or under certain circumstances. People recuperating from surgery or illness may find the regular reading posture impossible or may find it more soothing to listen than to read to themselves. And for many others, as the commercial producers advertise, books on tape allow busy people the opportunity to read while doing something else.

And future technologies will make live readers less necessary. Personal computers have had voice-synthesizing capabilities for some time. As they are now, these artificial voices are not for the faint of heart. They tend to read in a tinny monotone, giving equal value to every syllable. In his memoir, *Second Sight*, Robert V. Hines says his computer sounded like a foreign diplomat with a head cold. I asked a friend if the voice in her computer was male or female and she could not say for sure: "I don't even want to think about it." The program I use gives me a choice. The voice I prefer is decidedly male and has an earnest, well-meaning, though slightly adenoidal, quality. The female voices on the menu sound like the male voice talking falsetto, the computer performing vocal drag. Another program I've used consistently mispronounces my name, but so do many humans. When it encounters a word or phrase in capital letters, it spells it out letter by letter at breakneck speed. I have e-mail correspondents who rely heavily on capital letters for emphasis. My computer's readings of their messages become so much alphabet soup. But like many people who use voice synthesizers, I've adjusted. I've even grown rather fond of it. For one thing, unlike human readers, it never gets tired. It will read me the same sentence over and over without so much as a sigh of protest. I've come to think of it as plucky, even fearless, as it forges dauntlessly ahead through foreign languages, dialects, technical jargon without complaint or apology. I have it read me this paragraph. It sounds like it's blushing.

Voice-synthesizing technology improves all the time. Recently, designers discovered that with the simple addition of appropriately timed pauses, as if for breath, synthesized voices become more understandable. Apparently, human listeners derive meaning from the spaces between words and sentences as much as from the words themselves. Program the voice synthesizer to do this, and it suddenly sounds more human. My computer reads a period as a full-stop and a comma as a half-stop, which coincides with my sense of how this punctuation works. But the pause it makes for a semicolon is almost indistinguishable from the pause for a period. Also, being rather literal-minded, it reads a dash as an eighth-stop, and rushes breathlessly on. Most humans read a dash as a longer pause, a break in the rhythm of the sentence, like a phrase in parentheses. On top of all this, the computer also pauses at the end of every line of text whether there's punctuation there or not. To bypass this problem, I change the font size so the pause occurs at a different point in the line, then try to ignore these breaks. But when I ignore these pauses there's a risk I will also miss hearing when a pause is needed.

Patience helps. As with all new technology, kinks get ironed out over time. Very soon, users of synthesized voices will have greater control. The voices in computers will be digital recordings rather than artificially produced synthetics. Multimedia systems already allow users to create audiovisual productions, including recorded voices. You can, for a simple example, add "vocal Post-its" to a document, digital recordings of your own comments and queries, which can be activated when a reader clicks on a particular portion of the text. Your colleague or correspondent can hear your voice while reading your words, as if you were right there reading over their shoulder.

One day, I will be able to customize my computer's voice by loading digital recordings of voices – my own, friends', celebrities' – into the hard drive. I'll be able to alter and enhance aspects of these voices, to add or delete accents, emphases, and tonal qualities. I'll time the pauses to correspond to my punctuation. Then, using a CD-ROM or a scanner and a few deft keystrokes, I'll produce perfect (to me anyway) multi-voiced readings of any text I choose.

But even when this glorious future gets here, I might still listen to books read by human beings, live or on tape. I hope to one day become proficient enough at Braille to recapture an almost forgotten pleasure, that of reading silently, alone, without anyone's voice in my head but my own. But I suspect even then I would still want occasionally to pop a cassette into a player and have someone read to me. For one thing, I don't think I would stop having others read me my own prose, so I can hear for myself whether or not it stands up to someone else's voice. But I will also probably listen to other things too. I have come to value the random encounter of this kind of reading, the happy chance that allows me to hear something new and unexpected even in a text I thought I knew.

As the popularity of recorded books continues to grow, the prejudice against this method of reading will lose its grip. Sighted readers will quit apologizing, and the blind will have one less stigma to overcome. Still, this method may never be palatable for some. And if those people lose their sight I worry about them. If they disparage this method in advance, denigrating it as yet another distressing sign of the decline of literate culture, they doom themselves to the kind of despair the sighted presume is always the lot of the blind. And when they complain about being forced to read this way (as many do), they play into that prejudice, which insists that for a thing to be done right it must be done with the eyes. When I hear these complaints, I want to say, "Don't let them put those words in your mouth." Behind the eyes is the brain, where imagination, intellect, and memory reside. That's where reading happens. The ears and eyes are merely pathways. And then there are the readers to consider. Reading aloud to someone is an act of generosity that should never be underesteemed. It requires time, energy, voice, and imagination. Readers allow the text to inhabit their minds for a time, then give it voice. Such generosity never fails to move me.

NOTES

1.   F. Scott Fitzgerald, *Babylon Revisited and Other Stories* (New York: Scribner, 1960), 133–4.
2.   John Berger, *Ways of Seeing* (London: British Broadcasting Corporation and Penguin Books, 1972).
3.   Berger, 55.

Accidental Voices:
The Return of the Countertenor

Sherry Simon

John Dowland's melody *Flow My Tears* haunts the characters of Jeremy Podeswa's film *The Five Senses* (1999). The song floats down the corridors of the apartment building where most of the action takes place. Only at the end does one of the characters, the teenager Rachel, try to track down the source of the voice. She finds a door ajar and peeks in. What she sees is set up as a surprise. Although the song was sung in a high voice, the singer turns out to be a man.

Rachel's discovery re-enacts a moment that many have experienced over the last decade – *seeing* the countertenor for the first time. The singer in Podeswa's film is played by Daniel Taylor, whose blonde curls and small frame give him an androgynous look. But Podeswa's singer could as easily have been played by a bigger man like James Bowman or Alfred Deller. When Deller first began singing in the 1950s, audiences reacted to him with shock, "when, from that great frame and manly presence, there issued those flute-like sounds, ranging the register of the female alto."[1] Throughout his career Deller remained an oddity. And until recently, the sight of men singing in a high voice was still a novelty for most concertgoers.

The popular success of early music and Baroque opera since the 1990s has changed this. Two new generations of countertenors have come of age since Deller, and they appear regularly in the media. Some countertenors, like Andreas Scholl and David Daniels, have become stars of classical musical performance. But the mismatch between body and voice continues to exert a particular power. It's as if the visual dissociation, the break with naturalism, frees the listener to hear the voice as separate from the body.

"Voices are accidental things," says aspiring opera singer Thea Kronberg in Willa Cather's *The Song of the Lark*. The character is complaining about the fact that "exceptional voices" end up belonging to "common women, with common minds and common hearts."[2] Understandably, Kronberg expects voices to be linked in some necessary way to the person behind them. The countertenor introduces a new kind of skewing between voice and being, a new accidental relationship between container and content. Erased from the Western concert stage for a hundred and fifty years, the voice represents a lost tradition. Like Daniel Taylor's voice resonating through Podeswa's film, the countertenor is a phantom, only partly of our world. But in many other ways he is perfectly at home in the voice-morphing, gender-blurring present.

Why has the countertenor come so suddenly to prominence? There are several obvious reasons for his appeal. First there is the repertoire: the gorgeous Purcell and Dowland songs, for instance, that have received new life in the interpretations of contemporary countertenors. There is also the visual titillation provided by the high-voiced man, and the mythology of the suppressed voice-type which experienced a "miraculous return" through Deller. But these combine with elements that are less easy to define. The history of the countertenor throws open a field of questions about the voice and the way it inhabits the body. Once the voice has unlatched itself from gender roles and historical periods, what kind of truth does it express? No longer a representation of character but an "accidental thing," the voice takes on a life of its own. It is an enigmatic surface of sound, opaque and suggestive. Its power lies in its capacity to disturb, to invite listeners to hear the voice as simultaneously new and old, interior and exposed.

Scene One: And Then Came Deller...

From the 1700s until the mid-twentieth century, the high male voice was confined to English cathedral choirs and popular entertainment like the barbershop quartet. And then came Alfred Deller. The story of the moment when the countertenor voice re-entered history has all the awesome singularity of myth.

The story is told and retold of a day in 1943 when an English choirboy auditioned for the British composer Sir Michael Tippett and became the first countertenor of the modern era. A cathedral singer with no professional training, Deller (1912–1979), then in his early thirties, had made an unusual decision. Unlike his companions in the choir stalls of the cathedral, Deller chose not to give up his alto voice as he grew into his twenties. He continued to sing, in the choir or as a soloist, in the alto range – a range that was considered to be transitional for men, as they passed from young soprano voices to the mature tenor or bass range. Tippett had become fascinated with the songs of Henry Purcell (1659–95) and the Elizabethans, many of which are written for the countertenor. He had heard of Deller and asked to hear him sing. When Deller sang Purcell's *Music for a While* in "the voice for which it had been written," Tippett uttered appropriately grand words: "For me, in that moment, the centuries rolled back."[3]

It's true: Deller is a watershed. Before Deller, there was little interest in the repertoire and style of early English music. Philippe Beaussant, one of the most fervent promoters of the early music movement in France, says that the single strongest impulse for his return to the sound of the Baroque was Deller: "With him, Elizabethan music crossed three centuries; there was no intermediary stage, because there was no modern sound equivalent for Alfred Deller."[4] "It is as though," Deller's biographers explain, "an amateur archaeologist had stumbled upon a treasure of infinite value and found he possessed the gifts and perception to make himself the world's leading authority on it."[5]

How did Deller come to inaugurate a totally new moment in music history? There is something uncanny in the story of a man bearing a voice whose value is suddenly revealed. According to contemporary accounts, Deller was an unwitting vessel. Before meeting Tippett, Deller was a choir singer who, out of obstinacy, had not abandoned the alto register as choristers generally did. After his encounter with Tippett, he became the representative of a noble and forgotten tradition.

Biographies of Deller don't reveal much. Deller seems to have been conventional in many ways. He didn't like to travel and was uninterested in new sites or unfamiliar food. He had bouts of depression and remained religious all his life. He seems to have enjoyed family life and his son, Mark Deller, also became a countertenor. The "gift" of his voice was his overwhelming passion. Much of his energy was devoted to investigating and popularizing the repertoire of early English and Italian music.

The story of the "miraculous return" can only make sense if we introduce a character who generally remains unmentioned in Deller's story. This essential character – and the real villain – is Romanticism. The countertenor voice disappeared with the decline of the castrato, the onset of Romanticism, and the emergence of the "family of voices"[6] that have become familiar to us. The countertenor links us with a time before Romanticism, and for a writer like the French critic Dominique Fernandez the Romantics are guilty of all manner of crimes against the voice, by subordinating the voice to the demands of naturalistic drama and realistic gender roles. The periods before and after Romanticism share a taste for ambiguity and androgyny, for "pure" voice, as Rodolfo Celletti explains:

> [Baroque bel canto evokes] a sense of wonder through unusual quality of timbre, variety of colour and delicacy, virtuosic complexity of vocal display and ecstatic lyrical abandon. To achieve this, bel canto opera dispenses with realism and dramatic truth, which it regards as banal and vulgar, replacing them with a fairy-tale view of human feelings and of nature.[7]

Pleasure is to be found in the surfaces of voice, not in the pursuit of emotional depth or the pretense of naturalism. The countertenor reconnects to the time when voice was marvellous for its own sake, when its role was to unfold in a display of pure surface. This is hardly the "cult of the ringing tenor, who, in accordance with one of the many dubious conventions of Italian opera, must attack his high notes at full bellow, or be derided for a ninny."[8]

But while the countertenor enters our era trailing the glories of a former time, he decidedly connects with the values of today. This includes a vogue for all things androgynous. The countertenor has supreme theatrical value. The spectacle of gender reversals is as seductive and popular as the rediscovered Baroque repertoire. But there is more to be said about the qualities of the voice itself. The *New Grove Dictionary of Music* makes a huge leap by declaring that the countertenor voice does more than "revive" historical musical practice. It calls the voice one of the most important "innovations" in twentieth-century singing.[9] The return to pre-Romantic practices is compared to the modernist techniques of *Sprechgesang* – where the limits of the voice are tested and the melody is less important than the timbre of the voice itself – associated with Arnold Schoenberg and his *Pierrot lunaire* (1912), or the electronic manipulation of sonorities in Karlheinz Stockhausen and Luciano Berio.

This comparison seems difficult to understand at first. How can the reconstitution of a lost voice be considered avant-garde? Modernists like Schoenberg and Stockhausen wanted to disengage the voice from culture and history, to strip the voice of its traditional musical attributes (by making the voice shriek or talk rather than sing). The early music movement folds today's voice back into the past. But in both cases the voice is manipulated and hybridized. Herbert Lindenberger thinks that early music performance is actually "part and parcel of musical modernism." It emulates modernism by aiming to "shock complacent ears with new sounds."[10] The countertenor sound disturbs the listener accustomed only to the conventional sounds of the Romantic singer. The use of these voices to create strange sonorities, to produce the jolt of first-time hearing, to *épater le bourgeois*, is not to be discounted. Klaus Nomi, the iconoclastic pop-opera singer, was looking for these effects, exploiting barriers of gender and register.

But most of all, the countertenor invites us to dissociate the voice from the naturalistic link to psychology and gender that Romantic singing set as an ideal. *New York Times* critic Paul Griffiths praises the countertenor in a performance of Handel's *Rodelinda* for the sense of "separateness" and "artificiality" of his voice, "as if his voice were an instrument he was handling." For Griffiths this artificiality is positive, much preferable to the "usual voices...who sound as if they are making pretenses...."[11] As much as the countertenor caters to the contemporary taste for gender play and travesty, he also reopens a chapter in the history of singing. He is the instrument that will allow us to recover the "pure voice" adulterated by Romanticism.

Scene Two: The Trick with the Turntable

Gerard Corbiau's film *Farinelli* (1995) uses digital technology to re-create another phantom, the voice of the castrato. The film is an important moment in the recent fascination for things Baroque and the castrato voice in particular. Despite some unconvincing psychology, the film is successful in evoking the visual splendour of Baroque theatre, and the combined glory and pathos of the castrato. Most remarkable, however, is the electronically morphed voice (a soprano and a countertenor combined), which attempts to re-create the particular qualities of the castrato voice. The voice is indeed sumptuous. It combines the lightness and grace of a coloratura voice with density, strength, and warmth. It is precise, energetic, and elastic, attaining those qualities that are legendarily attributed to the castrato voice – the pneumatic vigour of a huge chest combined with the sweetness of an underdeveloped larynx, the embodiment of a "scandalous vocal plenitude,"[12] of a "vocal poetics of wonder,"[13] of a "faith in the expressive potential of singing, a faith so boundless that vocal timbre and vocal melody were all that was needed to create a reality independent of the real world."[14]

By combining the voices of a soprano and a countertenor, Corbiau reminds us that the castrato, in his time, was a cyborg, a hybrid created by the rudimentary technology of the time, a singing-machine. From the film we do get a sense of the unearthly qualities that listeners wanted. To produce the voice of an angel, the castrato had to be removed from the realm of the ordinary human. Like his protectors, men of the church who were figuratively unsexed, the castrato served a suprahuman ideal.

Farinelli uses technology to reconstitute a forgotten voice-type. But it is a reminder that the manipulation of the voice began far earlier than the electronic era. To the drastic methods of the churchmen we can add some more benign techniques. Take Wayne Koestenbaum, for example, a diva fan, who has written of the ways in which the listener's fantasies are projected onto the voice, the ways in which listening becomes fully active. He describes a trick that he invented as a teenager with his Victrola. He would tamper with the speed control of his antique Victrola turntable to alter the gender of the singer. "Turn Caruso into a woman by speeding him up; turn Galli-Curci into a man by slowing her down. Who hasn't tried this trick?"[15] The thrill of listening was intensified by the unexpected mismatch between pitch and gender.

Koestenbaum's trick with the turntable anticipates some of the developments on the contemporary music scene. What if we take a male baritone voice and speed it up to the soprano register? We would have the countertenor. What if we digitally mix a countertenor and a soprano? We get a reconstitution of the gender ambiguous castrato voice.

The castrato voice apparently entered Europe in Spain through the Mozarabic church, which integrated eunuchs from Islamic culture as singers as early as the ninth century. The church found a solution to a dilemma it had itself created (*mulier taceat in ecclesia*): how to represent the divine voice of the angel in the absence of women? The castrato voice then moved onto the stage of opera, where it became synonymous with Italian opera throughout the eighteenth century. Angus Heriot explains how its prominence was the result of cultural and musical particularities:

> The hegemony of the castrati can be attributed to several factors: their superior musical education which made them the best musicians; a certain taste for the artificial during the period that tolerated, better, appreciated travesty; and the apparently remarkable suppleness, agility, and singular tone the castrati voices were capable of achieving.[16]

The impressions of music historian Enrico Panzacchi reveal the delight of hearing a castrato in the Vatican chapel in the late nineteenth century:

> What singing! Imagine a voice that combines the sweetness of the flute and the animated suavity of the human larynx – a voice which leaps and leaps, lightly and spontaneously, like a lark that flies through the air and is intoxicated with its own flight; and when it seems that the voice has reached the loftiest peaks of altitude, it starts off again, leaping and leaping still with equal lightness and equal spontaneity, without the slightest sign of forcing or the faintest indication of artifice or effort; in a word, a voice that gives the im-

mediate idea of sentiment transmuted into sound, and of the ascension of a soul into the infinite on the wings of that sentiment.... Here, all my being was marvelously satisfied. Not the least mark of the passage from one register of the voice to the other, no inequality of timbre between one note and another; but a calm, sweet, solemn and sonorous musical language that left me dumb-struck, and captivated me with the power of a most gracious sensation never before experienced.[17]

Every age seems to manipulate the voice towards its own ends and discover its own voice disturbances. Some would argue that the true successor of the castrato is the contralto. For audiences in the early nineteenth century, she embodied an ambiguity similar to that of the castrato, a similar contrast between appearance and register. The low female voice exercised a particular fascination, and French fiction of this period repeatedly offers portraits of female singers who combine qualities of both genders, "who are in some sense beyond sexuality yet inspire an intense response of pleasure and desire in others."[18]

An 1849 poem by French poet Théophile Gautier is a particularly good illustration of this fascination. Describing the famous ancient Greek sculpture of the *Sleeping Hermaphrodite*, he imagines its powerful voice and gives it a contralto register:

> How lovely you are, oh strange timbre!
> Double sound, man and woman both,
> Contralto, bizarre mélange,
> Hermaphrodite of the voice.[19]

Gautier sees the statue as the expression of a new kind of beauty, an ambiguous, double beauty, bizarre and appealing. "It's Romeo, it's Juliet, Singing with a single throat, The raucous pigeon and the warbler, perched on the same rosebush." In the final stanzas, the poet enumerates a series of alto opera roles, both masculine and feminine, belonging to the contralto register and concludes: "It's you I love, O Contralto!"[20]

The contralto today is a familiar member of the musical family. The "intense response" which was a result of category confusion has disappeared, the cloak of novelty now draped over the shoulders of the countertenor. And so the countertenor voice turns out to be one more *frisson* in a history of vocal novelties.

Scene Three: Deller on Stage

Deller loved acting. He was a ham and adored disguises and practical jokes.[21] The one great disappointment of his career was not having the opportunity to sing contemporary opera. He did have one chance: Benjamin Britten wrote the role of Oberon in *A Midsummer Night's Dream* for Deller. But Deller's performance was considered wooden, and he was not able to project well. He was taken off the role after only a few nights and replaced by Russell Oberlin. Michael and Mollie Hardwick describe the deep sadness Deller felt as a result. He did sing in the recording under the direction of Britten, and his voice catches the role's dignity and eerie otherness, above all in the Purcellian solo *I Know a Bank Where the Wild Thyme Blows*. This song brings out all the strangeness of Deller's voice and illustrates well the kind of otherworldly roles that Britten composed for this voice.

You can get a sense of Deller's theatrical bent from comic roles like Mopsa in Purcell's *The Fairy Queen* (1972). Deller sings the part of a young maiden warding off the kisses of a peasant lad. The farcical duet is made all the more comic when we imagine the barrel-chested and goateed Deller playing up the incongruity of this love duet.

Deller's sound is entirely distinctive. It has the somewhat metallic and very androgynous tinge that you can still hear in some contemporary countertenors like René Jacobs and Paul Esswood. But it has more unevenness and a characteristic break across registers. It is this break that creates the full shock and oddity of his voice. For instance, in the English folk song *Three Ravens* (1955) Deller flips back and forth from a deep throat sound to very sweet but thinner high notes. Yet his voice is vigorous, bright, and supple.

Listening to Deller reminds me of what the French call *pleins* and *déliés* in calligraphy, distinguishing between the thick line you get when pressing down fully on the nib of the pen and the finer line you get when you turn the nib on its side. This variety in tone quality can be eerie. Deller's low notes are mysterious, his high notes gentle, occasionally dramatic or piercing. The variety in register is similar to what Elizabeth Wood calls "Sapphonics," a voice with a wide range, where the "defective" handling of bridges between registers turns out to be an engaging quality.[22]

There are two kinds of countertenor voice, one that is a high tenor (what the French call *haute-contre*) and the other that has a baritone base as its "fundamental" but maximally develops the headvoice. Deller belonged to the second category and said that: "Everyone has this voice: it's just a question of developing it."[23] But there is no end to the controversy surrounding this distinction, the long-standing quarrels constantly dredging up national stereotypes (the English countertenor, the Italian castrato), assumptions about "natural" versus "artificial" registers (the "falsetto" considered a perversion, a weak headvoice, different in nature from the real chestvoice)[24] and a heavy strain of misogyny. Being "for" the countertenor often counts as a vote against women singers. Deller's use of his huge range could be very effective, especially when, as in Britten's aria for Oberon, he jumps from low to high note, his voice changing radically in quality.

Deller received almost unanimous praise for his singing. It was not only the register that made his voice unique, says Tingaud, but the timbre of his voice and his very personal style of interpretation.[25] When he died, the *Musical Times* wrote that "for the sweetness and flexibility of his voice he stood without rival." Admitting that his "expressive subtleties (the colouring of a high note, the drawing back of a rhythm) could sometimes be called mannered," the review concluded that "Deller made us aware that the countertenor voice, far from being an object of contempt and derision, has a power and a character of its own, essential to the music composed for it...."[26] Most reviewers agree on this assessment – the combination of enthusiasm for the voice and reservations about what have been called "Dellerisms." And yet, as new generations of countertenors respond to the enthusiasm of listeners, Deller himself seems to be forgotten. Young countertenors take care to distinguish their voices from Deller's metallic and hooty tones, his unevenness. Deller's musical practices, his use of ornamentation, and especially his integration of sopranos into the Deller consort are relegated to what now seems like the Dark Ages of early music revival. Yet Deller is an historical figure of extraordinary significance. It is impossible to account for the current popularity of the countertenor voice without remembering its introduction via Alfred Deller.

What is certain is that Deller introduced a new set of questions about the relationship of voice to gender and sexuality, and to modes of performance. He began a new era in the history of singing. In what way does the voice belong to the body and what identity does the voice express? These questions have become lively issues of performance practice.

When playing a recently recorded Bach cantata, it is impossible to know who is singing the high parts until you listen for clues. The voices of boy sopranos will be athletic and boisterous, woman sopranos will be more interiorized and mature. For the alto register, the countertenor will have a veiled and dense sound, sometimes distinctly different from the mezzo-soprano but sometimes difficult to distinguish from a woman's voice. In the recent past, soprano and alto parts would automatically have been sung exclusively by women: this is no longer the case.

Early music elicits a shifting landscape of voices. Bach did not employ women singers because of the ecclesiastical prohibition against women, but it is said that in certain European cathedrals women stood behind the men and secretly reinforced their singing. Bach could count on well-trained boy singers, whose voices did not change until the age of seventeen or eighteen (while they change at twelve to fourteen today). Even a relative purist like Ton Koopman can justify using young women singers today, arguing that he cannot find appropriate boy soloists. Phillipe Herrewege, John Eliot Gardiner, René Jacobs have all given different and interesting reasons for their choice of voice combinations. Herrewege, for instance, enjoys using children, not only for their timbre but also for the emotion that is created in the contrast between their freshness and the gravity of the texts, which often mention death. Gardiner chooses contraltos for the more "sensual passages," countertenors for the more "abstract" passages. Jacobs prefers a contralto who is "humble and capable of creating emotion" to a countertenor who is "too narcissistic."[27] But what does it mean when two male voices sing Pergolesi's *Stabat Mater*? This is the lament of the mother for her son. Does the fact that it was originally written for castrati make the recording by Jacobs and the boy Sebastien Hennig less strange in contrast to the female duos we have become accustomed to?

Among other attributes the countertenor has inherited from the castrato is this aspiration to the ideal of "pure voice." Consider the following comment by Michael Tippett describing the countertenor voice:

To my ear it has a peculiarly musical sound because almost no emotional irrel-evancies distract us from the absolutely pure musical quality of the production. It is like no other sound in music, and few other musical sounds are so intrin-sically musical.[28]

What Tippett and others mean when they speak of "intrinsic" musicality refers to the relative absence of vibrato, the roundness of the sound that occurs at middle range, and the fact that the countertenor repertoire does not necessarily include dramatic inte-riorization or psychological role-playing. There is typically a flatness in the countertenor sound that makes it easier to capture as a quality exterior to the singer. Some coun-tertenors, like Paul Esswood, René Jacobs, and Alfred Deller, have an androgynous, lay-ered, metallic tone. But others, like Daniel Taylor and James Bowman, have a much lighter sound. These voices don't have the shocking dissonance that was so strong in Deller. Their voices don't seem hybrid in the way that Deller's was, always calling atten-tion to itself. The hybrid is created when two dissimilar and unexpected things are brought together. Deller's voice had a dissonant quality: it was unstable, making evident the friction between its different registers.

Today the countertenor voice is becoming naturalized, turning into a new idiom, in the same way that creoles become new languages. It's hard to imagine Purcell's music sung by anyone other than countertenors like Bowman or Taylor. How quickly the transition is made. These voices no longer strain against category definitions and expec-tations. And yet, at times, we sense that uncanny quality, the impression of a voice detached from the body that produces it, of an intriguing mixed message. Then the coun-tertenor voice once again becomes a phantom. Foreign and yet familiar, distant and yet close, it is a reminder that our accounts with the past are never settled.

NOTES

1. Michael Hardwick and Mollie Hardwick, Introduction to *Alfred Deller: A Singularity of Voice* (London and New York: Proteus, 1980), n.p.

2. Willa Cather, *The Song of the Lark* (Boston: Houghton Mifflin, 1943 [1915]).

3. Hardwick and Hardwick, 74.

4. Philippe Beaussant, *Vous avez dit "Baroque"?* (Paris: Actes sud, Coll. Babel, 1994), 84.

5. Hardwick and Hardwick, Introduction, n.p.

6. Roland Barthes, "The Grain of the Voice," in *Interviews 1962–1980*, trans. Linda Coverdale (New York: Hill & Wang, 1985), 36.

7. Rodolfo Celletti, *A History of Bel Canto*, trans. Frederick Fuller (Oxford: Clarendon Press, 1991), 9.

8. Hardwick and Hardwick, 79.

9. *New Grove Dictionary of Music Online*, "Singing: 5. 20th Century," < http://www.grovemusic.com /data/articles/music >, December 14, 2002.

10. Herbert Lindenberger, *Opera in History: From Monteverdi to Cage* (Stanford: Stanford University Press, 1998), 46.

11. Paul Griffiths, "Critic's Notebook: A Singing Voice on the Sexual Fringes," *New York Times* (July 14, 1998).

12. Wayne Koestenbaum, *The Queen's Throat: Opera, Homosexuality and the Mystery of Desire* (New York: Poseidon Press, 1993), 169.

13. Celletti, 8.

14. Celletti, 9.

15. Koestenbaum, 61.

16. Angus Heriot, *The Castrati in Opera* (New York: Da Capo, 1975), 87.

17. Quoted by Heriot, 36–7.

18. Felicia Miller Frank, *The Mechanical Song: Women, Voice, and the Artificial in Nineteenth-Century French Narrative* (Stanford: Stanford University Press, 1995), 115.

19. Frank, 107 (translation mine).

20. Frank, 107–109 (translation mine).

21. Jean-Luc Tingaud, *Alfred Deller: Le contre-ténor* (Paris: Editions Josette Lyon, 1996), 15.

22. Elizabeth Wood, "Sapphonics," in *Queering the Pitch: The New Gay and Lesbian Musicology*, ed. Philip Brett, Elizabeth Wood and Gary C. Thomas (New York and London: Routledge, 1994), 27–55.

23. Hardwick and Hardwick, 78–79.

24. Peter Giles, *The History and Technique of the Counter-Tenor: A Study of the Male High Voice Family* (Aldershot, UK: Scolar Press, 1994), 56–57.

25. Tingaud, 38.

26. "Obituary: Alfred Deller," *Musical Times* 120: 762 (September 1979).

27. "Bach," *Télérama* hors-série (January 2000).

28. Quoted by Hardwick and Hardwick, 75.

Tempaurality in *Twelfth Night*

Wes Folkerth

The idea that literary artifacts can provide information about the historical dimensions of acoustic experience has only recently come to be recognized in literary studies. The works of Shakespeare present a special opportunity for this type of research: first, because they come in the form of playscripts – scores written for acoustic actualization in theatrical performance; and secondly, because the words that constitute these playscripts refer so frequently to characters' acoustic experiences. In my own work I have focused on how Shakespeare's plays bespeak their author's experience of sound, an experience that is situated within a particular early modern sociohistorical context. This work proceeds from the assumption that the acoustic experiences of early modern English subjects such as William Shakespeare were affected by the attitudes, beliefs, and practices concerning sound and hearing that pertained to that cultural moment. More specifically, my work in this area has been concerned with attempting to identify the various early modern cultural dispositions, particularly the ethical and aesthetic attitudes, that Shakespeare consistently associates with sound and with hearing in his works.

Over the course of conducting and writing up this research, one critical comment in particular came to haunt me. There is a brief passage in Terence Hawkes' *That Shakespeherian Rag: Essays on a Critical Process* in which he likens the Shakespearean playtext to a sea-shell:

> [H]eld to the ear [it] apparently emits the sounds of the sea. But of course the sea-shell does no such thing: it produces no sound. In fact the sound we hear may simply be the sound of the circulation of our own blood.[1]

This passage was, and remains, troubling to me, because it suggests that the entire time I had spent trying to listen for instances of an early modern acoustemology, a specifically early modern epistemology of sound, in Shakespeare's plays, I was really only hearing myself.[2] My response to this in the book that resulted from this research was twofold: first, I argued that readers of the plays do sound themselves out with such a sea-shell, but added that such a device allows readers to listen to themselves in ways that they are less likely to in the everyday. The sea-shell enables readers to hear their own otherness.[3] The second part of my response was to bury the entire episode in a footnote, where Hawkes' typically useful provocation has since rested for me, awaiting and deserving further attention.

In the present essay I will try to respond to Hawkes' assertion by turning to the play *Twelfth Night* and suggesting that Orsino's acts of listening to music in that play advance nostalgia, and specifically the musical experience associated with it, as a "temp-aural" mode of subjectivity, one that situates subjective experience in, and opens it up to, time – specifically through the way in which musical performance (and by extension other modes of performance, including theatrical re-presentation) enables moments in time to be repeated, or echoed, and thereby recuperated and reflected upon. Although the play is a fairly typical representative of Shakespeare's "festive" comedies, a generic identity it shares with other works of the same period, such as *As You Like It* and *A Midsummer Night's Dream*, *Twelfth Night* may be set apart by the frequency, and espe-cially the tonal contributions, of its musical interludes. *Twelfth Night* is generally acknowledged as one of Shakespeare's most musical plays, one in which the use of music appears to have been considered quite carefully in terms of its contribution to the play's overall effect.

For those unfamiliar with the story's main plot, a young woman named Viola has survived a shipwreck, in which she believes her twin brother Sebastian has been lost, off the coast of Illyria. Viola disguises herself as a young man named Cesario to serve at the court of the local Duke, Orsino, who pines for the love of another local woman, Olivia. Over the course of the play Viola falls in love with Orsino herself, and Olivia with Cesario (Viola in disguise), who is sent by Orsino to woo her in his name. The play ends with the revelation of Sebastian's survival, which enables Olivia and Sebastian to become partners, and for Orsino and Viola, who then doffs her disguise, to do the same.

The first character to speak in the play, the Duke of Orsino, is a crucial figure to consider in the context of subjectivity and acoustics, both because he is so often dis-missed as a narcissist by his critics, and because he is so often represented as a listener in the play. What exactly *does* Orsino hear? Is he only hearing himself? And is what he hears at all related to what *we* hear when we listen to him describe what he hears? To begin it may be helpful to consider more closely whether Orsino might more properly be understood as a narcissist or as a nostalgic. While use of the latter term is somewhat anachronistic in this case, it would nevertheless appear that it better describes him. As Fred Davis notes in *Yearning for Yesterday: A Sociology of Nostalgia*, the term "nostalgia" was first used by the Swiss physician Johannes Hofer in the seventeenth century as a medical diagnosis, to describe the symptoms of homesickness felt by Swiss mercenaries.[4] Over time the term fell out of use in its original medical context, and the sense of phys-ical dislocation it denoted gave way to the temporal dislocation that was of course already latent, or implicit, in that description. Although Shakespeare would not have used the term "nostalgia," and would probably have thought of the same affective state in terms of "melancholy," I want to retain the term "nostalgia" for the present discus-sion because in *Twelfth Night* I find the role of temporality so central to this mood. It is a mood that permeates the play, and one that is specifically connected to music early on when the Captain who comes ashore with the shipwrecked Viola compares her brother Sebastian to Arion, the famous musician of classical myth who, during a nostalgic jour-ney to revisit his homeland on the island of Lesbos, is threatened by the ship's crew, so that he resorts to playing music to stave off their assault. After finishing his tune Arion jumps overboard and is carried to Tenaerus by a dolphin that has been attracted by the music: Arion apparently never completes his return home to Lesbos.[5] In *Twelfth Night*, nostalgia, or a temporally-inflected melancholy, is of course also readily discernible in the figure of Olivia, who is in a protracted period of mourning for her deceased father and brother, an emotion that she "would keep fresh/And lasting in her sad remembrance" (1.1.30–1).[6] Nostalgia is also prominently featured in specifically musical contexts at the very beginning and ending of the play, in the song Feste sings to draw the play to a close ("When that I was and a little tiny boy") as well as in the remarks of Orsino himself on the music that announces the start of the performance:

> If music be the food of love, play on,
> Give me excess of it; that surfeiting,
> The appetite may sicken, and so die.
> That strain again, it had a dying fall;
> O, it came o'er my ear like the sweet sound
> That breathes upon a bank of violets,
> Stealing and giving odor. Enough, no more,
> 'Tis not so sweet now as it was before.
> O spirit of love, how quick and fresh art thou,
> That notwithstanding thy capacity
> Receiveth as the sea, nought enters there,
> Of what validity and pitch soe'er,
> But falls into abatement and low price
> Even in a minute. So full of shapes is fancy
> That it alone is high fantastical. (1.1.1–15)

In this first speech, Orsino expresses the desire to hear certain music, even certain musical phrases, over and again. It is worth noting that Orsino is distinguished not only by the *intensity* of his musical experience, but more specifically by his desire to hear certain songs and melodies *repeatedly*. The self-absorption that many readers identify in his character is really only one facet of his tendency toward reflexiveness; another more positive facet is his capacity to think reflectively about the music that he hears, coupled with his evident desire to express to others his awareness of music's effect on him. That this reflectiveness is also one of the main characteristics of nostalgia is suggested by James Phillips:

> [I]f the nostalgic lives under this fate of an ever-increasing distance from the past, he also experiences a kind of recovery. In nostalgia, distant time is brought near. Indeed, paradoxically, it may be nearer than when actually lived.[7]

Intense affective states such as nostalgia, love, or the desire for revenge can work a strange magic on the experience of time, bending it, arresting it, speeding it up, sometimes simultaneously. Phillips observes that nostalgia "memorializes time" with its "tendency to crystallize into precious moments."[8] One such moment is of course the musical phrase with the "dying fall" that Orsino wishes to hear repeated at the beginning of the play. However backward-looking nostalgia may seem, the mood is characterized by a paradoxical focus on the present, which Phillips also notes. "It is to *this* world which nostalgia points," he observes, a world tantalizingly close to us, which we find "near because it is everywhere, yet distant because it must be approached through the categories of reflection."[9]

While *Twelfth Night*'s opening speech is often read as evidence of Orsino's exaggerated emotional self-indulgence, in recent years the Duke has gathered up a number of defenders as well, in addition to the play's heroine Viola, whose judgment we are not often invited to question over the course of the play. Yu Jin Ko has recently followed Peter Thomson's lead in noting that Orsino's music-listening habits are a part of a fairly complex strategy for coping with and managing the pain brought on by the awareness of the inevitability of time's (and love's) passing. Ko suggests that "if we accept the idea that possession of the desired object necessarily brings about decay of both pleasure and desire, then the sustaining of desire itself becomes the principal pleasure...."[10] In this scenario, time itself, or at least the attempt to replay it, becomes the solution to the problem of evanescence; the Duke's strategy becomes primarily one of substitution and deferral.

Listening to and replaying music is one way Orsino imagines at least temporarily breaking free of the hold that his strong emotions have on him – it is a form of substitution, just as he sends Valentine to woo Olivia in his stead, and as he sends Cesario (really Viola) to woo her afterward, just as hearing itself is replaced by other sensory domains in this speech. We discover in this speech that like the character Bottom, who declares upon waking from his dream that "the eye of man hath not heard, the ear of man hath not seen, man's hand is not able to taste, his tongue to conceive, nor his heart to report, what my dream was" (4.1.209–12), the Duke has a propensity for synaesthesia. His "high fantastical" fancy transforms the sounds he hears into very specific odours (violets, to be precise), music becomes food and the sight of his beloved purges the air of pestilence, which was commonly thought to enter through the nose – as Sir Toby will later note when he comments on Feste's sweet love song: "To hear by the nose, it is dulcet in contagion" (2.3.56–7).

For the Duke, the nostalgic desire to live intensely and fully in the moment is achieved when the senses begin to speak through each other. Listening to music puts Orsino in a heightened state of consciousness; it retunes his sensorium by opening channels and pathways between the senses, crossing the barriers that normally separate their discrete modes of engagement with the world. Hearing is for him a form of emotional amplification that floods the boundaries that describe and focus his affection for Olivia, thus preserving that affection. While it is the *sight* of Olivia that has brought Orsino to his present state of longing, listening to music is how he attempts to regulate it and preserve it without submitting it to the deteriorating effects of time. And to a certain extent this strategy has been a successful one: listening to music has only killed his appetite for more music, which is not so sweet now as it was before; it has not killed his appetite for Olivia herself. Orsino finishes his oration by submitting to fancy's sway over him, thereby raising his affection to a new level; his love has become amplified even as he has attempted to lessen its effect on him.

In the first chapter of *The Acoustic World of Early Modern England*, Bruce Smith identifies the sound [o:] as the most fundamental mode of entry into, and dialogic engagement with, the soundscape.[11] Bearing that in mind, it is interesting to note how often the Duke, whose very name begins and ends with this vowel, repeats the word "O" in his earliest speeches of the play, while he is listening to the sounds around him. In the opening soliloquy alone, the sound is repeated in numerous words, such as "love," "on," "so," "o'er," "sound," "violets," "odor," "no," "more," "before," "nought," "soe'er," "low," and "alone." Also repeated twice in the speech is the simple interjection "O," a word without a conventional linguistic referent, which represents language functioning in the way music does. "O" asks us to hear the tone of wonder in Orsino's speech, a speech which itself turns into a kind of music, a transformation that underscores the relation between acoustic experience and the temporality of subjectivity.

In the brief conversation that follows, Orsino notes that the first time he saw Olivia he was transformed, turned into a hart (deer) that is hunted because it loves. Orsino is keenly aware of the way he has been changed by this love, and now that he has been changed, he desires to stay in this state, to change no more. Throughout the play, he repeatedly insists upon his steadfastness, upon his capacity to resist the changes brought on by time, since he believes this the surest way to define himself as a true lover. In fact, his steadfastness is one of the traits for which he has evidently become renowned in Illyria. When Viola, disguised as Cesario, speaks with Valentine about the swiftness of the Duke's affection for "him," she inquires about what she calls "the continuance of his love." "Is he inconstant, sir, in his favors?" she asks, to which Valentine replies, with such certainty that his response may also suggest a touch of exasperation, "No, believe me" (1.4.7–8). Later, when the Duke directs Cesario how to woo Olivia, he commands his proxy to be the image of himself, particularly with regard to his constancy:

> Be not denied access, stand at her doors,
> And tell them, there thy fixed foot shall grow
> Till thou have an audience. (1.4.16–18)

Viola follows his direction, only to find herself suddenly the object of Olivia's affections. Before the play's second song, Orsino again speaks of the constancy of his love:

> For such as I am, all true lovers are,
> Unstaid and skittish in all motions else,
> Save in the constant image of the creature
> That is belov'd. How dost thou like this tune? (2.4.17–20)

While the sudden shift here from speaking of love to asking Viola her opinion about the music that accompanies their conversation may be played in performance as an ironic comment on the Duke's real lack of focus, the moment also serves as an elaboration of the strategy introduced in the opening speech of the play. That is, as he meditates on the power of his affection, he characteristically turns his attention to the music he hears in order to exert some control over love's power over him. Continuing this conversation with Cesario on the philosophy of love, Orsino asserts that inconstancy in love is too characteristic of men:

> For, boy, however we do praise ourselves,
> Our fancies are more giddy and unfirm,
> More longing, wavering, sooner lost and worn,
> Than women's are. (2.4.32–5)

By the play's final scene, however, Orsino appears to have undergone a change of sorts. When he meets Olivia onstage for the first time, he upbraids her for her own unwillingness to change. Olivia employs a musical metaphor in her rejection of him:

> If it be aught to the old tune, my lord,
> It is as fat and fulsome to mine ear
> As howling after music.

To which Orsino replies, "Still so cruel?" Olivia shoots back, "Still so constant, lord," to which Orsino retorts, "What, to perverseness?" (5.1.108–12) He is unable to reconcile the constancy of Olivia's affections with that of his own, and quickly shifts the focus of his love to Cesario, once it becomes apparent to him that she is actually a young woman.

In the 1942 film *Casablanca*, it is the character Ilse Lund who first asks the cafe's piano player, Sam, to play the song *As Time Goes By*, the tune his American friend Rick Blaine has forbidden him ever to play again. Later in the film, during a drinking binge brought on by the reappearance of his old love, Rick will ask Sam to play the song too – not with the famous line "Play it again, Sam," which of course never occurs in the film's dialogue, but with the simple prompt, "You know what I want to hear." Like *Casablanca*, Shakespeare's *Twelfth Night* is a work suffused with nostalgia, loaded with the weight of the past on characters' lives. And as in the film, this sense of the fullness of the past is represented primarily through the music that characters wish to hear – the popular songs such as *Come Away Death* and *When That I Was and a Little Tiny Boy* in Shakespeare's play, or *As Time Goes By* and *La Marseillaise* in *Casablanca*.

During his analysis of "flawed audition" in *Hamlet*, Peter Cummings perceptively notes that it is not only Shakespeare's characters that change, but the play's readers and audiences who do so as well, and that all of these changes are reflected and registered in sound: "We hear other things in texts as we grow older with them," he says, "as their lines and voices speak to us, just as we hear more subtle nuances in the human voices we know over time."[12] That strain again, and again, and again. The enduring popularity of Shakespeare's works is, I think, partly informed by modernity's nostalgia for a more aural relationship to culture, for forms of engagement with the world and with each other that are less based on the forms of mastery that have come to be associated with the visual realm, and more with the forms of wonder and intense affective experience that Shakespeare associates most closely with the domain of hearing. To conclude, I return to Hawkes' own strain again, and ironically come to recognize how the very constancy of my own desire to insist upon sound and hearing's relation to the temporal dimension of subjectivity, a relation I have come to think of as "tempaurality," only plays into his argument (I hear an echo of Orsino's "What, to perverseness?" in this realization). Perhaps I haven't listened well enough, or changed enough as the result of this listening. As Feste notes in the play itself, thus the whirligig of time brings in its revenges, and the rain it raineth every day.

NOTES

1.   Terence Hawkes, *That Shakespeherian Rag: Essays on a Critical Process* (London: Methuen, 1986), 43.

2.   "Acoustemology" is a portmanteau coined by the anthropologist Stephen Feld, who developed it during his work with the Kaluli people of New Guinea. Feld was searching for a term that would denote the special modes of knowing enabled by acoustic experience. See Stephen Feld, "From Ethnomusicology to Echo-muse-ecology: Reading R. Murray Schafer in the Papua New Guinea Rainforest," *The Soundscape Newsletter* 8 (June 1994). Available at < http://interact. uoregon.edu/MediaLit/WFAE/news_letter/08.html#Ethnomusicology > .

3.   Wes Folkerth, *The Sound of Shakespeare* (London and New York: Routledge, 2002), 129.

4.   Fred Davis, *Yearning for Yesterday: A Sociology of Nostalgia* (New York: Free Press, 1979), 1–2.

5.   For an account of the Arion story, see the entry in John Lemprière, *Lemprière's Classical Dictionary of Proper Names Mentioned in Ancient Authors Writ Large: With a Chronological Table* (London: Routledge & Kegan Paul, 1984).

6.   This and all subsequent quotations of Shakespeare's plays are from *The Riverside Shakespeare*, ed. G. Blakemore Evans (Boston: Houghton Mifflin, 1974).

7.   James Phillips, "Distance, Absence, and Nostalgia," in *Descriptions*, eds. Don Ihde and Hugh J. Silverman (Albany: SUNY Press, 1985), 67.

8.   Phillips, 66.

9.   Phillips, 72.

10. Yu Jin Ko, "The Comic Close of *Twelfth Night* and Viola's *Noli me Tangere*," *Shakespeare Quarterly* 48:4 (winter 1997): 397.

11. See Bruce R. Smith, *The Acoustic World of Early Modern England: Attending to the O-Factor* (Chicago: University of Chicago Press, 1999).

12. Peter Cummings, "Hearing in *Hamlet*: Poisoned Ears and the Psychopathology of Flawed Audition," *Shakespeare Yearbook* 1 (spring 1990): 83.

Polyphonic Aurality and John Cage

Robert Bean

I'm on the side of keeping things mysterious, and I have never enjoyed understanding things. If I understand something, I have no further use for it. So I try to make a music which I don't understand and which will be difficult for other people to understand, too.[1]
– John Cage

(bababadalgharaghtakamminarronnkonnbronntonnerronntuonnthunntrovar-rhounawnskawntoohoohoordenenthurnuk!)[2]
– James Joyce

Hearing, listening, and sonority can be difficult pleasures. More so in the case of a piece like John Cage's *Roaratorio: An Irish Circus on 'Finnegans Wake'*, in which the challenge to listening is intentional, and apprehension in a conventional, linear sense is impossible. Drawing upon James Joyce's *Finnegans Wake* as source material, Cage first produced *Roaratorio* for radio broadcast, and subsequently as a live performance, or "Musicircus." It engages such a heterogeneity of sounds and noises that disruption and disorientation are paramount. This piece exemplifies a complex, radicalized form of listening that to come to terms with it requires a distinct mode of auditory experience – what I call *polyphonic aurality*. This term, implying simultaneously the opening of numerous ears and the production of an incomprehensible sound collage, also alludes to a renewal of the collective act of hearing.

Dialogue and Polyphony

Polyphonic aurality, first of all, relates to polyphony, a form of contrapuntal composition and improvisation in use since the ninth century. Polyphony is a musical style in which more than one voice can be heard and comprehended simultaneously. Traditionally, the various strands of counterpoint that combine to create a musical texture are referred to as "voices." One of the most notable applications of counterpoint in the twentieth century has been the development of serialist music and the twelve-note technique of Arnold Schoenberg, a mentor to Cage in his student years. The twelve-note technique breaks down the harmonic hegemony of classical composition and replaces it with a system where there is no tonal centre to the music. This is accomplished by treating every note in the scale with equal importance through the use of the tone-row.

The importance of polyphony, however, extends beyond the strictly aural to encompass the realms of literature and theory. Counterpoint and polyphony, with their harmonic textures and strata of voices, can function as tropes for democracy, equity, and postcolonial difference in cultural theory.[3] Theodor Adorno, for instance, wrote a history of polyphony that posited it as a metaphor of the cooperative logic of a community. Its origin, he argued, lay in the "collective practices of cult and dance."[4] For Adorno, polyphony served as a striking counterexample to the isolated autonomy endemic to modern music. Because of this autonomy, music cannot retain or claim an immediate or integrated relationship with an audience or community. Given these circumstances, polyphony and modernity coexist in an antinomic relationship.

Cage's commitment to the principles underlying polyphony and counterpoint in musical composition can be discerned in his use of them as both a logic and a metaphor in his experimentations with sound, silence, composition, and performance. Creating *Roaratorio* in 1979 for the radio station WDR in Cologne, it was broadcast as a *Hörspiel* ("Ear-play") in the context of the station's Studio Acoustic Art projects. *Roaratorio* was the realization of Cage's intense interest in the writings of James Joyce, and it utilized a complex compositional process that synthesized the complete text of *Finnegans Wake* into a performance for music, voice, and recorded sounds.

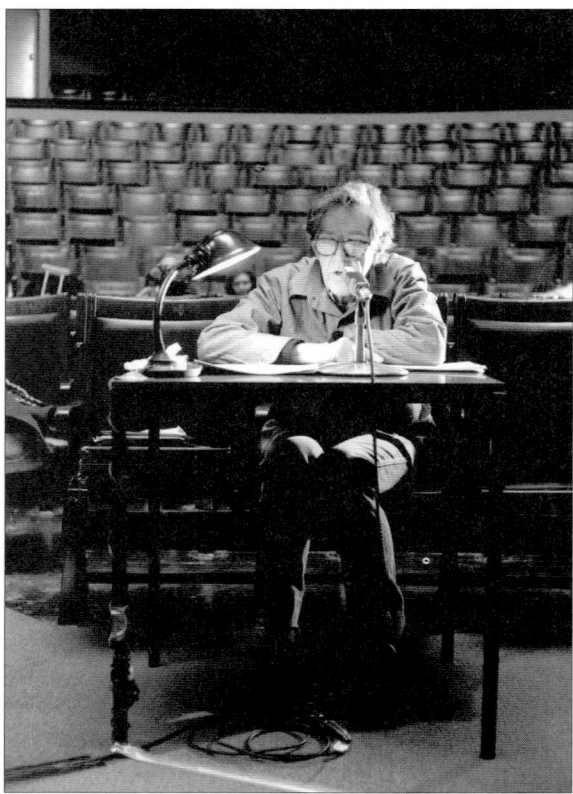

Vid Ingelevics
John Cage performing *Roaratorio*
1982
Convocation Hall, University of Toronto
Courtesy the artist

The structure of *Roaratorio* began with a text – "Writing for the Second Time Through Finnegans Wake." Cage notes that in the mid-sixties, Marshall McLuhan had encouraged him to base a work on the "Ten Thunderclaps" in *Finnegans Wake*, which he claimed represented "a history of technology."[5] Acknowledging that he owned a copy of *Finnegans Wake* but had never been inclined to read it, Cage devised a method of *writing through* the novel, as opposed to *reading through*. Writing through meant adopting a mesostic technique, a process that patterns lines of words in order to construct a central column of readable text. In the case of Cage, sentence fragments were excerpted from *Finnegans Wake* and arranged so that a vertical line spelled out the name of the author, James Joyce. This was an instrumental means of reducing *Finnegans Wake* to a publishable and performative scale – making the mesostic both an aural and visual palimpsest.

The system was straightforward: Cage looked for a word that contained the letter J but did not contain an A, followed by a word that contained the letter A but not the letter M, followed by a word that contained the letter M but did not contain the letter E, and so on. At times Cage felt it necessary to omit words to alter Joyce's more conventional syntax. Cage developed this editing process further and disqualified words with repeated syllables. With this additional limitation, Cage reduced *Finnegans Wake* from 626 pages of prose to forty-one pages of mesostics. Punctuation was also removed from proper, grammatical locations in the original text and dispersed erratically throughout the pages of the mesostics according to the chance procedures of the I-Ching. As Cage described it:

> [E]ach page is illustrated by its punctuation rather than clarified by its punctuation.... [P]unctuation as we know it commonly, is on the side of "law and order" and not on the side of what we could call "poetry and chaos."[6]

One of the mesostics that Cage created for *Roaratorio* condenses a page from *Finnegans Wake* where references to noise, radio, and the physiology of the ears are prominent:

patent number 1132 thorpeterson and synds Jomsborg selverbergen
wintriodic singulvAlvulous
tyMpan
bauliaughaclEeagh
culpable of cunduncing naul and Santry

or one watthour bilaws below till time Jings
hOst
indtil the teller oYne of an oustman in skull of skand
when he pullupped the turfeyCork by
grEats of gobble out of lougk neagk[7]

When producing the text for radio broadcast, Cage also began a *listing through* of the acoustic events described in *Finnegans Wake*. Amounting to somewhere between four and five thousand sounds, he organized them into the following categories:

> Thunderclaps
> Thunder rumbles and earthquake sounds
> Laughing and Crying (Laughtears)
> Loud voice sounds (shouts, etc.)
> Farts
> Musical Instruments (short)
> Bells, clocks, chimes
> Guns, explosions
> Wails
> Animals and particular birds
> Music (instrumental and singing)
> Water
> Birds (in general)
> Singing[8]

In his pursuit of Joycean sounds, Cage researched the place names mentioned in *Finnegans Wake* and conceived of travelling to and recording ambient sounds from each site. He selected 626 places, corresponding to the number of pages in the book, but due to the extensiveness of such a project, ultimately solicited recordings from the locations instead. *Roaratorio*'s resulting sound collage is an excessive cacophony of voice, Irish music, and vernacular sounds including radios, televisions, automobiles, barking dogs, and crying babies. Although there is a spatial density to the assemblage, the piece proceeds diachronically by way of Cage's voice, methodically reciting his series of mesostics. This recitation is performed in the tradition of the Cantus Firmus ("fixed song" or prescribed melody) of polyphonic composition. The work employs the heteroglossia of an Irish idiom already present in the language of *Finnegans Wake* with aleatoric segments of Irish music and prerecorded noise.

Roaratorio's carnivalesque nature was intensified when Cage adapted the work for a Musicircus, its live performance. Eliminating the central stage, the performers, and musicians, sound sources were located throughout the space with no distinct division from the audience. The chance sounds generated by the wandering, interacting audience are given equal value and priority in the overall work. This participatory structure interrupts the voyeuristic status of the audience and prompts them to become performers. For Cage, music was a social activity that brought together producers, audiences, and "cultures formerly separated" for experiences that would otherwise occur in isolation.[9] He was critical of the recording industry and the dependency it promoted in consumers. With this Musicircus, Cage conceded a degree of his authority to the crowd, who implicitly became co-producers of the musical event.

Prior to *Roaratorio*, Cage had never provided a score for a Musicircus. After completing *Roaratorio* for radio broadcast, he wrote the score, CIRCUS ON, which summarized and defined his creative process. CIRCUS ON exhibits the formal economy of a neo-Dadaist, conceptual artwork. It succinctly states basic instructions that anyone can adopt as a method for transforming a literary source into a Musicircus:

_____, _____ _____ CIRCUS ON_____
(title of composition)   (article)   (adjective)   (title of book)

means for translating a book into a performance without actors, a performance which is both literary and musical or one or the other.[10]

Fusing the collective, egalitarian principles found in counterpoint and polyvocality with his personal commitment to anarchy, Cage engineered a work that is, in Mikhail Bakhtin's terminology, *dialogical*. Bakhtin's concept of dialogism, as defined by Ken Hirschkop, is the relationship between "distinct voices in a narrative text, in which each takes its shape as a conscious reaction to the ideological position of the other; but even then it is a metaphor for a broader principle of discourse."[11] The systematic and obsessive mesostic procedure at the heart of *Roaratorio* – the searching for the proper name of "James Joyce," the eradication of syntax (or as Joyce would say "sintalks"), and the reconfiguration of punctuation – all add up to a Cagean version of dialogical experience that results in dissonance. (Ironically, while the mesostics render the name of James Joyce visible as text, Cage leaves the author's name inaudible.)

Listening Speaks

As a sound collage composed for broadcast, *Roaratorio* raises an apparent conflict between the monological technology of radio and the piece's basis in polyphony and dialogism. Radio, because it places aurality in the service of consumption, restricts the dialogical experience of speakers and listeners. Why would Cage create a nonlinear polyphonic work for voice and sound merely to have it reduced to a linear broadcast medium? Bertolt Brecht anticipated this paradox and its consequences:

> [R]adio is one-sided when it should be two-[sided]. It is purely an apparatus for distribution, for mere sharing out. So here is a positive suggestion: Change this apparatus over from distribution to communication. The radio would be the finest possible communication apparatus in public life, a vast network of pipes. That is to say, it would be if it knew how to receive as well as transmit, how to let the listener speak as well as hear, how to bring him into a relationship instead of isolating him. On this principle the radio should step out of the supply business and organize its listeners as suppliers.[12]

Implicit in Brecht's description of radio is its potential to serve as a communication technology that facilitates a reciprocal exchange.

Roland Barthes circumvents the problematic of unidirectional and non-dialogical radio by foregrounding the active component of aurality – the desire of listening. Listening, for Barthes, requires conscious effort and implies intention: "*Hearing* is a physiological phenomenon; *listening* is a psychological act."[13] Barthes describes three aspects to his genealogy of listening. The first is listening as an orientation to specific indices – animals listening for the sound of predators or prey, children listening for the footsteps of their mother. The second involves deciphering – listening to signs according to specified codes, an inherently human activity. The third posits an intersubjective listening of "who speaks" – an aural space where the phrase "I am listening" also means "listen to me."[14] In relation to the dialogic association of speaker and listener, Barthes notes that the silence of the listener is as active as the "locutor's speech."[15] From this perspective, *listening speaks*; it is a form of intersubjective exchange that is most typified by the analyst/analysand relationship and one that listens to, and recognizes, the desire of the Other. In its vernacular form, Barthes explains that *modern listening* includes "the implicit, the indirect, the supplementary, the delayed: ...the *shimmering* of signifiers."[16] Such a listening is equitable and reciprocal; it "grants access to all forms of polysemy, of overdetermination, of superimposition"[17] and consequently cannot be legislated or coerced through obligation.

Brecht's analysis of radio and listening is a response to the alienation that results from the propagandistic abuse of radio. His criticism predicates the listener as the subordinate and reified subject of monological speech. Barthes and Cage, however, contend that radio can engage the listener in an *aural polyphony* that is reciprocal with transmitted voice and sound. For Cage, the absence of sound is as significant as its presence. Consequently, the limitations that radio seems to impose can be transformed by the responsive awareness, or desire, of listeners.

The Sound of Words

Finnegans Wake is an apt subject for auditory experimentation and an ideal vehicle for Cage's exploration in writing and recording. In addition to transgressing the laws of grammar and symbolic structure, *Finnegans Wake* is an aural phantasm of polyphonic voices, multiple languages, and cacophonous sounds. Its phantasmatic quality is in part due to it being a representation of, according to John Bishop, "the reconstruction of a half-hour fragment of the dark," one that "invites its reader to sort these matters out...by studying what is seen," "in fact, under closed eyes."[18] Whether or not *Finnegans Wake* actually represents a dream, it is sleep, the period of absence that evades memory, that is at issue for Joyce. In his words, "that is what I want to convey: what goes on in a dream, during a dream. Not what is left over afterward, in the memory."[19] In this sense, *Finnegans Wake* is an invention of, and about, the unconscious and the analytic discourse that Barthes refers to as the site where *listening speaks*.

Joyce uses the initials HCE to identify the novel's protagonist, Humphrey Chimpden Earwicker, a nebulous human presence who functions cryptically as the apparatus for a character as well as an absurd motif that is iterated throughout the text. HCE is the central figure who falls asleep and becomes deaf and dumb. Yet there is general consensus that HCE also refers to the Latin words of the consecration – *Hoc est enim corpus meum* ("For this is my body"). This transubstantiation accurately identifies HCE, paradoxically, as both a presence and an absence. Earwicker is a nickname for the concept of "earwitness," as well as a reference to the protecting ear of mammals discussed in Vico's *New Science*.[20] The letters HCE repeatedly refer to forms of aurality throughout *Finnegans Wake*: "Hush! Caution! Echoland!"; "Hear! Calls' Everywhair"; "How chimant in effect"; "harbour craft emittences"; and so on.[21] HCE was also an acronym for "Here Comes Everybody," a phrase that Cage adopted as a metaphor for the participatory audiences of the Musicircus performances and the attentive, yet unstructured, listening that many of his compositions invited.

The significance of an embodied aurality in *Finnegans Wake* can be best found in a section describing a nonsensical play on radios, receptors, and the head of HCE, who appears as a sound-sensing contraption. As John Gordon notes, the complexity of language and mechanistic apparatus privileges the physiology of the ear:

> [T]he radio introduced at the start of the chapter is also the sleeper's head and trunk, his cranium ("a howdrocephalous enlargement"), brain ("harmonic condenser enginium"), mouth ("vitaltone speaker"), eyes ("circumcentric megacycles"), heart ("magazine battery"), arteries ("twintriodic singulvalvulous pipelines"), front and back ("up his corpular fruent and down his reuctionary buckling") – and the most prominent feature is the ears, the "umbrella antennas for distancegetting."[22]

The cybernetic morphology of Earwicker's hearing is a complex labyrinth of discontinuous and fragmented signification. Not only is H.C. Earwicker "equipped with supershielded umbrella antennas for distancegetting," even the components of his technologically enhanced ears – "hummer," "cstorrap," and "enville" – allude to the acronym HCE.[23]

At this point in *Finnegans Wake* the reader discovers an extensive inventory of audible inventions and, in Joyce's terms, "acoustic disturbances" that penetrate the ears of Earwicker. Many of these sounds are either emanating from the body of the sleeper (farts, snoring, teeth grinding, breathing, heartbeats, etc.) or from the "man made static" of the radio receiver that assembles the sounds of the world. Joyce poses the question of how any of these sounds can be heard at all. John Bishop responds by quoting these passages from *Finnegans Wake* – "our ears, eyes of the darkness" "see" in the night, and therefore serve as HCE's "aural eyeness."[24] In other words, it is sound and hearing that form the images of the night.[25]

Inevitably, for Joyce, the aural functions of the ears take precedence over the sense of sight. Sound is forever active in both the conscious and unconscious perception of the sleeping subject. Joyce presents an arduous array of phonemic play in the portmanteaus that describe the ability of the ears to manifest images throughout the night. One example of aural vision is a description of the "dectroscophonious photosension under suprasonic light control."[26] This combination of phonemes that correlate sound, hearing, and light through embodied sensation illustrates the etymological complexity Joyce utilized to reconfigure and predicate vision upon aural dynamics. The auditory space that the reader explores throughout *Finnegans Wake* is a territory of sensations that permeates the open, radio-receptive ears of Earwicker from a diversity of local, historical, and universal sources.

If for Barthes, *listening speaks*, and for Joyce, *hearing sees*, then for Cage, listening is the sensorial essence of experience. To Cage, the absence, as well as the presence, of sound attenuates the act of listening. In *Roaratorio*, Cage unravels the syntax from *Finnegans Wake* to foreground the sound of language itself. Layered with traditional Irish music and recordings of hundreds of sites and sounds referenced in *Finnegans Wake*, *Roaratorio* can be best described as sixty minutes of *prepared noise*. This creates an aesthetic of both anxiety and pleasure. Clamour often generates an atmosphere of discomfort, and Cage was accustomed to audiences leaving his performances because of boredom or irritation. He attributed this to a lack of understanding and a refusal to allow unfamiliar sounds into the experience of a composition. At the same time, the openness to listening that Cage offers can also be experienced as pleasure and astonishment. Our ears are invited to wander freely through the complexity of aural textures. It is possible at one moment to focus on the overall din, and then perhaps hear the drone of Cage's voice reciting mesostics. The next moment one may hear fiddles, Bodhrán drums, Uillean pipes, or a recording of a dog barking, glass breaking, or a child crying. This may eventually lead to a daydream that will displace the presence of sound entirely. The audience is encouraged to inhabit the invented racket of *Finnegans Wake*, perhaps to be inside of HCE's head as his dreams unfold in the night. Our ears are provoked long enough to re-experience the act of listening and to witness the "activity of sounds."[27]

At the beginning of this essay, I referred to the difficult pleasure of *Roaratorio* and the impossibility of listening to it in a conventional, musical manner. The act of hearing necessitated by this work, polyphonic aurality, a displaced mode of listening, is founded on the experience of inexplicability. *Roaratorio* invites analysis; yet any attempt at interpretation is sure to result in incongruity. Receptive to music that privileges all sounds, regardless of origin or affect, Cage radically rethinks the possibilities of aurality. Cage, like Joyce, transgresses the process of signification, resists symbolic meaning, and renews the art of listening.

NOTES

1. John Cage quoted by Kevin J. H. Dettmar, *The Illicit Joyce of Postmodernism: Reading Against the Grain* (Madison: University of Wisconsin Press, 1996), 51.

2. James Joyce, *Finnegans Wake* (London and Boston: Faber & Faber, 1975), 3.

3. See Theodor Adorno, *Philosophy of Modern Music* (London: Sheed & Ward Ltd., 1973); Jacques Derrida, *Monolingualism of the Other or the Prosthesis of Origin* (Stanford: Stanford University Press, 1998), Assia Djebar, *Fantasia: An Algerian Cavalcade* (London and New York: Quartet Books, 1985), Edward Said, *Culture and Imperialism* (New York: Vintage Books, 1993).

4. Adorno, 18.

5. John Cage, "Writing for the Second Time Through Finnegans Wake," in *Empty Words: Writings '73–'78* (London and Boston: Wesleyan University Press, 1973), 133.

6. John Cage, *Roaratorio* (Kew Gardens, NY: Mode Records, 1992), 38.

7. Cage, "Writing for the Second Time," 162.

8. Cage, *Roaratorio*, 71.

9. Cage, "The Future of Music," in *Empty Words*, 181.

10. John Cage, CIRCUS ON (New York: Henmar Press, 1979), 1.

11. Ken Hirschkop, Introduction, in *Bakhtin and Cultural Theory*, eds. Ken Hirschkop and David Shepherd (Manchester and New York: Manchester University Press, 1989), 2.

12. Bertolt Brecht, "The Radio as an Apparatus of Communication," in *Radiotext(e)*, ed. Neil Strauss (New York: Semiotext(e), 1993), 15.

13. Roland Barthes, *The Responsibility of Forms: Critical Essays on Music, Art and Representation* (Berkeley and Los Angeles: Hill & Wang, 1985), 245.

14. Barthes, 246.

15. Barthes, 252.

16. Barthes, 259.

17. Barthes, 258.

18. John Bishop, *Joyce's Book of the Dark: Finnegans Wake* (Madison: University of Wisconsin Press, 1986), 16.

19. Joyce quoted by Jacques Mercanton, "The Hours of James Joyce," in *Portraits of the Artist in Exile: Recollections of James Joyce by Europeans*, ed. Willard Potts (Seattle: University of Washington Press, 1979), 207.

20. For Vico, the mammalian ear evolved to be ever alert to the threat of predators, a significance that Barthes also acknowledges.

21. Bishop, 273-278.

22. John Gordon quoted in James A. Connor, "Radio Free Joyce: Wake Language and the Experience of Radio," *James Joyce Quarterly* 30:4 (summer, 1993): 831.

23. Joyce, 310.

24. Joyce, 14, 623.

25. Bishop, 286.

26. Joyce, 123.

27. John Cage, *Silence* (Middleton, CT: Wesleyan University Press, 1961), 10.

SUSAN HILLER

Witness, 2000
Installation views

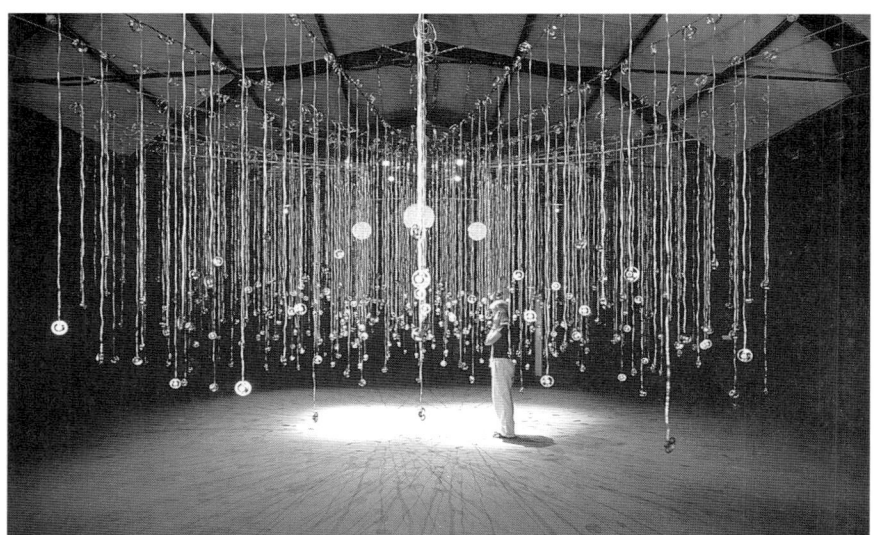

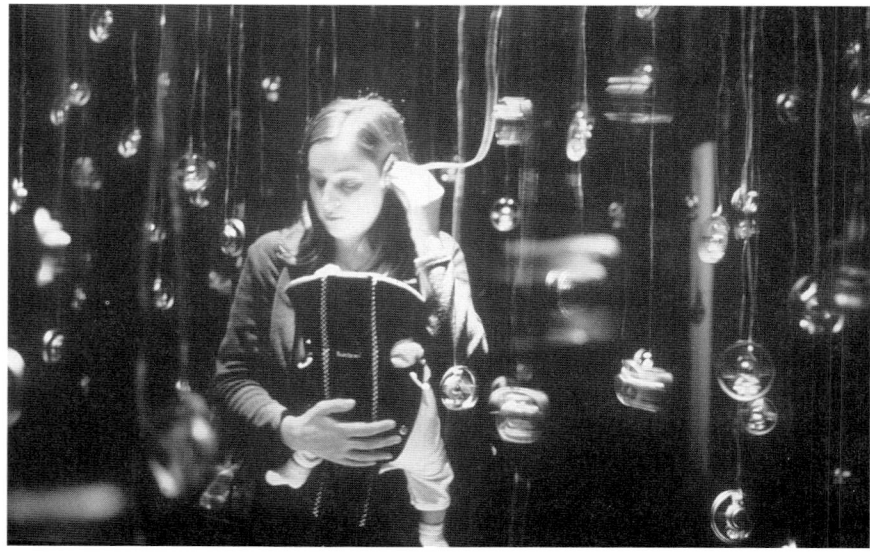

The Voice as Body:
An Interview with Mary Horlock

Mary Horlock: *The experimental recordings of the Latvian scientist Konstantin Raudive were a starting point for using sound in your work. Raudive believed he could capture the voices of the dead on tape. The idea of reclaiming what has been lost or overlooked is a fundamental concern in your work. Is this why Raudive interested you?*

Susan Hiller: I first heard about Raudive's work in the 1960s, before my practice was very well developed. The poetic idea of amplifying silence and finding that it isn't silent at all, but full of sound, was fascinating. The realization that "nothing" was in fact "something" seemed to support ideas I was forming about how to pay attention to what was out of sight or beneath or beyond recognition within our culture, and as an artist to try to picture it for myself and others. My interest in making the negative positive was encouraged tremendously.

I was also very attracted to the idea of using or misusing a scientific methodology in pursuit of what science would consider too mad or abject to bother with. Raudive's approach seemed incongruous but in an important way... It wasn't until the mid-1970s that I actually heard some of the amazing tape recordings Raudive made. Like many other things that our culture relegates to fantasy or delusion, hearing the voices within the soundscape of noise produced by amplifying tapes made in supposedly empty, supposedly silent rooms is somewhat a matter of having a wish or desire to hear something, and then trying to make sense of it. Personally I heard the voices clearly, but was never able to make the jump to supporting the hypothesis that they were the voices of dead people, who were said to have their own broadcasting station, although I've kept an open mind on that... But there certainly are voices on these tapes, speaking what seem to be words in a weird mix of languages. They are compelling, eerie, and if perhaps their only existence is as electronic artifacts or artifacts of the process of recording and amplification – it really doesn't matter.

In the installation Monument *(1980), viewers are invited to sit on a bench in front of photographs of memorial plaques and listen to a soundtrack of your voice. You call yourself "an audible Raudive voice," a voice from the past played back in the present, our present. Is the temporality of the spoken word the key to its appeal? How important is it that your voice, the artist's voice, and a female voice, was used?*

On one level, *Monument* is a memento mori, like all of Raudive's work. In order to hear the soundtrack, you need to participate in the work by listening privately in public.

I wanted people to be seen by others against a background of cultural inscriptions representing death – the photos you mention. My own voice improvising against a background of historical material seemed to emphasize, at that time at least, a kind of gendered exclusion from heroic, public forms of representation, and simultaneously, to question their relevance. Private and public come together in *Monument* in a fairly complex way.

The work emphasizes temporality on all levels, playing around with different kinds of "pasts" – the historical past, the past when the work was made and my voice recorded, the past of just a second ago when you were listening to an earlier bit of the tape...and so on. The unacknowledged uncanny aspect of sound recording, whereby the dead speak to us, dead musicians play to us, was very important and that's why the soundtrack references Raudive in its opening statement.

The intimacy of my voice speaking in your ear was a direct physical approach to viewers, a kind of seduction. At the time of *Monument*, this was really an unusual way for an artist to work, but I had been thinking a lot about the so-called tyranny of the visual and was looking for a more physical way to approach my work. If you sit on the park bench to listen to the *Monument* tape, in fact you can't really see the visual part of the work very well or at all, and that was deliberate. Touching someone's ears with your voice is actually a very intimate contact. In this sense, voice is physical, voice is body. Body is evoked and transmitted by voice, and not represented – this was one of the radical, political underpinnings of *Monument*, which was positioned "against" representation as some kind of fake immortality...

The way you use language is extremely evocative. In the Monument *soundtrack you create an aural collage, offering meditations on representation, memory, gender, heroism. You call this "automatic talking"; it flows freely without making claims to "explain" the piece. In other soundtracks, such as the video* Belshazzar's Feast *(1983–4), you use vocal improvisations, which cannot be translated into any recognizable language. Is the significance for you not so much in what is actually spoken, but how?*

Again, I would emphasize the idea of voice as body, the physicality of it and the intimacy. I would also mention again that yes, gender was important in my decision to speak. What I was trying to do was to speak "in the negative" about things that were not already in language. I tried a few different ways of doing this. In *Elan, Magic Lantern*, and *Belshazzar's Feast* I combined different modes of using my voice, speaking or whispering texts, chanting, etc., and in the two earlier works, combining this with excerpts from Raudive's tapes. My texts were never expository, they were exploratory and non-linear and they allowed for internal contradictions. I felt this would open up new spaces for thinking new thoughts.

It is hard to separate the aural from the visual in your works – they are so closely integrated. In Magic Lantern *(1987), we see circles of light appear, then fade, leaving afterimages, as the soundtrack shifts from your singing to samples of Raudive's recordings. The afterimage could be linked to echoes, to the memory of sound. Did the formal elements and narrative develop simultaneously?*

All the elements in a work need to cook together like ingredients in a recipe, to make something completely different. In this sense I'm a traditionalist. I'm not at all impressed by works that don't offer this unexpected something else. In making *Magic Lantern*, I realized that Raudive's voices within silence were somewhat analogous with retinal afterimages – which are subjectively perceived, but indisputably "real." *Magic Lantern* can't be documented very well, not only because documentation in the form of photographs can't give any idea of the soundtrack, but because at least half of the visual impact of the work comes from afterimages produced by the slide projections, which can't be photographed... The piece works with the visible and the invisible, the audible and the inaudible, coherent language and supposedly incoherent utterances.

Do you feel that sound goes further than imagery? In Dream Screens *(1996), for example, your piece for the Web, we click through colour screens while hearing recollected fragments of dreams, interspersed with heartbeats, pulsar signals, Morse code. Does sound multiply and diversify, perhaps in a way that images cannot?*

I do feel sound has a more direct effect than images, because of its physicality. There's something archaic, regressive about sound. We hear in the womb before we see, later we hear a burble of sound before we perceive separate objects... In *Dream Screens*, my idea was that the empty or blank colour fields could be sites of quiet contemplation in the midst of the proliferation of competing images on the Web. I imagined that people would find their favourite colour and stay there, dreamily, while listening to the sound. I wanted the soundtrack to spark off subjectively generated imagery that people would project onto the blank screens – this seems to have worked in earlier pieces like *Elan* (1982), where people often sit when it's exhibited to look at the "empty" central space while listening to the soundtrack.

In An Entertainment *(1990), you use footage taken from Punch and Judy puppet shows. Viewers are dwarfed by vast projections, and the amplified pulsions of sound – an accordion, clapping, Punch's screeching – make it very sinister. Likewise, the crescendo of beats in* Psi Girls *(1999) conveys an intense affect. If earlier works set up a scene for contemplation, what kind of engagement are you seeking here?*

My early works using sound featured my own voice and experimented with glossolalia, crypto-languages, signifiers without signifieds. As well as creating a contemplative or meditative setting, these works conveyed a strong physicality. "Voice" evokes "body" more strongly and directly than any visual representation. This is how I would explain

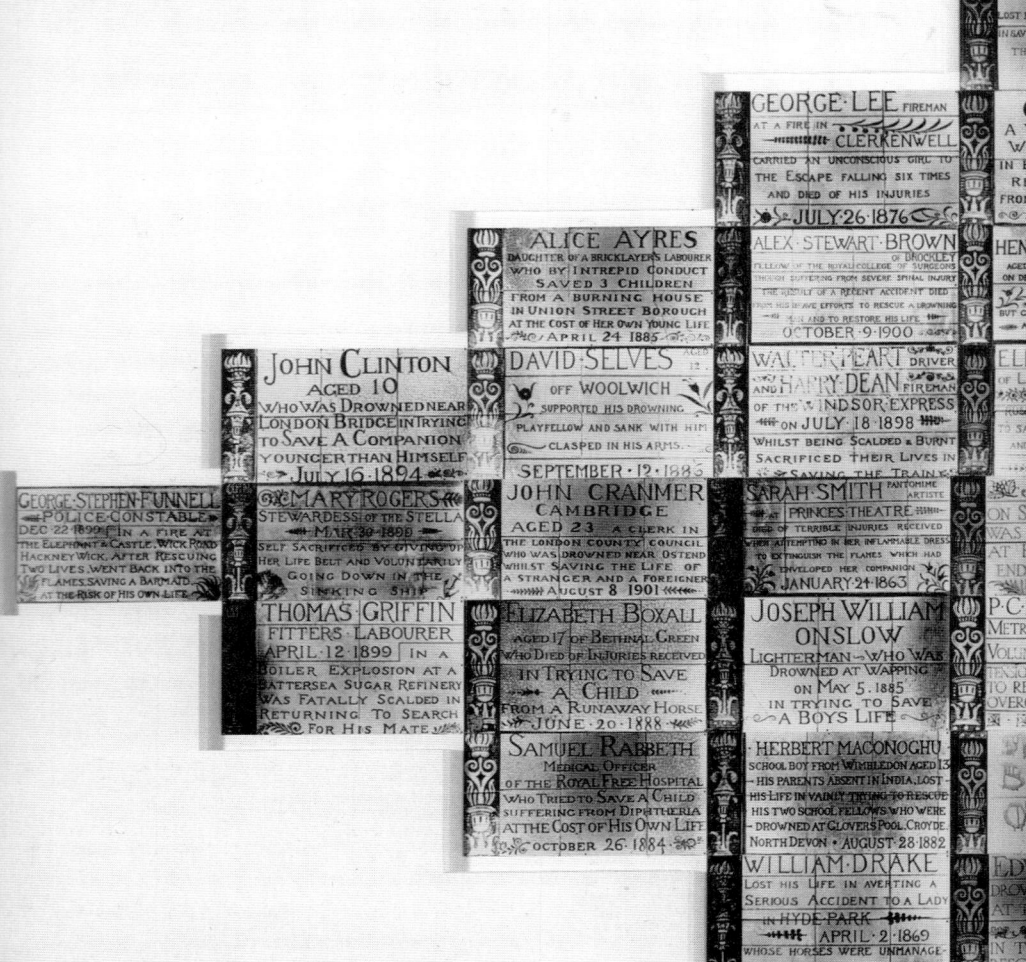

Monument, 1980
Installation view

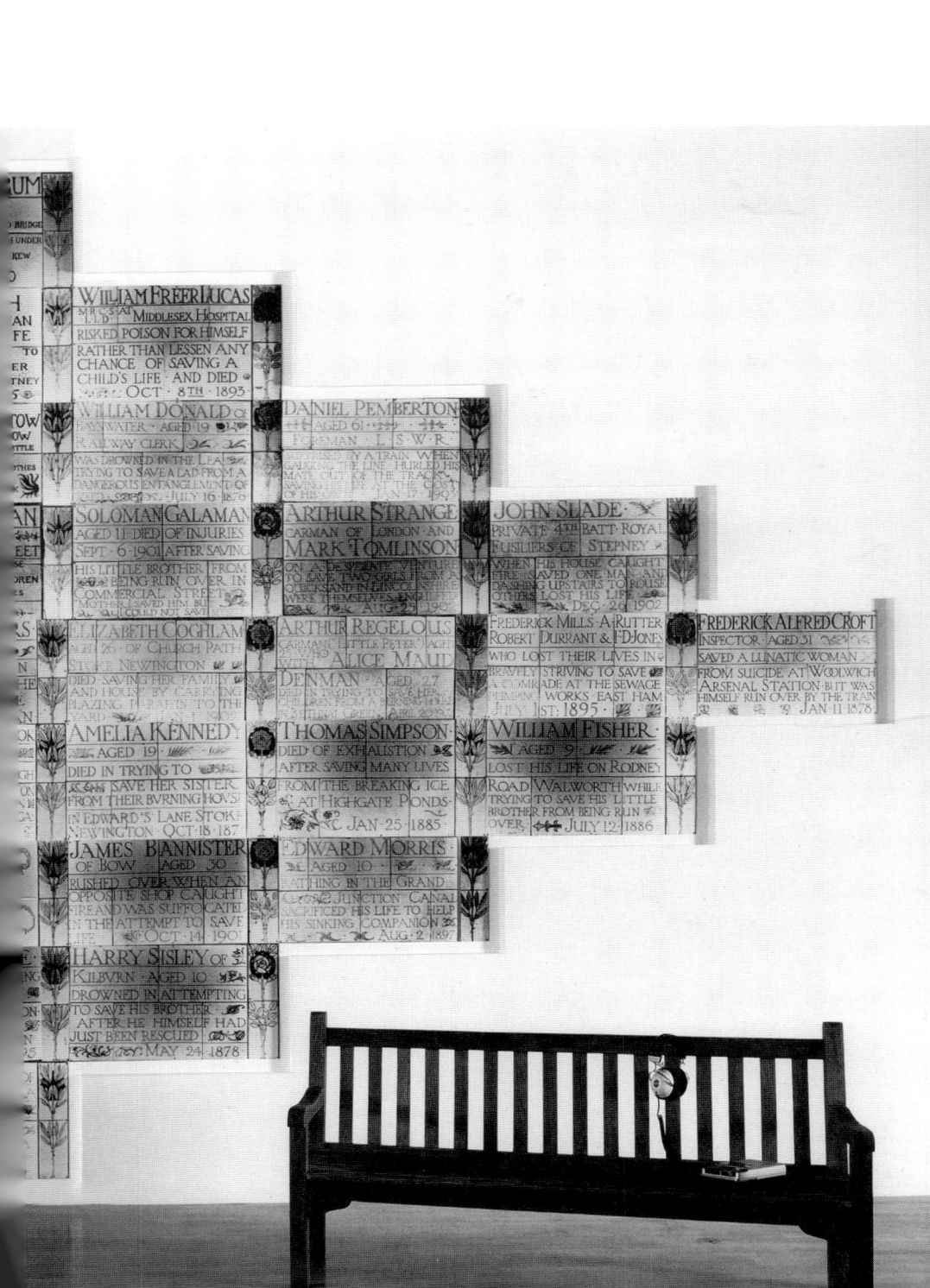

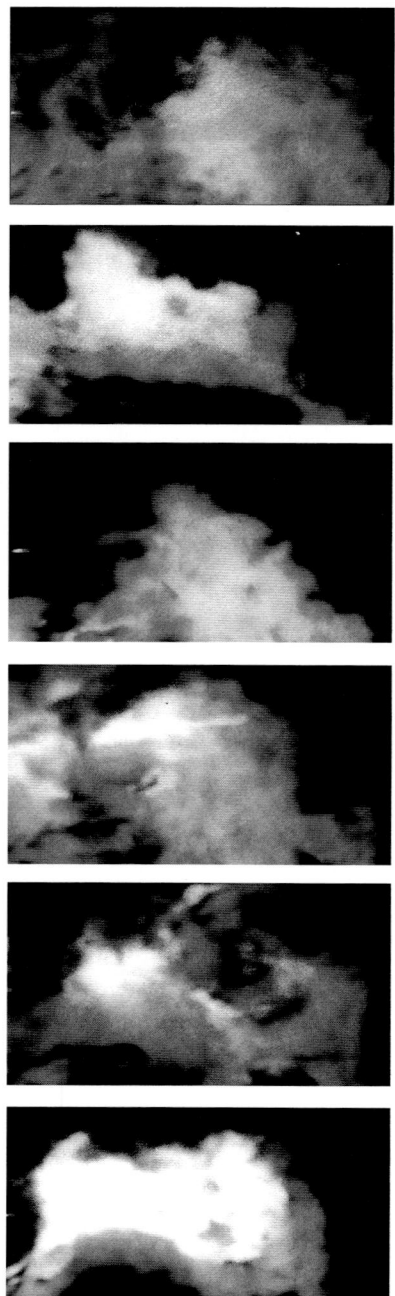

Belshazzar's Feast, 1983/84
Video stills

the evolution of my use of sound – moving from a personal source to a social source, always emphasizing the physical power of sound.

In *An Entertainment* I amplified and exaggerated the disturbing effects of the real combination of crowd noise, fairground music, and the smacking, hitting noises of Punch and Judy. I wanted to make adults feel what children feel, and since we are desensitized and habituated as adults, I needed to heighten all the sounds. In the same way, I turned the tiny puppet theatre inside out and made it huge, with ourselves small in scale surrounded by an unpredictable, powerful assault of visual and sound effects.

In *Psi Girls*, I took a field recording of a gospel choir as my sound source. *Psi Girls* is one of a proposed trilogy of video installations looking at aspects of belief in supernatural or magical powers. I'm particularly interested in the way belief occurs out of context. There is an unacknowledged continuity of older religious beliefs in our secular society that finds its place in popular culture, cinema in particular. You could think of this dislocation in terms of Freud's "return of the repressed," because we have religion and superstition in many places outside churches, and increasingly so. *Wild Talents* (1998) was the first of these works, *Psi Girls* the middle one, and I'm working on the third now. In *Psi Girls*, the link between cinema magic and traditional religion hinges on the soundtrack. Gospel music has a driving rhythm that pushes hearers toward belief. I made it loud and distorted. The soundtrack alternates between two minutes of silence and two minutes of this pulsing beat. The music ends with a burst of static that's matched on the five screens by interference patterns. Then, silence. The room seems to echo with the absent sound. Physically, watching the visuals when the music is on gives viewers a very different take on the images than watching in silence. Silence allows for a more distanced scrutiny, a calm evaluation. The musical sections lead to a kind of immersion – people have told me they want to get up and dance, or they feel their hearts pounding – these bodily responses go along with a feeling they may be watching real events, maybe this cinema magic is real, etc. They want to have that feeling again, and when the silence then situates them more distantly, they want to be back inside so they wait for the music to begin again... Then there's the opposite response from other viewers, who feel lost in the noisy sections and wait for the silence so they can see things clearly and figure out what's going on. Personally I would say I'm trying to clear a space in between the dualism of belief/disbelief, and that's what this work is about.

Witness (2000), like Psi Girls, *focuses on the paranormal. Here, you had only sound to work with (recorded sightings of* UFOs, *no image documentation) and yet you made it an incredible spectacle; there is a vast collection of personal testimonies from all over the world, being spoken simultaneously through tiny speakers in semi-darkness. How did you come to this presentation?*

For quite a long time I've been looking at our culture's representation of the uncanny aspects of the so-called paranormal or supernatural. This focus goes back to some of my earliest works of the 1970s. It's what I mentioned earlier, a position that questions our official version of reality, while not replacing it with any other orthodoxy. Formally, I've always taken a cultural artifact as a starting point and built up a work from that, keeping its original nature as a sign. In *Witness* I began with people's personal testimonies about these sightings and experiences as they appeared on the Internet – which I gradually came to realize was functioning as an international confessional. The idea of embarrassing secrets brought out to share in public is what a lot of my work seems to be about, and *Witness* deals in private experiences of what once would have been considered mystical or religious visions of angels or whatever… I tended to be interested not in the famous examples, but in people who began their stories by saying something like, "Well, I'm embarrassed to say this happened to me but I feel I need to tell people about it…" I'm not questioning the truth or falsity of the stories, they are simply social facts that exist.

To place viewers in the position of listening to so many stories was to invite their cooperation. I wanted to make an ambience that was intimate and somewhat mysterious, to make a setting where empathetic visualizing might occur as the stories were heard. In fact, when I found what seemed to me to be the perfect tiny speakers to use, the whole formal shape of the piece very quickly fell into place, because it replicates the cross-in-a-circle design of the speakers on a much larger scale. This shape itself refers obviously to classic UFO design and, beyond that, to what is a widespread mystical diagram…

The idea of so many voices all speaking at once is something like the sense I have of the vast sea of stories we live within, and the option to listen to individual stories is a choice left up to viewers as they wander through this structure.

In Witness, *as in* Monument, *visitors are given "listening devices." In* Monument *we activate the piece by donning headphones and in* Witness *we pick up one of any number of earpieces. By so doing we agree to participate: did you want to make your audience more conscious of their role as "listener"?*

I want the viewer to become complicit, to take on the role of detective, analyst, collaborator, activator, or whatever. The main thing that interests me in my large public works is to become, when something is "finished," a participant myself. So I make the works for myself as an other, if you understand my meaning… The idea is to find out something new through a focused experience that only the work can provide. If I knew ahead of time what it might mean, how it would affect my feelings and thoughts and the feelings and thoughts of other people, I suppose I wouldn't bother. What I think art provides is something like an instigation or an enhanced awareness of how we are all collaboratively and creatively implicated in making a culture…

Psi Girls, 1999
Installation views

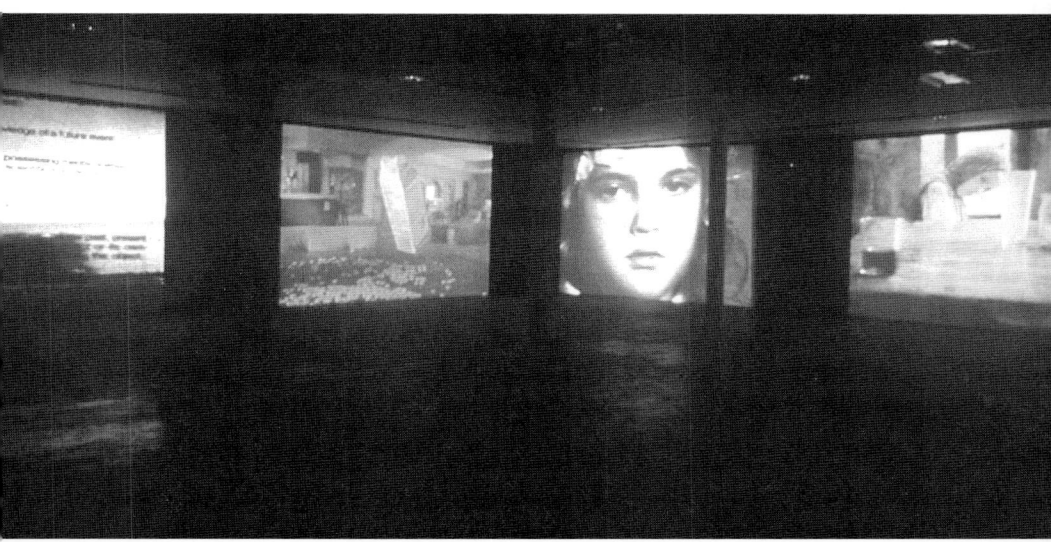

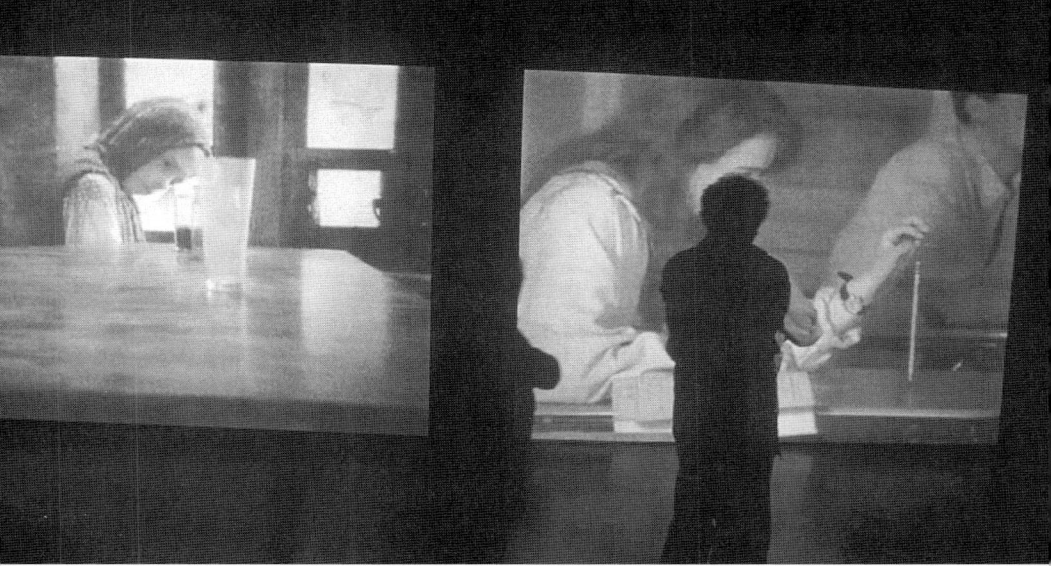

Via Caruso

A photograph taken in Atlanta, Georgia, on April 24, 1916, shows Enrico Caruso (1873–1921) singing an excerpt from the opera *Samson and Delilah* by Camille Saint-Saëns (*"Vois ma misère hélas! Vois ma détresse"*) for Helen Keller, the renowned blind, deaf, and mute writer (1880–1968). Keller tries to capture something of the voice of the great tenor by placing her fingers on his lips and throat. She, therefore, literally listens through her fingers, through her sense of touch. Apparently, they both cried afterwards and Caruso exclaimed, "I have sung the best in my life for you," to which Keller echoed, in writing:

> What a magnificent experience it was when with ravished fingers I felt Caruso's voice in passages from *Samson*! Spellbound, I followed him as in a perfect glory of tone, he sang compassion for the captive, lamenting his loss of vision and the strength with which he had wrought in the light of day. Then Caruso's voice swelled and surged in harmonious billows as he sang of Samson's reviving courage and the might with which in the dark he tugged the pillars of the temple until the roof crashed down on his enemies, the Philistines. Indeed it was unforgettable, the animation of Caruso's face and his rapt response to the sphere-born harmonious sisters, voice and verse.[1]

Since she could not really hear the full voice of Caruso, what was it that Keller (substituting for Delilah?) actually experienced at that moment? Was it only tactile vibrations that she felt in her hand or some other mysterious presence, a sixth sense capturing perhaps the spiritual outlook of the sound? Who knows? (Delilah's famous aria from that same opera was titled *"Mon cœur s'ouvre à voix."*)

Paradoxically, Caruso was to sing later in silent films and, according to ear specialist Dr. Alfred Tomatis, he was partially deaf (on the right side).[2] In retrospect, then, as an occasional mute, deaf, and blind artist (via Samson), Caruso came to share peculiar links with Keller.

The couple Caruso-Keller becomes, through this photograph, the central duet of an imaginary opera (opera often being an art of extremes where individuals lose their senses…). Here, the tenor loses his head. Caruso's head has been cut out of the vertical photograph, then framed and installed horizontally underneath (much like a recording of his split, distanced voice being placed on a turntable, the record player as such

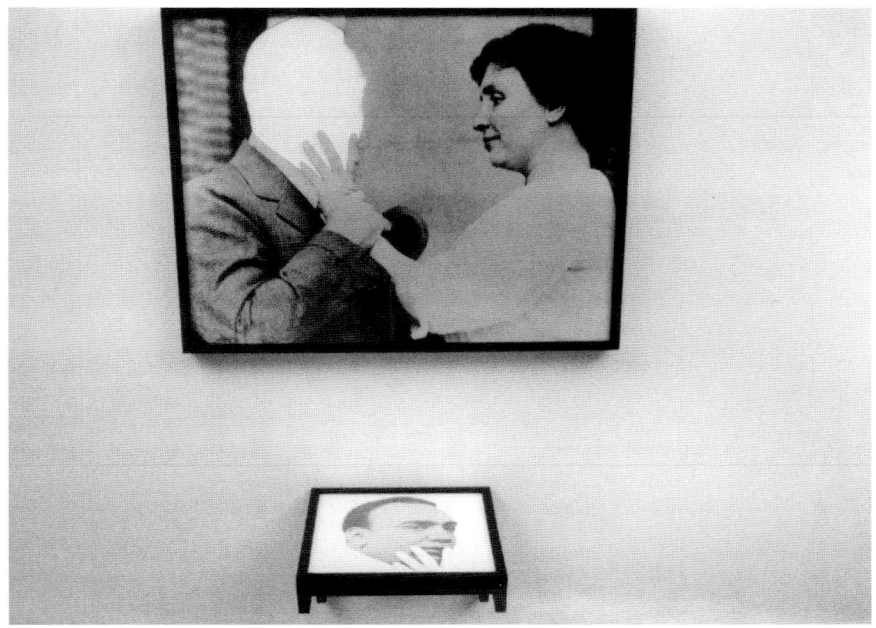

becoming a small portable opera house). Which brings to mind the sound devices that Keller touched when visiting with Alexander Graham Bell at the 1893 World's Columbian Exposition in Chicago – prototypes of the telephone and phonograph.[3]

Keller's hand is seen touching the empty space left by the cut-out head in the large silent photograph. And we, the public, witness her listening to an absence, feeling an empty shape, a mute void. This staging of an immaterial play in space becomes a screen, or mirror, for the viewer's own projection, this time via Helen Keller.

NOTES

1.   Francis Robinson, *Caruso: His Life in Pictures* (New York: Bramhall House, 1957), 129.

2.   Alfred Tomatis, "L'heureuse surdité d'Enrico Caruso," in *L'oreille et la vie* (Paris: Robert Laffont, 1990), 89–128.

3.   Dennis Wepman, *Helen Keller, Humanitarian* (New York: Chelsea House Publishers, 1987), 54.

SOUND, MEDIA, AND THE ENVIRONMENT

Philip Auslander

Jodi Brooks

Gabor Csepregi

Andra McCartney

Looking at Records

Philip Auslander

Intellectual property expert Paul Goldstein predicts that, in the very near future, recorded music and other entertainment commodities will be distributed by means of a system he calls the Celestial Jukebox, which he describes as "a technology-packed satellite orbiting thousands of miles above Earth, awaiting a subscriber's order – like a nickel in the old jukebox, and the punch of a button – to connect him to any number of selections from a vast storehouse via a home or office receiver...."[1] Goldstein concedes that the notion of a satellite is metaphoric, but insists that some such delivery system, whether celestial or terrestrial, is the wave of the future.

The development of a new system of cultural distribution along the lines of the Celestial Jukebox is well underway; witness the popularity of downloaded MP3 files as musical commodities. This development will radically change our relationship to recorded music. Above all, it entails the dematerialization of the musical object, a change so fundamental as to constitute a paradigm shift. Throughout the history of recorded music, the consumption of music has been accomplished through the consumption of recordings as material objects. Arguably, the first such material object – though not strictly speaking a recording – was the mass-produced printed score, which became a consumer commodity in the nineteenth century with the increased popularity of domestic music production and the piano as a home appliance. Subsequent material objects associated with the consumption of music include the piano roll, the Edison cylinder, the 78-rpm disc, the LP, the 45-rpm single, the twelve-inch single, the cassette, and, ultimately, the CD. For well over a century, the consumption of recorded music has meant the purchase and ownership of objects of this kind, the material supports for the music itself.

In the twentieth century, the consumption of recorded music was often achieved through media that do not require ownership of a musical object, such as the traditional jukebox and radio. It is the case, however, that the primary function of these media is to create a market for musical recordings and, thus, to promote sales. The transaction that is initiated when a listener hears a recording on the radio is not complete until that listener has acquired a copy of the recording.

When the Celestial Jukebox is fully developed, either we will be able to download music onto a material support of our own choosing (e.g., recordable CDs and DVDs or other large-capacity discs) or, conceivably, we will not need to record it at all, since the jukebox will feature a limitless library from which we can retrieve whatever we want whenever we want it, for immediate use. Such a system of distribution will bring about a major change in consumer culture and cultural consumption. Recorded music will be consumed as a commodity in itself, apart from a specific material support. We will no longer need to buy and own a particular material object to have access to particular music. (I will return to the implications of this development.)

Historically, one consequence of the reification of music in recordings is the century-old separation of the aural experience of music from its visual experience. Dave Laing indicates that the critical impact of the gramophone when it became widely available in the 1890s was "a vital shift in the experience of listening to music: the replacement of an audio-visual event with a primarily audio one, sound without vision."[2] The advent of recording technology brought about a crucial change in the sensory economy of music consumption that made hearing the dominant sensory mode in that subsector of cultural production.

In this respect, the music industry is perhaps different from other subsectors of commodity capitalist economies. French Situationist theorist Guy Debord, who "grafted…antiocular discourse onto the Western Marxist totalizing critique of reification and fetishism,"[3] argues that sight is the central sensory trope of capitalist economies. In his major work, *The Society of the Spectacle* (originally published in 1967), Debord argues that commodity capitalism works by substituting images for reality.[4] In his most succinct definition of the spectacle, Debord states bluntly that "The spectacle is capital accumulated to the point where it becomes image."[5] For Debord, "The spectacle's function in society is the concrete manufacture of alienation,"[6] which it achieves by presenting the social world as a visual object for the consumer's contemplation rather than something upon which the individual can act. "The spectator's alienation from and submission to the contemplated object works like this: the more he contemplates, the less he lives; the more readily he recognizes his own needs in the images of need proposed by the dominant system, the less he understands his own existence and his own desires."[7] Because Debord focuses on the visual as the sensory modality of the society of the spectacle, his theory demands that all cultural production be assimilated to a visual model. It seems to me, however, that Debord's model is not sufficiently fine-grained to account fully for the operation of reification and commodification in cultural subsectors that provide experiences appealing centrally to senses other than vision. Here, I shall examine musical recordings through the lens of Situationist social theory. My purpose in adopting Debord's ideas as my framework is twofold. On the one hand, I wish to show how they can illuminate the workings of commodification within a particular subsector of cultural production. I also hope, however, to suggest a limitation to Debord's totalizing condemnation of the visual as the central tool of commodity capitalism by proposing that the visual may prove to be a site of resistance in cases where cultural commodities engage other senses primarily.

For an account of music and recording, I turn to another *homme de gauche*, Jacques Attali. In *Noise: The Political Economy of Music*, first published in 1977, some ten years after *The Society of the Spectacle*, Attali offers a brief history of music's progressive reification and commodification that echoes Situationist themes. For Attali, as for Laing, the decisive turning point in this history is the use of sound recording technology to produce musical commodities. In Attali's historical account, this moment marks not only a change in the sensory experience of music, but also the end of music as a significant social discourse and its relegation to the status of a mere commodity like any other:

> [W]ith the stockpiling of music [in recordings], a radically new economic process got underway…. Stockpiling then becomes a substitute, not a preliminary condition, for use. People buy more records than they can listen to. They stockpile what they want to find the time to hear. Use-time and exchange-time destroy one another. [M]usic is no longer heard in silence. It is integrated into a whole. But as background noise to a way of life music can no longer endow with meaning.[8]

For Attali, the way that music is objectified in recordings deprives music of its use-value. Musical recordings become objects to collect and stockpile, not to hear. Attali's analysis of music can be seen as a particular case of Debord's claim that under the spectacle, "the totality of use has been bartered for the totality of abstract representation."[9] In Debord's terms, sound recordings are abstract representations of music, objects that become visual signs for music whose very proliferation subordinates the actual use of music to its status as commodity object.

The question I wish to pose in relation to this Situationist analysis of recorded music is: what does it mean to look at records? (By "records" I mean all sound recording media, and I am referring to the objects themselves, not their packaging.) At first glance, the reification of music in sound recordings seems to be a perfect illustration of Debord's association of the ocular with commodification. Since, as Attali suggests, most consumers own more musical recordings than they have time to listen to, the recording becomes an object of exchange and contemplation: an image of music that substitutes for music itself. This analysis implicitly describes the process of commodification as a sensory conversion: recording subordinates music's existence as sound to its new existence as a visible object, and music thus enters the spectacular world of the commodity.

When I think of my own practices as a lifelong record collector, I have to admit that this Situationist analysis seems accurate as far as it goes. I always look at my new acquisitions before playing them and derive pleasure simply from looking at them, a pleasure that is partly an anticipation of realizing the use-value contained in the recording, but also partly the unabashed pleasure of commodity ownership. The pleasure of looking at records also entails the pleasure of looking at their packaging, including LP covers and CD booklets. To a certain extent, this packaging, too, can fuel the anticipation of hearing the music by providing images associated with those who made it. But I am focusing here on the less-acknowledged practice of looking at the recording itself. Lest it be thought that my practice is purely idiosyncratic, I hasten to add that anecdotal evidence gathered from many collectors of musical recordings suggests that I am far from alone in looking at records before or in place of listening to them. This is surely contemplation in Debord's sense of the term, the visual experience of the sign of music that substitutes for a real experience of music, and an experience through which I surrender to the commodity.

But I do think there's more to this story. The Situationist analysis is concerned solely with the fact of music's having been objectified and made visible, not with the specific implications of that visibility in a cultural subsector whose primary sensory modality is the aural. In the realm of recorded music, Debordian contemplation – the passive act of perception that links the spectator to the commodity and robs the spectator of agency – takes the form of listening, not looking. It is this kind of alienated listening that Attali describes when he says that recorded music is now a part of everyday life, but only "as background noise to a way of life music can no longer endow with meaning." In the context of commodified music, the ear more than the eye is implicated in subordinating the spectator to the spectacle. The continuing importance of radio as a means of promoting recorded music even in the age of music video evidences how deeply the process of commodification implicates the ear in this subsector of cultural production.

Even though to look at a record is to play into the hands of the spectacle in the way I discussed a moment ago, it is also a perverse act, given that the object of the gaze was produced as a commodity to be consumed through the ear. The nature of this perversity may become clear through a consideration of striking cases. In *The Recording Angel*, a collection of essays on the culture of recorded music, Evan Eisenberg describes an encounter with a man named Clarence, who lives in a tiny house filled from floor to ceiling with records. This is how Clarence describes one part of his collection: "I collect anything with [the name] 'Clarence' on it. I don't like rock and roll, though I think the names are fabulous, but there's a Negro rock and roller named Clarence and I have all his records."[10] Clarence, it seems, buys these records for what might be called a literary characteristic: the appearance of a certain word on the labels. He has no interest in listening to the music on them, which he actively dislikes, only in seeing his own name on the labels. (I must confess to having done the same thing. Once I heard that the rock group Living Colour had recorded a song called *Ausländer* (1993), I had to acquire it. I bought a twelve-inch vinyl disc featuring several dance remixes of *Ausländer*. My name is proudly emblazoned on both the record's label and its sleeve.) Clarence goes on to discuss another record collector, who has amassed an enormous collection of which Clarence is jealous. Eisenberg ends the piece with a dramatic essayist's flourish: "The thing about this collector in Brooklyn. He's deaf."[11] We cannot know, of course, why this deaf man collects records, but it's clear that he's not listening to them. Whatever pleasure he gains from records he must access through their visual and tactile qualities.

Both Clarence and the deaf man are obsessive collectors, and that makes them worthy of the essayist's attention. But another aspect of these anecdotes is more relevant to my argument: we may feel that these men who collect records they either have no interest in hearing or cannot hear are highly idiosyncratic individuals who buy records *for the wrong reasons*. That response in itself indicates that there is something perverse about insisting upon treating an aural commodity as if it were a visual or tactile one. Such individual redefinitions of the use-value of objects seem perverse because they challenge the spectacle that seeks to impose its own regimens of consumption on spectators; such individual redefinitions of use-value therefore constitute acts of resistance to the domination of the spectacle.

In 1961, Debord addressed a conference on everyday life by means of a tape recording of his presentation that was played at the event. He explained his choice in the following terms:

> It is desirable to demonstrate, by a slight alteration of the usual procedures, that everyday life is right here.... This slight discomforting break with accustomed routine could serve to bring directly into the field of questioning of everyday life...the conference itself, as well as any number of other forms of using time or objects, forms that are considered "normal" and not even noticed, and which ultimately condition us.[12]

Debord's strategy of using the tape recorder was intended to throw into relief the conventions of normal conference procedure that go unnoticed and therefore remain unquestioned. I am suggesting that Clarence's and the deaf collector's perverse uses of aural commodities as visual objects function in much the same way – they are forms of consumption that throw into relief the ways in which we are conditioned, to use Debord's term, to accept that certain objects should be consumed only in certain ways, a conditioning that undoubtedly reinforces the power of the spectacle. I would further suggest that my own practice of looking at records, though perhaps less distinctive than the activities of a Clarence or a deaf record collector, involves the same implicit resistance. The moments at which I am looking at the record instead of listening to it are not just moments at which I am under the contemplative spell of the commodity; they are also moments at which I am consuming that commodity in a way that goes against the grain. Here, the difference between looking at the recording itself and looking at its packaging becomes very clear. To look at a recording represents a way of consuming the object that challenges its sensory economy. Looking at the packaging offers no such challenge. To look at an album cover is to use and consume that cover the way one is supposed to – as a visual object. To look at a record is to use and consume it against the intended use. Crucially, these acts of resistance to the spectacle engage the sense of sight, the very sensory modality that Debord places at the heart of the economy of the spectacle. A significant flaw in Debord's theory is that his totalizing antiocularcentrism renders his social theory insufficiently supple to account for sensory economies in which sight is not the dominant mode of reification and commodification. I contend that the visual can function as a site of resistance within those subsectors of the society of the spectacle where commodification and consumption are defined in terms of a sense other than vision.

Treated as visual objects, records offer other opportunities for resistant readings of the spectacle. One of Debord's central themes is that "The spectacle...is in effect a false consciousness of time."[13] Under the spectacle, time has lost its relationship to lived experience and has become a commodity in itself. "[T]he time of the spectacle [is] in the narrow sense, the time appropriate to the consumption of images, and, in the broadest sense...the image of the consumption of time."[14] Looking at vinyl records is germane to this issue, for the grooves on the surface of a vinyl record constitute a visual representation of time. Vinyl records reify time in that they make time tangible: in handling a record, one is handling a chunk of time, in a sense. The division of time into bands and its distribution over the two sides of a disc are other ways records transform time into something one can see and touch. Records also commodify time; as Attali points out, to buy a record is to buy musical use-time. In these ways, records are means by which time is rendered spectacular.

Looked at from another angle, however, vinyl records also offer a resistant reading of spectacular time. It is significant that there is no consistent relationship between the visual representation of time on a vinyl record and the actual use-time of the music. Side six of George Harrison's album *The Concert for Bangla Desh* (1972), for example, contains only two songs totalling just over seven minutes of music, yet it looks the same as other discs containing up to four times as much music, or more. (In fact, the grooves on side six of the same album occupy more surface area than those on side four, which contains almost five more minutes of music!) In other words, the grooves on the surface of a vinyl record do not constitute a rational representation of use-time: on the surface of an LP, seven minutes of use-time can look identical to twenty-five minutes of use-time. Since there is no direct correlation between the musical use-time of an album and its visual appearance, the visual representation of time on a vinyl record asserts itself as arbitrary, abstract, and capricious. Understood in this way, the surface of a vinyl record makes visible the means by which the spectacle induces false consciousness of time through images of time purveyed by commodities.

The prospect of looking at the music side of a CD raises a different but related issue. When we look at the shiny side of a CD, we see ourselves looking back, mirrored by the commodity. Looking at a CD, we both contemplate the commodity and see ourselves contemplating the commodity. The look of contemplation reflected back by the shiny surface of the commodity dramatizes "the spectator's alienation from and submission to the contemplated object." The way this musical commodity reflects our contemplative gaze back upon us offers the possibility of self-consciousness concerning that gaze and its implications. Again, this effect is possible because to look into a CD is to use the object in a perverse way that invokes a sensory modality other than the one for which it was produced. To look into a mirror one has purchased would not create the same effect.

The CD is also an important development in the last issue I will take up here, the issue of the dematerialization of the musical commodity. To look at the progression of the material forms of music media – from shellac or vinyl discs to CDs to direct downloading from the Internet or the Celestial Jukebox – is to witness the progressive dematerialization of the musical object. The general historical progression of music media has been in the direction of disappearance: the trend has been toward smaller and smaller objects (78-rpm disc to 45-rpm disc to cassette to CD) and now to no specific object at all. If my suggestion here that treating music recordings as visual objects allows for consumer practices and readings that resist the domination of the spectacle, then it would stand to reason – especially if one is willing to indulge in a bit of Situationist paranoia – that the spectacle would have an interest in seeing to it that musical commodities disappear from the visual realm. I'd like to conclude, however, with a different point, one that further challenges Debord's antiocularcentrism. As we have seen (a word I use advisedly!), Debord's antiocularcentrism stems from his premise that reification and commodity fetishism operate through the conversion of reality into images that are deployed as if they were real, inducing false consciousness in the spectator. The conversion of music, which exists first as intangible sound, into visible objects is an example of this process. But the historical progression of music media constitutes a serious problem for Debord's anti-ocularcentrism. I would argue that the trend we are seeing now toward the disappearance of specific physical objects and the consumption of music as pure digital information (MP3 files and such) constitutes a *hypercommodification* of music, in which musical sound becomes a commodity in itself, unmoored from physical support in a way that was never previously possible. That this process of hypercommodification entails the disappearance of music, its removal from the realm of the spectacular object, presents a major challenge to Debord's thesis that commodification is an ocular phenomenon.

NOTES

1.   Paul Goldstein, *Copyright's Highway* (New York: Hill & Wang, 1994), 199.
2.   Dave Laing, "A Voice Without a Face: Popular Music and the Phonograph in the 1890s," *Popular Music* 10:1 (1991): 7–8.
3.   Martin Jay, *Downcast Eyes: The Denigration of Vision in Twentieth-Century French Thought* (Berkeley: University of California Press, 1993), 426.
4.   Guy Debord, *The Society of the Spectacle*, trans. Donald Nicholson-Smith (New York: Zone Books, 1995), sec. 6.
5.   Debord, sec. 34.
6.   Debord, sec. 32.
7.   Debord, sec. 30.
8.   Jacques Attali, *Noise: The Political Economy of Music*, trans. Brian Massumi (Minneapolis: University of Minnesota Press, 1985), 101.
9.   Debord, sec. 49.
10. Evan Eisenberg, *The Recording Angel* (New York: Penguin, 1987), 7.
11. Eisenberg, 9.
12. Guy Debord, "Perspectives for Conscious Alterations in Everyday Life" (1961), available at < http://hamp.hampshire.edu/ ~ cmnF93/debord.txt > .
13. Debord, *The Society of the Spectacle*, sec. 158.
14. Debord, *The Society of the Spectacle*, sec. 153.

"Worrying the Note":
Inaudible Beats in the Gangsta Film

Jodi Brooks

I'm developing an idea that I call Black visual intonation (BVI). What it consists of is the use of irregular, nontempered (nonmetronomic) camera rates and frame replication to prompt filmic movement to function in a manner that approximates Black vocal intonation.... Nonmetronomic camera rates, such as those employed by silent filmmakers, are transfixing precisely because they are irregular. The hand-cranked camera, for example, is a more appropriate instrument with which to create movement that replicates the tendency in Black music to "worry the note" – to treat notes as indeterminate, inherently unstable sonic frequencies rather than the standard Western treatment of notes as fixed phenomena. Utilizing what I term alignment patterns, which are simply a series of fixed frame replication patterns (and I have 372 at this point), the visual equivalencies of vibrato, rhythmic patterns, slurred or bent notes, and other musical effects are possible in film. You could do samba beats, reggae beats, all kinds of things. This is just a beginning for trying to talk about certain possibilities in Black cinema.[1] – Arthur Jafa

In his essay "69," filmmaker Arthur Jafa proposes a black film practice structured through the tonal and rhythmic principles of black musical traditions. In so doing he also suggests a framework for reading films, turning attention to a range of rhythmic practices possible in the moving image. The beats that Jafa proposes here are *visual* beats, produced through variations in camera speed and other such procedures that enable a visual equivalent of "worrying the note." And certainly the forms of rhythmic articulation possible in film are not limited to those of the soundtrack and can arise from a variety of means, including performance, editing, shot duration, or any combination of these, each of which can serve to solicit the spectatorial ear. Whether one's interest is filmic samba and reggae beats or, more generally, the various rhythmic structures possible in film, Jafa's essay offers a useful starting point for addressing the moving image's "inaudible beats."

While questions of rhythm played a significant role in classical film theory, they have played a considerably smaller role in contemporary film theory debates. What if film was approached in terms of questions of rhythm and music? How might such an approach enable a rethinking of the relations between structurings of time in cinema and the temporal structuring of experience in modern life? And how might such inaudible beats operate as (to borrow a concept from Paul Gilroy) "time signatures"?

This essay looks at the inaudible beats and rhythmic structures that characterize the gangsta or hood film, a cycle of films that strode on to the screens in the late 1980s and 1990s. Referred to as "gangsta films," "hood films," "New Jack cinema," and, somewhat less enthusiastically, "homeboy cinema," the gangsta or hood cycle is a somewhat diverse group of films, embracing comedies such as *Friday* (F. Gary Gray, 1995), melodramas like *Boyz N the Hood* (John Singleton, 1991), and action films like *Set It Off* (F. Gary Gray, 1996). While the parameters of the cycle are particularly malleable, one of the things that connects these films is a particular form of rhythmic play and the ways that this rhythmic play underlies their structuring of time.

Rhythmic play – delaying, stretching, and anticipating the beat – is central to this cycle of films. These are films in which the beat is frequently interrupted; films in which time fractures, repeats, stretches, collapses, and in which different rhythmic structures are set against one another both across the body of the film and within distinct scenes. In *Friday* for instance, Craig (Ice Cube) and Smokey (Chris Tucker) spend the bulk of the film on the front porch of Craig's house, sitting out the day, watching the activities of the street, and getting stoned. Time is swollen and heady, sculpted through the heightened sensory perception of dope. Erupting through the surface of this structuring of time are a number of slapstick routines that fracture the regular beat of the everyday, introducing different rhythms and establishing a form of counterpoint as the basis for scenic construction. The (new) rhythm to be taken up and played with in these sequences is often (and quite literally) introduced through the arrival or return of a neighbourhood character or family member, who "carries" this new rhythm into the scene. The local bully, Deebo, for instance, makes his entries via the off-key and off-the-beat comically menacing, grating creak of his pushbike, establishing the syncopated beat that then stands as the basis for the comic sequences revolving around his character. Likewise, Smokey's involuntary twitches and spasms – a side effect of an evening of angel dust – provide a kind of prelude to his slapstick eruptions. The spasmodic gestures that characterize Smokey's scenes begin with localized facial twitches. As these twitches begin to take hold and set the beat, they spread across his body and then across the scene, operating as a kind of gestural break beat. These slapstick sequences evolve out of small interruptions in the film's representation of the everyday, an everyday marked by both waiting and dead time. Sometimes it is done through the release of a gesture or expression across a face or a body, at other times through the juxtaposition of performance styles. While *Friday*'s juxtaposition of different rhythms and metres produces a structuring of time in which a seemingly stationary everyday is constantly being ruptured by play and remapped as a site for storytelling and performance, the rhythmic operations of most gangsta films produce a somewhat different kind of temporal fissure. If a specific rhythmic structure in these films could be located, it would be that of the fall, a fissure in the unfolding of time itself. It is a rhythmic structure that I will call, for want of a better term, the caesura – the suspended or, in some instances, elided beat.

The first section of this essay focuses on this particular rhythmic structure, a visual beat that returns, repeatedly, both within and across many of these films. This rhythmic structure operates as a kind of "time signature," a concept that is borrowed from Paul Gilroy's book *The Black Atlantic: Modernity and Double Consciousness*, where he uses the term to refer to the temporal structure of a social practice or cultural form.[2] In the second section I will look at how this time signature, like the beats that Jafa addresses, "worries the note." While Jafa is not referring to the gangsta film in the above quotation, this idea of "worrying the note" is particularly valuable in that it not only offers a way of describing and being attentive to the complex "beats" that punctuate many of these films but also brings attention to what these beats "worry" or destabilize. In gangsta films, what the inaudible beats worry is the generic cliché.

Part 1: "Tragic Magic"

What does Wesley Brown's "tragic magic" mean when he says, "I played in a Bar Mitzvah band. And it was a great job until I got hit by that tragic magic, and I start playing a little bit before the beat, a little bit behind the beat. I couldn't help myself. I lost the job."[3]
– Arthur Jafa

In one of the most exquisite edits in James Edward Olmos' *American Me*, the anticipation of the fall of the beat is stretched to breaking point. It is a cut that moves the viewer forward in story time – from the central character Santana's teenage years in juvenile hall to his adult years in Folsom – without, in fact, moving anywhere. Santana and his friend J.D. are shown in medium-shot in the prison grounds playing handball, the radio playing in the background. As the ball is hurled towards the wall, the film moves into slow motion. With the ball's return, the film picks up speed but has moved on to the next decade, the two friends still playing handball, in the same positions, in an identical ball court, in a different prison, the radio soundtrack now having moved on to the sounds of the next decade. Between the moment that the ball is hit and its return, chronological time is swallowed, leaving behind the stretched outline of its absence. In this extended instant, chronological time – the time of historicism and the structuring of time generally credited to the camera-projection apparatus – is arrested and collapses. When narrative time and apparatus time seem to regain their pace, they have been vacated, mechanized. Like a photographic flash that freezes and momentarily erases that which it blindingly illuminates, the edit sculpts what Peggy Phelan would call the "affective outline" of missed experience.[4] This edit inscribes a fissure in linear time that not only marks each instant as dead(ening) repetition but infects and ruins any idea of time unfolding.

This kind of teasing of the beat is central to many gangsta films. It stages a kind of falling, a fissure in the unfolding of time itself, a rhythmic operation that deals not so much with the falling of the beat in terms of its *placement*, but the falling, through elision or excision, of the beat itself. The affective impact of the edit in *American Me* arises, in part, from the ways that the film both plays with and thwarts the spectator's anticipation of the fall of the beat. It gains its *force*, however, from the place and role of this elided beat in the film's articulation of a form of social experience and its temporal structure.

Whether it takes the form of the repetitive, circular time of Allen and Albert Hughes' *Menace II Society* (1993) or the swollen and playfully interrupted "stoned" time of *Friday*, the contemporary gangsta film is characterized by a particular experience of time. The present is both charged and missed, both summoned as a moment of possibility and laid out as the too-late. If one of the key things at stake for the young (and not so young) characters in these films is the attempt to occupy, harness, and rupture time from their place in the post-industrial ghetto, this struggle also choreographs the films themselves. The key battle in these films becomes one over time itself, and this tension is not only played out at a thematic level, but infuses every cinematic element – performance, mise-en-scène, and narrative structure.

In his 1952 novel *Invisible Man*, Ralph Ellison describes invisibility in terms of a structuring of time, an outlining a form of experience that shares a number of similarities with that found in the gangsta film:

> Perhaps I like Louis Armstrong because he's made a poetry out of being invisible. I think it must be because he's unaware that he *is* invisible. And my own grasp of invisibility aids me to understand his music.... Invisibility, let me explain, gives one a slightly different sense of time, you're never quite on the beat. Sometimes you're ahead and sometimes you're behind. Instead of the swift and imperceptible flowing of time, you are aware of its nodes, those points where time stands still or from which it leaps ahead. And you slip into the breaks and look around. That's what you hear vaguely in Louis' music.[5]

In the final chapter of *The Black Atlantic*, Gilroy cites this passage in the context of discussing a recurrent time signature in black expressive cultures (and black popular music in particular). Gilroy's project is "to rethink modernity via the history of the black Atlantic and the African diaspora in the western hemisphere," and "to reconceptualize the orthodox relationship between modernity and what passes for its prehistory."[6] Gilroy, like Walter Benjamin, is interested in historically specific social forms of memorative communication, and one of the central concerns of the book is how "black expressive cultures practice remembrance" – more specifically, how "this active remembrance [is] associated with a distinctive and disjunctive temporality of the subordinated."[7] It is here that Gilroy's concept of the time signature takes on a central role, particularly in the closing chapter of the book, where he turns to black popular music when discussing the black Atlantic as a "non-traditional tradition."[8] The time signature that Gilroy identifies is characterized by a "syncopated temporality" and "temporal disjunction" in which the caesura comes to the fore.

One does not need to look far for examples of this time signature in either black popular music and its many offshoots or in the work of many black Atlantic writers. Like Ellison's account of the experience of invisibility, this time signature is characterized by a stalling and withholding of the beat, and in this respect Gilroy's time signature certainly correlates with familiar arguments about rhythm in black popular music practices. But Gilroy's proposal of this time signature, particularly as it can be traced in the Ellison passage, foregrounds something that is less readily commented on. For Gilroy, as for Ellison, what is crucial in this time signature is not only the way that the anticipation of the fall of the beat operates as what James Snead has called a "horizon of expectations."[9] It is not only the experience of an out-of-step-ness – of being behind or ahead of the beat – that is important. Rather, it is that these spaces around the beat are both potent and occupied (as when Ellison writes "you slip into the breaks and look around"); they are the very place and means through which experience is made transmissible. Here the caesura, one could say, is not so much the content of a tradition but transmissibility itself. It is precisely this idea of never being quite on the beat, of being behind or ahead of the beat and "slipping into the breaks," that characterizes the structuring of experience in many gangsta films and constitutes the cycle's dominant time signature.

Questions of time, memory, and historical experience underlie the gangsta film in a number of ways, from its workings with genre and its structurings of story and plot duration to its uses of cinematic techniques such as slow motion and leader to jar the sense of a continuous, linear time. Time is both compressed and dilated, fractured and arrested. One of the most notable ways this structuring of time is produced is through contracted plot and story durations, a feature of many of these films. The stories take place over a period of days, weeks, or perhaps a few months, but they rarely entail the lengthy plot and story durations that characterize genres like the epic and the woman's film. *Friday* covers a period of less than a day (with a few flashbacks), the period in which one of its central protagonists has to find the money (or replace the drugs) owed to "Big Worm," his Mr. Whippy-driving dealer. Gray's *Set It Off* takes place over a period of roughly two weeks, and Allen and Albert Hughes' *Menace II Society*, while framed by pixellated footage of the Watts uprising and a prologue that snapshots the protagonist's childhood, takes place over one graduating summer. While such contracted plot and story durations could be understood as serving the cycle's often commented upon "documentary effects" (as a journalistic "slice of life") – an issue to which I will return later – here, however, this contraction instead foregrounds affect. These stories unfold in a period that is both dilated (the present is flattened out and stretched) and compressed (this present is nevertheless charged to breaking point). Even gangsta films with longer story and plot durations – such as John Singleton's *Boyz N the Hood* and James Edward Olmos' *American Me* – are characterized by this kind of compression and dilation. Here, too, the story seems to take place in one extended instant – the dilated instant of the fall of the protagonist – producing the effect and affect of a contracted plot duration in which time is telescoped. Whereas the classical gangster film is generally structured around the rise and fall of the gangster, in the contemporary gangsta film there is no rise and fall, but rather random, chance-like moments in an arrested and repetitive present. Missed experience is infused at the very heart of the present, for if these presents are charged, they are also marked by the "too late." This structuring of time is best exemplified by *Menace II Society* and is one of the film's most remarkable, though rarely discussed, features. Time is precisely what does not move in this film, and like O'Dog's relentless viewing of the surveillance video of his shooting of the grocery store workers, each claim on the present seems to miss it, becoming instead a reproduced and reproducible image. While the two genres that would be closest to the gangsta film in terms of plot duration would be, significantly, the teen pic and the disaster film, in the gangsta film the story often seems to have taken place before the opening credits have left the screen. Scenes take on the qualities of a repeat, a replay, or a return, and the viewer is positioned like a witness, watching the events unfold in an order that is both random and predetermined.

This structuring of time – in which the present is always "missed" – is also produced through the use of voice-over in *American Me* and *Menace II Society*. In both of these films the temporal location of the voice-over is at odds with that of the image. *American Me*, for instance, has a relatively straightforward plot. The film revolves around the life of Santana (Olmos), the film's central protagonist and narrator, and opens with Santana in prison reading what is later revealed to be a letter to a woman with whom he had a brief, though significant, relationship. The film then moves back in time, crossing to his conception, the result of the gang rape of his mother by American soldiers during the Zoot Suit Riots, his childhood in an East L.A. barrio, his arrest for breaking and entering, his imprisonment in juvenile hall, and his adult life in prison. But the sequential logic and order of the plot are undermined by the voice-over narration. Narrated, like *Menace II Society*, by a central protagonist who speaks from the moment of death, the film has a particular tense structure and temporal location. Santana's voice-over narration, structuring the film in the key of remembrance, offers a form of recollection in which each memory only traces the subject's absence. Each of these films is narrated through a kind of retrospective gaze in which images of the central protagonists' lives flash forth with an insistence that grants them the structure of shock experience. Narrated from the moment before a death marked as inevitable, *American Me* (like *Menace II Society*) is written through by departure – the departure not only of the character through death, nor even simply of the narrator-character's departure from a previous self, but of the narrator-character's non-coincidence with each moment in which he finds himself. As with the elision of the beat that takes place in the handball sequence, the relation between the voice-over and image results in a temporal fissure in which the present is "missed."

Part 2: Missed Beats

Much of the critical debate around the gangsta cycle has focused on its (assumed) claims to an authentic black urban experience, particularly in terms of the "masculinist privilege" and Oedipal agendas that frequently underlie this authenticity. Valerie Smith, for instance, has undertaken a detailed critique of this cycle of films in terms of what she calls their "documentary effects"[10] and Sharon Willis has taken up Smith's arguments and examined the ways that these "documentary effects" are anchored in the role of the "native informant" in the marketing and public discussion of much recent black American cinema (in which directors and performers have been presented or read as "authentic" representatives of a black urban ghetto).[11] And certainly it would be hard to overlook or dismiss the force of these claims to authenticity in the circulation and discussion of many gangsta films, and indeed in some of the films themselves. What tends to get overlooked in such discussions is the way many of these films play with and undermine their own "documentary effects" through quotation or sampling. If the withholding and elision of the beat underlies the time signature of many gangsta films, it is also the means through which these films complicate or destabilize the documentary impulse that has frequently been identified at their core.

Generic quotation operates in a number of ways in the gangsta film. Many of these films make direct reference to the classical gangster film by incorporating the viewing of these films into their narratives. In Ernest Dickerson's film *Juice*, the fall of Bishop (Tupac Shakur) into madness is signalled by his enthusiasm for the "top of the world" sequence in *White Heat* (Raoul Walsh, 1949), and in *Menace II Society*, Caine (Tyrin Turner) blankly watches classic gangster films in his hospital room after being shot. These direct references tend to operate somewhat didactically – the characters make sense of their lives and their opportunities through the figure of the Hollywood gangster.

This kind of direct reference, however, is only one form of quotation deployed in the gangsta film. Found more frequently is a form of quotation or sampling in which the film unexpectedly slides into a generic quotation, destabilizing familiar generic signs and undermining their "documentary impulse." In *American Me*, for instance, these "documentary effects" are frequently complicated through the use of generic clichés and quotations from other films. To take but one example, in the scene where Santana and J.D. meet with a local mafia head in an attempt to take over the drug market in East L.A., the film's gritty urban realism is destabilized through a slide into Coppola's *The Godfather*. The scene opens with Santana and J.D. being shown into the lounge room of the dealer's sumptuous home, but when they are led into the garden to meet with this "godfather," the scene seems to have moved into a quotation. Ponderously inspecting his rose bushes, this godfather is so haunted by Brando's godfather that the status of the "documentary effect" of the scene is thrown into question. It is as if these characters have just wandered onto a set where *The Godfather* is always being played. The slide into *The Godfather* places repetition at the core of the scene and, by extension, at the heart of the film. In their interweaving and refiguring of various representations of the urban ghetto and gang culture from television news reportage, Hollywood cinema, music videos, and gangsta rap, these films – to varying degrees – complicate any attempt to separate the ghetto and the figure of the gangsta from the technical media. If the slide into the generic cliché would seem to move the scene outside the field of a documentary or gritty urban realism, it also seems to move it out of a sense of linear, continuous time, by bringing time to an arrest in a reproduced and reproducible image. While this may seem to be a long way from the nonmetronomic camera movements that Jafa speaks of in his proposal of a filmic worrying of the note, the gangsta film's summoning, suspension, and repetition of clichés can also be understood as a rhythmic operation.

What if the hood film was approached less in terms of the forms of gritty urban realism it deploys than in terms of the ways that it works with clichés? It is not simply that these films critique clichés, nor that they produce clichés (though they can be seen to do both). The gangsta film also mobilizes the cliché as a kind of arrested image and stages its exhaustion and collapse. In this respect one could say that it foregrounds the temporal structuring of the cliché, infusing the generic cliché with the temporality of the photograph.

The film that I want to discuss in closing worries the note through the sampling of clichés. F. Gary Gray's second feature, *Set It Off*, stages complex rhythmic "beats" through its pacing, editing, narrative structure, and articulations of the everyday. This film is frequently seen as one of the most commercial (and by implication, least "authentic") of the recent cycle of gangsta films, and my focus on Gray's film is partly motivated by its place in and relation to the cycle. *Set It Off* stages the temporal structuring of missed experience – as fissure and as a falling – through the exhaustion and fracturing of clichés. Here clichés seem to be summoned only to expire, leaving in their place suspended beats. For as Pascal Bonitzer suggests, clichés always carry their own expiry:

> Clichés are not called "tartes à la crème" [custard pies, a French idiom] for nothing. The proof of the custard pie is that someone gets it in the face. It proves itself by bursting, spreading, crumbling, dripping.[12]

As the close of *Set It Off* approaches, Cleo (Queen Latifah) is killed in a hail of bullets by the LAPD. Diegetic sound cuts back to a distant hum as she drives through a police blockade and the film moves into slow motion. As Cleo's getaway car grinds to a halt, so too, it seems, does the filmic apparatus. Blocked on all sides by cop cars and helicopters, Cleo not only has no escape, she cannot move in relation to the genre. The camera pulls back to an aerial long shot and Cleo seems to be swallowed by the image, her body now barely visible in the frame. The filmic devices that are used in this sequence are by no means exceptional. Slow motion is, after all, one of the most common devices used in action sequences to spectacularize the body's movements in space and time, particularly for the "fall" of a body. Nor is the muting of diegetic sound that remarkable. It too is a familiar device in popular cinema. Yet this generically familiar scene – the extended and spectacular death of the gangster – nevertheless stages something that is considerably less familiar in popular cinema even when, as in this film, the figure of the classical gangster is assumed by a black lesbian character. What is found in this scene is a kind of collapsing and evacuation of time as the generic cliché of the gangster's death is seemingly infinitely extended.

The scene of Cleo's demise is, of course, a reference to Arthur Penn's *Bonnie and Clyde* (1967). In Penn's film, the deaths of Bonnie and Clyde are staged through various forms of arrest (the use of jump cuts, still frames, and shots filmed at differing speeds) that serve to signal the characters' flash-like, and almost exquisite, grasp of their anticipated deaths. In *Set It Off*'s quotation of this scene, Cleo finds herself being scripted into a generic cliché that is neither exquisite nor tragic, but almost banally predictable. For it is not only Bonnie's and Clyde's deaths that are evoked here: this scene also summons Sonny's death in Coppola's *The Godfather* – a scene that is itself an homage to Penn's film. In this respect it appears as if it is the generic cliché that is summoning Cleo into its path rather than the cliché itself being summoned or quoted. Pummelled by relentless slo-mo bullets, Cleo – unlike Bonnie, Clyde, or Sonny – progresses through the police blockade as if she were moving through a film set or a computer game. Knowing the script better than her cinematic predecessors she also extends the scene, rising, bullet-ridden, from her car and unleashing a final spray of silent gunfire. Cleo's death is oddly unplaceable in narrative time – both claiming and expiring a cliché, she is marked as dead before her body hits the ground.

Woven into Cleo's death sequence is another generically familiar scene – the television image of the criminalized black body. At this point the film moves between two iconographies by intercutting shots of two other characters into the shootout – Cleo's girlfriend Ursula (Samantha MacLachlan) and her gun dealer and friend Black Sam (Dr. Dre) – both of whom are watching the shootout on a news report in separate locations. Each of these characters turns away from the television at the point when Cleo has fallen – and become a familiar televisual image. The film returns to the aerial shot of the scene, though now Cleo's body is virtually invisible. Like film running off a spool, this scene seems to simply expire to the point where there is no longer anything to see but a vacated space, an arrested image.

Like Ellison's account of invisibility, this expiring of the cliché charts an experience of time in which the beat is always "missed." *Set It Off* diverges from some of its better-known predecessors in a number of significant respects. Revolving around four young black women in South Central L.A., the film shifts away from one of the contemporary gangsta film's central narratives – the crisis of black masculinity in the urban ghetto. The "set it off" of the film's title refers to the action that will both kick-start a heist and provoke a series of traumatic events. Catastrophes punctuate this film from the first scene. In the first half hour, one character witnesses a murder during a bank robbery, then loses her job; another's brother is killed by the LAPD when he is misidentified as one of the bank robbers from the opening sequence; and another loses her son to welfare and is deemed an unfit mother when the child swallows cleaning liquid. These events follow on from one another with clock-like regularity but little causal relation. All of these events seem to take place in the fraction of an instant and with unbearable predictability. The characters are progressively located in a time that does not move and does not count. Working as night-shift janitors in a city office block, even their claims on public space take place after hours and in spaces that are temporarily vacated. While these events narratively serve to explain why the four women decide to hold up banks, they also serve to place crisis at the core of the film.

The "set it off" of the title refers above all, however, to the characters' attempts to remap time and charge themselves into it. The way that Cleo "rescores" scenes for action entails one such form of remapping. With each car the women steal to undertake a robbery, Cleo adds the music and sets the pace, replacing the stolen vehicle's "shit" music with one of her own CDs. But over and above the function of music to energize and redirect the moment, *Set It Off* also charges time through the ways that it works with duration. The women's first bank job takes place in one uninterrupted shot with the camera awkwardly following their movements. The scene has a slapstick element to it that has disappeared by their next job, and with their second and third robberies the full force of action-film editing is mobilized and the characters become both initiators and orchestrators of the event. By the close of the film, the characters' attempts to set off time take the form of rupturing time by staging its collapse. If Cleo's demise collapses narrative time by being unplaceable within it, the film's next death – that of Frankie (Vivica A. Fox) – also performs a numbing of time, in this case by extending the moment of her death through an ever-expanding shot/reverse-shot structure. The sequence immediately follows Cleo's death and opens abruptly with Frankie frozen in the foreground of the frame, a barrage of cop cars behind her. This moment is simultaneously extended and erased by the slow motion reverse shots of Stony (Jada Pinkett) – now the only one of the film's central protagonists still alive – being moved into the position of witness and audience as the tourist bus on which she is escaping progressively moves into centre frame. This shot, which is repeated a number of times and intercut with shots of Frankie, operates as a kind of horizontal wipe. As the bus progressively fills the screen, its movement across the frame brings Stony into centre frame as if pushing a blank space offscreen. While the traditional wipe edit seems to push or slide the previous shot off the screen, the wipe effect found in this sequence serves to establish a blank space in the unfolding of the event.

In his essay "Off the Gangsta Tip," Tim Brennan suggests that "[i]f the great ally of the country-western lyric is the pun, the ally of the rap lyric is the caesura."[13] While there would clearly be a number of problems with referring to these films as "rap films,"[14] the gangsta cycle engages in rhythmic play that is comparable to that found in rap. The elision of the beat – central to the time signature of these films – produces a temporal collapse or breach that shares a number of similarities with the temporal structuring of missed experience. By opening a space around the beat, the claims of the latter to constitute the present through the relentless production of the new are both laid bare and thwarted. The gangsta film's story seems to take place in – and through – a suspended beat, a kind of "off time" that ceaselessly returns and demands spectator and character alike to navigate.

While it is easy to locate such forms of rhythmic play in music, film often seems wanting in regard to this kind of rhythmic complexity, reluctant to play with the beat and, as Ralph Ellison writes, make one "aware of [time's] nodes, those points where time stands still or from which it leaps ahead." But perhaps this is in part because of how film and photography have come to be understood; they are rarely addressed via their relation to music and rhythm. The bases for such an approach are many and varied, from Eisenstein's theory of montage to Barthes' notion of the photograph as music in *Camera Lucida*, in which the relationship between the punctum and the studium is described in terms of counterpoint.[15] But it is perhaps Walter Benjamin who has gone furthest in this direction. Benjamin's theory of film and practices of the image more generally are inextricably tied to questions of time and rhythm, most famously in his essay "Some Motifs in Baudelaire."[16] His redemptive reading of film relies, to a large degree, on his understanding of film's rhythms of reception and representation and their relations to the temporal structuring of experience in modernity. Questions of rhythm – including the affective force of rhythm on the body of the spectator – are of central importance to Benjamin's theory of film. Film mimetically embraces the temporal structuring of modern experience, and this temporal structuring can be used as the basis for a new form of narrativity. Being attentive to film's inaudible beats provides a way of addressing the relations between structurings of time in cinema and temporal structurings of experience. By being attentive to the gangsta film's inaudible beats one finds a structuring of time in which time is always missed.

NOTES

I would like to thank Viki Dun, Patrice Petro, Lesley Stern, and Cathryn Vasseleu for their comments and suggestions on this paper, and Dana Polan for arranging access to the Cinema-TV library at USC.

1. Arthur Jafa, "69," in *Black Popular Culture*, ed. Gina Dent (Seattle: Bay Press, 1992), 254.

2. Paul Gilroy, *The Black Atlantic: Modernity and Double Consciousness* (Cambridge, MA: Harvard University Press, 1993).

3. Jafa, 253.

4. See Peggy Phelan, *Mourning Sex: Performing Public Memories* (London and New York: Routledge, 1997).

5. Ralph Ellison, *Invisible Man* (London and New York: Penguin, 1965), 11.

6. Gilroy, 17.

7. Gilroy, 212.

8. Gilroy, 198.

9. James A. Snead, "Repetition as a Figure of Black Culture," in *Out There: Marginalization and Contemporary Culture*, eds. Russell Ferguson, Martha Gever, Trinh T. Minh-ha, and Cornel West (New York: The New Museum of Contemporary Art; Cambridge, MA: MIT Press, 1990), 221.

10. Valerie Smith, "The Documentary Impulse in Contemporary U.S. African-American Film," in Dent, *Black Popular Culture*.

11. See Sharon Willis, *High Contrast: Race and Gender in Contemporary Hollywood Film* (Durham and London: Duke University Press, 1997).

12. Bonitzer quoted in Alison Smith, *Agnès Varda* (Manchester and New York: Manchester University Press, 1988), 43.

13. Tim Brennan, "Off the Gangsta Tip: A Rap Appreciation, or Forgetting about Los Angeles," *Critical Inquiry* 20 (winter 1994): 683.

14. See Jacquie Jones, "The New Ghetto Aesthetic," *Wide Angle* 13:3–4 (July-October 1991): 33.

15. Roland Barthes, *Camera Lucida: Reflections on Photography*, trans. Richard Howard (London: Flamingo/Fontana, 1984).

16. Walter Benjamin, "Some Motifs in Baudelaire," in *Charles Baudelaire: A Lyric Poet in the Era of High Capitalism*, trans. Harry Zohn (London and New York: Verso, 1989).

On Sound Atmospheres

Gabor Csepregi

For more than a quarter of a century, members of the acoustic ecology move-ment have warned us about the significant noise-level increase in our immediate sur-roundings. They observe, not without some worry, that we not only live in an over-stimulated world, but also tend to become indifferent to vociferous sounds. Whereas in many public places an unpleasant smell prompts an immediate nauseated revulsion, disturbing and debilitating noise rarely arouses even a slight disapprobation.

Some eminent philosophers and sociologists of our time fare no better. To be sure, they publish noteworthy studies on the complex relations our body entertains with the urban environment, showing convincingly how, in our everyday life, tech-nological devices gradually give way to a bodily disengagement and desensitization. They fail, however, to relate these deep-seated problems of modern geography and technology to our auditory experience of the world, forgetting that in a large city our body comes into repeated contact not only with stone and metal but also with sound. The acoustic consequences of the mechanized and rationalized city seem to be con-sidered a secondary, negligible process. Or, we may add, they simply exchange their ear for a better eye.

True, there are some notable exceptions.[1] In his incisive and thought-pro-voking analysis of contemporary culture, George Steiner expatiates at some length on the psychological causes and effects of the all-pervasive "sound-capsule" that encloses us in almost every moment of our waking life.[2] How, he asks, does the new and stag-gering "decibel-culture" influence and shape our perception of the world, our contacts with others, and our own self-awareness? What are the underlying motives of such a widespread imposition of, and addiction to, a "perpetual sound-matrix"? What kind of values are promoted by the "musicalization of our culture"?

I would like to reflect on these central issues, focusing my attention on the human responsiveness to background music. I have chosen this particular form of auditory experience because, it seems to me, our whole being is nowadays immersed in music: we are unable to work, study, eat, ride a bus, or drive a car without music. We are no longer swimming but, almost literally, drowning in the grand sea of music. As a magazine editor recently remarked, "an obligatory orchestration cram[s] every inch of public space.... And it's not just in public spaces. Private life...is equally lit-tered with dissociated musical fragments."[3]

The Primacy of Atmosphere

We know how much sound, colour, and light can modify the way we experience living spaces. A cathedral appears handsomer when organ music is heard: we sense the music's harmonizing influence as the resonating tones of a chorale penetrate the transepts and the nave. Likewise, in a theatre we notice a change as the lights are turned off and people suddenly cease to talk with each other. To be sure, the sounds or lights do not modify the material aspects of these spaces; they merely evoke a momentary and latent significance that we experience as atmosphere.

What are, more precisely, these atmospheres that we consider as distinctive components of gardens, museums, or libraries? They are affective qualities that we detect in our immediate surroundings. Because they touch and move us, in the deepest senses of these terms, atmospheres are, in the words of Gernot Böhme, "stirring emotional powers (*ergreifende Gefühlsmächte*)."[4] We may resist these powers or yield to their compelling influence, but we cannot eliminate them. Wherever we are, in a small room or in the middle of an ocean, we are constantly exposed to a particular atmosphere. Although we do not always notice it, the contact with an atmosphere, according to Böhme, is just as much a fundamental feature of human existence as are consciousness or embodiment.

The nature and function of atmospheric emanations have been illustrated and analyzed with remarkable subtlety by Hubertus Tellenbach.[5] Just as it is for Böhme that the experience of atmosphere is pivotal in human life, similarly for Tellenbach, the "atmospheric mode of being human" is one of the most important fields of study for philosophical anthropology.

Our sense of smell, Tellenbach points out, gives us primary access to an atmosphere. Hospitals, schools, churches, apartments: all give off a peculiar odour, endowing the whole spatial structure with a certain tonality. Odours, like sounds, detach themselves from their sources, permeate the lived space, and induce a reaction. There is, however, a difference in the way we are affected by odour and sound. Whereas the former encompasses us rather gently, discreetly, without inducing a shock or a significant resonance, the latter – sound – exerts a more compelling influence and elicits a more marked response.[6]

Newborn babies achieve a primary mode of contact with their mothers through their olfactory and gustatory senses. They sense not only the scent of a perfume and the taste of the breast, but also an "emotional essence," namely the specific atmospheric tone of their mother. "There is," writes Tellenbach, "in nearly all sensory experiences, a surplus which remains inexplicit."[7] To detect a particular atmospheric quality means to reach beyond the factual, the objectively given: to hear, beyond the sound, the timbre of a voice, and to see, beyond the shape, the glimmer of a colour.

The atmosphere of a city, Maurice Merleau-Ponty tells us, consists of a self-evident and specific "emotional essence" or "style," diffused throughout the streets, squares, and buildings.[8] As we arrive there for the first time, we instantly apprehend this essence, and each subsequent and explicit perception merely confirms the validity of our primary mode of communication.

Likewise, we are able to grasp, sometimes with great accuracy, the inner state and character of a person speaking or gesticulating. We "hear through" the voice or "see through" the movement, to use Nicolai Hartmann's expressions.[9] Our first impression of a man or a woman occurs by virtue of such an immediate experience of a distinctive atmospheric quality.

Indeed, a particular atmospheric nimbus permeates human beings and endows their movements, gestures, and words with a certain tonality. The personal atmosphere reminds us of the phenomenon of expression: a glance, a vibration of the voice, a gesture of the hand discloses a "breath," a "halo," or a "fine cloud" that constitutes, in the words of Eugène Minkowski, the "spiritual aspect of a personality."[10] All of us have encountered strong personalities who, in spite of their lack of striking physical traits, exert on us a distinctively vivid impression: they seem to radiate energy, dynamism, and conviction.

In fact, a personal atmosphere pervades the lived space around every encountered person. We sense a particular presence or aura and, with it, a certain tonality (joy, vitality, sincerity, sadness) that, like perfume, gradually infiltrates the whole surroundings. Children are keenly responsive to the atmosphere created, consciously or unconsciously, by their parents. As J. Rudert remarked, the parental atmospheric radiation is a "kind of spiritual food" that children need for healthy growth.[11] Their personality is considerably shaped by the atmosphere they "breathe in" at home. For the same reasons, students may resent or enjoy their learning experience in the classroom. In general, an atmosphere permeates every sector of our life-world and influences, to a greater or lesser degree, the characteristics and outcomes of human activities.

The atmosphere is neither identical with, nor totally independent from, some objectively given traits. In a sense, it is everywhere and nowhere. Therefore, we do not always feel able, nor do we need, to account for our ways of replying to situations. We may stroll through the streets of a foreign city without being able to pin down why we feel ill at ease. "In entering an apartment," says Merleau-Ponty, "we can perceive the character (*l'esprit*) of those who live there without being capable of justifying this impression by an enumeration of remarkable details, and certainly well before having noted the color of the furniture."[12] Clearly, we seem to receive two types of "messages" from our surroundings: while, and even before, apprehending the physical characteristics of a room, we sense the lifestyle of its inhabitant. Yet, notwithstanding its obviousness and specificity, the atmospheric quality may resist our efforts to explain it conceptually.

The Power of Sound

To gain a better understanding of these atmospheric experiences, let us return to our perception of sounds. We do not necessarily have to hear music or ambient noise in order to detect a sound atmosphere. In our daily conversations, we hear not only words but also the tone of the voice and, not infrequently, we need to rely on the "musicality" of a sentence in order to apprehend its true meaning. As Erwin Straus pointed out, "a conversation contains more than mere content; it contains something which cannot be expressed in writing."[13] The way in which we greet the other, begin a sentence, stress syllables, words, even whole sentences, the various bodily elements (eye contact, facial expression, distance) shape the whole context of the verbal communication and convey a particular atmosphere. Since we apprehend, often unconsciously, sounds with their affective meanings, the choice of certain phonetic elements already elicits a particular atmosphere. There is a rich and informative literature on the emotional quality of vowels and consonants and the tonal melody and rhythm of speech.[14] Pauses, coughs, stammers, hesitations, and silences are also integral and necessary parts of every "conversational music." David Abercrombie repeatedly emphasized the importance of silent stress in the spoken language: "This stress is felt by the speaker and (because he would do the same if he were speaking) 'empathized' by the hearer."[15] I would suggest that speakers' "phonetic empathy" is ultimately tied to their participation in a particular atmosphere and it is thanks to their ability to discriminate accurately an emotional quality that they come to a successful linguistic understanding. In other words, a genuine conversation, in which silence plays an important role, is rooted in, and constituted by, as Tellenbach would put it, a shared "atmospheric togetherness."[16]

We hear different sounds when we say goodbye to our conversational partner and find ourselves in a store, an office, or a factory. In all these places, perceptual information is tied to a communication with an atmosphere. We are linked to these spaces, says Tony Hiss, by both the "pin-point focus of ordinary perception" and the "broad-focus of simultaneous perception."[17] What are, then, the specific features of the more inclusive approach to sounds?

Tellenbach's expression "atmosphere as an envelopment" seems particularly appropriate to characterize our experience of sounds. Sounds, as I have said, detach themselves from their source and pursue us. We are able to turn away from visible objects, but unable to preserve a distance between ourselves and the sounds.[18] Colours "cling" to objects; sounds "move away" from them and "enjoy" an autonomous existence. We see clearly the red light in front of us, but are at a loss as we try to figure out from where the ambulance is coming. We can easily impose our will onto the visible, but not onto the audible; we can close our eyes at any time, but not our ears. In his phenomenological analysis of sounds, Erwin Straus has emphasized the semantic relationships among the German *hören* (to hear), *horchen* (to hearken), and *gehorchen* (to obey).[19] Indeed, when sounds emanate from a resonating body, we can't run away and, like schoolchildren in the classroom, must obey. The acoustic sphere entails an element of possessiveness; we are seized by sounds and delivered to their influence. No wonder that, since Ulysses encountered the sirens' chanting allurements, sound has always been considered a unique means of enticing, manipulating, and imposing one's own will on others, or breaking down a resistance.

Helmuth Plessner relates both the volume and impulse of rhythmically articulated sounds to the phenomenon of "insistence (*Eindringlichkeit*)."[20] No other sensory element makes its way and soaks into us as does a sound: it provokes resonances at levels deeper than a colour or a tactile quality.[21] Not only strident sounds, such as a piercing cry, but also gentle melodies penetrate and reach the depths of our being. Sometimes their effect is indelible. A simple tune, heard many years earlier, can suddenly, in the most unexpected moment, come to our consciousness and assert its spell. "It is music," writes Steiner, "which can invade and rule the human psyche with a penetrative strength comparable, it may be, only to that of narcotics or of the trance reported by shamans, saints and ecstatics."[22] However important and thorough the recent studies on the physiological conditions of our senses may be, they are unable to tell us anything about the *sovereignty*, *invasion*, *penetration*, and *depth* of the sounds. These categories resist the narrow and exclusive demand for the quantifiable. Yet each of them is an essential element of our daily encounter with auditory atmospheres and central for our understanding of our immediate response to its particular meaning.

The decisive factor here is our ability to echo vivid or discreet effects, to resonate tonal impressions (pitches, intervals, chords, etc.) and to detect unexpected deviations. The words *echo* and *resonance* refer to the stirring intensity and penetration of sounds that either correspond to or contradict our auditory habits.

That is not all, however. Our auditory sensibility cannot be reduced to a unidirectional attunement. Certainly, sounds come to us, press upon us, and resonate in us. But, just as we like to approach flowers and smell their pleasant perfumes, so, in the same manner, we like to focus actively on some sounds and reinforce their effect.[23] Minkowski uses the French *aspirer* when he refers to the active aspect of our atmospheric experience.[24] With all our being, we are able to detect and "breathe in" a particular sensory or moral atmosphere without, of course, taking, literally, a larger quantity of air into our lungs. It is worth remarking that, for Minkowski, the act of *aspirer* – as well as that of seeing, tasting, or touching – is not only a distinctive mode of sensory contact with an object but, above all, a fundamental way of being in the world. Thanks to a phenomenological approach, we are truly able to grasp the function and significance of this vital and dynamic category of human life.

I have already alluded to the various responses to atmospheres: streaming traffic on a busy street induces a different reaction than a peaceful meadow. In general, a natural environment seems to arouse in us a higher degree of sensory and atmospheric alertness than does the ambient noise of a large city. As Hiss observes, "A quiet place that offers no threat seems to invite people to redistribute their attention, and any number of subtle perceptual cues can then come into play."[25] The possible affect of an atmospheric quality on our behaviour and mood cannot be ignored by all those who consciously create or modify our immediate surroundings. Architects, city planners, landscape designers, artistic managers, or party hosts must be well aware of the correlation between an atmosphere and the way we respond, act, and feel. Likewise, performers and lecturers must learn to correctly apprehend and modify a prevailing atmosphere.[26] They all should know that atmospheres can exercise a significant power over human sensibility that, as Paul Valéry observed, is not only a "faculty of sensing" but also a "mode of reaction," "mode of transmission."[27] Yet responses to atmospheres are neither automatic nor consistent. Music tends to unite the listener with the singer and thus create a "community of consonance," as Straus describes it. But a particular song, instead of inducing a vivacious participation and an experience of intimacy, can sometimes produce adverse effects. The character and intensity of our responsiveness depend on a great variety of factors, such as taste, culture, and living habits, as well as our will, awareness, desire, and momentary mood. These determine the way we react to music, whether we display an attitude of enthusiastic acceptance or one of strained resistance.

The Din Around Us

Our active response to our surroundings, claims Tony Hiss in his valuable book *The Experience of Place*, goes together with a "sort of unhurried feeling," a "feeling there is time enough to savor all the sights and sounds and other sensations coming in."[28] Once again, here the act of savouring denotes more than just a particular mode of sensory contact; it also implies a fundamental human attitude in which intimacy, calmness, presence, serenity, and liveability predominate. Thus, when we savour the charm and mystery of fog, or the sadness and melancholy of the requiem, we respond, with relaxed or rapt attentiveness, to a singular event. The intensity of our experience notwithstanding, these "objects" do not appear obtrusive or disturbing. Although the music of a requiem is carefully studied and rehearsed, we do not have the impression of being subjected to a constrained or artificial atmosphere. In spite of our sorrow, we may find a deep satisfaction in the markedly suggestive and enriching music that discloses a specific atmospheric colouration.

We come to an altogether different awareness of the atmosphere when, in a state of passive reception, we hear music not as a unique aesthetic event, but *as* a background and *in* the background. If I single out this kind of atmospheric experience, it is due to its ubiquity and to the widespread tendency to use it for the attainment of specific objectives. Indeed, in most public spaces, background music is played in order to create an atmosphere and, thereby, induce the appropriate mood and behaviour. There is a deliberate effort to envelop people almost everywhere with an artificial "acoustic bell," to use Rüdiger Liedtke's expression.[29]

Entering into this kind of packaged and inescapable atmosphere, we do not perceive it as a surplus, which we might actively welcome, but as an imposed and passively apprehended medium. Whether good or bad, classical or popular, music is forced on us, reducing us to a state of receptivity. Of course, there is no question here of attending to an artistic form, of making a creative response to an organized and meaningful musical movement. In this case, the aesthetic content (both cognitive and emotive) of a musical work is either devalued or distorted. The background-music atmosphere is independent of the active and conscious dimension of our auditory sensibility; it is apprehended semi-consciously and passively as a flow of dispersed and, for many of us, annoying sounds. Hanns-Werner Heister therefore considers background music a "disturbance," a "form of noise" that, despite some claims about its positive affects, results in a lack of concentration, nervousness and even exhaustion.[30] Music in the background, adds Heister, is an obtrusive and irritating "expropriation of our senses" and a sort of "undefinable 'terror' that operates through 'pleasant' means." Of course, one could object that there is no "terror" whatsoever when an aural tapestry is voluntarily introduced into a workplace or a private living room. But unless sounds are actively attended, the self-chosen background music still appears as a highly disturbing and distracting element and, obviously, weakens the human ability to feel, understand, and discriminate the rightness and beauty of tonal forms.

However conjectural, and even questionable, these observations on the self-chosen music's debilitating affects may appear, there is a general consensus concerning one point: the constant, indiscriminate, and widespread exposure, nay addiction, to music, from morning to night, at home and in the workplace, leads to a gradual decay and atrophy of our sensibilities. Not only our ear but all our senses lose their susceptibility to subtle qualities, forms, and nuances. It is our sensibility that, according to Louis Lavelle, "reacts to the subtlest and most remote happenings" and "distinguishes their finest differences."[31] The astute and quick communication between ourselves and the world requires gaps and contrasts, namely those existing between sound and silence. But the nonstop stream of sounds, the permanent "acoustic bell" hanging over our heads, leaves no room for silence, which has become a "matter of the greatest luxury," Valéry contends, and spreads in space a noisy and restless vulgarity.[32]

It may be argued that the relentless and undue quest for fierce auditory impressions is also linked to this obtuseness or atrophy of our sensibility for fine distinctions. When our ear is no longer bound to sounds with delicate fibres, only coarse impressions penetrate its thick and opaque tissues. In Western societies, there is a tendency to crave forceful and even violent sensory impressions: we yearn for loudness, vividness, and shrillness in order to feel and find some pleasures in our otherwise dull life.[33]

I am inclined to share the views of Liedtke, who discusses these problems in some detail. "The uncontrolled exposure to music," writes Liedtke, "whether voluntary or not – leads to alienation, dehumanization, apathy, stereotyped thinking, collapse of cultural-ethical values, uniformity of taste."[34] Let us pause for a little to examine the phenomenon of apathy. There seems to be a symmetry between the ongoing contact with sounds and a general state of passivity. The impulse towards action requires not only sensory alertness but also the wealth and unity of feelings, thoughts, and fantasies, and these can hardly emerge and flourish in the midst of a constant and all-pervasive sound-matrix. Doubtless, the alarming passivity of many can be, in part, provoked by a loss of immediate bodily contact with the world. But beyond the scarcity of bodily engagements and the rapid rise of abstractness, the constant exposure to intense sensory impressions appears to be a non-negligible cause of a widespread passive behaviour.

In this context, Harry Heft has observed that a high noise level in the home environment hinders the proper development of children's perceptual and motor skills.[35] Important aspects of cognitive development in infancy, such as verbal and motor imitations, are significantly impaired when children are exposed to constant noise in their home. Television and radio, for example, not only reduce the frequency and intensity of common activities (meals, games, walks) but also create such an auditory and visual confusion that children stop paying attention to their parents' words and gestures. A prolonged exposure to noise also affects children's ability to discriminate and learn, and distracts them from the playful exploration of their immediate environment. In a word, the inability to escape from noise at home brings about the general reduction of motor activity and exploration.

In a remarkable lecture, delivered in 1937 at the Ferenc Liszt Academy of Music of Budapest, Béla Bartók had already tied "machine music," as he put it, to some obnoxious effects. He noticed that, for many people, listening to music on the radio had become "nothing more than a caress of a kind of tepid bath, a kind of coffee-house music, a droning in the background so that one can perform other tasks with less boredom and with hardly any attention to music."[36] According to Bartók, radio broadcasting had unfortunately created a superficial and inconsistent approach to musical forms. As a result of doing many things at the same time, he argued, people had become accustomed to hearing sounds without serious concentration and commitment.

I have no space here to adequately discuss the cardinal problem of distraction. I will merely point out that background music appears to be a striking example of the general tendency to place entertainment and amusement above serious and concentrated awareness, and to make suggestibility and gullibility more important than independent thinking and self-determination. The flow of scattered images presented by television and the unending stream of sound blaring from radios, Walkmans or CD players sacrifice coherence and continuity for a shallow familiarity with a fragmented world. Background music is more than just a particular form of entertainment; it represents a comprehensive alienation both from our concrete surroundings and from some natural and vital human activities, such as reading, singing, and engaging in conversations. It also conveys a judgment on the quality, occupation, and purpose of everyday life. Heister is not far from the truth when he views it as a specific kind of manipulation, "vital to a system of domination."[37]

It would be worthwhile to disclose and analyze, in more depth, the motives and interests of all those who, by creating a sound-culture everywhere and by nurturing a widespread addiction to music, seek to seduce, manipulate, and control. By doing this, we could perhaps encourage people to become more aware of the psychological and social influence of sound atmospheres, and of the necessity of consciously selecting them.

NOTES

1. Among the happy few, R. Murray Schafer is doubtless one of the most important. See his *The Tuning of the World* (Toronto: McClelland & Stewart, 1977) and *The Thinking Ear* (Toronto: Arcana Editions, 1986).

2. George Steiner, *In Bluebeard's Castle: Some Notes Towards the Re-definition of Culture* (London: Faber & Faber, 1971), 89–95.

3. J. Bottum, "The Soundtracking of America," *Atlantic Monthly* (March 2000): 56–57.

4. Gernot Böhme, *Anthropologie in pragmatischer Hinsicht: Darmstädter Vorlesungen* (Frankfurt am Main: Suhrkamp Verlag, 1985), 199.

5. Hubertus Tellenbach, *Goût et Atmosphère*, trans. Jean Amsler (Paris: Presses Universitaires de France, 1983); "Die Begründung psychiatrischer Erfahrung und psychiatrischer Methoden in philosophischen Konzeptionen vom Wesen des Menschen," in *Philosophische Anthropologie: Erster Teil*, eds. Hans-Georg Gadamer and Paul Vogler (Stuttgart: Georg Thieme Verlag, 1974), 175–179.

6. See Eugène Minkowski, *Vers une cosmologie: Fragments philosophiques* (Paris: Aubier-Montaigne, 1967), 116.

7. Tellenbach, *Goût et Atmosphère*, 40.

8. Maurice Merleau-Ponty, *Phenomenology of Perception*, trans. Colin Smith (London: Routledge & Kegan Paul, 1962), 281. See also Jean Ladrière, "La ville, inducteur existentiel," *Vie sociale et destinée* (Gembloux: Duculot, 1973), 139–160.

9. Nicolai Hartmann views the acts of "seeing through" (*Hindurchsehen*) and "hearing through" (*Hindurchhören*) and their correlates, the "affective tones (*Gefühlstöne*)," as constitutive elements of human perception. *Ästhetik* (Berlin: W. De Gruyter, 1953), 42–49.

10. Minkowski, 119.

11. J. Rudert, "Die persönliche Atmosphäre," *Archiv für die gesamte Psychologie* 116 (1964): 295. See also Otto Friedrich Bollnow, "The Pedagogical Atmosphere," *Phenomenology + Pedagogy* 7 (1989): 5–76.

12. Maurice Merleau-Ponty, *The Structure of Behavior*, trans. Alden L. Fisher (Boston: Beacon Press, 1967), 173.

13. Erwin W. Straus, *The Primary World of Senses: A Vindication of Sensory Experience*, trans. Jacob Needleman (New York: Free Press of Glencoe, 1963), 196.

14. See, for instance, Ivan Fónagy, *La vive voix: Essais de psycho-phonétique* (Paris: Payot, 1983), 57–151.

15. David Abercrombie, "A Phonetician's View of Verse Structure," *Studies in Phonetics and Linguistics* (London: Oxford University Press, 1965), 21. For example, the meaning of a quibble like "A sound atmosphere is not always a sound atmosphere" can be accurately understood from the tone of the voice and the felt silent stress.

16. Tellenbach, *Goût et Atmosphère*. There are, of course, situations in which the participation in an atmosphere does not guarantee a successful communication. When people are inclined to distort their atmospheric experience, or are unable to comment upon the contrast between various orders of messages, their entire communicational behaviour is doomed to failure. See Gregory Bateson, "Toward a Theory of Schizophrenia," in *Steps to an Ecology of Mind* (Northvale, NJ: Jason Aronson Inc., 1987), 201–227.

17. Tony Hiss, *The Experience of Place* (New York: Vintage Books, 1991), 3–26.

18. On the relation between the visible and audible, see Straus, *The Primary World of Senses*, 367–379.

19. Erwin W. Straus, "The Forms of Spatiality," in *Phenomenological Psychology*, trans. Erling Eng (New York: Basic Books, 1966), 16.

20. Helmuth Plessner, "Anthropologie der Sinne," in *Philosophische Anthropologie: Zweiter Teil*, eds. Hans-Georg Gadamer and Paul Vogler (Stuttgart: Georg Thieme Verlag, 1974), 22–23.

21. There is a difference, says Anthony Storr, between seeing and hearing a suffering person: "At an emotional level, there is something 'deeper' about hearing than seeing; and something about hearing other people which fosters human relationships even more than seeing them." *Music and the Mind* (New York: The Free Press, 1992), 26. See also Vladimir Jankélévitch, *La musique et l'ineffable* (Paris: Seuil, 1983), 7–9.

22. George Steiner, *Errata: An Examined Life* (London: Weidenfeld & Nicolson, 1997), 72–73.

23. See Schafer, *The Tuning of the World*, 212–213.

24. Minkowski, 118.

25. Hiss, 34.

26. See P. E. Vernon, "The Ear is Not Enough," in *Pleasures of Music: An Anthology of Writing about Music and Musicians from Cellini to Bernard Shaw*, ed. Jacques Barzun (Chicago: University of Chicago Press, 1977), 33.

27. Paul Valéry, *Cahiers*, vol. 1, Collection "la Pléiade" (Paris: Gallimard, 1973), 1206.

28. Hiss, 3.

29. Rüdiger Liedtke, *Die Vertreibung der Stille: Wie uns das Leben unter der akustischen Glocke um unsere Sinne bringt* (München: Deutscher Taschenbuch Verlag, 1985).

30. Hanns-Werner Heister, "Music in Concert and Music in the Background: Two Poles of Musical Realization," in *Companion to Contemporary Musical Thought*, vol. 1, eds. John Paynter et al. (London: Routledge, 1992), 66.

31. Louis Lavelle, *The Dilemma of Narcissus*, trans. W. T. Gairdner (London: George Allen & Unwin, 1973), 84. See also Paul Valéry, "Le bilan de l'intelligence," in *Oeuvres*, vol. 1, Collection "la Pléiade"(Paris: Gallimard, 1957), 1069–1071.

32. Valery, *Oeuvres*, 1426. Erik Satie emphatically deplored the eradication of "exquisite and gentle silence" and its replacement with "bad music." Perhaps his own "invention," the *musique d'ameublement*, served not so much as a joke but as a counterbalance to the "silly ritornellos" which, in his opinion, brought nothing but torment and ugliness into human life. See his *Écrits*, ed. Ornella Volta (Paris: Éditions Champ Libre, 1981), 24–25. On the cardinal theme of silence, see Jankélévitch, *La musique et l'ineffable*, 161–190; Steiner, *Errata*, 143–152.

33. See Bernd Riede, "Schadet Musik? Über einige negative Aspekte der Musik in unserer Gesellschaft," *Universitas* 49 (1994): 1183–1190. See also Josef Pieper, "Über Musik. Ansprache während eines Bach-Abends," in *Nur der Liebende singt: Musische Kunst – heute* (Ostfildern bei Stuttgart: Schwabenverlag, 1988), 33.

34. Liedtke, 212.

35. Harry Heft, "High Residential Density and Perceptual-Cognitive Development: An Examination of the Effects of Crowding and Noise in the Home," in *Habitats for Children: The Impacts of Density*, eds. Jochaim F. Wohlwill and Willem van Wliet (Hillsdale, NJ: Lawrence Erlbaum Associates, 1985), 39–75.

36. Béla Bartók, "Mechanical Music," in *Essays*, ed. Benjamin Suchoff (Lincoln: University of Nebraska Press, 1976), 296.

37. Heister, 65.

Soundscape Works, Listening, and the Touch of Sound

Andra McCartney

> Touch is the most personal of the senses. Hearing and touch meet where the lower frequencies of audible sound pass over to tactile vibrations (at about 20 hertz). Hearing is a way of touching at a distance and the intimacy of the first sense is fused with sociability whenever people gather together to hear something special.[1]
> – R. Murray Schafer

Several years ago, I attended a college dance – a college that had a large program for the deaf. Some of the most expressive dancers that night were the deaf students. They took their shoes off, and felt the music through the soles of their feet, reaching up to animate their whole bodies in motion. They expressed with their actions what composer R. Murray Schafer writes above: sound is the language of vibration, and we hear this language with more than our ears. David Burrows describes this full-bodied hearing by distinguishing between hearing and seeing a bell:

> The ringing reaches me with the intimacy of a touch, and this intensifies the feeling of self-confirmation. To see the bell I must turn toward it and focus on it, reach out myself and touch it with my attention; and nothing would be easier than to withdraw my touch by shutting my eyes or looking away. The sound, like the touch of a hand moved by a will other than my own, is not so easily ignored: I cannot shut non-existent earlids. And sound goes beyond touch, which respects the perimeter of my skin, and beyond its degree of intimacy in seeming to be going on within me as much as around me.[2]

Hearing is done not only with the ears, but also with every fibre of our beings as vibrations of sound move into our bodies. Sound touches us, inside and out. And this feeling of being touched by sound is heightened by technology: when microphones amplify and record sounds, they not only involve the ears, but also every other part of the body.

Soundwalks in Research, Public Education, and Sound Art

A soundwalk is an exploration of, and an attempt to understand, the sociopolitical and sonic resonances of a particular location via the act of listening. Soundwalks originated as a research tool by the World Soundscape Project, a team at Simon Fraser University in the 1970s led by Schafer. Travelling to various towns and villages in Canada and Europe, they sought to measure and record sonic environments. Each research expedition began with a soundwalk to orient the team to the area. However, these soundwalks were not recorded, nor were their results discussed specifically in the resulting documents. The role of soundwalks seemed restricted to orientation only.

Later, a member of that research team, composer Hildegard Westerkamp, recorded soundwalks in the region around Vancouver. Her aim was different: she wanted to sensitize listeners to their immediate environment by playing it on community radio.[3] Her involvement with Vancouver Cooperative Radio gave Westerkamp a place to actualize ideas about sound ecology, particularly through her show *Soundwalking*. She took listeners to various locations in their immediate area, then played back the sounds of these environments, framing and contextualizing them with on-air commentary. Sometimes, as in a program about Lighthouse Park, she would read excerpts of writings (in this case, Emily Carr). The shows often made a political point acoustically. For instance, in *Under the Flightpath* (1981), roaring jets can be heard as long-term residents claim that they don't even notice the planes.

For Westerkamp, the main element of a soundwalk is not only orientation, but also dialogue and composition. It is possible to use a soundwalk for orientation when in an unknown environment, as a mariner would use sounding to understand unknown waters:

> [G]o for an orientation walk in the city, any city, asking people for directions. Besides not getting lost that way, you will also get to know a little of the character of a city by listening to the way people answer. Listen to the sounds and melodies in their voices, listen for accents.[4]

Dialogue can involve responding to the call of a bird or animal, finding echoes in landscape formations and building structures. Both orientation and dialogue are necessary for the third element – soundwalk composition:

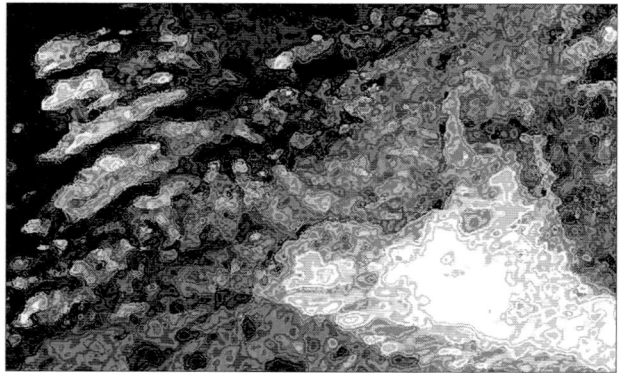

Andra McCartney
Textures, 1998
From the on-line interactive project *The River*
www.earthear.com
Courtesy the artist

Go out and listen. Choose an acoustic environment which in your opinion sets a good base for your environmental compositions. In the same way as the architect acquaints himself with the landscape into which he wants to integrate the shape of a house, so we must get to know the main characteristics of the soundscape into which we want to immerse our own sounds. What kinds of rhythms does it contain, what kinds of pitches, how many continuous sounds, how many and what kinds of discrete sounds, etc.? Which sounds can you produce that add to the quality of the environmental music? Create a dialogue and thereby lift the environmental sounds out of their context into the context of your composition, and in turn make your sounds a natural part of the music around you. Is it possible?[5]

Westerkamp sometimes uses soundwalks as the basis of compositions – as in *Kits Beach Soundwalk* (1989) – and sometimes uses stationary field recordings, usually recorded herself. Either way, she always seems present in the work. To hear one of Westerkamp's compositions is to be drawn into her evocation of an acoustic environment, to feel her presence, and to experience her relationships with different sonic events.

Touching Sound Through Amplification

From the earliest days of sound recording, practitioners and theorists remarked upon the heightening of sound through touch and, conversely, touch through sound when using microphones. Pierre Schaeffer was one of the earliest composers to work with tape recordings of "concrete" sounds in Paris during the 1940s. Schaeffer described his recording technique in terms of using his fingers as if they were sound-sensing devices, extensions of his ears:

> It is necessary to fasten the mike to the tip of the fingers, and that everything one experiences reach the mike and be formulated by the mike…. This is the musical exercise par excellence.[6]

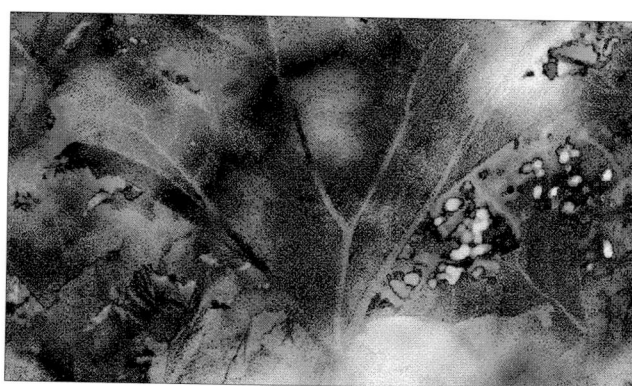

Andra McCartney
Elephant Skin Plant,
1998-2000
From the interactive artwork *Soundwalking Queen Elizabeth Park*
Courtesy the artist

With the variety of microphone types and pickup patterns available today, it is possible to go further with this exercise of extending the placement of artificial ears. Microphones, for instance, can be attached to headphones, creating a listening perspective similar to one's own ears, with breathing sounds particularly present. If placed near the belt, it is as if the navel has grown ears. Other parts of the body will facilitate other perspectives. With a stereo microphone, monitored on headphones, listening can be extended to places that one's hands and legs cannot reach. Leaning over the edge of the pier, a microphone can be dropped down to water level, allowing the ears to focus on the sounds of water approaching as the cable descends. If the microphone enters a drainage pipe, listening can become metallic, resonant, echoing.

Schaeffer's compositional process often unfolded directly from the experience of recording:

> Always [put] the mike at the tip of the fingers, and [let each] "thought," each movement of the back of the throat, of the cerebellum be transcribed into suitable sounds on tape by the mike. Formulat[ing] as one goes along....[7]

This is similar to the way I observed Westerkamp doing soundwalk recording. Rather than beginning with a defined objective (except that of listening), she reacted to interesting sounds, allowing her movements to be affected by events as they happened. During a soundwalk in Vancouver's Queen Elizabeth Park, an airplane passed overhead, with its characteristic falling glissando. Westerkamp guided the microphone towards the air vents of a nearby building, timing her motion so that in one continuous gesture the sound of the airplane was swallowed by the rising amplitude of the broadband vent sound.

While Schaeffer was aware of a heightened sense of touch during the recording process, his works did not maintain this link to textures and surfaces. He developed a compositional process that attempted to sever sounds from their sources by removing the attack of the sound, or processing it to limit its anecdotal properties. He removed the sounds' connections with everyday existence, which he increasingly understood as being deficient. In contrast, some composers who work with recorded sounds are particularly interested in transmitting a sense of their experience of a place, a trace of their presence, to the listener. Composer and theorist Katharine Norman refers to this as "realworld" composing. In her description of the work of composer Michel Redolfi, Norman emphasizes how it is possible to keep in touch with an environment audibly:

> In his recordings the sounds from the California desert are at times inseparably fused with the signs of his intervention: sounds travel as he moves the microphone about, we hear the sound of the microphone being handled, scrunching gravel, a rock moved and replaced. In fact all the natural but telltale signs of a mediating human being who, in this quest for the "desert tone," literally scratches the surface to activate aurally reticent surroundings.[8]

In a section of one of my own multimedia pieces, *Soundwalking Queen Elizabeth Park* (1998–2000), sound is particularly linked to the sense of touch. *Elephant Skin Plant* features a sound excerpt based on a close-miked recording of my finger stroking the leaf of this impressively large and statuesque plant, a stroke that took about fourteen seconds. The microphone, held in the hand, amplified the contact with the plant's surface, allowing the monitoring of sounds normally inaudible as well as intensifying the experience of touch. At the same time, the finger felt the textures of the surface, in this case rough, prickly, and bumpy. This biofeedback loop led to a heightened perception of both senses, through their interlinked association with each other. I eventually slowed the sound down during the composition stage, in order to hear the intricacies of the leaf's topography in more detail. This process of slowing sound increases the sensation of tactility: the bumps and ridges become much more evident. Tactile exploration, remarks Constance Classen, finds pleasure in gradual revelation, in "making sense of something not all at once, but in stages."[9] After layering various speeds of sound, filtering the frequencies to emphasize the finger's bumpy journey from stem to tip, I then scanned a single photograph of the leaf, and zoomed in close, focusing first on one part, then another, making sense of the whole through a close examination of different areas – adding vision to the fusion of tactility and sound.[10]

Presence, Place, and Engagement

A soundwalk is an improvisation with the sounds of a place. While saxophones and bongo drums are playing instruments, a microphone is primarily a listening instrument. Whereas a jazz improviser works with melodic and rhythmic lines and harmonic progressions, a soundwalk recordist improvises with perspective, motion, and proximity. In a jazz solo, it is possible to hear how intimately the soloist knows the other members of the band, how well he or she can anticipate their progressions, the energy that is born of surprises in the way the band works together. In a soundwalk recording, it is partly how well recordists know a place that determines a recording's success. Can they anticipate the weather? Do they know the environment well enough to plan a walk at a time when particularly interesting sonic juxtapositions occur? And then there are the surprises: an unusual sound occurs, out of the blue. Can presuppositions be let go of to deal with this new situation? The power and subtlety of a good soundwalk recording depends on the ability to respond to a sound environment actively and with full agency, and to remain in constant dialogue.

Soundwalks, however, are not innocent encounters. Using focus and perspective, it is possible to alter the dynamic hierarchy of sounds within a place. The microphone allows the recordist to discover and attend to the subtle sonic emanations of very small sounds. Often masked or too quiet to be heard normally, these sounds can be elevated into audibility. Their social significance may be heightened or altered dramatically. Soundwalks thus record a specific interaction with a place, one in which the microphone constructs a particular experience, and within which the recordist's motion remains audible. These sounds trace the movements of everyday life, and are predicated on an ethics of place. Often soundwalks take place in busy urban areas. In order to avoid using sound recordings as a means of surveillance, it is important for the recordist to turn away from passing conversations, focus on the background ambience, and treat all recorded sounds with respect. To this way of thinking, the recording process is less like a mining of the sound environment, or a capturing of sounds for later manipulation, than a gleaning of unnoticed ambiences to be brought into active awareness.[11]

What is the source of the attraction to tracing one's movements through precise locales? I believe it is due to the holding power of places. For philosopher Edward Casey, the power of places is based on a combination of memory and novelty:

> Minimally, places gather things in their midst – where "things" connote various animate and inanimate entities. Places also gather experiences and histories, even languages and thoughts. Think only of what it means to go back to a place you know, finding it full of memories and expectations, old things and new things, the familiar and the strange, and much more besides. What else is capable of this massively diversified holding action?[12]

Casey speaks of returning to places one knows, and Westerkamp's recorded soundwalks were initially played back to people who probably knew those particular sites. Her community radio listening audience could easily get into a car or bus, or even walk to where the recordings had been done. While she utilized electronic technology in the sound recordings, the broadcasting maintained an emphasis on the local. Westerkamp has since created soundscape compositions that speak of particular places and distributes them on CD for international audiences, yet wonders about the meaning and importance of such works to people in quite different environments. Such dispersed production and presentation tends to radically dislocate sounds from their sources, flinging them across the globe. To what extent do places continue to have meaning and holding power when heard in other, disparate locales?

The aim of soundwalks is to maintain presence and proximity in a work that takes a sound experience out of context, shorn from its original moorings in a particular place. Regardless of distance, soundwalks do maintain a level of presence. For those who have been to the soundwalk locations, it often leads to recollections of their visits. Others are reminded of places in their experience that were similar. It is sometimes the sense of human presence that is meaningful – a number of listeners remark on the feeling as if they were walking with the recordist, a form of sonic companionship. Often it is the emphasis on everyday sounds that is a revelation, causing people to listen differently in their daily lives. For some, it engenders an urge to begin like-minded activities and practice soundwalking themselves.

The contrast between visual and aural experience, and how it affects one's relationship to the landscape, is vividly conveyed by Constance Classen's discussion of a scene in Jean-Paul Sartre's *Being and Nothingness*. An individual standing in a park, seeing but unseen, dominates the space with his or her gaze until someone else enters. Authority is then displaced as the viewer becomes an object seen by another. But for someone who is blind, Classen notes, the situation is different. A blind person alone in a park would hear nothing outside of his or her own sounds. But when movement and activity commence, the world emerges into being. This changes the situation from one of domination to one of engagement:

> The world thus exists for the listener not as a stable scene, but as a dynamic sequence of sounds. It is too changeable, too transient, to be dominated – as one dominates a landscape through sight – it can only be attended to and engaged with.[13]

A soundwalker's engagement with the landscape is at once sonic, tactile, and kinaesthetic. It is defined through what is heard of others' sounds, through interactions with the surroundings, and by the recordist's own movements. Amplification translates the subtlety of touch into an audible play with surfaces and textures. In soundscape works, traces of tactility are embedded that help to link distant and everyday places. They explore auditory experiences and memories of natural and urban environments, and attend to and reflect upon the depth of daily rituals.

NOTES

1. R. Murray Schafer, *The Tuning of the World* (Toronto: McClelland & Stewart, 1977), 11.

2. David Burrows, *Sound, Speech and Music* (Amherst, MA: University of Massachusetts Press, 1990), 15–16.

3. Hildegard Westerkamp, "The Soundscape on Radio," in *Radio Rethink: Art, Sound and Transmission*, eds. Daina Augaitis and Dan Lander (Banff: Walter Phillips Gallery Editions, 1994), 87–94.

4. Hildegard Westerkamp, "Soundwalking," *Sound Heritage* 3:4 (1974): 25. For more information on Westerkamp, see Andra McCartney, "Soundwalk in the Park with Hildegard Westerkamp," *Musicworks* 72 (autumn 1998): 6–15, and McCartney, *Sounding Places with Hildegard Westerkamp*, Electronic Music Foundation Website, < www.emf.org/artists/mccartney00/ > .

5. Westerkamp, "Soundwalking," 25.

6. Pierre Schaeffer quoted in Carlos Palombini, "Technology and Pierre Schaeffer: Pierre Schaeffer's *Arts-Relais*, Walter Benjamin's *technische Reproduzierbarkeit* and Martin Heidegger's *Ge-stell*," *Organized Sound* 3:1 (1998): 3.

7. Schaeffer quoted in Palombini, 4.

8. Katharine Norman, "Telling Tales," *Contemporary Music Review* 10:2 (1994): 106.

9. Constance Classen, *The Color of Angels: Cosmology, Gender, and the Aesthetic Imagination* (New York: Routledge, 1998), 148.

10. For other work, see Andra McCartney, *Le terroir sonore du phare Lachinois* (2000), < www.givideo.org > and "Soundwalking Blue Montréal," *Soundscape: The Journal of Acoustic Ecology* 1:2 (winter 2000): 28-29, < www.andrasound.org > .

11. Agnes Varda, *The Gleaners and I* (Paris: Ciné-Tamaris, Zeitgeist Video, 2001).

12. Edward Casey, "How to Get from Space to Place in a Fairly Short Stretch of Time: Phenomenological Prolegomena," in *Senses of Place*, eds. Steven Feld and Keith H. Basso (Santa Fe: School of American Research, 1996), 24.

13. Classen, 142.

ACOUSTIC HEGEMONY AND CONTESTATION

Charles Hirschkind

Daniel Fisher

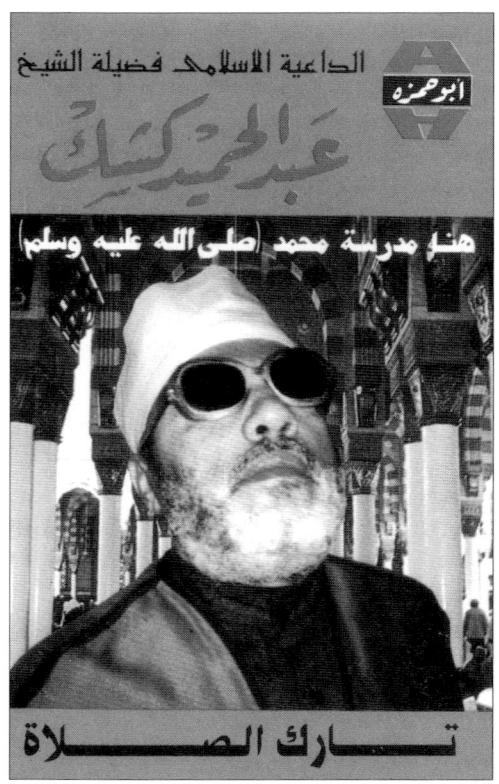

`Abd al-Ḥamīd Kishk, *Tarak al-ṣalāt* ("The Failure to Pray")

On the obligatory character of prayer and the consequences,
in this life and the next, that follow upon one's failure to
perform the act

Civic Virtue and Religious Reason: An Islamic Counter-Public

Charles Hirschkind

Since the rise of modernization theory in the 1960s up through present concerns with globalization, a growing body of anthropological and sociological scholarship has explored the impact of modern media technologies on religious practice. Scholars have frequently approached this topic in terms of a polarity between what are assumed to be two contradictory processes, the deliberative and the disciplinary. Analyses focusing on the deliberative aspect have emphasized the possibilities of argument, contestation, and dialogue that have been afforded by the advent of universal modern literacy, the diffusion of printed texts, and the operation of electronic mass media. Following conventional histories of the Protestant revolution, this scholarship has given particular emphasis to the role of print and other media technologies in propelling a democratization of religious authority. The new object-like quality of religion and the universal accessibility of religious texts, it is argued, transform ritual speech into individual assertion, oral mnemonics into analytical memory. Equipped with these newly found sophistications and the autonomous reasoning that they facilitate, a growing number of individuals engage with and revise the religious traditions they have inherited.

Scholars emphasizing the disciplinary functions of religious media, on the other hand, have stressed the ideological over the dialogic aspects of the phenomenon. Media technologies, in this view, enable an extension of an authoritative religious discourse. The resultant public is less a sphere of discussion than of subjection to authority, part of a project aimed at promoting and securing a uniform model of moral behaviour. In short, the public arena constituted by the media practices of religious actors tends to be identified *either* as a deliberative space of argument and contestation between individuals, *or* as a normative space for education in community-oriented virtue. The assumption is that the more truly deliberative a public, the weaker its disciplinary function, and vice versa. This way of framing the inquiry reflects, in part, a tendency within liberal thought to view the individual as necessarily in conflict with the community and the forms of collective discipline that undergird it.

I want to rethink this polarity between deliberative and normative models through an interrogation of the practices of public sociability tied to the production and consumption of cassette-sermons in Egypt. In Cairo, where I conducted fieldwork for two years, cassette-recorded sermons of popular Islamic preachers, or khuṭabā' (sing. khaṭīb), have become a ubiquitous part of the contemporary social landscape. The recorded voices of these orators can be heard to echo from within cafés, butcher shops, private homes, and most forms of public transportation throughout the city. Beyond its use as a form of pious entertainment, taped-sermon audition in Egypt has become a popular technique for the cultivation of Islamic virtues, and thus, for the creation of the modes of public sociability these virtues uphold.

I will argue that the emphasis placed on the recuperation and cultivation of Islamic virtues by preachers and sermon audiences in Egypt needs to be seen in light of the role ascribed to those virtues in creating the ethical conditions for a domain of public deliberation and argumentation, a domain that over the course of this century has come to be seen by many Egyptian Muslims as necessary for the revival and strengthening of the Islamic community (*umma*). In contrast to a space for the formation of opinion through intersubjective reason, this arena is geared to the deployment of the disciplining power of ethical speech, a goal that takes public deliberation as one of its modalities. As such, these emergent practices cannot be understood as simply a modernizing turn toward an increasingly individualized form of rational piety, nor as the deployment of religion for the task of consolidating a national culture. Rather, they need to be analyzed in terms of a particular articulation of personal and political virtues within contemporary Islamic discourse.

Cassette-*Da'wa*

From their inception in the early 1970s, the production and consumption of sermon tapes has been associated with the broad movement known as *al-da'wa* (literally, a summons or call), and almost all of the preachers who make use of this medium refer to themselves, and are referred to by others, as *du'āt* (sing. *dā'iya*), i.e., those who undertake *da'wa*. The term *da'wa* has historically encompassed a wide range of meanings. As found in the Quran, it generally refers to God's invitation, addressed to humankind and transmitted through the prophets, to live in accord with God's will. Over the early centuries of Islam's development, *da'wa* came to be used increasingly to designate the content of that invitation, and in the works of some classical jurists it appears to be interchangeable with the terms *sharī'a* (the juridical codification of God's message) and *dīn* (often translated as "religion").[1] *Da'wa* also, however, carried another sense from early in Islam's historical career, one that has been central to contemporary Islamic thought: that of a duty, incumbent upon some or all members of the Islamic community, to actively encourage fellow Muslims in the pursuance of greater piety in all aspects of their lives.

The notion of *da'wa* seems to have received little systematic elaboration from the late medieval period until early in the twentieth century. While the "rediscovery" of the notion cannot be tied to any particular figure or institution, its current salience owes primarily to its development within Islamic opposition movements in the early twentieth century, most notably the Muslim Brotherhood. From the late 1920s, Ḥassān al-Banna, the founder of the Brotherhood, revived the classical notion of *da'wa* to define the goals of the organization, namely, the restoration of the Islamic community (*umma*) in the face of its increasing secularization under khedival rule.[2] The Brotherhood was particularly critical of the marginalization of Islamic doctrines and practices within the projects of

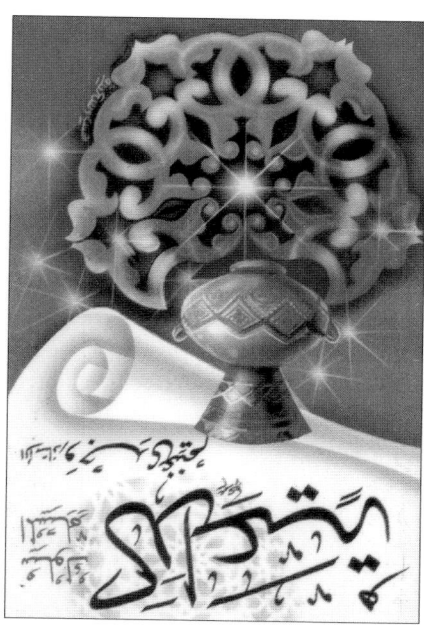

Wajdi Ghunīm, *Sulūk al-muslim ka dāʿiyya*
("The Conduct of a Muslim in His Capacity
as Moral Advocate")

A discussion of the activities and styles
of conduct incumbent upon Muslims in
the performance of their duty as moral
advocates

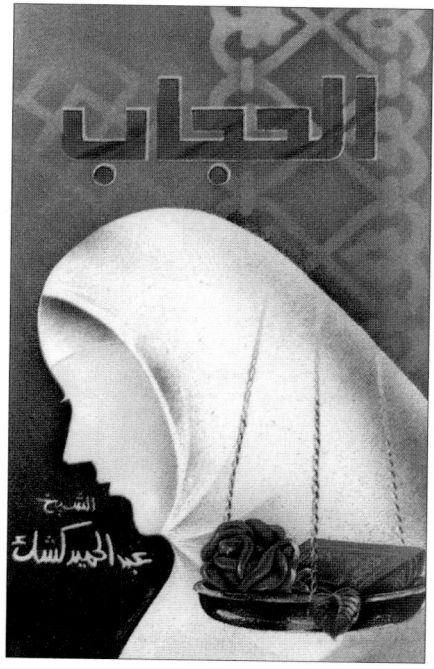

ʿAbd al-Hamīd Kishk, *al-Hijab*
("The Headscarf")

A discussion of the doctrinal
bases for the duty of wearing the
headscarf, and the importance of
the practice in the context of
contemporary society

social and political reform being promoted by nationalist thinkers, as well as of the failure of the established institutions of Islamic authority to oppose this process. By employing such modern political methods as print and recorded media, large-scale rallies, and training camps for the task of Islamic reform, the Brotherhood quickly went from a local grassroots association encouraging pious conduct to an international organization embodying considerable religious and political power and authority.

As elaborated by al-Banna, *da'wa* defined the mode of action by which moral and political reform were to be brought about. Brotherhood members were advised to go to mosques, schools, cafés, clubs, and other public locations to speak with whomever would listen about Islam, the Brotherhood, and the task of building a pious Muslim society. The Brotherhood also encouraged the Islamic practice of *isti'dhān*, wherein a member of the mosque assembly asks permission to address the gathering on matters relevant to the Muslim community. This practice, one that became increasingly widespread during subsequent decades, had the effect of enhancing the dialogical structure of social discourse within the mosque, thereby expanding its role as a key site of public discussion. Mass media also became central to the Brotherhood's effort. Books and short tracts by contemporary religious writers, as well as magazines covering national and international events considered relevant to Muslims, were widely circulated and competed with the more secular oriented publications of the nationalist movement. For *da'wa* speech and print (and later, audio media), the sermon provided a paradigmatic rhetorical form, a practice that stood in contrast to the European models of political oratory increasingly adopted by Egyptian secular nationalists. Al-Banna's sermons in particular became massively popular in Egypt and other Arab countries and were widely distributed in book and pamphlet form.

While the Brotherhood was eventually banned by the Egyptian state and many of its members imprisoned or driven underground, *da'wa* itself did not disappear. On the contrary, over the last half century *da'wa* has increasingly become a space for the articulation of a contestatory Islamic discourse on state and society, a discourse embodied in a diversified array of institutional forms including educational centres, preaching associations, thousands of private mosques, and an expanding network of publishing houses and other media. As a result, there now exists a vast literature offering instruction in the practice of "individual *da'wa*," understood as an ethical form of speech and action aimed at improving the moral conduct of one's fellow community members. The concept has also become a key point of reference for a wide variety of other activities in some way oriented toward promoting and fortifying the ethical practices that constitute Islamic modes of piety and community – from providing social services to the poor, to tutoring children at mosques, to selling Islamic books or tapes. This extensive network of commercial, welfare, and spiritual associations has provided the institutional framework for the emergence of a domain of practice and critique that, to a certain extent, remains autonomous from the interests and policies of the state.

Taxi Talk

The kind of discursive arena I am suggesting here can be illustrated through a conversation that I overheard during a taxi ride through downtown Cairo, a conversation that is rather typical of the kind of public interactions for which cassette-sermons have played a constitutive role. Taxis in Cairo frequently pick up more than one passenger. In this case I was sharing the ride with two other people, a teenage boy and a young woman who wore the *al-hijab* (headscarf). The taxi driver, who had a long beard and was dressed in a *jalabīyya* (a shirt-like garment worn by men in Egypt), was listening to a sermon tape by the popular preacher 'Umīr 'Ab∂ īl-Kāfi. At a certain point during the ride, as the tape came to an end, the boy sitting in front next to the driver asked him if he had any song music he might put on instead. After a few moments of awkward silence, the driver responded that music was *harām* (forbidden) in Islam. The boy looked surprised and irritated, but kept quiet and turned away. The driver, noting the boy's irritation, said, "Don't just look away, tell me what you're thinking. We can talk, there's no problem." "How can singing be *harām*?" said the boy, "Who told you that?" The driver replied, "Do you or don't you believe in the Quran and the *sunna*?"[3] The boy responded that of course he did. "Shouldn't we do everything in our lives to follow the *sunna*? Doesn't it tell us not only the rules of God, but as Muslims? Isn't it also a model for us?" Again, the boy, now getting impatient, concurred. On a roll, the driver moved to clinch the argument by means of a *hadīth*, an account of one of the Prophet's deeds or sayings: "When the Prophet used to hear songs, he would put his fingers in his ears, and considered music to be one of the devil's snares [*madkhal al-shaiṭān*]." The boy quickly retorted that the driver's *hadīth* was "*da'īf*," a classificatory term referring to a category of *hadīth* whose authority is of the weakest kind. Not ready to concede the point, the driver continued: "Do you believe there is nothing that is *harām* in religion [*dīn*]?" "Of course," the boy countered, "but I must know where the proof [*dalīl*] is for the *harām*. Someone can tell you today that driving a car is *harām*, and you'll stop driving. Then later you'll find out it was wrong, and start to drive again, unless you found out from the beginning whether what was called *harām* was really *harām* or just an erroneous invention." The driver, realizing now that he had better take another tack, asked: "Don't you think that drinking alcohol is *harām*? Do you know why? Because it interferes with prayer. It's the same with songs, when you hear songs your mind goes somewhere else and you can't pray." The boy retorted vigorously: "Alcohol is one thing, but the Quran says nothing about music. I pray, fast, and do all my obligations of worship [*i'bādāt*], and what is wrong if I hear songs as well? I am not doing anything *harām*!" At this point, the woman sitting in the back next to me entered the debate:

> But all the words of songs are about love and all of these things, so that when you go out you think about that rather than think about God. Your ears get used to hearing the songs, until you don't like to listen to the Quran. Well, then songs are prohibited so that at an adolescent age you don't think about things

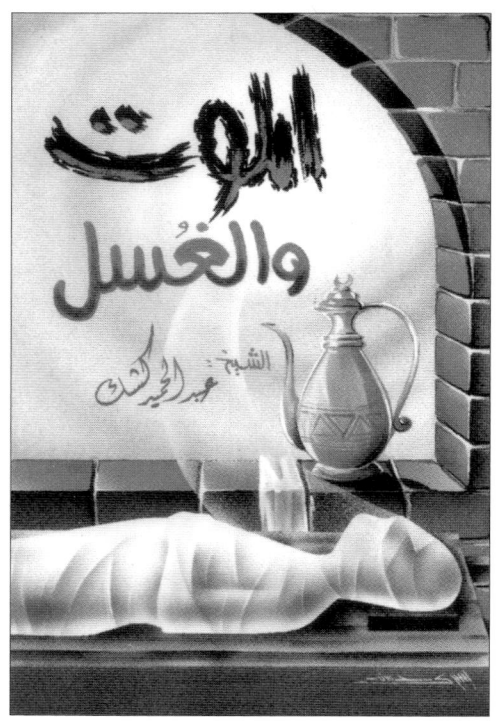

ʿAbd al-Ḥamīd Kishk, *al-Maut wa al-Ghusal*
("Death and the Preparation of the Corpse for Burial")

A description of the events that befall the soul at the moment
of death, as well as the doctrinal requirements for the preparation of the body by those who survive the deceased

that would lead you to illicit desire [*shahwāt*] and sin [*al-dhanb*]. Especially in this era and time, when the world is full of seductions that are always seeking to occupy your thoughts [*tishaghallak 'ala tūl*]. The sermon, on the other hand, makes you think of God, and brings you feelings of humility [*khushū'*] and regret [*nadam*].

She then quoted a verse from the Quran, but the boy immediately pointed out to her that the verse made no mention of music. "Yes," she concurred, "but it leads you to the reasoning of why music is *harām*." The driver nodded in agreement. The boy, not to be defeated, countered, "Love is not *harām* in Islam."

This conversation reveals a number of characteristics of a kind of public deliberation that has become increasingly prevalent in Egypt in recent decades. Note, to begin, the rather unstructured and informal character of this exchange. Circulating outside the boundaries of prescribed ritual practice, cassette-sermons have helped to create the context for this type of public argument, one that, as seen here, cuts across generational and gender lines in ways not possible within the ordered, sex-segregated space of the mosque. The relation between the speakers is not that of teacher to pupil but of relative equals, their speech structured around a presupposed orientation to correct Islamic practice. As opposed to the position of *khatīb* within the mosque, which is reserved only for men, the duty of *da'wa* falls to both men and women.

In addition, and contrary to what has often been suggested, reference to authoritative Islamic sources does not close debate. Instead, the lines of argument pivot precisely upon the proper interpretation of those sources. Whereas in liberal society religious authority is generally understood to impose undue constraints on free and open discussion and is thus unwelcome within the secular public sphere, here it provides the foundation upon which opposing viewpoints are articulated.

The exchange also points to a new familiarity with bases and styles of Islamic argumentation, evidenced, for example, in the boy's knowledge of the specific *hadīth* as well as its classification within the authoritative traditions. The advent of modern mass education, literacy, and the wide availability of written texts has equipped recent generations of Muslims in the Middle East with new competencies in traditional and contemporary Islamic scholarship. Cassette-sermons and recorded mosque lessons, likewise, enable listeners to expand and bolster their knowledge of Islamic traditions in moments of the day when the sort of concentration demanded by written texts would be impossible – and to do so, moreover, without the literacy skills required by such texts. All of the men I worked with had sought to acquire competence in these traditions, a task that has become easier with the proliferation of new institutions of Islamic learning associated with the revival movement, such as mosque study groups, private Islamic institutes, *da'wa* centres, and a vibrant market in Islamic books and tapes.

For many of those I worked with in Cairo who listened to cassette-sermons, *da'wa* entailed a commitment both to learn Islamic virtues and to encourage those around them through personal appeal to abide by Islamic moral standards – an activity they understood to be a duty placed upon them as Muslims. Sermon tapes helped one pursue both of these commitments. Sermons are listened to as a disciplinary practice geared to ethical self-improvement: a technique for the cultivation and training of certain forms of will, desire, emotion, and reason, conceived of as intellectual and bodily aptitudes or virtues that enable Muslims to act correctly as Muslims in accord with orthodox standards of Islamic piety. In addition, cassette-sermons provide a point of reference when discussing religious issues with acquaintances, or an inexpensive and easily accessible media form through which others might be encouraged to attend to their religious duties. Tapes are frequently exchanged between friends or acquaintances, both informally and in the context of mosque study groups, a type of association that many of the young men I worked with had at some point been involved in. Indeed, it is the difficulty of controlling a media form that can be so easily and inexpensively reproduced and circulated that has enabled the cassette tape to evade, to an extent far greater than other media, the regulatory purview of the state.

While the commercial aspect of the cassette-sermon should not be ignored, I would caution against placing too much emphasis upon it for the following reasons. First, the majority of the *khuṭabā'* whose sermons are available on cassette have no formal contractual relations with the tape companies and receive no remuneration from the sales of their tapes. Indeed, many *khuṭabā'* encourage people to record, reproduce, and disseminate their sermons, and even commercially produced tapes usually include a written statement prompting the buyer to copy the tape and make it available to others as part of doing *da'wa* work and as a means to receive beneficence from God. Moreover, the majority of tapes listened to in Egypt circulate outside of the structures of sale and marketing, through the practices of borrowing and exchange mentioned above. Many mosques in Egypt are now equipped with tape libraries that regular attendees can borrow from without charge.

In this way, cassette-sermons have played an important role in the transformation of *da'wa* in Egypt since the 1970s, as *da'wa* changed from an organizing principle within specific institutions to becoming a popular form of public practice and participation. Due largely to the mass popularity achieved through cassette circulation, popular preachers – most notably Shaykh 'Abd al-Ḥamīd Kishk (who died in 1996) – became rallying points and exemplary figures within an emerging counter-public of *da'wa* practitioners. Many of the young men I encountered explicitly identified cassette-sermons as an alternative to the televisual and press media promoted by the state. As one man told me, pointing to his cassette recorder: "This is the only mass media [*al-i'alām*] I need. The [state-controlled] television and the newspapers never discuss the important events and issues. We would never find out about what is really going on even here in Egypt without these tapes."

What I want to draw attention to here, however, is how *da'wa*, as developed first within the Brotherhood and later in many other institutional locations, became the conceptual site wherein the concerns, public duties, character, and virtues of an activist Muslim citizen were elaborated and practiced. In the case of the men I met in Cairo, this practice was woven into their daily activities. When speaking with colleagues at work, one might remind the others to thank God for their successes. While riding a bus, one might point out to a fellow passenger the error of getting angry with the slow driver. Da'wa may even take the form of conversations among friends, in discussions over whether one may pray in a mosque built over a tomb, or whether donations collected at the mosque should go to Bosnia or be used to buy school-books for the needy in the neighbourhood.

The *Dā'iya* as Muslim Citizen

While the ethical and social norms of citizen conduct are oriented around the notion of a broad unity of practicing Muslims, an *umma*, they also are grounded in political technologies of modern national citizenship. That is, while *da'wa* provides conceptual resources grounded in a long tradition of Islamic practice and scholarly inquiry, these resources are put to novel uses within a contemporary situation shaped by modern political institutions, pedagogical techniques, and media forms, as well as by notions of civic responsibility grounded in the idea and experience of national citizenship. As in other modernizing states, in Egypt the process of recruiting citizens into the structures of national political life produced expectations, aspirations, and participatory demands before the administrative, ideological, and security apparatuses that could accommodate these demands had been fully developed. In this context, *da'wa* became one of the critical sites for the expression of those demands engendered by political modernization, especially among those ill-versed in the literacy of newsprint. Resituated in this way, these demands gave new impetus and direction to a project aimed at fortifying the bases of the Islamic community. The elaboration of *da'wa* as a civic duty, in this sense, involved neither what has been termed "retraditionalization" nor, on the other hand, simply the instrumentalization of a traditional category within a modernizing or secularizing project.

As opposed to the national public sphere centred around the press and televisual media, the *da'wa* public reveals a more marked supranational focus evident, for example, in the considerable attention given within sermons to the plight of Muslims worldwide as well as the interest shown by cassette-sermon audiences in such issues. As one man told me after hearing a tape by an Egyptian *khaṭīb* on Muslims in the U.S.:

> When one hears these things, like that people in the U.S. or in Bosnia are taking up Islam, one is stirred. You ask yourself, if they are turning to Islam there, how is it that I as a Muslim am not even committed in my practice? What do they have over me? We are all equals after all. So hearing this moves me toward committing to Islam, and reforming my practice.

In this way, as numerous scholars have pointed out, mass media have transformed the political and religious context wherein Islamic virtues are cultivated and practiced, endowing it with a distinctly transnational focus for participants of this movement. This tendency has been further enhanced by the fact that many of the *khuṭabā'* whose tapes are listened to in Egypt are from other Muslim countries, particularly Saudi Arabia and, somewhat less frequently, Jordan and Lebanon. Furthermore, the leading contemporary *khuṭabā'* and other significant figures of the *da'wa* movement carry on ongoing associations with mosques and *da'wa* centres not only in other Arab countries, but also in Europe, the U.S., and Canada.

Note also that this practice does not map onto the constitutionally demarcated separation of public and private but rather traverses this distinction in a way that is often uncomfortable to those with secular-liberal sensibilities. *Da'wa* is undertaken in the street, on public transportation, at the workplace, or in the home. It may take place between friends or co-workers, though it also occurs between total strangers, as in the case of the taxi ride cited above. From a liberal perspective, *da'wa* is seen as encouraging an unwarranted intrusion into the privacy of others, especially as it entails entering into what are considered to be personal matters of religious faith. *Du'at* render public issues that the liberal state relegates to the private sphere of individual choice – the modesty of one's dress, the precision of gesture in prayer, the danger of gossip, and the proximity of unrelated men and women in both the workplace and the home, as well as questions of Quranic interpretation and religious authority. For liberals, these issues tend to be viewed as either insignificant (e.g., precision in prayer, gossip) and thus unworthy of public attention or, alternatively, as matters of individual preference (e.g., dress, gender relations) and as such protected by private law. *Da'wa* for this reason constitutes an obstacle to the state's attempt to secure a social domain where national citizens are free to make modern choices, as it *re-politicizes* those choices, subjecting them to a public scrutiny oriented around the task of establishing the conditions for the practice of Islamic virtues.

Politics and Ethics

Thus, the media and associational infrastructure put into place by the *da'wa* movement has created the conditions for a kind of publicness, one grounded in certain classical Islamic concepts but reformulated in response to a variety of contemporary conditions.[4] That is to say, reformers like al-Banna and 'Abd al-Ḥamīd Kishk revived a notion of *da'wa* as a civic duty, the performance of which, conceptually and historically, had long been defined as a condition for the vitality of the Muslim collective. In its contemporary elaboration, *da'wa* defines a kind of practice involving the public use of a mode of reasoning whereby the correctness of an action is argued and justified in the face of error, doubt, indifference, or counter-argument. I say "public" precisely insomuch as to assume the position of *dā'iya* (the one who does *da'wa*) is to adopt the rhetorical stance of a member of the Islamic *umma* acting on behalf of that particular historical project (and

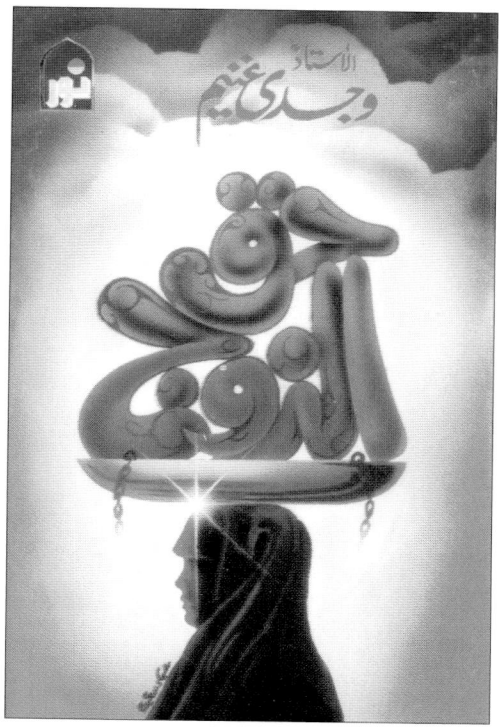

Wajdi Ghunīm, *Ḥaqq al-zauj*
("The Rights of the Husband")
A description of the various rights owed to husbands from their
wives, children, and extended family

thus not simply as an individual concerned for his or her own moral conduct). In this sense, although such a *da'wa* public has only become possible with the contemporary emergence of a range of Islamic institutions, it is less an empirical entity than a framework for a particular type of action. It is constituted whenever and wherever individuals enter into that form of discourse geared toward upholding or improving the moral condition of the collective as a whole. As a type of activity aimed at shaping other practices through persuasion, exhortation, and deliberation, it is fundamentally a political practice, and hence is distinct both from the web of personal relationships and public representations of cultural identity (e.g., public ceremonies, Islamic media productions), neither of which are grounded in processes of deliberation. Indeed, *da'wa* emerges not at a point of commonality, but precisely at one of difference, where a discrepancy in practice makes argument necessary.

While *da'wa* frequently takes the form of discussion and deliberation, its paradigmatic speech genre is the sermon. Notably, the interpretive norms informing Islamic homiletic traditions foreground the capacity of ethical speech – particularly speech imbued with the language of the Quran and the teachings of the *sunna* – to move the sensitive heart toward correct practice. A well-crafted sermon is understood to evoke in the listener the affective dispositions that underlie ethical conduct and reasoning and which, through repeated listening, may become sedimented in the listener's character. Enabled in part by the mediatization of sermons on cassette, the norms governing sermon practice have been extended by the *da'wa* movement to the dialogical context of public discourse. Within this arena, speech is deployed in order to construct moral selves, to reshape character, attitude, and will in accord with contemporary standards of pious behaviour. The efficacy of an argument here devolves not solely on its power to gain cognitive assent on the basis of its superior reasoning, as would be the case in some versions of a liberal public sphere, but also on its ability to move the moral self toward correct modes of being and acting. What joins the practice of delivering or listening to a sermon with that of arguing with a neighbour is a conception of the rhetorical force of ethical speech to shape character. Deliberative and disciplinary moments, in other words, are thoroughly interwoven and interdependent within this arena.

As conceived by its participants, the *da'wa* public constitutes that space of communal reflexivity and action understood as necessary for perfecting and sustaining the totality of practices upon which an Islamic society depends. For the *du'at* (those undertaking *da'wa*) I spoke to over the course of my fieldwork in Cairo, this practice has been necessitated by the erosion of the Islamic character of society under the impact of what is most often referred to as *al-ghazwa al-fikri* ("ideological conquest," i.e., Western cultural imperialism), and particularly its forms of consumerism and sensualism that are seen to be corrosive of the virtues enabling one to live a Muslim life. In this context, *da'wa* responds to the need for an individual and communal praxis to uphold what is perceived to be an enfeebled Muslim community. The scope of this practice is not limited to issues of personal piety, but necessarily extends to address such matters as the methods and content of education, appropriate styles of popular entertainment, modes of public conduct for men and women, and even appropriate forms of employment. In short, as a project aimed at securing the conditions necessary for the practice of Islamic virtues, *da'wa* entails an intervention into, and transformation of, the activities and institutions that constitute the community. By promoting the cultivation of sensibilities and the adoption of certain goals, the movement shapes the form of collective life and culture that its adherents, as Muslims and national citizens, will endorse, the arguments they will find persuasive, the projects they will contribute their energies to.

Contestatory Religion

Although the practice of *da'wa* does not presuppose the idea of the nation so much as that of the collective of those who practice Islamic virtues, national institutions are a necessary object of the *da'iya*'s discourse insomuch as they shape the conditions of social existence for Muslims in Egypt. As is well known, through the processes central to modern nation-building, such institutions as education, worship, social welfare, and family have been incorporated to varying degrees within the regulatory apparatuses of the modernizing state. Whether one is entering into business contracts, selling wares on the street, disciplining children, adding a room to a house – in all births, marriages, deaths – at each juncture the state is present as overseer or guarantor, defining limits, procedures, and necessary preconditions. As a consequence, in Egypt as elsewhere, modern politics and the forms of power it deploys, have become a condition for the practice of many personal activities. When the state acts in ways that foreclose the possibility of living in accord with the Islamic standards promoted by the movement – such as forbidding schoolgirls from wearing headscarves, broadcasting television serials that show what is considered indecent public behaviour (e.g., kissing), or cutting back on the amount of time dedicated to learning the Quran in schools – *khuṭabā'* use the mosque sermon to publicly criticize these actions, a critique that is then quickly distributed on tape.

The Egyptian state is anxious about the loyalties and sensibilities of the religious subject being forged within the *da'wa* movement, and has sought, in response, to establish a network of secular cultural institutions as a prophylaxis. Thus, within the government-controlled press one can find numerous articles calling for the development and expansion of after-school cultural activities – music, literature, debating clubs, arts, and sports. For "normal young people," Islam – as individual spiritual practice – should stand as a brief interlude between the two primary modes of existence around which the times and spaces of daily life are arranged, work and leisure. Indeed, it is precisely this disjuncture between the kind of public subject fashioned within the *da'wa* movement and one who will perform the role of national citizen inhabiting a private domain of unconditional immunity that has made culture a site of considerable struggle. For *khuṭabā'* and their audiences, the danger of Western cultural forms and popular media entertainment lies in the fact that they engender emotions and character attributes incompatible with those that in their view enable one to live as a Muslim. As a *khaṭīb* I worked with told me, echoing a widely held opinion, "the enemies of Islam use *fann*, *adab*, *thaqāfa*, and *mūda* [art, literature, culture, and fashion] to attack Islam," a comment explicitly acknowledging the Western and secular genealogy of these categories of discourse and practice. Much of the criticism found in cassette-sermons is directed at media entertainment, film stars, popular singers, and television serials. Thus, Shaykh Kishk's most well-known sermons are his critiques of the immensely popular national icons, the singers Umm Kulthūm and Muḥammed 'Abd al-Whāb, while the *khaṭīb* 'Umar 'Abd al-Kāfi is best known for having convinced a number of famous film actresses to give up their acting careers.

The state's attempt to control *da'wa* has met two serious obstacles. One is grounded in the limited resources and capacities of the economically enfeebled Egyptian state. The second, on the other hand, owes to the very heterogeneity of the state itself. Many of the state-administered religious organizations include sizable factions sympathetic to the same religious arguments that their own institutions have been called on to officially denounce and combat. It is also notable that most of the well-known Egyptian *khuṭāba'* of recent years – e.g., Muḥammed Mitwalli al-Sha'arāwi, Muḥammed al-Ghazāli, 'Abd al-Sabbūr Shahīn, 'Abd al-Ḥamid Kishk – have all been affiliated at some point in their careers both with state institutions *and* with major opposition movements, primarily the Muslim Brothers. Shayhk Kishk, one of the most unequivocally oppositional public voices in the last thirty years, was never entirely outside of the official structures he so powerfully criticized. While Kishk worked for a brief period as an itinerant *khatib* within the system of mosques belonging to the private *da'wa* association al-Jam'iyya al-Shar'iyya, for most of his life he preached for the Ministry of Religious Affairs at the al-Malik mosque in the al-Hadaiq al-Qubba quarter of Cairo. He retained his position as *khaṭīb* at this mosque from 1964 until 1981, despite having become one of the most virulent critics of the Egyptian government and having been subject to all forms of state repression, including two periods of imprisonment.

In short, while the state has tried to harness the Islamic pedagogical, juridical, and homiletic institutions to a variety of national goals (many now tied to issues of state security), this has not led to the wholesale abandonment within these institutions of practices and discourses that articulate with the field of *da'wa*. As a result, many of those active in *da'wa* don't categorically identify the state as an enemy or antagonist. Rather, among those involved in the movement one finds a plurality of arguments and opinions in regard to the state, ranging from outright condemnation, to distrust and ambivalence, to indifference.

While in practice *da'wa* may entail an oppositional stance in regard to the state in the various ways I have described, this type of public does not in its present form play a mediatory role between *state* and *society*. In other words, the practice of *da'wa* does not take place within or serve to uphold that domain of associational life referred to as civil society. Rather, the *dā'iya's* narrative locates itself within the temporal frame of an Islamic *umma*, and in relation to the succession of events that characterize its mode of historicity. In this regard, when asked where the effect of the *da'wa* movement was most evident, rarely did those I spoke with refer to "Egyptian society" or "the nation." Instead, when indicating the positive impact of *da'wa* most of them would refer to specific popular neighbourhoods where in their view residents' neighbourly conduct accorded with Islamic standards: assistance was provided to the sick and poor by the community, those behaving improperly (e.g., drinking, swearing, fighting, dressing inappropriately) were readily confronted by community members, most people prayed and attended mosque regularly. While participants of this movement clearly considered themselves to be Egyptian citizens, they also cultivated sentiments, loyalties, and styles of public conduct that stood in tension with the moral and political exigencies, and modes of self-identification of national citizenship. In this sense, they constitute what I have called a counter-public.

Dialogic Conditions

Cassette-sermons have played a central role in the creation of the public domain I have thus far described. By allowing the sermon to move outside the more rigid framework of the mosque, the cassette medium enabled this oratorical form to become a key instrument of *da'wa*. Traditionally, the Friday sermon occurs within a highly structured spatial and temporal frame, as a duty upon the Muslim community as established in the exemplary practices of the Prophet.[5] As a traditional and obligatory component of Muslim weekly routine, the *khaṭīb*'s performance anchors its authority in its location and timing, in the *khaṭīb*'s competent enactment of a role established within the practices of Muslim societies. During the initial years of their use, taped sermons permitted an infinite extension and replication of this performance but remained beholden to it, a mere supplement, and not a departure or transformation, of a long-standing authoritative Islamic oratorical form. Sermon speech was now displaced outside its assigned locus but only as a re-presentation of an original founding performance to which it referred. However, with the increased popularity of such tapes, the development of tape markets, new practices of listening, association, commentary, and tape-based *khuṭabā'*, taped sermons have become increasingly independent from the mosque performances that they reproduce: a signifying practice of their own, related to but not subsumable within mosque sermons.

The fact that taped sermons may be widely distributed and repeatedly listened to has meant that they are now subject to a higher degree of public scrutiny in terms of both scholarly rigour and general argument, a fact that has further accentuated the dialogicality of the practice. For example, in late 1996, the widely acclaimed Egyptian *khaṭīb* Muḥammed Hassan put out a re-recording of his most popular sermon, on the death of the Prophet, which was prefaced by a studio-recorded apology for certain errors in *ḥadīth* citation he had made in the original. The question of an error in a *khaṭīb*'s discourse, which earlier would have been solely a concern of religious specialists, had become a topic to be addressed before the mass public of sermon listeners, many of whom now take an active interest in these issues. In this way, *khuṭabā'* are now subject to assessment by increasingly well-informed audiences.

Hassan's apology illustrates the way the contemporary sermon, as the privileged rhetorical form of the *da'wa* movement, has come to reflect the set of demands placed on it by the new public context wherein it now circulates. Within this sphere, taped-sermons mediate multiple forms of argument and contestation. *khuṭabā'*, for example, not only provide a critical commentary on trends within society, actions taken by the state, and international events seen as important to Muslims, but also commonly draw attention to erroneous positions put forward by other *khuṭabā'* or religious scholars. Likewise, sermon listeners frequently disagree with arguments made by *khuṭabā'*, both in content and in style. Many of my informants, for example, felt that Shaykh Kishk's style of criticizing public figures directly and openly, at the time of the regime of Anwar Sadat (1970–1981), was a violation of the ethics of public criticism within Islam. This points to another level of dialogue mediated by cassette-sermons: namely, tapes frequently serve as a catalyst for arguments between listeners about the responsibility of the *khaṭīb* in relation to the national state.

The Virtues of Civic Debate

Within *da'wa* literature and among the young men of my study, the performance of *da'wa* is understood to be predicated upon a prior cultivation of the virtues. They play more than an instrumental role: as with other practices that Muslims consider duties – such as prayer, fasting, or alms giving – *da'wa* has conditions of enactment that include a particular set of virtues. In this sense, it is both an activity that upholds the possibility for the virtuous performance of other Muslim practices and a virtuous act in itself.

As I mentioned earlier, much of the Islamic print and audio media today concerns the qualities the *dā'iya* must possess in order to perform the civic duty of *da'wa*. Such discourses fall within a long and continuing tradition of Islamic ethical and pedagogical writings on the virtues that uphold individual piety. Where they depart from this tradition is in addressing the virtues, not simply from an ethical point of view, but also from a rhetorical one, as conditions for the persuasiveness of speech and action within the public domain of *da'wa* practice. Virtuous conduct, in other words, is seen by the movement both as an end in itself and as a means internal to the dialogic process by which the reform of society is secured.

The virtues of the *dā'iya* as cultivated and practiced within daily life tend to be understood behaviourally, as disciplined ways of being and acting, ways for which the body's performances and expressions constitute an integral part. They are cultivated gradually through disciplinary practices, such as prayer, Quranic recitation and memorization, *ḥadīth* study, and listening to sermons, as well as by undertaking the practice of *da'wa* itself.

Some of the virtues specific to the practice of *da'wa* are addressed within *da'wa* literature under the term *adab al-da'wa* (loosely, etiquette of *da'wa*), and include those qualities that ensure the orderliness and civility of public interaction. Much of *da'wa* print and cassette media focuses on the task of developing these qualities. A tape by the popular *khaṭīb* Wajdi Ghunīm entitled "The Muslim as *Dā'iya*" provides the listener with a list of thirteen requirements that every individual in his or her capacity as *dā'iya* must adhere to. Among these he includes friendliness, gentleness of speech (*al-rifq wa al-līn*), and temperateness, as well as neatness and cleanliness. Throughout the tape, Ghunim provides numerous illustrations of how *da'wa* should be undertaken, as in the following:

> Say we are sitting and speaking with a fellow who then gets upset. I'll say to him, O' my brother, may God be generous with you; O' my brother, may God open your heart and mine [*yashraḥ ṣadrak wa ṣadri*]. Or say someone is sitting nearby smoking a cigarette, and then comes and offers you one. Take advantage of the opportunity. Don't try to take the pack of cigarettes away from him. No. *da'wa* always entails politeness [*adab*]. Say to him: O' Brother, may God restore you to health. I ask God that you stop smoking. May God protect your chest [*ṣadrak*] from your act.

The prior cultivation of such virtues as friendliness, temperateness, and gentleness of speech ensures that *da'wa*, as a public act, will be conducted in a calm, respectful manner, protected from the kind of passions that would vitiate the act and the social benefit that it seeks to realize. The *adab* of *da'wa*, in other words, entails not a simple suppression of the passions, but their moderation or attunement in accord with an authoritative model of the virtues. A speech devoid of passion – what Muhammed Hassān, referring to certain modern media styles, calls "cold culture [*al-thaqafa al-barida*] addressing only the intellect [*al-adhan*]" – lacks the rhetorical force to move the moral self toward correct behaviour – the central aim of *da'wa* public discourse.

Also necessary for the practice of *da'wa* is the virtue of courage (*shaja'a*). Indeed, courage was one of the qualities most often cited by the men I knew in identifying the excellence of a particular *da'iya*. The exemplary figures here are again the *khuṭaba'*. One of the most commonly mentioned attributes of a true *da'iya-khaṭīb* is his courage to speak the truth in the face of the quite real danger of arrest and torture by the Egyptian state. Tales of Shaykh Kishk's feats of courage while in prison, including standing undaunted before attack dogs brought to his cell, are widely known and frequently recited by *da'wa* participants. In addition, many of the young men I knew in Cairo cited a lack of courage as largely responsible for the failure of people to enact *da'wa*, and worried that Egypt would become like the U.S. where (they had heard) no one dares to speak or take action in public on the behalf of others out of fear.

The virtues of sincerity (*ikhlas*), humility (*khushū'*), and fear of God (*taqwa* or *khauf*) are also frequently associated with the performance of *da'wa* and are given great emphasis in sermons and manuals on the practice. As elaborated within classical Islamic moral doctrine, these dispositions endow a believer's heart with the capacities of discrimination necessary for proper moral conduct and reasoning. In the rhetorical context of public deliberation discussed here, this understanding has implications for both speaker and listener. For the speaker's discourse to result not merely in abstract understanding but in the kind of practical knowledge that impacts on how one lives, it must be imbued with those virtues that enable it to reach the heart of the listener. Alternatively, from the perspective of the listener, without having first imbued the heart with the requisite emotional dispositions, he or she will be incapable of actually grasping and digesting what is at stake in the discourse. The virtues, that is to say, are a condition for the effectiveness of both the dā'iya's utterance and the listener's audition. As affective-volitional dispositions sedimented in one's character, they form the evaluative background enabling one to act and speak reasonably and effectively within the public realm.

The kind of public arena that has been created by the da'wa movement in Egypt is both normative and deliberative, a domain for both subjection to authority and the exercise of individual reasoning. It is less an empirical structure than a framework for a kind of action, one intertwining moments of learning, dialogue, and dispute, as practices necessary for the moral guidance of the collective. In this sense, one does not undertake sermon audition and the associated practices of da'wa with a preformed or unchanging set of interests and goals. Rather, one comes to acquire an understanding of the good and the virtues that enable its realization in the course of participation in this domain. This learning is not simply a process of acculturation or ideological indoctrination, insomuch as both of these notions fail to capture the extent to which one's participation within this arena necessarily involves practices of argument, criticism, and debate. Although some shared orientations and languages are a prerequisite for this type of public engagement, and one participates with the assumption that there is a proper and divinely sanctioned form of life to which one aspires, this does not imply a uniformity of thought and action. Rather, the aim is to uphold those practices understood to be essential to an Islamic society, practices whose proper form, however, must be continuously determined by public acts of guidance, argument, and discussion by all members of the collective.

My argument is that da'wa should not be viewed as simply an Islamic rendition of the normative structure of the public sphere, one enabled and produced through an incorporation of Islamic symbols and culturally grounded frames of reference. To focus solely on the process through which the concepts and modular institutions of modern liberal-democracy have been inflected by non-Western traditions is to fail to explore the often parallel projects of renewal and reform launched from within the conceptual and practical horizons of those traditions. This is not to reinstate the binary of tradition and modernity, but, on the contrary, to point to processes that cannot be adequately analyzed via this opposition. It is for this reason that I find unhelpful discussions of contemporary Islamic movements in terms of the notion of an "invented tradition," a modern institution in the guise of an ancient one. An approach adequate to the historical form I have described here will necessarily understand tradition as a set of discourses and practices that, while enabled by modern power, nonetheless articulate a politics and a set of sensibilities incommensurate with many of the secular-liberal assumptions that attend that power. Of course, the Islamic tradition is not the only framework within which the actions of the participants of the *da'wa* movement are meaningful, nor by any means the most powerful.

Lastly, note that while debate and argumentation are ascribed a salient role within the Islamic counter-public I have examined here, this does not imply a move toward liberalism. Indeed, many of the social norms that the practice of *da'wa* has helped to strengthen in Egypt would not be acceptable for most liberals. *Da'wa* is not geared toward securing the freedom of individuals to pursue their own interests, but rather, their conformity with a divine model of moral conduct. This model is not static, a labour of timeless repetition, but involves an historical dynamism derived precisely from the sort of practices of reasoning and argument foregrounded by the *da'wa* movement, practices that depart from the assumption of an authoritative corpus by which the status of current practices may be assessed. Thus, while liberals may wish to take strong issue with this tradition of public reasoning, those concerned with democracy and its cultural conditions and possibilities in the contemporary world will want to pay close attention to religious movements of this kind.

NOTES

All unattributed quotations are from conversations I recorded during research conducted in Egypt between 1994 and 1996. Translations mine.

1.   On the history of the concept and practice of *da'wa* and its classical origins, see Isma'il Al-Faruqi, "On the Nature of the Islamic da'wah," *International Review of Missions* 65 (1976): 391–409; Milo Mendel, "The Concept of 'ad-Da'wa al-Islamiyya': Towards a Discussion of the Islamic Reformist Religio-Political Terminology," *Archiv Orientalni* 63 (1995): 286–304; Jacques Waardenburg, "The da'wa of Islamic Movements," *Actas, XVI Congreso Union Europeenne d'Arabisants et d'Islamisants* (1995): 539–549.

2.   Mendel, 295.

3.   The *sunna* refers to the Prophet's exemplary behaviour as witnessed by a contemporary and passed down via an authoritative chain of transmitters.

4.   My own discussion of the Islamic public sphere overlaps with Armando Salvatore's "Staging Virtue: The Disembodiment of Self-Correctness and the Making of Islam as Public Norm," in *Islam – Motor or Challenge of Modernity, vol. 1, Yearbook of the Sociology of Islam,* ed. Georg Stauth (Hamburg: Transaction Books, 1998) and "Self-Empowerment, Communicative Action and the Market in the Formation of an 'Islamic Publicness': Some Theoretical Reflections," unpublished paper (Humboldt-Universitat zu Berlin, Fakultatsinstitut Sozialwissenschaften, 1996).

5.   The most thorough and interesting anthropological works on Islamic sermons are Patrick Gaffney's *The Prophet's Pulpit: Islamic Preaching in Contemporary Egypt* (Berkeley: University of California Press, 1994) and Richard Antoun's *Muslim Preacher in the Modern World: A Jordanian Case Study in Contemporary Perspective* (Princeton: Princeton University Press, 1989).

Local Sounds, Popular Technologies: History and Historicity in Andean Radio

Daniel Fisher

In the Bolivian and Peruvian Andes, radio broadcasting and listening have been intricately involved with the production and elaboration of place-based notions of identity and agency. While radio has a lengthy history in the Andes as a site of political organization and cultural objectification, radio's particular characteristics, both in terms of the media's perceived historicity and in terms of a phenomenology of listening, are rarely questioned for how they may speak to epistemologies of place and person. Here I explore the historical soundscape of Andean radio, foregrounding the synaesthetic, place-making engagements that radio's mobilization entails, and addressing radio as a site for the elaboration and allocation of cultural value. Radio and sound have played significant roles in the historical constitution of indigeneity, as well as in the making of contemporary Andean social life. Bringing together the history and historicity of sound technologies in the Andes, I will analyze several issues raised by the "indigenization" of Andean radio.

Andean Radios

Between the 1930s and the 1950s, Bolivia's highland miners and rural peasantry began to establish radio stations in the context of great social and political restructuring. This involved the consolidation of labour unions' political legitimacy at a national level, the enfranchisement of indigenous and non-literate populations previously at the margins of national political discourse, and a revaluation of indigenous cultural forms as elements of a national history and populist politics. These developments corresponded simultaneously to an increased efficacy and radicalism on the part of organized labour in Bolivia, and to the recognition by both political elites and marginalized groups of a newly constituted "popular" sphere and its power in maintaining or securing the privileges of their own constituencies and class factions.[1] As central technologies in the development of organized union activity in Bolivia and cultural objectification in Peru, radio stations played a central part in the advent and subsequent transformation of these "national" social topographies.

In the process these stations became prominent features of many mountain communities, broadcasting everything from radio plays and music to political bulletins and news, utilizing Aymara and Quechua, in addition to Spanish, as broadcast languages. More recently, between 1979 and 1982 these stations enabled widespread resistance to a series of military coups in Bolivia.[2] As various political factions sought to reestablish military leadership of the state following the demise of the Banzer regime, rural radio stations and their DJs aided in the organization of nationwide strikes – strikes that by 1982 proved crucial for preventing the continued domination of a military elite. Chaining their signals from station to station, rural-based miners' radios countered a military blackout of other forms of national communication (e.g., newspapers and television) – broadcasting troop movements and calling general strikes, often in the face of direct military attack.

In such contexts radio broadcasting can be understood as a technology central to the elaboration of a "popular," workers' public, as the following appeal, broadcast during the 1980 military coup of Luis Garcia Meza, suggests:

> Brother if you are listening to us, brother son of the mine worker, of the peasant, of the factory worker, brother if you have not such a high military rank, you are aware that the Bolivian *pueblo* is your own brother, it is because of this that we call on you not to fire against your own brothers, against your own fathers....[3]

This broadcast pragmatically indexes differences in social standing and cultural background between low-ranking soldiers and their officers, gathering the former into a masculine, familial *pueblo* of miners and other workers. Such incidents have also entered a national discursive archive of popular heroism, providing a potent figure of popular struggle for labourers, activists, and academics alike, kept alive by the place of media in contemporary struggles against neo-liberal formations of global (and local) capital.

Looking at Bolivia and Peru, it is possible to discern two different national trajectories for radio. In the former, radio's development was in large part shaped by its location in the midst of labour politics and civil unrest. In Peru, however, where mining and labour politics have not figured so centrally in the history of radio, the media has played a more overtly "cultural" role. The mandate for Radio Tawantinsuyo in Cusco, Peru, for example, may be interpreted as an elite project of self-definition through the elaboration of discursively constructed, but sonically materialized, place-based identities. Raul Montesinos Espejo founded Radio Tawantinsuyo in the early 1940s and his numerous activities exemplify long-standing nationalist and regional figurations of Andean identities and Andean places.[4] His endeavours to distinguish an Andean identity and Inca pride should be understood in the context of a racial marking of the highlands as *mestizo* and "Indian" by turn-of-the-century coastal elites, and thus in the context of *Cusqueño* elites' complementary efforts to distinguish themselves as more "Peruvian" and "cultured" than what they characterized as effeminate, Europeanized *Limeños*.[5] The very naming of the station itself as *Tawantinsuyo*, which is a Quechua compound term meaning the four corners or states of the Inca empire, conjoined history and place with the sounds of an "Andean" authenticity. Montesinos' aesthetic sensibility here joins a regional aspiration for an explicitly Andean radiophony.

In January 1999, for three *soles* each (about $1.50 Canadian), DJs at Radio Tawantinsuyo read personalized birthday messages, greetings, and news on the air, carrying these *mensajes* beyond the confines of Cusco to small towns and hamlets throughout the adjacent sacred valley and beyond. Such *mensajes* circulate within a broader sonic mediascape given life through the social index of genre, and reproduced and managed by the various projects and perspectives of DJs at stations such as Radio Tawantinsuyo. *Huaynos*, for example, are a form of Quechua love song whose melodic and rhythmic structure has been historically played by small ensembles of guitar, *charango*, and flute as well as by larger groups of brass instruments, such as trumpet and sousaphone. When I asked Juan Quispe[6] (a music producer and DJ at Radio Tawantinsuyo) to elaborate on different types of *huaynos,* he responded by outlining a general typology of *Peruvian* music. Quispe manages small bands who take this generic form to electric bass and guitar and self-produces cassette tapes for circulation in Cusco's sacred valley. Quispe distanced the African-influenced genre of *musica criolla* (made popular in North America by such performers as Susana Baca) from the *campesino huayno* (an Andean genre itself a hybrid, decidedly "modern," tradition) by reference to the former's "professional," "educated" listeners. Such typologies are given social life in the circulation of radio sounds, and Quispe may entail his audience in his practice, discursively mobilizing genre to make explicit socially audible distinctions. These "classes" of music, as Quispe called them, suggest that in musical discourses around Cusco, social difference resonates in sounds that index social categories; correspondingly, such categories may have ramifications for how sounds are experienced and valued.

The ways in which such systems articulate genre with a social project can be heard in the words of Mario Molina, a *Cusqueño* DJ and music producer, speaking to the filmmaker John Cohen in *Dancing with the Incas*:

> Because I was born here, I listen to the music that they play on the *pincullu*. I find it both nostalgic and peaceful. I feel this music in my soul. Just like a man who knows the music of Chopin or Schubert. He listens and he also feels the same sensation. The music relaxes him, it feeds his spirit. So I wonder why these foreigners who come here, when they talk about our music, indigenous Peruvian music, they always label the music "ethno." As though it were a music that's a bit primitive.
>
> Because many tourists come to this city another type of music is presented. It is put on by owners of restaurants frequented by tourists. Perhaps it is the wrong type of music. It's Latin American music – more than anything it has the influence of Bolivia, and some from Argentina with the sambas they play. The instruments played are not the authentic ones. They play guitar, panpipes and the bomba. These are not from here. The music I record is not of that type. Those who record here themselves buy

the recording on cassettes and records. The music is recorded here and returns to the puna.[7]

For Molina, his radio and recording practices explicitly engage discourses that peripheralize Andean musics as "ethno," and he sees himself returning the sounds of the Andes to the Puna, crafting a new circulation of sound that stresses the local in the production and consumption of the authentically Andean. He thus inverts a hierarchy of style and positions his endeavours within a broader, international social field.

One can join such positioned aesthetics and "contextualizing" aspects of socially mobilized sound with the construction of particular places in the Andes, both in the discursive metaphors used to describe those places and in the ways in which Andean radios resound in particular experiences of audition. Attending to such sounds as aesthetically ordered, socially dense phenomena that both resound in places and do the social work of signifying those places may enrich our understanding of Bolivian revolutionary broadcasts and the linkage of song and city on Cusco's Radio Tawantinsuyo. The local in the Andes, made manifest in *mensajes*, musical form, or the sounds of revolution, "gathers" the nation and region within a sonic space. And these DJs' voices may concretize the imagined space of Peru's sacred valley in the sounds of its many radios, a space made familiar by the non-present voices of *locutores* (radio announcers) bearing news of kin and clan, *affine* and *ayllu*.

In Bolivia, the dynamic of national form and local sounds has been explored in the context of folklore contests, and Bolivian radio stations often serve as "stages" for performances and broadcasts of folklore, featuring the songs and sounds felt to be most indigenous or most representative of "Bolivian" culture as articulated along lines of both regional indigenous and Hispanic histories. Such objectifications of cultural form have not gone unnoticed by anthropologists, who have questioned how the staging of culture in such contests becomes one means for the creation of gendered national identities as well as for the navigation of the institutions and practices of the state by marginalized social actors.[8] Here I want to place such different Bolivian and Peruvian radiophonic pragmatics in dialogue with a series of questions that look to approach radio in its specificity as a sonic medium, and to draw out the implications of that specificity for the sensorial density of what might be termed "place-making engagements."[9] In their day-to-day operations, stations such as Radio Tawantinsuyo or Radio Pio XII in Siglo XX, Bolivia, continue broadcasting *mensajes*, providing a sonic dimension to the space of the Andes by connecting towns, villages, and rural hamlets with each other and with these areas' urban centres.

Such suggestions of an emergent, socially differentiated public sphere and expanded sonic space can be deepened by conjoining Edward Casey's insight that "perception remains as *constitutive* as it is constituted," with Keith Basso's suggestion that symbolic vehicles "shape geographical experience and facilitate its communication."[10] Linking Quispe's sociology of aesthetics with Molina's evocation of the affective resonance of emplaced sound suggests how one's "sense of place" is amenable to symbolic manipulation, how places are aesthetically reproduced and transformed and, ultimately, how they resonate with social history. Andean radio carries its history in the discursive fray of social differentiation that surrounds the sounds, but also in its mix of musical genre and broadcast idiom.

This political phenomenology can aid in an instructive reading of European and North American studies of sound, space, and technology. Acoustic space, to follow R. Murray Schafer's terminology, refers to those characteristics of sound that enable the perception and conceptual construction of space, as well as to spaces that are socially dominated and ruled through sonic practices.[11] Schafer's conceptualization entails a dialectic whereby sounds' reverberation gives us perceptual access to spaces, while also providing one means of controlling place, investing it with authority and power. Jody Berland's discussion of radio in Canada opens this rather abstract dialectic to the specifics of institutional histories. In Canada, she argues, much of radio's power to local-ize the consumption of global forms historically derives from the local authority of the radiophonic voice.[12] It is this local voice, for Berland, that misleadingly interpolates a lis-tening community and a marketable audience in the interests of a non-local dynamic of consumerist desire. Yet if North American radios have historically delivered audiences to producers, in the Andes these consumers might better be conceptualized as "citizens" or constituencies, sonically hailed as Bolivians or Peruvians to membership in a place-based *pueblo*. Thus, when Quispe broadcasts *huaynos* on Peruvian regional radio, he uses a pragmatics of genre to lay claim to a social territory, and ties this to a radiophon-ically constituted Peruvian *campesino* space.

I would further suggest, looking to the works of Susan Buck-Morss and Jesus Martin-Barbero, that if in Europe and Mexico film enabled the very *perception* of the crowd and the mass as a "new collective protagonist," radio in the Andes made the space of these nations audible places.[13] Indeed, Andean radio must be questioned as centrally implicated in the mass-mediated constitution of a "popular" class and "national" space. Martin-Barbero has termed such processes, in the different context of Mexican cinema, the "degradation" of the nation: a "downward" shift that expanded the boundaries of cit-izenship beyond elite restrictions on membership and participation and placed the "national" within reach of newly constituted "masses," – made it familial by including, as Martin-Barbero puts it, "the idler, the drunkard, the sentimental slob" – a list to which we should also add, in Bolivia and Peru, the miner, the soldier, and the factory worker.[14]

Sound and Social Agency

The dialogue established above suggests how radio practices might be understood to constitute social space and social order. The radio voice of DJs like Molina or Huallpa in Cusco, Potosi, or La Paz may thus constitute locality by connecting the farms, hamlets, and cities announced in both *mensajes* and musics with the sound of the "popular" itself, making the nation as audible as the hamlet in the vocal and technologically sonic index of its presence. Static, hiss, and the bombastic oratorical style of Quechua and Aymara locution, then, may themselves resonate with the space and sense of a social collective, tying it to the positioned audition of particular engagements.

Yet I would also emphasize that the perceptual imbrication of place, person, and the familiarization of social belonging radio may entail are likely underdetermined with respect to the kind of collectivities and social projects to which sound technologies may be applied. Other histories, other kinds of sedimented social practices, and other ideologies of person and place are at work in the Andes, and these can begin to be glimpsed in Thomas Solomon's ethnographic discussion of Bolivian acoustic and aesthetic ideologies and their centrality in constructing felt relationships to places.[15]

Dividing the year into roughly two seasons, corresponding to ecological and temperate shifts between rainy and dry periods, people in the social group Ayllu Chayantaka employ a system of musics and instruments with which they performatively give sonic presence to a yearly agricultural cycle, making a sensuous linkage between seasonally changing sounds, ecological transformations, and the tactile aspects of musical instrumentation. Solomon thus highlights how Chayantaka musical instruments and song types resonate with a felt correspondence between season and sound.[16] Wind instruments, for example, have physical characteristics that are iconic with the lack of fertility of the dry season or with the dampness of the rainy season, and the pitch and size of stringed instruments also make tactile a "presence or lack of fertility."

Looking to Solomon's discussion of the shifting valence of *Sirinas* (that he describes as a kind of "place spirit" found in the central Andes at springs and rivers) provides a means to bring these sonic agencies to the changes occurring as radios become more audible in places like Northern Potosí. *Sirinas*, Solomon relates, are the sources of musical power and beauty, and are also connections to underworld waterways and the land of the dead.[17] *Sirinas'* powers, which are called forth through musical production, regulate the flow of water and the cosmological order, and are strongly associated with Chayantaka senses of fertility and reproduction. For Solomon this also explains why they are understood as endowing instruments with the power to seduce:

> That music should, on the one hand, attract the rain that makes fields productive, and on the other hand, attract and seduce girls, making them also potentially productive, makes perfect sense. Marriageable girls, like newly sown fields at the start of the rainy season, are the embodiment of potential fertility.[18]

While young men in the Andes have long strolled through hamlets playing *charangos* in attempts to seduce young women, recent decades have seen the replacement of *charangos* with radios by hopeful suitors, perched on village walls or dancing at mountain fiestas.[19]

At one level, this suggests that the sedimented social practices of Andean history are made audible in these moments of seduction – where new technologies are indigenized by Andean notions of sound and its gendered manipulation. Or, in a different anthropological domain, the iconicity of sound and season suggests one manner by which Andean radiophony may transform the audible as a field of social praxis. If Solomon's work suggests that the reproduction of seasonal change and social order occurs through the sonic manipulation of cosmological forces, then contemporary practices of sounding might expand the audible as a domain for social action and agency, and with that expansion provide new means for reproducing the social. Radio now may widen the realm for a social agency, and with it the topography of sonic emplacement.

History and Historicity

On its own, Solomon's work may suggest a genealogical understanding of Andean sonic agencies and perhaps something of a nostalgic search for origins that would locate Andean practices in a deep indigenous past, essentializing Andean sonic practices by finding their "truth" in their indigenous location. Further, radio's sonic presence is often equated with the "orality" of indigenous life-worlds and the past of an almost-disappeared indigenous tradition. As such, particularly in the Andes, radio may become identified with indigeneity, the "voice" of the people, and the sound of the past. So while radio may transform the audible, it also serves as an icon of locality in an era when the televisual may speak of high-class distinction or the dissolution of the nation in the face of North American cultural imperialism.

I thus wish to conclude by complicating what might otherwise lend itself to an essentializing narrative of cultural origin, loss, or redemption as "Indians" are moved from an "allochronic" essence, existing outside of time, to a more "modern" relationship with technology, change, and the state.[20] Radio has long held a significant place in Bolivian popular politics, and grasping the place of the Andes as constituted by radio requires reaffirming how radio itself has been tied to the expansion of a "rural proletariat" since the 1920s, and more recently to nostalgic memories of mining and "Indians" since the privatization of the tin industry in the mid-1980s.

As Bolivian unions gained political power, they became viable actors on a national stage, represented by their newly bourgeois delegates at international indigenous congresses, which began to take place in the 1940s. And yet the emergence of indigeneity as positively valued cultural capital resonated unevenly across a racialized social hierarchy, and it is clear that as often as not Andean radio addressed workers and citizens rather than "Indians."[21] The social group construed as these stations' addressee was one of workers, miners, and their family members – an index perhaps of the stigma that indigeneity may still carry for many Andeans. Further, the communities to which this essay refers have been shaped in large part by their historical involvement with colonial-era resource extraction, "modernized" in the twentieth century and threatened with dissolution in a new-millennium Bolivia in which populations move across a national and international landscape, much as they do elsewhere.

Since the mid-1980s the relevant public addressee seems to have changed as development groups, missionaries, and the state itself have all sought to address Quechua and Aymara speaking citizens, subjects, and clients. Such projections of an audience as a collective public in need of development unfold in different idiomatic forms, and figure a wide array of imagined indigenous and peasant futures in development projects ranging from language maintenance and revitalization to New Tribes missionization and other, corresponding forms of Christian salvation.[22] Exemplifying the latter, North American and Australian New Tribes missionaries seek to bring various stations to air across Bolivia: the Johnson Family carries the gospel in both indigenous languages and Spanish to air twelve hours a day in San Borja, while Ross and Kelly Patterson of Bell Block Baptist Church in New Plymouth bring the gospel and the occasional Quechua music-and-dance festival to the air in Cochabamba.[23]

For urban elites and intellectuals, radio's locality in the Andes may also signify radio's indigeneity and historicity – a medium that resonates with past progressive struggle and authentic community in the face of its dissolution in a neo-liberal era of privatization, dispersal, and the perceived increasing dominance of the televisual. To others, the history of Andean radio may carry the positive valence of indigenous agency, now broadcast across the cities and regional centres of Latin America, such as Lima or Buenos Aires, to which many mountain families have been drawn in the past several decades.[24] The power of radio as a figure of locality and political activism can be seen particularly in the value that Bolivian migrants to Sweden place on radio as a means to counter neo-liberal dissolution and exploitation through the voices of *reporteros populares*.[25] Documenting global inequality and the exploitation and devastation of Bolivia's mining communities as much as an ongoing antagonism between labour unions and the military, the Friends of Radio Pio XII look back from the Church of Sweden with economic support for the work of Pio XII, and utilize online media to document and argue for the material survival and democratic inclusion of Bolivia's miners.

Reviewing Quispe's practice, one can see a decidedly futurist orientation that nowhere evinces a nostalgia for village pasts or *campesino* sociality. For Molina, the radio dial is a place to press a cause about the specificity, refinement, and value of Andean pasts for Andean futures. Here, against McLuhan's romance of the electronic village, local processes of sociality objectify both local and extra-local as Molina counters primitivizing touristic representations and Quispe looks to anthropology students for high-tech equipment from abroad. Thus, while indigenous radio may speak to a romance of indigenous national history, it has been an undeniably powerful, affordable, and accessible means of constituting and carrying out contemporary social projects – as Quispe, Molina, and Bolivian miners' radios make evident.

Listening to these sound practitioners suggests that it might be appropriate to think of the sonic as a domain of social action and emplacing power, as a technology constitutive of the audible, but also as a site for the objectification of the past in the sounds of a dated media.[26] The meaning of radio discourse, then, rests as much in the medium and its meaning as in its message. But this medium does not lead of necessity to a corruption of the autochthonous and indigenous, nor does it rehabilitate some dying indigenous commune. Rather, in a reversal of terms, perhaps it aids in the constitution of indigeneity by giving it a space in which to resound, a microphone from which to speak.

In a "post-Marxist," neo-liberal era of Latin American identity politics, it becomes an ethnographic, researchable question how particular Andeans make meaning from radio sounds, words, and musics. The meaning of radio is not reducible to discursive contests over "Indianness" (even if it provides an important complication to such contests). Understanding aesthetic engagements as sonic emplacements and radiophony as the transformation and amplification of audibility as a site for social action, we might question the juncture between the discursive allocation of indigeneity and historicity, and particular instances of sonic signification as dialectically implicated in the production of place and person.

People act on the social by working with sound, and in so doing they make places experientially dense and affectively significant, they make collectivities knowable, and they make mass and historical events *experiential* objects of perception that refract on the constitution of personhood and local agency. One analytic opening for addressing such sonically keyed cultural production consists in asking after the particular ways in which the abstracted space of Bolivia or Peru may resonate on the radio, in asking how sounds echo places (and in places) in ways that are neither determined by essential aspects of a spatial world nor woven of whole cloth by ahistorical auditors. The historical resonances between sound and the flow of water and power through spatially organized Andean cosmologies call attention to the ways that perception, place, and sonic agency are intertwined, while the contemporary projects of missionaries and migrants demand a future-oriented perspective on the constitution of Andean soundscapes and an understanding of how they resonate with politically dense histories of sound and social agency. Places and peoples thus emerge as resonant materializations of history, and sounds the material of their making.

NOTES

1. For accounts of this history from various disciplinary perspectives see Herbert Klein, *Bolivia: The Evolution of a Multi-Ethnic Society*, 2nd ed. (Oxford: Oxford University Press, 1992); Maria de la Cadena, *Identity, Race, and the Struggle for Indigenous Self-Representation: De-Indianization in Cusco, Peru (1919–1992)* (Ph.D. Dissertation: University of Wisconsin, Madison, 1996); Jesus Martin-Barbero, *Communication, Culture, and Hegemony: From the Media to Mediations* (London, Newbury Park: Sage, 1993); June C. Nash, *We Eat the Mines and the Mines Eat Us: Dependency and Exploitation in Bolivian Tin Mines* (New York: Columbia University Press, 1979).

2. Alfonso Gumucio Dagron, "Las Emisoras Mineras en Tiempos de Crisis," in *Las Radios Mineras De Bolivia*, eds. Alfonso Gumucio Dagron and Lupe Cajias (La Paz: CIMCA–UNESCO, 1989), 85–96; Robert Huesca, "A Procedural View of Participatory Communication: Lessons from Bolivian Tin Miners' Radio," *Media, Culture & Society* 17:1 (1994); Alan O'Connor, "The Miners' Radio Stations in Bolivia: A Culture of Resistance," *Journal of Communication* 40:1 (1990): 102–110.

3. My translation from the Spanish of Gumucio, 94.

4. Abel Fernando Mujica Escalante, *Una Vida y un Rumbo: 50 Años de Cusqueñismo, Radio Tawantinsuyo y Raul Montesinos Espejo* (Cusco: El Diario del Cusco, 1999).

5. *Cusqueños* and *Limeños* are Peruvian labels for residents of Cusco and Lima. See de la Cadena, passim.

6. Unless drawn from published sources, all proper names have been replaced with pseudonyms to protect contributors' confidentiality.

7. John Cohen, *Dancing with the Incas* (1991).

8. Stuart Alexander Rockefeller, "'There Is a Culture Here': Spectacle and the Inculcation of Folklore in Highland Bolivia," *Journal of Latin American Anthropology* 3:2 (1998): 118–149; Mark Rogers, "Spectacular Bodies: Folklorization and the Politics of Identity in Ecuadorian Beauty Pageants," *Journal of Latin American Anthropology* 3:2 (1998): 54–85; Thomas James Solomon, *Mountains of Song: Musical Constructions of Ecology, Place, and Identity in the Bolivian Andes* (Ph.D. Dissertation, University of Texas at Austin, 1997).

9. See Thomas J. Csordas, "Somatic Modes of Attention," *Cultural Anthropology* 8:2 (1993): 135–156; Solomon, passim.

10. Edward Casey, "How to Get from Space to Place in a Fairly Short Stretch of Time: Phenomenological Prolegomena," in *Senses of Place*, eds. Steven Feld and Keith H. Basso (Santa Fe: School of American Research Press, 1996), 19; Keith Basso, "Wisdom Sits in Places: Notes on a Western Apache Landscape," Feld and Basso, 56.

11. R. Murray Schafer, *Voices of Tyranny, Temples of Silence* (Indian River, ON: Arcana Editions, 1993), 31–32.

12. Jody Berland, "Radio Space and Industrial Time: Music Formats, Local Narratives and Technological Mediation," *Popular Music* 9:2 (1990): 178–192.

13. Susan Buck-Morss, "The Cinema Screen as Prosthesis of Perception: A Historical Account," in *The Senses Still: Perception and Memory as Material Culture in Modernity*, ed. C. Nadia Seremetakis (Chicago: University of Chicago Press, 1994), 45–62.

14. Martin-Barbero, 449.

15. Solomon, passim; see also Pierre Bourdieu, *Outline of a Theory of Practice* (Cambridge: Cambridge University Press, 1977); Ian Keen, *Knowledge and Secrecy in an Aboriginal Religion: Yolngu of Northeast Arnhem Land* (Oxford: Clarendon Press, 1994).

16. Solomon, 93–199; see also Henry Stobart, "*Tara* and *Q'iwa* – Worlds of Sound and Meaning," in *Cosmologia y Musica en los Andes*, ed. Max Peter Baumann (Vervuert: Iberoamericana, 1996), 67–82.

17. Solomon, 248–250.

18. Solomon, 250.

19. Thomas Abercrombie, personal communication with the author; see also Nathan Wachtel, *Gods and Vampires: Return to Chipaya* (Chicago: University of Chicago Press, 1994).

20. Johannes Fabian, *Time and the Other: How Anthropology Makes Its Object* (New York: Columbia University Press, 1983).

21. Gumucio, passim.

22. For a recent account of language maintenance and revival projects see A. Luykx, "Across Andean Airwaves: Satellite Broadcasting in Quechua," in *Endangered Languages and the Media: Proceedings of the 5th Foundation for Endangered Languages Conference*, eds. C. Moseley, N. Ostler, and H. Ouzzate, September 20–23, 2001 (Bath: FEL, 2001), 115–119.

23. The Johnsons, < http://www.solomonsporch.org/chimaneradio > , accessed 01/12/03; Radio Mosoj Chaski, < http://tunari.it.uts.edu.au/rmc/ > , accessed 01/12/03.

24. Alejandro Grimson, *Relatos de la Diferencia y la Igualidad: Los Bolivianos en Buenos Aires* (Buenos Aires: Federacion Latinoamerican de Facultades de Comunicacion Social, 1999); Jose Antonio Llorens, "Andean Voices on Lima Airwaves: Highland Migrants and Radio Broadcasting in Peru," *Studies in Latin American Popular Culture* 10 (1991): 177–190.

25. Radio Pio XII, < http://www.caritas.se/radiopio/ > , accessed 01/12/03.

26. See Douglas Kahn, *Noise, Water, Meat: A History of Sound in the Arts* (Cambridge, MA: MIT Press, 1999).

ANN HAMILTON

speaking the hand's pace, 2003
Video stills

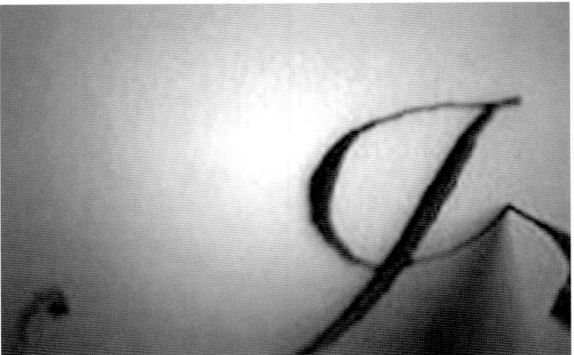

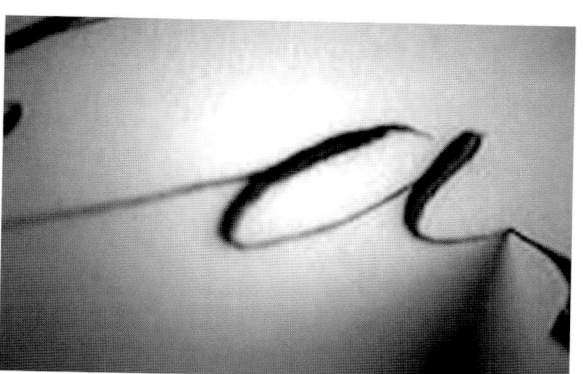

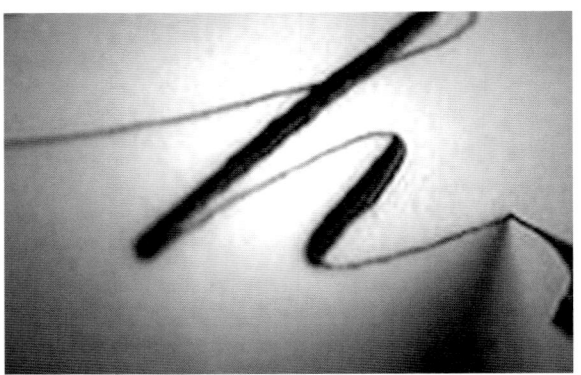

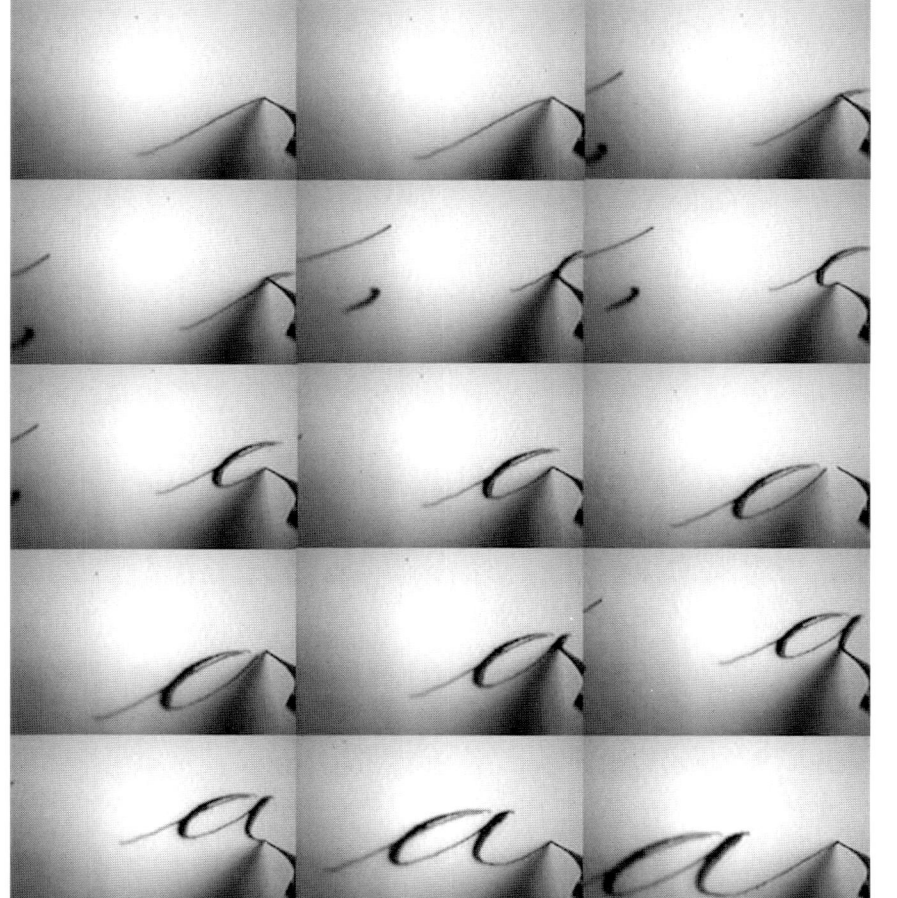

DANIEL OLSON

Silence, 2001/03

You have the right to remain silent.

AURALITY AND ALTERITY

Kanta Kochhar-Lindgren

David Howes

Robert Desjarlais

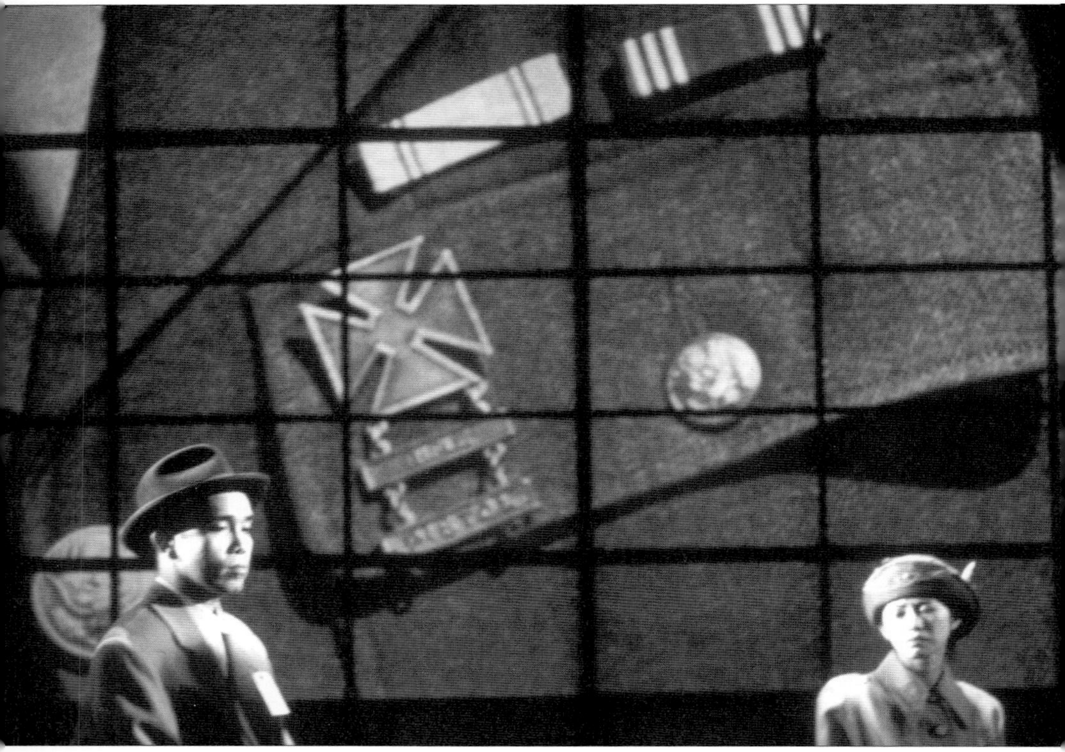

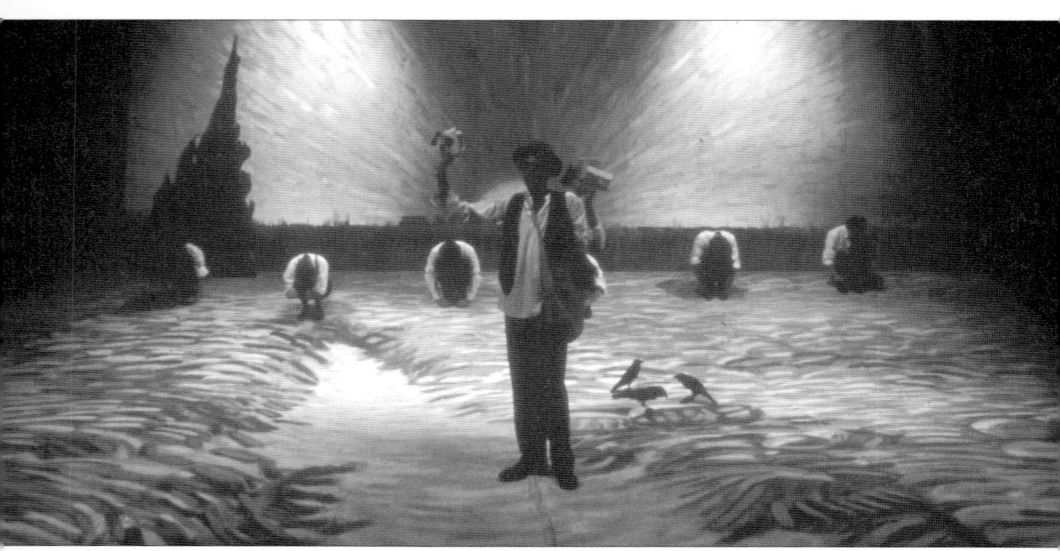

Performing at the Edge of Hearing: The Third Ear

Kanta Kochhar-Lindgren

Ping Chong's *East/West Trilogy* chronicles a series of cultural collisions that have grown out of the history of colonialism. In this compound performance work, he grapples with the political and historical obsessions that drive a group of people to exert power, often through violent means, over another group. As an archetypal example of postcolonial theatre, *Trilogy* acts as a site of resistance by simultaneously recovering and revising lost history, and reinserting it into the cultural imaginary. In order to do so, Chong uses theatrical structures that involve a series of shifting images sustained through multiple storylines, time frames, and geographical locations. As a result, who speaks and why is unsettled and reconstituted.

It is significant to note that relatively little work has been done on the practice of listening in relation to postcolonial theatre. Chong's work serves as a vital vehicle for attending to the importance of listening to that which has traditionally been ignored, denied, or erased, and how this alters not only our personal and historical senses but also the very act of "hearing." Postcolonial theatre – occurring at the edge of hearing – forces us to grapple with the conditions for "hearing" the other that also account for the ways in which we are "deaf" to "the Other." *The third ear*, my neologism that draws from psychoanalysis and the work of Jean-François Lyotard, can be seen as an improvisational method for listening to what cannot be literally heard or understood. Often it involves crossing sensory frames and the experience of synaesthesia. Thus unmoored sensorially, the new can be better heard.

Trilogy is divided into three parts. *Deshima* (1990) focuses on the history of Japan from the encounters with Dutch traders to the internment of Japanese-Americans in the U.S. during World War II, and makes links between Japan and Van Gogh. *Chinoiserie* (1995) deals with Chong's childhood in the U.S. and includes sections on the building of the transcontinental railroad by Chinese workers. *After Sorrow* (1997) addresses the aftermath of the Vietnam War through the personal histories of Chong and performer/choreographer Muna Tseng.

Within the trilogy, there are three striking moments at which hearing the multiple "voices" of the narratives activates the uncanny space of the third ear. In the progression from *Deshima* to *Chinoiserie*, the first two performances, the voice of the Other, to which Westerners have been historically and culturally insensitive, awakens the third ear and its corollary, the listening body. In the third section, *After Sorrow*, an electronic recording transmits the voice of the Other from the past so that it can be heard in the present. In all three cases, listening to that which cannot literally be heard requires an auxiliary, or third, ear, which enables the tracking of the ambiguous articulations of sound, silence, and image.

Ping Chong, *Deshima*, 1990. Performance stills. Photos: Brendan Bannon (top), Bob van Dantzig (bottom). Courtesy the artist

Deshima illuminates the interconnection of voices, hearing, and spatiality, addressing the complexities of hearing at perceptual and sociocultural levels. Originally, Deshima was the name of a compound built in 1598 off the coast of Nagasaki as a living space for Dutch foreigners, a place where they could be retained without contaminating the native Japanese populace. As the trilogy progresses, parallels unfold, ranging from the detention of the Japanese practiced in the United States during World War II to the treatment of Chinese railroad workers during the 1800s, to everyday stories about contemporary racism at elementary schools and restaurants. These examples outline the efforts of certain groups to impose a physical, and subsequently psychic, regulatory bonding upon the foreign. The polyphony of voices from the cultural imaginary that Chong presents has become so charged that it crosses the boundaries of cultural distance and history into the present.

It is not, however, a matter of simply adding these emerging accounts to an already existing body of stories. Nor will it suffice that such accounts, as Michel de Certeau warns about the stories of the Other, "be transformed into texts in conformity with the Western desire to read its products."[1] These cultural tendencies to dismiss the stories of Others by trying to minimize or contain them reflect a failure to hear beyond the boundaries of what one considers familiar. This sociocultural tendency to circumscribe an unknown within the known parallels the variations on the "Deshima" patterns Chong addresses in his trilogy. Given these observations, what are the responsibilities of "listening"? What, then, is heard when the voice of the Other speaks? Given such restrictions, can one hear another? Although the technologies of power obfuscate the ability to hear, de Certeau remarks that there is, nonetheless, a kind of excess or remainder:

> Perhaps at the extreme limit of these tireless inscriptions [of social symbolic codes], or perforating them with lapses, there remains only the cry: it escapes, it escapes them. From the first to the last cry, something else breaks out with them, the body's difference.[2]

The activation of the third ear engages a modality for hearing difference – the cry as well as the body – and for resisting the "machinery of representation."[3]

Homi Bhabha, who could well be describing Chong's trilogy, shows how old binaries are opened up by a different kind of temporality and its cultural productions:

> Private and public, past and present, the psyche and the social develop an interstitial intimacy. It is an intimacy that questions binary divisions through which such spheres of social experience are often spatially opposed. These spheres of life are linked through an "in-between" temporality that takes the measure of dwelling at home, while producing an image of the world of history.[4]

Bhabha further explains that the subject who inhabits this "in-between" space experiences a "borderline existence," "a hybridity, a difference 'within.'" This space is one where the subject "inhabits a stillness of time and a strangeness of framing."[5] The third ear couples a listening to the sounds of difference, the cry that de Certeau identifies, and the stillness that Bhabha describes. These articulations of the body are voices that emerge prior to, or outside of, the moment of language, disrupting the official "machinery of representation."

Chong's trilogy provides, in addition to compelling historical and cultural stories, many striking perceptual moments, especially when the elision between sound and image unsettle what Trinh T. Minh-ha calls "securely anchored audio-visual habits."[6] Trinh, in her essay "Hole in the Sound Wall," writes about the cinematic use of image and sound:

> The eternal chatter that escorts images is the oppressive device of fixed association. To bring out the plural, sliding relationship between the eye and the ear and to leave more room for the spectators to decide what they want to make out of the statement or a sequence of images, it is necessary to invent a whole range of strategies that would unsettle such fixedness.[7]

In each of his works, Chong "unsettles such fixedness" through cutting and splicing texts, images, and the split bodies of speech and movement to create an uncertain relationship between the eye and the ear.

In *Deshima*, an all-Asian cast plays both the colonizers and the colonized, which complicates the questions of who, exactly, is speaking. Such techniques of forcing gaps, delays, and detours in the construction of meaning involve, according to Trinh, "the crossing of an indeterminate number of borderlines, one that remains multiple in its hyphenation."[8] This staging approach reflects the larger sociopolitical space of the "interstitial intimacy" between public and private, and it also opens up new possibilities for spatiality, its relationship to the non-normative body, and hearing. As a result, these gaps and delays necessitate a new way of listening as the performance progresses through an historical, sociocultural, and perceptual trail of silences and signs.

Deshima, the first section of the trilogy, was originally commissioned by the Dutch government to honour the 100th anniversary of Vincent van Gogh's death. The work, while focusing on the history of Japanese, Dutch, and U.S. relations in the Far East, also includes numerous references to Van Gogh and questions the interrelationship of art, commerce, politics, and religious power. Structurally, *Deshima* presents a series of trans-spatial and trans-temporal visits to a variety of locations, and it reflects de Certeau's axiom that "every story is a travel story – a spatial practice."[9] The original performance, in Holland in 1990, explored a kind of doubling of the story by creating stories within stories, as the audience was physically moved from scene to scene in a hydraulic boxcar. Suzanne Westfall remarks that "[r]arely is a theater audience so literally and vividly immersed in foreign worlds."[10]

Chong uses sound, such as texts, singing, music, and sound effects, so that he can strategically place the silences; silence becomes a disruption in the fabric of sound. The first section of *Deshima* covers the political and commercial exchange between the Dutch and Japan in 1598, the second focuses on the conversion of the Japanese by the Portuguese Jesuits, and the third section depicts a 1941 radio broadcast of a frenetic jitterbug dance hour. In each of the sections there is lengthy text and the second two sections add singing and music.

Throughout the piece, actors give the impression that they are performing the rhetoric of politics, commerce, religion, and, eventually, the public face of racial terror without really listening to themselves or to what the others are saying. In the first section, for example, the Daimyo (or Japanese lord) and Dutch trader, who have been trying to arrive at a satisfactory trade agreement, talk at once and declaim in various ways how disgusting they find each other. In the next scene the Priest is so subsumed with the rhetoric of martyrdom that he does not hear when the converted ask questions about the violation of their native culture. In the dance scene, the radio announcer spews a series of racial invectives as labels for the top ten popular songs. The dancers who display such physical excellence are vocally silent.

The first example that invokes the space of the third ear in *Deshima* occurs at the end of a long section focusing on the release of the Japanese from internment camps; it is transmogrified through the use of a "soundless music box." Chong overlays songs, historical facts, and tapes of General MacArthur and the Japanese surrender in order to underscore the context of the Japanese detainees' release and subsequent welcome home on V-J Day. In a long modern dance scene, the various individuals dance with their suitcases. These dancers are silent, but their bodies speak of their longing and their need to reclaim their personal space through the interaction with their personal belongings. There is a contrast between the sound and soundlessness of the scene that is answered by a powerful moment of complete silence.

One woman who has been looking through her belongings picks up a music box and opens it. She leans forward as if hearing the music, but no sound emanates from the box. The woman then takes a long time to leave the stage, crossing from downstage left to upstage right. She seems suspended, listening to the soundless music, walking along the long diagonal. The question emerges whether this passage is a release from the painful experience of internment or an anticipation of the future. Because of this uncertainty, both are possible interpretations.

There are several reasons why this section is particularly useful to the larger discussion of the third ear. First of all, the scene draws attention to the listening of something that, ostensibly, cannot be heard, and the listening is evoked not through sound but through its corollary, the image of listening. In this almost private moment, transfixed as it is between hearing and seeing, the viewer's first impression is that the woman hears something that the audience cannot. Since the scene is silent, one must imagine its melody.

Perhaps the woman listens to music, her memory of music, or she is now deaf and struggles to hear the music of her memories through the silence. Music, associated with memory, provides reassurance and repeatability of the past. Silence underscores that this reassurance is missing. However, this space is more than a form of nostalgia; it also creates a space of desire, but one whose object cannot be readily identified. What desire wells up out of soundlessness? Can the nature of her desire be grasped, or does this "gap in the sound wall" make audience members wilful, superimposing their desire on this silence? The silence is a vortex that disrupts meaning.

The image of the woman listening to the soundless box itself is also embedded within the larger "image" of being released from the internment camp. The woman, as she departs from the enclosure of the camp, is now freed and trails across the stage, like the music that cannot be heard trailing from the box she holds in her hand. The physical trail of silence reiterates the sonic trail of silence, bringing into question the location of the "voice of the Other." This scene of double "soundlessness" provides an example, then, of the conjunction of the personal and the political.

Despite the fact that the woman is physically free, there are several reasons why she cannot be heard. There is no sound; there is not a thing to hear. In this case, what is "heard" is the emptiness of loss and pain. Bound by an audist bias for communication through sound, i.e., speech, viewers are ill-equipped to read the event. Also, given the way in which sound is linked with particular cultural meaning, the sounds of another culture are inaudible, except through the third ear – connections occur through the silences. These trails mark off a liminal space of the in-between that oscillates over the silent, visual, kinaesthetic trajectory to create a relay system for the ambiguous signs of the uncanny space of the third ear – listening to that which has no aural existence. The deafened space marks a rupture in the cultural fabric as well as the historical and political failures to deal with the individual. It is through the (non-) "hearing eye" that the failure, and the possibility of restitution, is conveyed.

This scene refracts back on a number of earlier parts of *Deshima*. As a result one can understand certain aspects of the work, particularly other silent sections, not only as they unfold but also retroactively. For example, this silent section is reminiscent of the silence of the woman in the waltz section. Ostensibly about honouring the Dutch government, the scene turns on itself when, after the stage has almost cleared, one of the men makes a move toward a woman and starts to undress her, revealing her Javanese dance costume. She rebuffs him and, half-dressed, travels along the same diagonal as the woman with the music box.

Near the end of *Deshima*, Chong deconstructs the performance. The performers cross back and forth over the stage – clearing it, calling one another by their "real" names and, in various forms of undress, attempting to restore their "real" identity. At the very end, the performers build a dream scene, based on Van Gogh's *Crows in the Field*. Through the use of this image, Chong reminds the audience one last time of the silences of another outsider, Van Gogh, who spoke through his paintings. Questions are raised, finally, about the relationships of art, history, and silence. The silences speak, and, uncannily, that which has been hidden becomes visible. The recovery of marginalized voices is momentarily accomplished, and with it the recognition of a more inclusive humanity.

Chinoiserie, the second part of the trilogy, is Chong's autobiographical account of growing up Chinese American. In this performance, Chong uses the motif of baseball to depict an interest in, and the failures of, American life. The stage itself is structured to reflect and contain the multiple splits between voice, text, song, movement, and music. Chong delivers most of his commentary from a position downstage right, marked off by a lighted podium and his partially visible manuscript. The other four performers are in the upstage right with their own lecterns, lamps, and scripts.

Slides are projected onto a screen that is upstage centre. The musicians are opposite the four performers upstage left. In the centre-stage space there is a large carpet to which the performers go when they move and speak the text, or they move and others speak from the sidelines. From the periphery of the space the sound and the text are emphasized, and in the centre space the body and the visual are emphasized. This piece forces the suturing of two idioms – voice and body. In addition to presenting the voice and body in disparate stage locations, when the performers do move to the centre space, they perform in a stylized fashion that emphasizes the gaps between the order of the body and the order of speech. These gaps mark the failures of the body and voice to synchronize and also mark the doubling of stories as the voices and bodies depict their disparate narratives.

At the end of *Chinoiserie*, Chong uses sign language to say, "You believe in the goodness of mankind." When he signs a second time, a slide appears, which also states "You believe in the goodness of mankind." Chong communicates silently but visually, through the use of sign and text. Nevertheless, the closing scene is marked by ambiguity. The shift to a visual-spatial mode through the use of sign language ruptures the expected reliance on speech as explanation. It propels the audience into a region where they do not hear, but are momentarily deafened. Not only is there the surprise of no sound, but also the concomitant speechlessness or non-use of the voice. It appears that

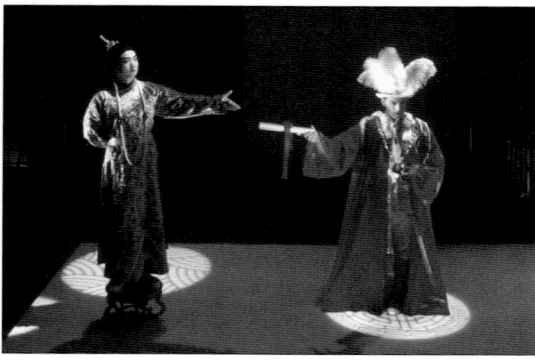

Ping Chong
Chinoiserie, 1995
Performance stills
Left: Shi-Zheng Chen and Ric Oquita
Right: Shi-Zheng Chen and Aleta Hayes
Photos: Walker Art Center
Courtesy the artist

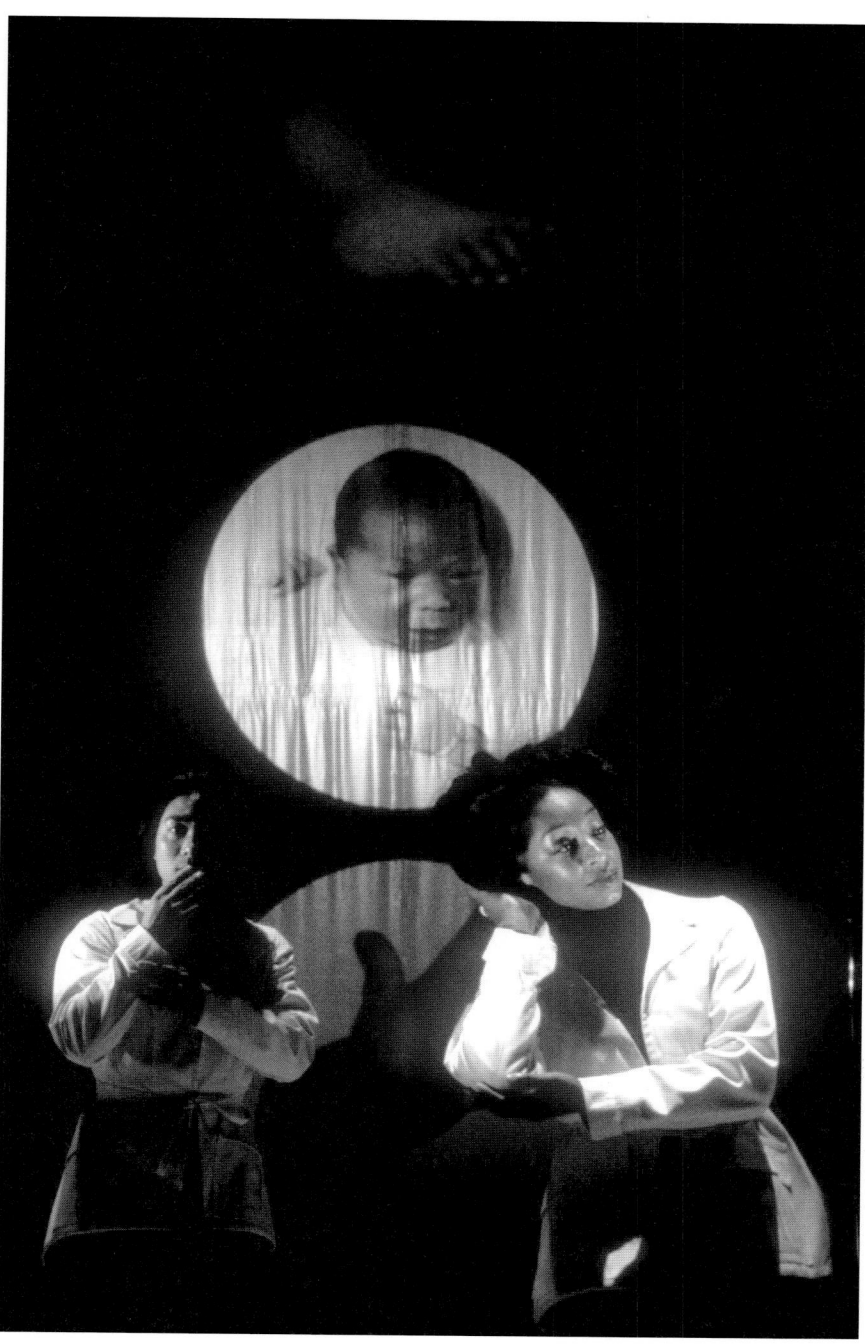

the voice does not serve what Chong wants to say, as language presents itself from another part of the body, the hands. Who is deaf, the audience or Chong?

The text echoes his own signing, and at the same time these "lines" also refer to the opening story of *Chinoiserie* in which Chong recounts an encounter he had with a friend while they were eating dinner at a Chinese restaurant. This friend had wanted to know why the Chinese didn't use forks. Chong, who wanted to remain a "good" Chinese, managed to keep a straight face and did not, he recounts, "murder" her. He received, a few minutes later, the message "You believe in the goodness of mankind" from a fortune cookie. At the very end of this section, the lights fade out as Chong begins to sign the statement a third time.

In this moment Chong aligns himself with deaf politics, just as elsewhere he works with ethnic politics. For a moment, the politics of deafness and the politics of race merge. H-Dirksen L. Bauman expands on the relationship between the signifying systems of eye and ear:

> Deafness does more than disrupt the system of "hearing-oneself-speak"; it creates an embodied linguistic system which, unlike speech, is not fully present to itself. Signers, unless gazing in the mirror, do not fully see themselves signify. While they may see their hands, they cannot see their own face perform much of Sign's grammatical nuances. The eye, unlike the ear in the system of "hearing-oneself-speak," can only partially "see-oneself-sign." There is always a trace of non-presence in the system of signing.[11]

Chong signals the non-presence of the other, perhaps his own non-presence. However, this moment also acts as a mirror to the audience, and it acknowledges the ambiguous lack of awareness embedded in the statement, "You believe in the goodness of mankind."

This moment also raises the complex dialectic of hearing/non-hearing that relies on being seen by the other. In an instance of inversion, where the outsider looks back in through signing, viewers are confronted with a space of doubled distance. Lennard Davis, a deaf studies theorist, has noted this conjunction between the categories of deafness and race:

> The Deaf are, in a sense, racialized through their use of sign language as a system of communication. They are seen as outside citizenry created by a community of language users, and therefore ghettoized as outsiders.[12]

Chong sends back the message he received vis-à-vis the fortune cookie, using another visual-spatial medium to do so. In a sense, fortune cookies are a created Chinese fiction, so he creates a fiction as a response.

Chong asks us to confront the silences of the body and image to hear what cannot literally be heard, but only surmised. For Chong, the text is the handmaiden of these silences, a progression that he constructs with painstaking care. He complicates these moments with successive layers of silence, speech, text, image, and the moving body, and insists on the process-based nature of personal and cultural restitution.

The tone of the work is utopian; to the extent that an audience can be moved by and hear what has not been stated, the voices of the marginalized can be reclaimed, and the public and private spaces of cultural exchange can be transformed. The very last slide shown in *Chinoiserie* reads: "To be continued in the twenty-first century."

Finally, the last part of the trilogy, *After Sorrow*, deals with the aftermath of the Vietnam War from a Southeast Asian perspective. This piece begins in China and gives voice to a young Chinese bride at the turn of the twentieth century. It also includes the personal stories of Muna Tseng, Chong's co-collaborator on the project and the work's only solo live performer, and Chong himself as immigrants, and their relationships to their deceased brothers. The work ends with the story of a Vietnamese woman who speaks about the son she lost in the Vietnam War.

The first section of the trilogy, *Deshima*, addresses the splits between the foreign and the domestic at the political and historical level. In *Chinoiserie* the emphasis is on the body, gesture, and the voice in the social context. The last section arrives at a crucial place – that of the issue of communication in the personal and familial realms. The question then emerges: how is the chasm between the self and others to be traversed? De Certeau suggests that it is a certain system of citation that bridges the gap:

> These voices narrate interminably the expectation of an impossible presence that transforms itself into its own body that traces what it has left behind. These quotations of voices, "glossolalia," mark themselves on an everyday prose that can only produce some of its effects – in the form of statements and practices.[13]

Chong echoes the issue many times in the middle section of *After Sorrow*, as the two performers share stories with a constant refrain of "The things they share. The mystery of the other."

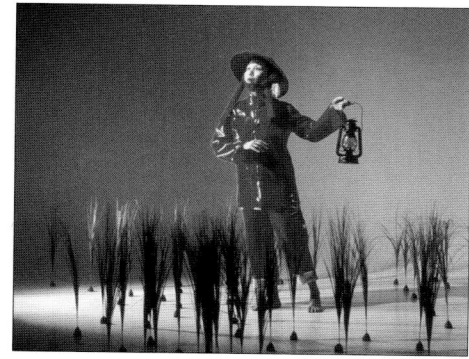

Ping Chong
After Sorrow, 1997
Performance still (Muna Tseng)
Photo: Beatriz Schiller
Courtesy the artist

Chong answers these questions through the form of the performance itself:

> She is here this very evening
> Before your very eyes, dancing.
> He is here too as an afterglow,
> A digital hop, skip, and jump,
> A voice in a room tapping
> Against the thin membrane of
> Your collective eardrum
> Rippling across the room
> As undulating as sound waves,
> Dancing with her dancing
> As a voice would and might
> And is doing here and now.
> He is a dancing voice against
> Her dancing body together and apart
> And this very moment,
> This exact moment,
> Will never be the same again.
> It is that fragile.[14]

In the most immediate sense this section describes quite literally what is occurring on the stage. Tseng dances in front of the audience, and occasionally she speaks. Chong, however, has recorded his voice on tape; the audience hears what he has to say, but does not see him at all. His own voice has become a deferred presence.

In this case, the body and voice of the other are overlaid, appearing to be together. But they are also apart, the disjunction created by the use of mechanical devices. In this manner, sound travels across time and space and is a "dancing voice." But since much of this piece is about "dancing voices" from the past, it becomes uncertain how much of this section is not only literal, but also metaphorical. A number of individuals emerge from the past as the voices of Tseng, live, and Chong, tape-recorded, overlay the movement and visual sequences projected on the scrim.

Voice, in this section, is an "afterglow," which strikes across the audience's "collective eardrum." What is this moment that exceeds the hearing of the individual, and allows the personal and immediate to merge with the distant? "Distant" as in far away or in the past? The possibilities increase through the use of technology. There is a circuitry that passes between individuals and groups. The issue of "sensory recovery" is tinged with haunting. This section is sensory recovery in that it brings various people back to be heard once again. Their voices iterate through the voices of Tseng and Chong, but it is haunting because it is always partial, never complete.

From these mute spaces of cultural imaginary in each of the three works, *Deshima*, *Chinoiserie*, and *After Sorrow*, history is reconfigured as a complex intersection of the political, social, and personal. Chong attempts through his many stagings of the multiply fragmented body of history to re-render history for the men and women whose voices have been previously lost in the silent archives of non-normative history.

What has been hidden and then brought to light must be not only "seen," but also heard, by what Trinh has called the "ear below the eye."[15] Opening up the past so that it can be heard anew, the anamnesis that Lyotard invites readers to consider, relies on just this moment of suspension, where judgment and precast expectation are shunted aside. The voice of the other always resides in the interminable spaces of silence. But these multiple thresholds of silence must continue to unfold, becoming intelligible through sounds and images staged in the *aporia* of language and pictoriality to generate the necessary communication.

In his many uses of sound, silence, and the moving body, Chong attempts to speak what has not yet been spoken. *Deshima* starts with the larger political/historical picture and funnels down to include more personal elements. *Chinoiserie* is yet more personal and *After Sorrow* the most personally rooted of the three sections of the trilogy. In this poetic documentary, Chong must first sift through various cultural histories before realizing his own individuality. Cultural loss is finally met with personal loss, and even "after sorrow" there is still the nostalgia for what Lyotard calls the *domus*, or the "inscription of the awakening."[16] In this moment of empathic exchange and recognition, there is hope for communication, new narratives, and the transformation of the voice.

NOTES

In 1999 Ping Chong added *Pogaji*, a fourth part, to his series on the history of East/West encounters – this time focusing on Korea since the sixteenth century. In the interest of space, my commentary on this section will be featured in an upcoming publication.

1. Michel de Certeau, *The Practice of Everyday Life*, trans. Steven Rendall (Berkeley: University of California Press, 1984), 159.

2. De Certeau, 147–148.

3. De Certeau, 147.

4. Homi Bhabha, *The Location of Culture* (New York: Routledge, 1994), 13.

5. Bhabha, 13.

6. Trinh T. Minh-ha, *When the Moon Waxes Red: Representation, Gender, and Cultural Politics* (New York: Routledge, 1991), 205.

7. Trinh, 206.

8. Trinh, 107.

9. De Certeau, 115.

10. Suzanne Westfall, "Invasion of a Cornfield: Ping Chong's *Deshima*," *American Theatre* (January 1993): 11.

11. H-Dirksen L. Bauman, "Derrida and Deafness: Phonocentrism, Audism and Sign," MLA Conference Paper (1996): 3.

12. Lennard Davis, *Enforcing Normalcy: Disability, Deafness, and the Body* (New York: Verso, 1995), 78.

13. De Certeau, 154.

14. Ping Chong and Co., *After Sorrow* (1997).

15. Trinh, 104.

16. Jean-François Lyotard, *The Inhuman: Reflections on Time*, trans. Geoffrey Bennington and Rachel Bowlby (Cambridge, UK: Polity Press, 1991), 198.

Sound Thinking

David Howes

The theory of oral-aural mentality was invented by the communications theorists Marshall McLuhan and Walter Ong to account for what they took to be certain characteristic features of the social and cognitive organization of non-literate societies.[1] According to this theory, in the absence of writing, speech is necessarily the dominant mode of communication. This has the following consequences: 1) primacy is accorded to sound; 2) hearing is the dominant sense; 3) the intellect is associated with hearing; 4) knowledge must be cast in verbal formulae, such as rhymes or commonplaces, in order to be memorable; and 5) the individuation (or rational structuring) of ideas, as of people, is comparatively slight. The last point builds from the idea that hearing is an inclusive, emotional sense. By contrast, the theory goes, thought in literate societies tends to be rational or objective, and lineal or tied to a single (individuated) point of view. This is because the transition from orality to literacy involves the exchange of "an eye for an ear" and the separation "of the knower from the known" (given that knowledge can henceforth be exteriorized in writing and no longer need depend on memory per se).

I would like to test the theory of oral-aural mentality against the ethnographic record for a particular Melanesian culture area, namely the Massim region of Papua New Guinea, where literacy has made relatively scant inroads to date. The evidence suggests that the theory overlaps with aspects of the indigenous reality, but rarely for the predicted reasons. This lack of congruence stems from the fact that the theory of oral-aural mentality rests on some peculiarly Western assumptions about the nature of the senses, the function of language, and the representational powers of mind – assumptions that need to be exposed and contested. I want especially to contest the idea that it is by reference to a single "dominant" sense that societies can be categorized, and that technologies of communication are the determining factor with respect to the shape of a given society's epistemic order. It is remiss to focus exclusively on technologies for the communication of the word. Cultures invariably rely on other media besides language for making sense of the world. Non-verbal media, such as body decoration and currency (in the instant case, *kula* valuables), warrant careful study as alternative expressions of a given society's epistemic order or way of sensing the world.

The Sensory Dynamics of the *Kula* Ring

The Massim region, which lies off the southeastern tip of Papua New Guinea, is known for the natural beauty of its volcanic islands, coral reefs, and emerald lagoons. Its most famous social institution is the *Kula* Ring, a vast inter-island circuit of ceremonial exchange first described by Bronislaw Malinowski in *Argonauts of the Western Pacific*. Two sorts of valuables move against each other around the Ring: necklaces (*soulava* or *bagi*) and armshells (*mwali*). The former circulate clockwise, the latter counter-clockwise. Every man of the *kula* (only a few women participate) must therefore have at least two partners, one to his geographical right, from whom he receives necklaces in exchange for armshells, and one to his left, from whom he gets armshells in return for necklaces.

Malinowski described the operation of the *Kula* Ring from the standpoint of the Trobriand Islands. Other ethnographers who have contributed to knowledge of this institution include Reo Fortune on Dobu, Géza Róheim on Duau (Normanby Island) and Nancy Munn on Gawa. My own research in the area was concentrated in Bwaiowa (southeastern Fergusson Island).

Throughout the area covered by the *kula*, people are organized into small, matrilineal, exogamous land-holding groups, called *dala* in the north and east, *susu* in the west and south. One key characteristic of this Massim form of social organization is the tension that exists between the individualization of the person or "expansion outward" of the self and the conservation of the resources of the group. Expansion outward, or "penetrating the matrilineal boundary that sets off the self from others," as Annette Weiner defines this process, is accomplished through bestowing gifts on others and receiving gifts in turn.[2] This giving represents a strain on the resources of the *dala* or *susu*. Nevertheless, the fame that the individual achieves through exchange reflects back on the matrilineage, and makes the group's own fame climb higher too. As a result, it is generally the case that the individual is perceived as an extension of the group in the Massim world, rather than as standing in opposition to the group.

According to Malinowski, what animates the *kula* is "the love of give and take for its own sake."[3] There is never any question of bargaining for an armshell or necklace, for example. Weiner, who also carried out research in the Trobriands, has questioned Malinowski's construction. According to her, the *kula* is not about "giving for the sake of giving, but creating one's own individual fame through the circulation of objects that accumulate the histories of their travels and the names of those who have possessed them."[4]

"Fame" in the language of the Trobriands, as in other Massim languages, is signified by the word *butu*, which also means "noise, sound." The circulation of *kula* objects is thus understood by Massim people themselves to be geared to the production and circulation of sound. This suggests that to understand the *kula* from within, it is imperative that ears are trained on the analysis of this institution. Most studies to date have focused on the objects of *kula* exchange, not its sounds. These studies have yielded many important insights into the economic and social dimensions of the *kula*, but they remain incomplete. What is needed is a full-bodied sensory analysis of ceremonial exchange in the Massim world. The following analysis of *kula* exchange begins with the gustatory dimension and culminates with the acoustic.

Hospitality in food is one of the mainstays of a man's reputation in the *kula*, and eating well is one of the main reasons for going on a *kula* expedition. At the same time, the activity of eating ranks lowest in the hierarchy of *kula* activities. The ordinary members of an expedition must subsist on their own provisions until the first *kula* gifts have been received, and the leaders (canoe owners) will not touch the local food until they have received their fill of valuables. The agonism of exchange takes precedence over the pleasures of eating.

Malinowski records that "abstention from food is to [the Trobrianders] a virtue and to be hungry, or even to have a sound appetite, is shameful."[5] This attitude is deeply entrenched in the Massim world. There would appear to be three reasons why having a good appetite is cause for shame. All three have to do with the importance attached to "the work of expanding outward" in the Massim world. The first pertains to the way eating interferes with one's capacity for giving. The least productive way to dispose of one's food resources is to consume them oneself. It is considered better, in the sense of more productive of renown, to use appetite-dulling magic on oneself and one's kin so that the food remains available for distribution to overseas *kula* visitors. The advantage of this course of action, as a Gawa man explained to Nancy Munn, is that the visitors "will take away its noise...its fame.... If we ourselves eat, there will be no noise, no fame, it will disappear.... Gawa would have no *kula* shells."[6]

The second reason is that eating is felt to weigh a person down and induce lethargy. On ceremonial occasions, a person wants to feel buoyant and quick, like a canoe bobbing on the sea. The third is that eating is supposed to spoil or dull the lustre of a person's body decorations. The underlying rationale for these beliefs is that eating is an act of *interiorization*, associated with sluggishness and the darkness of the inside of the house. *Kula* beauty magic is aimed at the *exteriorization* of the person, which is accomplished by scrubbing off the body's habitual coating of "hiding darkness" and extending the body in light by means of the paints that give an "expansive quality of sharp brilliance to the body that intensifies visibility and presence."[7] Seeing the flashing body and face of the *kula* visitor is supposed to make the host's senses swim, or "move his mind" as the expression goes, and "loosen" his grip on the valuables he holds, so that he relinquishes them.[8] It is for this reason that the act of appearing or "being seen"

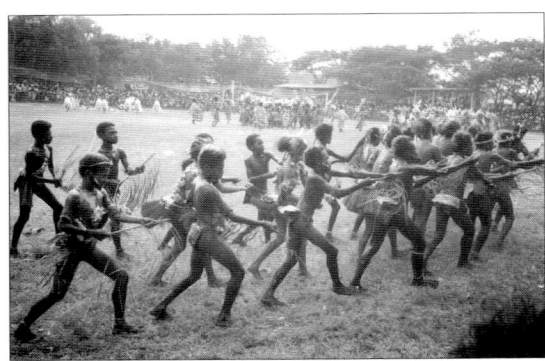

Trobriand youth corps at the
Port Moresby Show
Papua New Guinea, 1990
Photo: the author

ranks higher than the act of eating in the hierarchy of *kula* activities, and no self-respecting leader of a *kula* expedition will consume local fare until valuables have been acquired. It should be noted that there is more to Massim body decoration than meets the eye. Virtually every act of self-decoration extends the body through the medium of smell as well as light, since all of the local cosmetic substances (the native pigments and oils) are either naturally fragrant or are made aromatic. In this way, all of the senses lead inexorably to the aural dimension of *kula* exchange.

Being the Talk of the *Kula*: Attaining Thunderdom

A Massim "man of influence" will pride himself on the fact that there are islands where people have "never seen my face, but they know my name."[9] Such renown stems from the circulation of the man's name in connection with the shells of note, also distinguished by name, which have passed through his possession. This is the aural dimension of *kula* exchange, a dimension that is regarded by Massim people themselves as more extensive than the olfactory or visual dimensions, and that has been the subject of greater symbolic elaboration. The reason for this greater elaboration seems to be that there are no geographic limits to the distance at which a person's name can be spoken, whereas there are limits to the distance at which a person can be seen or scented.

The acoustics of *kula*ing are best broached by examining the steps involved in attaining *kula* stardom – or perhaps "thunderdom" would be a better word, since the process is actually one of becoming a name with no face, quite different from stardom as known in the West. This metaphor is suggested by the closing lines of a Trobriand *kula* spell: "My fame is like thunder/my treading is like earthquake."[10] These words encapsulate the aspiration of every man of the *kula*.

The handsome young man of the *kula*, who is just starting out (usually with the aid of a shell supplied by his father or mother's brother), pays much attention to his body decoration. He goes places to be seen, but more importantly to listen. Listening is a more productive activity than being seen in two ways. First, by appearing to listen and

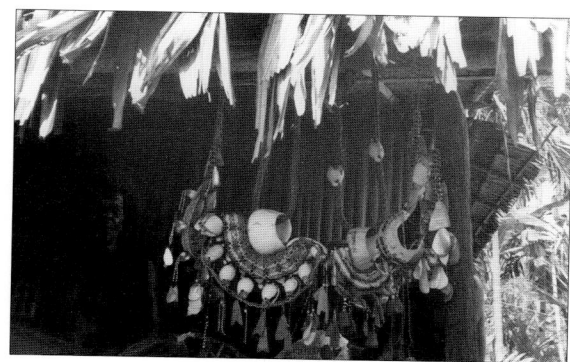

Kula armshells (*mwali*)
Dobu, Papua New Guinea, 1990
Photo: the author

lending assistance to his sponsor (father or mother's brother), the youth becomes known to the latter's partners as trustworthy and dependable, and therefore stands in better stead of inheriting the older man's *kula* paths. Second, it is only by listening to the discourses of more senior men that the youth can acquire the knowledge of the names, transaction histories, and current locations of shells, as well as the speaking skills necessary to obtain shells.

"*Kula* speech" includes discourse about the identities and locations of shells, and the rhetorical skills necessary for persuading partners to relinquish shells. A "man of influence," or "big man," is one who has mastered this speech and thereby established himself as a "name" – that is, one "to whom others should 'listen'...or to whose requests they may be influenced to 'agree.'"[11] A man's name, in this sense, condenses all of the acts of persuasion he has accomplished in the course of his *kula* career. Junior men feel themselves to be lacking a name. Indeed, the problem for the junior man is precisely that he is a face with no name. His aspiration is to become a name with no face. He wants to grow out of being seen and into being talked about or heard. That is the trajectory of thunderdom.

The successful *kula* career involves a progression from the realm of sight to that of sound. This hierarchization of the sensory qualities of the person is manifest in other ways as well. Consider, for example, the names of the categories into which shells are classified on the island of Vakuta, southern Trobriands.[12] On Vakuta, the highest standard or class of *bagi* (necklaces) is called *Bagiriku*; *riku* means "earthquake" or "to shake." It is said that when a man hears the name of a valuable belonging to this category, his body will "shake with desire." The second-highest class is called *Bagido; dou* means "to call, to beckon." Necklaces of this category are said to "call" armshells to them. The name of the highest class of *mwali* (armshells), *Mwarikau*, contains a reference to "blindness" (*kau*), which may be interpreted as connoting age, given that failing sight is culturally associated with advanced age. The second-highest category of armshells is called *Mwaributu*; *butu* means "noise, sound," and "news, rumour" – hence "fame."

All valuables belonging to the above-mentioned classes are distinguished by the fact that they possess individual names and individual histories, in addition to the requisite tactile and visual qualities (diameter or length, smoothness, colour, etc.). It is striking that the names of these categories make no reference to the latter qualities: rather, the references in the names are all to the sonorous and motile qualities or acoustic and kinetic *effects* that the valuables are deemed to produce.

Bwibwi is the term used to denote the range of shell appendages or attachments, such as trade beads, seeds, other types of shells, and bits of plastic or tin. These attachments indicate the status and classification of a shell; for example, five cowrie shells attached to the lip of an armshell signify that it belongs to the *Mwarikau* category. According to Shirley Campbell, the attachments indicate status but do not add to it: they are "mere decorations."[13] This is an unfortunate choice of words. Things that look to be merely decorative are typically packed with symbolic significance in the Massim. For example, the sensory qualities of the media used to decorate or "extend" a person's body are not only indicative but *constitutive* of the value of that person. That the same goes for shell decor becomes apparent when we examine the sensory effects produced by the attachments.

Basically, the appendages serve to extend the boundaries of the valuable by virtue of their motility and the way they make a chiming or tinkling noise. It is fitting that the attachments enlarge the body of the shell, extending it outward in space, given the connection between beautification and exteriorization that was noted earlier. It is also fitting that they impart motion (specifically a trembling motion) to the shell, since the essence of a valuable lies in its mobility – its being for transmission. The main function of the attachments, however, is to "signify success in *kula* exchange through sound," hence the significance of the tinkling or chiming noise they make.[14] This function is particularly evident on Vakuta, where *kula* exchange takes place mostly at night. The man who has just won a valuable has a friend carry it off to the beach. "In response to the [chiming] sound of *bwibwi*, villagers will call from the dark to inquire for whom the carrier walks."[15] News spreads quickly, and soon the man's name and that of the valuable are on everybody's lips.

The sound of the *bwibwi* chiming is the first ramification of the success of the man who has just won a valuable on the *kula* exchange. The news is understood to be relayed by various creatures, such as the monitor lizard, who trumpets on the island of Tewara (off Dobu). "The women staying at home [on Dobu] hear the sound and send round word that their men folk have secured valuables."[16] It is much the same in the Trobriands: returning home from Dobu, the *kula* voyagers' waiting kin "profess to hear thunder roar and feel the ground shake – nature's witness to the success of the voyage and the spreading fame of the men."[17] Upon the men's safe arrival home, songs are composed and performed by the women to commemorate the successful expedition:

> [Women, rather than men, are] the others who transform the selves of the male actors by converting the latter's particular acts and material acquisitions into a verbal discourse that circulates apart from them, the artifacts, and the relevant momentary events. At the same time that [these] chants are about fame and its processes, they also make famous what they chant about.[18]

Noise and mobility are the source of a shell's "history" (literally, its being talked about) as it circulates through different hands, and in time acquires its own individual path and its own personal name. Most shells, however, like most men, never attain status in the upper ranks of *kula* exchange. They are judged too small to warrant a name in the first place, so there is no way of keeping track of them. They arrive in numbers on an island, and leave in numbers, or as it is put in Gawan parlance, "disappear." In effect, they pass unseen, even though their number makes them empirically more visible than the larger, older, slower-moving *mwali* and *bagi*. This point brings out nicely how being an object or a face with no name is "not to be" among the Massim. Existence, like beauty, is in the ear of the beholder.

Making Sense in the Massim World

In light of the ethnographic evidence adduced thus far, the tenets of the theory of oral-aural mentality include:

1) *Primacy is accorded to sound*. Primacy *is* accorded to sound or "noise," as opposed to light, in the Massim world. However, this follows from the importance attached to "expansion outward" and other such cultural values, not simply from the absence of writing. Sound is valued because of its power to intensify a person's presence. Sound is also credited with greater expansive potential than light because a person's name can be spoken at a greater remove than he or she can be seen. Hearing, not sight, is the distance sense in the Massim world.

2) *Hearing is the dominant sense*. It *is* possible to construe hearing as the dominant sense in the Massim world. For example, it is associated with both socialization and sanity, as one can gather from the following Duau childrearing maxim: "If a child runs about too much to other villages and does not listen to father and mother, when his parents die he will be like *uwauwa* [mad], not knowing how to do things properly."[19] It is of related interest to note that the chief god of the Trobriand underworld is supposed to have large ears that flap continually.[20] We might speculate that the exaggerated ears of this deity can be seen as iconic of the extended role of hearing in Massim culture.

However, this interpretation of the cultural salience of hearing is misleading to the extent that it deflects attention from the fact that even greater value and importance is attached to "being heard." It is the same with the other senses: being seen is valued over seeing, being smelled is valued over smelling and not eating (so there can be more food to distribute to others) is valued over eating. The way sensing the world is conceptualized in Massim psychology is, in an interesting sense, exactly the reverse of the way perception is conceptualized in Western psychology. In the Massim, perception has to do with the *production* of effects in others, as opposed to the *reception* of incoming stimuli. This ex-centric conception of the perceptual process is consistent with the cultural emphasis on "expansion outward." The *self-outered*, as opposed to self-centred, directionality of Massim sensory psychology may also be seen to go along with the exchange-oriented, as opposed to consumer-oriented, character of Massim society.

3) *The intellect is associated with hearing*. There is support for the proposition that intelligence is associated with hearing rather than, say, sight in the Duau childrearing maxim quoted above. Mental disorder is conceptualized as a kind of hearing disorder. However, the intellect is not actually thought to be situated in the ear or head. Malinowski records that "The seat of *nanola*, 'mind', is located in the throat, in the larynx, as they say, this being the place from which a person speaks."[21] It follows that hearing is not yet knowing in the Massim, at least not in the same way that "hearing is understanding" for

such ear-minded peoples as the Suyà of Brazil or "seeing is believing" in the West.[22] In the Massim, for something to be known it must first be voiced.

In the Massim world, then, thinking seems to involve speaking and hearing oneself talk at the same time, either inwardly or outwardly. Malinowski's account of how spells are learned both confirms this point and brings out how the memory is thought to be situated in a different part of the body from the mind, namely the belly:

> A man will be said to have a good *nanola* when he can acquire many formulae, but though they enter through the larynx, naturally, as he learns them, repeating word for word, he has to stow them away in a bigger and more commodious receptacle: they sink down right to the bottom of his abdomen.[23]

The idea that the memory resides in the belly explains why a novice sorcerer is obliged to drink salt water to purge his belly before receiving instruction from his mentor. It also explains why the sorcerer must refrain from food while practicing his art. The belly is regarded as a receptacle for words that are interiorized by repetition, and the place from which magic exits. For the belly to contain or yield knowledge (read: "noise-force"), it must first be empty of food.

Awareness of this antithesis between eating and "sound thinking," as the Massim conception of cognition might be called, would appear to be on the wane, as implied in the following Trobriand incident:

> One day I asked some men where magic resided. Bunemiga shook his head and said, "I think our ancestors made a mistake about that because they said magic stayed in the belly. If that were true, then when we defecated we would lose all the magic. Our ancestors were wrong about magic. I think it stays in our heads."[24]

For the ancestors, however, the digestive tract was not the only tract that led to the belly, and words were not assimilated the same way food is. The mutual exclusivity of eating and memorization is still recognized on Gawa. There, "eating" is a metaphor for forgetting. Bunemiga, it seems, has already forgotten how to remember.

4) *Knowledge must be cast in verbal formulae, such as rhymes or commonplaces, in order to be memorable.* Orality theorists, such as Donald Lowe, go so far as to claim that "The metric recitation of rhythmic formulas and commonplaces provides a communicational grid to *determine* knowledge in oral culture. Only those phenomena which fit existing formulas and commonplaces can be preserved as knowledge."[25] Thought therefore tends to be formulaic, rather than analytical.

Supporting this proposition is the fact that Massim magical speech is strongly formulaic, contains many puns and is heavily repetitive. However, the repetition is considered to be more for the purpose of intensifying presence than storing knowledge, and the puns are typically esoteric and inventive rather than commonplace.[26] Furthermore, it is not solely in the verbal structure of the spell that knowledge is stored and communicated. The physical medium into which the spell is spoken is of *equal* importance. Indeed, the medium is intrinsic both to the conceptualization and to the communication (or effectiveness) of the message. For example, a spell to make a canoe speed along is uttered into a bundle of pandanus leaves, which always flutter even in the slightest wind and thus suggest movement. The spoken word is therefore more dependent on its material embodiment in Massim practice than the theory of oral mentality would allow.

The theory of oral mentality also fails to accord adequate importance to modes of thought and communication other than speech in oral societies. Knowledge may be encoded in non-verbal forms as well. For example, Patrick Glass has shown that knowledge of the male role in procreation was emblazoned on Trobriand war shields. The apparently abstract designs are, in fact, anatomical diagrams. Such knowledge could not be verbalized precisely "for fear of offending 'the ears of the spirits.'"[27] This, then, is a case of knowledge *having* to be encoded non-verbally for cultural or religious reasons.

A further limitation of language that orality theorists often fail to appreciate is that words, particularly "hard words" as they are called in the Trobriands (that is, words spoken in anger or that state the truth), can be all too memorable. Annette Weiner noted a marked reticence among her Trobriand informants as regards making explicit their thoughts and intentions: these are, in fact, *supposed* to remain hidden. Rather than define a situation by speaking about it, Trobrianders often prefer to express their thoughts and emotions through food gifts, *kula* shells, and other nonverbal media, such as body decoration.[28]

As we have seen, *kula* shells and body decorations constitute extensions of the senses. These nonverbal media of communication may convey very detailed or analytical appraisals of a person's worth (i.e., the esteem in which a man is held by his *kula* partner) or a situation's significance. Where, then, does the idea that thought in oral societies is "nonanalytical" come from? It comes from the orality theorist assuming that speech is paramount, and looking only to linguistic usage for evidence of "analytic" modes of thought. Not finding anything but formulae used in public oratory, magic, and mythtelling, the orality theorist concludes that thought in oral societies is nonanalytical. But this is a foregone conclusion if those are the only places the analyst is prepared to look!

5) *The individuation (or rational structuring) of ideas, as of people, is comparatively slight.* This branch of the theory of oral mentality holds that thought in oral cultures tends to be diffuse or "participatory" (meaning emotional) as opposed to "rational." The theory, according to Lowe, holds that "Speech is assimilated directly by the ear, without the mediation of the eye. And we are moved more by sound than by sight, since the former surrounds us, whereas the latter distances."[29] Personality structures are also deemed to be more collectivist than individualist (or sociocentric instead of egocentric) in oral cultures because hearing is a more "social" sense.

Giancarlo Scoditti's account of the apprenticeship of prowboard carvers on Kitava provides an instructive context for the examination of this proposition. One of the stages in the initiation rite for an apprentice carver involves the carver-initiator uttering a spell as he and the initiate bend over a pool of water. The spell is supposed to induce the apprentice to see himself as the reflection, or mirror-image, of his instructor:

> The mind of the initiate, as the mind of his mirrored image, the carver-initiator, is "wrapped" or "enveloped" [in the course of the rite] by an external power, sometimes thought of as the mythical hero Monikiniki.... The performers [who have become as one] are momentarily "blind." During the performers' blindness the hero Monikiniki, represented...as "Shout," spreads his creative power upon them, and they in their turn "spread" the same power, as "images," upon the commoners.[30]

The carver-initiator is the link between the initiate and the culture hero Monikiniki, just as the prowboards he has carved mediate the initiate's first "vision" of the abstract model (the ideal form of the prowboard) he will later reproduce in his own work. The purpose of the rite is to transform this relation of mediation into one of identification. Hence its strong "participatory" or "confused" character, as McLuhan and Ong would say.

While it is certainly possible to point to various cases of "mystical participation" in Massim culture, such as the above, there is an equal if not stronger accent on differentiation. People distinguish themselves from each other by means of the food taboos they keep and, significantly, by means of the sounds they make. For instance, rattling one's lime spatula in one's lime gourd is a chiefly prerogative in the Trobriands, something commoners are forbidden to emulate.

People are above all differentiated by their faces. A child's face is supposed to resemble its father's visage, both in those cultures where physiological paternity is recognized and in the Trobriands, where it is not.[31] The significance of this resemblance lies in the fact that it is through the father that the individual is connected with the world outside the confines of his or her own matrilineal sub-clan (*susu* or *dala*). As Nancy Munn puts it, facial appearance is "the domain of relationality to the other or to an extrinsic, external order."[32] The "expansion outward" of the individual is thus already visible, already implicit, in the features of that individual's face at birth. The individual's life will be spent establishing ever more interfaces with the external world through food distribution, courting, *kula*ing, and so on – in short, all the arenas where a person's own individual fame can be enhanced through exchange.

De-Essentializing the Senses

We can conclude, then, that there is no intrinsic connection between orality and aurality. The significance of hearing in a given culture's epistemic (and aesthetic) order is not explicable in terms of the presence or absence of writing. In fact, as Constance Classen observes, "there is as much sensory diversity among so-called oral cultures as there is between such cultures and the [literate] visualist West."[33] Some "oral cultures" privilege smell, others privilege touch; it happens that many oral cultures attach fundamental symbolic significance to sound and hearing (as in the case of the Massim world), but there are also those that privilege sight. In any event, it is not which sense is treated as dominant that gives a culture its distinctive character. Rather, it is the specific manner in which the senses are distinguished from and combined with each other in practice, according to the culture's sensory model. In the case of the Massim world, the senses are ordered and used so as to maximize the "expansion outward" of the individual. This gives rise to a distinctive mode of being-in-the-world, one in which suppressing the appetite, feeling buoyant, and appearing (and smelling) radiant accumulate in their effects so that the person comes to be heeded and talked about far and wide.

NOTES

Part of the research on which this essay is based was made possible by grants from the Social Sciences and Humanities Research Council of Canada and Concordia University.

1. See Marshall McLuhan, *The Gutenberg Galaxy* (Toronto: University of Toronto Press, 1962) and Walter J. Ong, *Orality and Literacy* (New York: Methuen, 1982). Aspects of the theory of oral-aural mentality can be found reiterated in the works of numerous anthropologists such as Jack Goody, *The Domestication of the Savage Mind* (Cambridge: Cambridge University Press, 1977) and Stephen Tyler, *The Unspeakable: Discourse, Dialogue and Rhetoric in the Postmodern World* (Madison, WI: University of Wisconsin Press, 1987). Certain of its tenets also figure as commonplaces in the work of cultural theorists such as Donald Lowe, *History of Bourgeois Perception* (Chicago: University of Chicago Press, 1982) and Derrick De Kerckhove, *The Skin of Culture: Investigating the New Electronic Reality* (Toronto: Somerville House, 1995).

2. Annette Weiner, *The Trobrianders of Papua New Guinea* (New York: Holt, Rinehart & Winston, 1988), 159–61.

3. Bronislaw Malinowski, *Argonauts of the Western Pacific* (New York: E. P. Dutton, 1961), 167.

4. Weiner, 9.

5. Bronislaw Malinowski, *Coral Gardens and Their Magic*, vol. 1 (Bloomington: Indiana University Press, 1965), 227.

6. Nancy Munn, *The Fame of Gawa: A Symbolic Study of Value Transformation in a Massim (Papua New Guinea) Society* (Cambridge: Cambridge University Press, 1986), 49.

7. See Munn, *The Fame of Gawa*, 89–101. See further Malinowski, *Argonauts*, 336; Weiner, 69.

8. See Nancy Munn, "Gawan *Kula*: Spatio-temporal Control and the Symbolism of Influence," in *The Kula: New Perspectives on Massim Exchange*, eds. Jerry W. Leach and Edmund Leach (Cambridge: Cambridge University Press, 1983), 278, 284–86.

9. Weiner, 143; Munn, *The Fame of Gawa*, 106.

10. Malinowski, *Argonauts*, 199.

11. Munn, "Gawan *Kula*," 277. See further Susan Montague, "Trobriand Gender Identity," *Mankind* 14:1 (1983): 33, 42.

12. See Shirley Campbell, "Attaining Rank: A Classification of *Kula* Shell Valuables," in *The Kula: New Perspectives on Massim Exchange*, eds. Jerry Leach and Edmund Leach (Cambridge: Cambridge University Press, 1983).

13. Campbell, 234.

14. Campbell, 234; Munn, *The Fame of Gawa*, 114.

15. Campbell, 236.

16. Reo Fortune, *Sorcerers of Dobu* (New York: E.P. Dutton, 1963), 221.

17. Weiner, 139.

18. Munn, *The Fame of Gawa*, 112–13.

19. Géza Róheim, *Psychoanalysis and Anthropology* (New York: International Universities Press, 1950), 198.

20. Patrick Glass, "The Trobriand Code: An Interpretation of Trobriand War Shield Designs," *Anthropos* 81 (1986): 47, 56.

21. Malinowski, *Argonauts*, 408–9 and *Coral Gardens*, vol. 1, 445. The same association is found on Dobu and in a weakened form on Gawa. See Fortune, 168; Munn, *The Fame of Gawa*, 68.

22. See David Howes, ed., *The Varieties of Sensory Experience: A Sourcebook in the Anthropology of the Senses* (Toronto: University of Toronto Press, 1991), 175–78; Tyler, 149–70.

23. Malinowski, *Argonauts*, 409. See further Munn, *The Fame of Gawa*, 228, 290 n. 32.

24. Annette Weiner, *Women of Value, Men of Renown: New Perspectives in Trobriand Exchange* (Austin: University of Texas Press, 1976), 252.

25. Lowe, 3 (emphasis added).

26. See Malinowski, *Argonauts*, 441, 448, 452.

27. Glass, 60.

28. See Weiner, *The Trobrianders*, 39 and *Women of Value*, 86–7, 212; and Annette Weiner, "From Words to Objects to Magic: Hard Words and the Boundaries of Social Interaction," *Man*, n.s., 18 (1983): 690. See further Munn, *The Fame of Gawa*, 68.

29. Lowe, 7.

30. Giancarlo Scoditti, "Aesthetics: The Significance of Apprenticeship on Kitawa," *Man*, n.s., 17 (1982): 74, 79.

31. See Bronislaw Malinowski, *The Sexual Life of Savages in North-Western Melanesia* (New York: Harcourt, Brace & World, 1929), 204; Weiner, *Women of Value*, 123; Munn, *The Fame of Gawa*, 142–43.

32. Munn, *The Fame of Gawa*, 143.

33. Constance Classen, *Worlds of Sense: Exploring the Senses in History and Across Cultures* (New York and London: Routledge, 1993), 122. In *The Color of Angels: Cosmology, Gender and the Aesthetic Imagination* (New York and London: Routledge, 1998), Classen goes on to document the sensory diversity internal to Western culture.

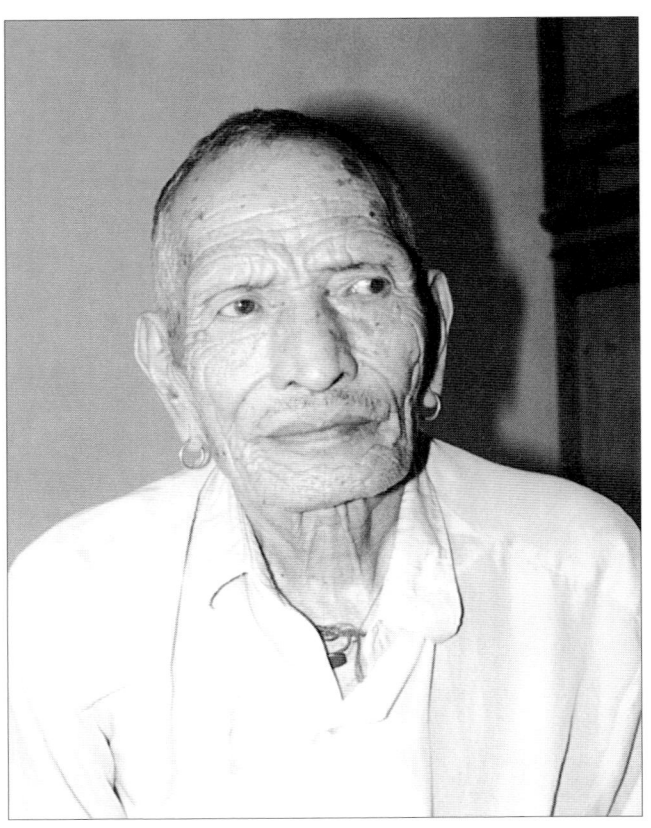

Ghang Lama
1998
Photo: the author

Echoes of a Yolmo Buddhist's Life, in Death

Robert Desjarlais

"Shyi mandi mareko hoina. Sareko ho." I hear these words as I drive south along Interstate 84, gliding past Worcester and Hartford and a world of unknown places as the magnetic trace of a voice recorded months before sounds through an unreliable tape deck set on the seat beside me.[1] Time and again during these weekly commutes from Boston to New York and back again, I listen to the voice and try to soak up the sounds and grammars of the sentences heard. I wonder about the welfare of the speaker, hoping that the old man is alive and well and talking still while asking myself why there isn't more of an anthropology of voice, of the histories of voicings in their many particulars as they are heard and echoed by others who speak or write in turn.

Shyi mandi mareko hoina... "Dying does not mean dying."[2] The voice belongs, if a voice can ever belong to its speaker, especially once it is recorded and resounded electronically, to an elderly man often called "Ghang Lama" or "Hill Lama" by other members of his community, many of whom identify themselves as "Yolmo wa" or "Yolmo people," an ethnically Tibetan Buddhist people who for two centuries or so have lived in hamlets and villages along the upper ridges of the Yolmo or Helambu Valley of north-central Nepal. Ghang Lama, also called "Mheme" (pronounced "mhem-mhē") or "Grandfather" by family and friends, lived in a village in the Yolmo region until some twenty years ago, when, in seeking a more comfortable life in the city, he moved with his second wife and daughter to Chabahil, an ethnically mixed neighbourhood on the eastern outskirts of Kathmandu, about a mile west of the Tibetan neighbourhood of Boudhanath. Born in 1916, the second son of a respected priest from a prestigious lama lineage, Mheme raised a daughter and three sons with his first wife, who died in 1964. He remarried two years later, and his second wife soon gave birth to a daughter, as yet unmarried and living still with her parents. Much of his life had been spent either farming or practicing "the lama work," with the former taking priority in his youth and the latter gaining importance as he grew older, in part because his weakening body prevented him from working as he once did, and in part because he wanted, as many Yolmo men and women do, to prepare well for death. "Now the most important thing to do is to die," he told me.

...Sareko ho. Dying "means moving." Ghang Lama took his death to be quite imminent when I came to know him well, in the summer of 1997, when he was in his early eighties, his body seemingly comprised then of frail bones, a weather-lined face, and steady, gentle eyes: he felt that the "burning flame" he knew to be lodged in his forehead was slowly dimming, and that, with his *tshe* or "life" expiring, he hadn't much time left. For several months that summer and again in the winter and spring of the following year, I worked with him to elicit and record his "life story" (*jīvan kathā*). Much of

this work entailed travelling from Boudhanath, where I was staying at the time (in the home of his first son, in fact), to Mheme's house in Chabahil, and visiting and talking with him and his family. Often at first I was accompanied by Mheme's grandson Norbu, a twenty-three-year-old man who had lived and studied in India until he was 18, when he returned to Nepal with his parents and siblings to set up a home in Kathmandu. Norbu, who speaks Nepali and English fluently, helped me to explain to his grandfather what I hoped to accomplish, and then joined me in my initial conversations with him. Several months after I left Nepal in 1997, Norbu himself travelled to New York with the help of a sponsor letter I wrote on his behalf. When I returned in 1998, Nogapu, a Yolmo friend, agreed to help me understand Mheme's use of Yolmo, a Tibetan language that most Yolmo wa consider their native language. Mheme took an immediate liking to Nogapu, in part, I think, because Nogapu, like Mheme but unlike Norbu, grew up in Yolmo, spoke Yolmo fluently, and knew village life well.

Dying does not quite mean dying. Fair enough. But does the same principle hold for a society and culture that has changed substantially in the past two decades? This was a question on the minds of many Yolmo wa living in Kathmandu in the 1990s, when young people and (usually wealthier) families continued to migrate from the Yolmo region to the city in search of employment, better education for their children, and more *kyipu* or "comfort" than could be found in any village. People spoke often of the consequences of these dispersals: houses in Yolmo were being boarded up; mostly elderly people and impoverished farmers remained in the villages; the forests were growing wild again; children studying in Kathmandu were learning Nepali rather than Yolmo as their first language; and many youths were, like Norbu, leaving Kathmandu to look for better paying jobs in places like New York City. Many I spoke with, young and old, were concerned that traditional Yolmo culture was eroding away, with the histories and lifeways of "the old days" soon to be lost with the passing of the most senior Yolmo wa. In response to these concerns, several organizations had been created with the aim of cultivating and preserving aspects of Yolmo society. "If we don't collect the stories, if we don't know the history, everything will be lost," one member of a Yolmo student association told me in speaking of the work he and other students sought to do in their free time. Given that many Yolmo wa would agree that a death is often "the death of memory,"[3] my plans to record the life histories of elderly Yolmo men and women were well-received by acquaintances when I returned to Nepal in 1997 after an eight-year absence. And while neither Mheme nor I put it in so many words when I introduced the subject to him, I believe he also found that our work together could substantiate something of his life and time, especially if we conversed not in Nepali but in Yolmo, a language that, he felt, embodied so much of Yolmo culture. "We should not leave the Yolmo language," he once said pointedly to Norbu, who, to Mheme's chagrin, knew but a few words. To later insist, after Norbu had left for the States, that our conversations take place in Yolmo was therefore to make a political statement about the value of this language and the need to preserve it as well as the cultural heritage encoded within it.[4]

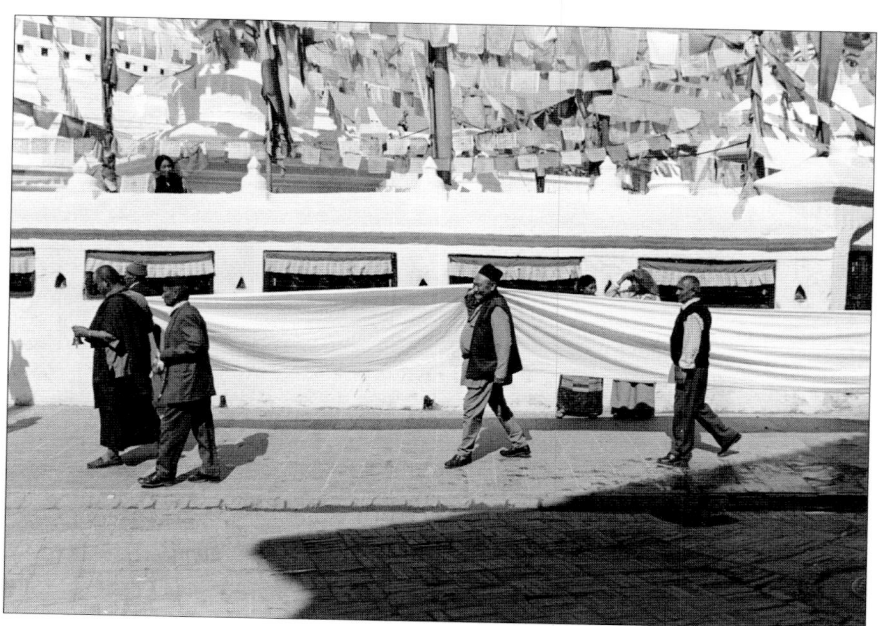

Yolmo funeral procession
2001
Photo: the author

What is "dying," what is "moving," how does a culture shape the makings of a life or the meanings of a death? What does it mean to generate a life story in a place where people often advance the idea that a life is, by nature, impermanent, ephemeral, perhaps ultimately illusory, and yet also highly consequential? Through a mix of Nepali, Yolmo, and English, profoundly co-constructed, multi-authored traces of a life took form: while Yolmo wa do have some culturally patterned ideas of biographies and life histories as the oral or written recounting of an individual's significant doings and travels while alive, I soon realized that Mheme would not be talking freely and at length about his life as though recounting an artfully formed story without prompting. Rather, much like others who told me something about their lives, he seemed to expect that our conversations would build on a protocol of questions and answers, in which he would respond, sometimes concisely and sometimes at length, to specific questions that I posed; perhaps he had gleaned from previous observations that this was how I sometimes went about my research, or he had spotted reporters interview people on television, or, alternately, a complex set of motives and expectations led us to proceed in this manner. In any event, as his daughter Maya served us cup after cup of salt-butter tea, and the tape recorder, set on a rickety chair between us, quietly "picked up" traces of our words, my companions and I asked the lama a range of questions about his life, from memories of childhood to his thoughts about the fate of Yolmo culture.

What interests me most here are less the specifics of the man's biography than what he understood was going on when I came to talk to him and his words took form on paper – what, in effect, the act of inscribing his life on paper meant for him. The likes of such an inquiry are seldom to be found in life history research in anthropology. While detailed narrations of non-Western lives are commonly generated, as are reflective essays that examine in sophisticated ways how ethnographers came to regard those lives or engaged dialogically with their informants, rarely have anthropologists seriously examined how life history informants themselves make sense of the act of setting their lives to paper. Nor have they considered the potential consequences of such an act, or, significantly, the personal sensibilities or cultural metaphysics that shape the act and its consequences as perceived by those involved. I would like to try something along these lines by mulling over a few of Mheme's words and the meanings apparently implicit in those words. My aim is to convey what I think he in part thought our engagements were about in order to detail the various ways in which a written account of his life might come to "echo" in his life or after his death.

Such an inquiry also requires an attempt to understand something of the pragmatic import of people's engagements with one another. It requires an attempt, that is, to estimate the potential social significance and real-world effects of various utterances and actions – how people do things with words, as well as how words and actions do things on their own, in particular social worlds. Anthropological inquiries of this sort usually investigate how certain actions, such as a lengthy pause or a laugh or a sigh, build to certain identities or understandings, with conscious intention or not, in the course of a conversation or two in order to understand more precisely how discursive meanings take form through social engagements. Here, the focus is broader and more diffuse, concerned, as it is, with the meanings that emerged, in the span of a year and beyond, with meanings that are emerging still, out of the heteroglossic invocation of a life. And since what I have come to know of this invocation is similarly tied to the emergence of meanings in time, my writing reflects, in some ways, my shifting awareness of what is at stake, and what my responsibilities might be, in the writing of that life.

As for such meanings, it strikes me that in order to make sense of what my work with Ghang Lama meant for him, one first needs to consider *how* things mean for him and other Yolmo wa. This is to say that those who live outside the folds of Yolmo culture must try to suspend their own notions about how signs signify and explore something of the ethnosemiotic sensibilities of these people and how those sensibilities contributed to the ways in which the lama thought of his life and the textual inscription of that life. To do this effectively, one needs to attend to how he and other Yolmo wa think of the interrelated workings of such matters as language, time, bodiliness, personhood, life, and death, and what it meant for an aged man to tell something of his life at a time when he thought that life to be ending.

A Logic of Echoes

One rainy afternoon in the spring of 1998 Mheme used a word with multiple, intershading connotations that has greatly influenced how I have come to think about his life and the meanings he and I have invested in his life story. In trying to elicit Mheme's thoughts on good ways to die, Nogapu and I had asked if it was better if family members kept quiet in the presence of a dying person, which is something I had heard other Yolmo wa speak of. "It's good, for sure," he said in response, then continued:

> If no noises are made, it's good. If it's quiet, we can die well.... If it's quiet, we can get the way easily. If the noisy sounds come, then the dead person becomes confused. He gets confused, the poor man. If he dies and is lost, what can we do?

He then went on to describe what happens to a dead person during the *bardo* or "intermediate" state between one life and the next, and ended by detailing what the soul encounters when it tries to leave the deceased's body: namely, amplified features of that person's body as perceived by the itinerant soul as it journeys through it:

> We need not go somewhere else, far away. After we die, if we have long hair, we can see lice and a bear and tiger. The hair appears like a jungle. We can see a bear and a big tiger. The forehead appears like a plain, and the nose appears

like a big hill. When they say the soul goes out, it's our own body that frightens us. Our shadow [*dhip*] frightens us. Whatever we do, our shadow does the same thing. That's called an echo [*bhaja*]. When we make a loud sound, an echo is heard. If we say "wey!", it also says "wey!" That's called *bhaja*. "Good echo" [*bhaja zangbu*] is said: if we've done good, good comes. If we've done bad, bad comes.

After a pause, he continued:

Bhaja is like imagining. If we imagine good things, then, after we die, they echo in what we see. If we make a loud noise, a bad echo [*bhaja*] comes. If we pray "*Om mani-padme hum,*" a good echo comes. If people are crying and fighting and making a lot of noise, then it's no good. If one dies when it's very quiet, it's good. Noises are no good.

A cluster of subtly overlapping meanings infused Mheme's uses of the Yolmo word *bhaja*. He first used the word in speaking of echoes. *Bhaja* in this sense means very much what "echo" does in English: the repetition or reverberation of a sound. Its nineteenth-century Tibetan equivalent, *brag-cha*, which is also translated as "echo," appears to have literally meant "rock-noise" or "rock-clamour."[5] As Mheme observed, "When we make a loud sound, an echo is heard. If we say 'wey!' it also says 'wey!'" But for Mheme and other Yolmo wa, visual echoes of sorts can also occur; as the soul tries to journey beyond its corporeal abode, features of the deceased's body (hair, forehead, nose) "appear like" elements of a landscape (jungle, plain, hill). An element of mimesis is therefore at work here, for echoes, be they acoustic or visual in nature, simulate the phenomenon they resound or revision. From this perspective, as Mheme noted, a person's shadow can be seen as a *bhaja* or illusory visual echo of that person, while the thoughts of the dying person or the cries of grief-stricken family members can reverberate in the liminal, phantasmagoric world encountered in the hours after a death. As he put it, "*Bhaja* is like imagining. If we imagine good things, then, after we die, they echo in what we see. If we make a loud noise, a bad echo comes." For this reason, bereaved family members should not mourn a loss too vocally since their cries will be heard as noises by the deceased, with the din of any noises sounding in direct proportion to the intensity of the cries: "How many teardrops, that much rain comes. The sound of crying brings thunder," Mheme explained.

Such mimetic acts mesh well with the "homological" or "analogical" thinking of many South Asian and Himalayan peoples, in which images and objects are understood to resemble or ritually stand for other, often sacred, images or beings. Aspects of Ghang Lama's world often involved such homologies, and mimesis was for him a common, but by no means the only, means of thought and being. He and other lamas tried when meditating, for instance, to imagine their bodies as resembling the divine forms of great bodhisattvas; the king's palace, he told us, was but "a very small model" of a deity's palace in heaven; and, like other Yolmo wa, he said he learned how to do things largely by watching others and then copying what they did. It is important to note, however, that a strong temporal dimension often inhered in the mimetic echoes Mheme spoke of. Certain acts or images repeated or were repeated in turn. In general, then, it is not simply a question of copies or simulations, as many modern Western discussions of mimesis suggest, but about repetitions and re-presentations in time. When it comes to such repetitions, any copies are like the original, but not quite – much as, for Mheme, dying is like dying, but not quite. Intrinsic to ideas of repetition, especially among Yolmo wa, are ideas of death and rebirth. In its most basic configuration, a logic of echoes implies a logic of change, loss, and death in that one sound or form replaces another in time, and earlier forms dissolve in time. To repeat is to occasion a death in some way. An echo can therefore signify a loss; it can indicate the absence of something once present, something that can only be represented through a reverberation of some sort.

Yolmo wa understand an echo to be something immaterial and unreal. One hears the echo "as though" one was hearing the actual sound, but usually while knowing well that it is not the actual sound. Since the repeated sound is secondary to the original, it is commonly taken to be an illusory, insubstantial trace of the original. *Bhaja*, then, can also mean "illusion," and Ghang Lama and others use the word in this sense as well.[6] "That is only the heartmind imagining," Mheme once said of phenomena encountered by a deceased person soon after dying. "There's not really a body. It's only an illusion [*bhaja*], for sure." Mheme might have had this connotation in mind as well when he observed that "*Bhaja* is like imagining," for, as a good Buddhist, he would at times understand and encourage his interlocutors to realize that much of life, including a person's body and self-perceptions, is an illusory apparition. Echoes, then, are on a par with other illusory phenomena, such as mirages and hallucinations, in that, despite their differences, they all involve perceptual phenomena that are understood to be not materially real. As a Yolmo lama put it one day when explaining to me the illusory nature of *bhaja*, "We say from our Tibetan books, '*bhaja tabu, gyuma tabu, migyug tabu*' [like an echo, like an illusion, like a mirage]." One such book, read often by Yolmo lamas, relies on similar thinking in advising its listeners to recognize all phenomena of waking life as being "like a dream, a magical illusion, an echo, a fairy city, a mirage, a reflection, an optical illusion, the moon in water, lacking even a moment's truth-status, definitely untrue, and false."[7] For Yolmo wa, *bhaja* can be understood as an "as though" phenomenon: as an apparition that appears, but only appears, to be real.

In fact, Yolmo lamas like Mheme advise, as do their Tibetan counterparts, that the images perceived in the hours and days after a person dies are best understood as apparitions of this sort. Mheme, like other Yolmo lamas, often reads a Tibetan text called the *Bardo thos grol* (usually pronounced as *Bardo Thedol* in Yolmo), a title that can be translated as "Liberation Through Hearing/Understanding in the Between," although the

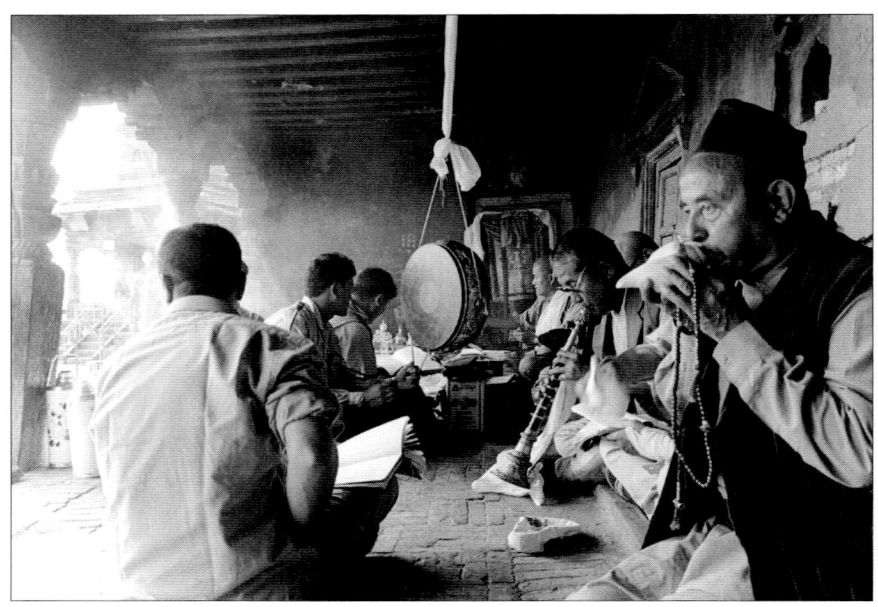

Yolmo priests performing a cremation rite
2001
Photo: the author

text is more famously known in the West as *The Tibetan Book of the Dead*.[8] One of the main reasons for reading this text to oneself while alive, or to others when they are dying or have already died, is that readers or listeners can gain a better understanding of the nature of the apparitions encountered during the "between" and so not be so frightened by or attracted to them in the liminal dreamworld after dying. One passage, for instance, encourages any recipients of its instructions to develop and affirm an understanding that all sights and sounds perceived are one's "own":

> May I know all sounds as my own sounds!
> May I know all lights as my own lights!
> May I know all rays as my own rays!
> May I know the between's reality as mine![9]

Elsewhere the text advises its readers to recognize that all visions encountered in the death-between are "but empty images," the product of one's "own creations," with one's body itself "born by apparition."[10]

For Mheme and other Yolmo wa, such selfsame manifestations are a kind of *bhaja* in that they entail mimetic apparitions of a person's thoughts, utterances, or perceptions. Yet the presence of such manifestations points to the fact that a logic of echoes also implies a logic of traces, of lingering consequences, in that something of an original sound or phenomenon can carry on in subsequent reverberations. An element of mimesis still applies with any echo, for the secondary phenomenon simulates, in some respect, an initial phenomenon or action. An echo contains traces of its predecessor. To repeat is to continue living in some way. Dying does not quite mean dying.

All this helps to explain why the word *bhaja* among Yolmo wa can also refer to a "residue" or "trace" of some sort, particularly of something that no longer exists. The residuum left in an empty teacup, for instance, can be said to be a *bhaja* or "remainder" of the tea that once filled that cup. A ghostly presence, in turn, can be thought to entail a *bhaja* of a person who once inhabited a household, and Yolmo wa often worry that a family member might leave such an unwelcome remainder behind, since such a ghostly trace can have harmful effects on the living. A good death, consequently, is one in which a deceased person does not leave a dangerously strong "echo" behind. When speaking to the spirits of the deceased at funerals, for instance, bereaved family members will often tell them not to "give a *bhaja*" in death or not to "leave a *bhaja* behind." In voicing such concerns, they have in mind the possibility that the deceased might remain attached to his or her former life circumstances and, in effect, "cling" to cherished loved ones or possessions. "His *bhaja* is left behind with his youngest daughter," a sentence I once heard, suggested that a father's ghostly presence was clinging to his daughter; the attachment was threatening to pull the daughter into death as well. Apparitions of the deceased are fitting exemplars of *bhaja*: they occur after the fact, as ghostly traces of beings once alive, as illusory afterimages of former presences, like the original, but not quite.

Invested in Mheme's understanding of the physics of echoes, then, were two somewhat opposed but characteristically Buddhist messages: the understanding that everything is impermanent, that nothing lasts forever, that life is transient, shifting from form to form; and the idea that traces remain, residues linger, rebirths occur, and actions have consequences long after the actions themselves are completed. Life is impermanent and, some say, ultimately illusory, yet the actions a person undertakes in life can effect powerful reverberations. Milarepa, the great eleventh-century Tibetan saint, sang of similar notions in a song of his:

> All that which manifests
> Is unreal as an echo,
> Yet it never fails to produce
> An effect that corresponds.
> Karmas and virtues therefore
> Should never be neglected.[11]

Manifestations of a life, unreal as echoes, produce further, corresponding echoes.

Something of Mheme's understanding of the consequential force of human actions in the world can be heard in his statement, cited above, that "'Good echo' is said: if we've done good, good comes. If we've done bad, bad comes." That is, if people act in morally good ways, good will result, whereas if they harm others, misfortune will plague them sooner or later. In more general terms, and as Milarepa reminded his audience, this is the principle of karma (or *le*, or "work"), as basic and commonsensical to Buddhist peoples as the law of gravity is to others, in which, quite simply, any moral act, good or bad, brings about a correspondingly positive or negative result, either in this or in a future lifetime. The principle, central to Yolmo notions of time and causality, resounded in many aspects of Mheme's life, in his understanding of the moral consequences of actions in a sequence of lives, and in his assumption that good comes of good and bad results from bad: a person who gives alms, he explained, will later prosper; crippled or disfigured bodies were the result, he said, of previous sinful actions, while a person who did not repay his loans in one life would need to work as a servant in the house of his lenders "after being born again." The force of karma sometimes involves a mimetic economy of meaning and action whereby the consequences immanent in certain actions entail "results" echoing in time.

For Ghang Lama and many other Yolmo wa, karmic principles intensify when a person dies. The shadowy images that a recently deceased person encounters in the intermediate state between lives are often held to be manifestations of that person's karmic and psychic dispositions. Both of the key features of Yolmo echoes – reverberation and illusion – thus pattern what a recently deceased person perceives. The nature of a person's rebirth, in turn, is profoundly conditioned by the way in which that person lived in previous lives. In fact, much of Mheme's talk with me seemed to be concerned with what had happened while he was alive, and, by implication, what might happen when he dies – how, in effect, his life might echo in his death. Such musings, along with the way in which he went about his life, led me to conclude that his world was very much shadowed by an anticipatory consciousness; his thoughts and actions were geared toward anticipating and preparing for the future and, in particular, for his death. "This is work for later, not for now. This is work for the time of dying," he once told Norbu and me, referring to the religious texts he read daily in order to augment his spiritual merit and so increase the chances of a good fate after dying: "One reads as much as one can. If one reads more, one reaches heaven." And yet despite all his preparations, all his spiritual practices, and all his efforts to develop a spiritually pure heart, he still feared what might happen immensely.

In our conversations, Mheme's words often quietly designated him as a spiritual teacher of sorts. I think such a role made a lot of sense to him while talking with us, given that many Yolmo wa knew him foremost as a lama, as "one who knows," and given that one of the main forms of biographical representation known to him were the *nam-thar* or "full liberation [stories]" of Tibetan Buddhist lore, in which the spiritual development and fruition of a spiritually great person's life is portrayed in writing with the intent that the portrait will serve as a supreme example for others also seeking liberation.[12] While Mheme never said that his life story would in fact be like a *nam-thar*, I do believe he sincerely wanted to teach us and others something, and much of what he conveyed to us, about his life or life in general, could indeed be heard as a primer on meritorious ways to live a life, with his words and deeds exemplifying, perhaps, a good life in modern, spiritually flawed times. Yet what his next life might entail, where and in what sentient form he might be reborn, and what might happen when he met up with the Lord of Dharma after dying were unknowns that troubled him a great deal. At the same time, Mheme, I believe, was also trying then to think of death, his death in particular, in terms that did not involve the complete loss of the "I" known to him, or the end of life in a world of familiarity and loved ones from which he did not wish to part. To die, he therefore held, did not entail a complete annihilation but rather meant a re-becoming, another echo, or, more prosaically, a "move" into a new life.

People Will Say

Mheme knew well that anyone who might have the occasion and skills to look perceptively at his life story would also generate a sense that "he was [like] this," and he clearly sensed that the contents of any account of his life would affect his family's reputation once it was published and people had a chance to read or hear or talk about it. Such an awareness is a terrifically important one among many Yolmo wa, for one's *mhin* or "name" is forever tied up with how one (and one's family) acts in life and what people say about those actions.

"People talk," Yolmo friends have often told me. They talk, in either critical or laudatory tones, about the "work" one does, good or bad, and of how well one talks or performs certain actions. Many activities that Yolmo wa engage in, or think of engaging in, therefore have an intersubjective air (and ear) to them from the start – subjective consciousness often implies an awareness of the consciousnesses of others – for there is always the chance that others will comment on those activities, sometimes in quite critical terms. Such *gyap-tam* or "back-talk," which quickly spreads from household to household, does not just apply to oneself, but to a person's entire family. If a person acts in what others consider a shameful or sinful manner, it can "cut the nose" of other family members, causing them to lose face, as it were, and find themselves to be similarly disgraced. Good talk also regularly occurs, but it is the gossip that seems to spread most quickly. Something of the anticipatory, consequential logic of karmic principles resounds in both forms of commentaries, for the moral implications of one's actions can echo in what others later say about those actions: bad actions inevitably incur critical talk, the cultural logic goes, while good actions result in praise.

Such talk can have powerful consequences. Along with leading one to feel ashamed or shy around others, and therefore hesitant to show one's face in public arenas, a person can lose the respect of others, who will then be reluctant to associate with or marry into that person's family. It therefore becomes crucial for children to maintain the reputations and good names of their parents, and thus to "save" or "hold" their noses. People say that sons need to work well, marry someone from a good family, and hopefully "do something with their lives," as Mheme put it once, while daughters need to be known as skillful, hospitable, chaste women. Many try to lead morally good lives, and encourage or insist that other family members do so as well, in part to gain the respect of others and avoid any "cutting" talk.

Ghang Lama's family, respected by other Yolmo wa, has so far been free of the scabrous talk that has fallen on a few families. And while he and his family are, like other Yolmo families, forever worried about the possibility of such gossip, the old man appeared confident in what others might say or know about him, and he approached our conversations with a certain degree of comfort and candidness. It struck me that he thought his words and actions (and candidness) would bear out that he was, in fact, a good man, and he tried to convey as much when talking with us. "I say that me and my sons are very good," he asserted on one occasion. The phrase "I say that..." (*Ngai mai...*) characterized well his stance in many of our exchanges, for his words had the effect, usually indirectly, of "saying" what he and his sons were like: namely, good people who faced a lot of hardships but who continued to practice dharma and act in morally good ways.

What troubled him more, apparently, was how much prestige he and his family might carry through the years. Ultimately, this was a question of what others might say about him and his family, especially if his sons or grandsons acted or failed to act in certain ways, as he noted on several occasions:

Now, afterwards, some [of my family] are that way, others are that way [they live in different places]. Now there is a worry about what they are doing, whether they are fighting with people. If something happens, people will say he's so-and-so's son, so-and-so's grandson. With this, won't there be sorrow, won't there be worry?

Such eventualities, good or bad, could be traced back to Mheme's life and character, for Yolmo wa commonly understand that the moral consequences of a person's actions can eventually affect that person's children or grandchildren, such that a son's violent or drunken demeanour, for example, can indicate wrongdoings or spiritual failings on the part of that man's father. Mheme understood that a bad son or grandson can result from a bad father or grandfather, and he worried over the possibility that the demise of his family might indicate, to some, moral flaws on his part.

Faced with these potential legacies, Mheme seemed to sense that the life story could effect a good echo, and so help to shore up the genealogy of his family's name. Much was riding, in short, on what people might say about the life and actions of this hard-working man. His afterlife will correspond in many ways to his afterimage. That afterimage will emerge, in part, from how others speak of him. For my part, any words I might write about his life and circulate among others could very well feed into such back-talk in as yet undetermined ways. At the least, I find I need to write well of Mheme's life, to say that he was a good man, which, I should say for the record, is an easy, straightforward thing to do, since, like his children and grandchildren, he is, in fact, a good and virtuous man, without significant sins or moral failings to speak of.

The Poor Man

"He was a good man. But he's dead." As was often the case when we spoke, Mheme anticipated what might occur after his death and how his life might echo in his afterlife. In his estimation, one that closely accorded with what many Yolmo wa think about the implications of acts-in-time, his reputation and social identity will be defined even more by what others say about him once he passes from his body and so can no longer speak or act on his own. His appreciation of the lasting legacy of people's talk, and of how people can be remembered in death, was evident in how he described his mother and father to us when asked what they were like:

> My father was a hard man. He was hard. People said he was a hard man, but his heart was good. People also said that he was a good man, my father.... All the Tamang people [another ethnic group who lived in the same region] were saying that she [my mother] was a very good woman. They said this because she would cook food for them.

In characterizing people who have died, he related what others have said about them. Voices again persist beyond a body's life. Mheme expected people to talk about him as well after he died. Although it remains to be seen how others will speak of him and whether that talk will maintain the good name of his parents, he did seem to anticipate what they might say.

"How will people remember your life after you die?" Norbu and I once asked him.

"Even today villagers remember me," he answered. "They say, 'Don't stay in Kathmandu, come to the village.' For good people, people will always speak good of them. For bad people, people will always say bad things of them."

"After you die, do you think people will say good [things] about you?"

"I think they will. Because I have never done bad to anyone, never ruined anyone, never talked rudely to anyone. Everyone says I am a straight lama [*theka lama*]. The Tamangs say I am a straight lama, even today."

In effects similar to the cause, people speak good of good people and bad of bad; because of his actions, people will continue to say that Mheme is "straight" – upright, honest, direct. Yet, for Mheme at least, when it comes to talking about a recently deceased person, the import of such words does not simply shape that person's "name" or reputation. As with so many other kinds of talk among Yolmo wa, such as curses and the mantras of lamas and shamans, this kind of eulogistic, postmortem talk entails a physical force that can have powerfully real consequences in the world. As Mheme explained it, what people say about a person after he or she dies influences where that person is reborn, for the gods listen to and heed such talk, which can then affect one's fate. "After people die," he told us, "if the people talk good about the person, then he reaches heaven, because the gods also hear the people talking." He then pointed at the tape recorder and said, "This thing picks [up] when we talk. Similarly, the god picks [up] when people talk about us. It's like that, above."

On another occasion, with the tape recorder rolling, Nogapu and I asked him where a person's soul travels to once it separates from the body in death:

> If people did good things, then the soul will go to a good place. If people did bad things, the soul will go to a bad place. If people do really good, then the Buddha will take them. If they've done sins, then they'll be taken down to hell. If they've done good, performing good rites [*pūjā*], talking well of others, then they'll go to heaven. That is our thinking.... If someone is bad – Ah!, and the people say "He should die, because he's bad!" – then he reaches hell, because many people are saying that about him. If someone is good, people will say good things, and then he reaches heaven.

"By oneself it's not enough," Mheme told us, implying that a person cannot reach "heaven" by his or her efforts alone. Though a person travels alone and friendless in the death-betweens, others need to help from a distance. As with the vocalizations of grief that can disturb a person's death if too intense, the voicings of others can, for Mheme, powerfully influence the nature of one's journey and existence after death. The lamas who perform the funeral rites need to guide the soul toward a good "way," and the deceased's family and friends (and enemies even) have to act and speak on the dead person's behalf. Death and the fate of the deceased are imminently social affairs. There are, in fact, several activities that people can undertake on behalf of a dead person in the weeks following a death. Along with performing the funeral rites well, mourners can light candles to help illuminate "the way" after death; they can accept food distributed in the deceased's name; and they can participate in the group chorusing of prayers, known collectively as *mani*, that occur at various times in the ritual process; the prayers and the wealth distributed increase the deceased's store of karmic "merit" (*ghewa*) and so increase the chances of a good rebirth. Mheme also noted that it is important for people to speak well and compassionately of the deceased: "We need to say '*nyingjwa*' to the person who is dying, even if he's our enemy."

Nyingjwa, or *snying-brtse-ba* in Tibetan, literally means "compassioned one" – one, that is, who is receiving, or deserves to receive, *nying je* or "compassion" from others. In contexts such as these, however, its pragmatic import can perhaps be best heard in translation as "loved one," or "poor, unfortunate one." As such, the phrase, often used when speaking of deceased loved ones or acquaintances, designates the respectful compassion one feels for a suffering or dying person. "It means he's a good man," Nogapu said when asked what the word meant. The old man continued:

> We need to do some *mani* [prayers], and pray to the gods – we need to do this. We shouldn't cry. Everyone needs to die. Our enemies also need to die. If we say "loved one" [*nyingjwa*] to our enemy when he's dying, he can get the nice place. If everyone says, "He's a bad person," then he goes down, down. If one or two people say he's good, then it helps a bit. If everyone says he's bad, then the gods also believe this. If people say he's a very good person and everyone says, "He's dead," then he can go to the Buddha. If one person tries to pick up a heavy stone, it won't rise. But if many people try to pick it up, it can be lifted. It's the same with saying *mani*.

There was a lot on the line for Mheme when it came to the voicings of others. What people say about him after his death, he understood, and the extent to which they collectively voice *mani* prayers, will help to determine the nature of his rebirth. He seemed to anticipate that any writings about him would contribute to such a judgment. He mused, for instance, that people reading certain aspects of his life story, such as his sufferings and his dharmic career, might voice the mournful, *nyingjwa*-like statement that, "He was a good man. But he's dead." Notice how these words closely echoed his observation, expressed a month later and noted above, that "If people say he's a very good person and everyone says, 'He's dead,' then he can go to the Buddha." His words anticipated the mourning to come, as well as how an account of his life might help to shape any laments voiced on his behalf.

One reason Mheme invested in the recording of his life, in short, was to convey that he was an important, morally good person, and so effect good talk about himself before and after he died. Like the many texts he read daily in preparing for death, this, too, was "work for later." "A good read" might prompt people to speak compassionately about him; divine beings would ultimately be listening. As it is, the presumed consequences of such talk lead me to wonder if, and to what effect, the present chain of words will be heard by the gods. Such are an ethnographer's concerns and responsibilities when local realities and interests are taken seriously. For what it is worth, I do not take my responsibilities here lightly, in part because my life has become greatly interwoven with the lives I wish to write about, and certain ethical duties come with those ties. At the same time, through the course of my engagements with Yolmo lives some recesses of my mind seem to have acquired, in rather visceral, preconscious ways, many of the sensibilities toward action, time, and meaning that I have been trying to understand, such that when I put pen to paper the metaphysics of Yolmo lives echo powerfully in the soundings of my own thoughts. One consequence of this is that what, and how, the life history work apparently means for Mheme has been converging at points with what, and how, that work means for me. Another related consequence, one in accord with a logic of karmic echoes, is that I have come to appreciate a wealth of potential long-term "pragmatic effects" resulting from our engagements together, effects that I would not have anticipated before getting involved in such work, given that the inhabitants of my Euro-American world, including its theorists of language, tend to conceive of the significance of acts-in-time in ways quite different than Yolmo wa do. For the record, then, and to help with the burden to come: *nyingjwa*.

Responses

What I have come to gather, then, is that any written accounts of Mheme's life will likely effect diffuse and as yet undetermined remainders/reminders that will work through a complex nexus of local semiotic principles to establish certain absences, presences, identities, and remembrances. Traces of "the old ways," of Yolmo history and culture, of a lama's deeds and sufferings, and of skilful, virtuous ways to live and die might transfer to and remain among others. Particular, and heavily co-authored, understandings of Yolmo engagements with life and death might also echo through texts such as this, much as novel ideas of biographic writing and its worldly (and otherworldly) consequences might resound in the minds of non-Yolmo authors and readers. And yet while it now seems clear that writings about Mheme will instantiate an array of echoes for different readers, it remains to be seen if some of these writings will function in more ghostly ways. For some time, in fact, I have been worried that any meanings invested in writings about him could potentially effect, or be understood as bad, disturbing *bhaja* among some Yolmo wa, including his family members. This is not an easy question to think through, since there are some representations of deceased loved ones, such as photographs, that people usually welcome, and there are others, such as ghosts, that are greatly feared.

The implications of any *bhaja*, whatever its origin, reside largely in the mind of the beholder. But while that message is clear to me, my mind is not any more at peace for it. I feel I can speak well of Ghang Lama, and so help to effect good echoes of his life, however illusory they might ultimately be. I therefore plan to continue to write about that life, and in more direct ways than I have done here. Still, in thinking about what and how this work might mean for Mheme and others, I find myself increasingly entangled within the meanings emerging from that work. I worry about the potential effects of my writings. I am now accountable to a set of lives powerfully geared to the voicings of others. I listen to the tapes. Caught within a particular engagement with time, bracing for a death, I am haunted, at times, by the words of this good man.

NOTES

1. This essay draws from ethnographic research I conducted among Yolmo people in 1988–89, 1997, 1998, and 2000. The most recent field studies were supported by grants from the American Philosophical Society, the Howard Foundation, the Guggenheim Foundation, and Sarah Lawrence College. Special thanks to Mheme Lama, Lhatul Lama, Norbu Yolmo, Nogapu Prakash Sherpa, Pramod Yolmo, Binod Yolmo, Temba D. Yolmo, and Karma Gyaltsen Yolmo for their generous help on this project.

2. The first two words of Mheme's quoted utterance, *Shyi mandi...*, were in the Yolmo language, followed, after a brief pause, with the remaining words all in Nepali (*...mareko hoina. Sareko ho*), as though the inequation noted by the utterance ("Dying does not mean dying") prompted or necessitated a transfer from one language to another.

3. Ruth Behar, *The Vulnerable Observer: Anthropology that Breaks Your Heart* (Boston: Beacon Press, 1996), 42.

4. In general, then, conversations with Norbu present were conducted in Nepali, while those with Nogapu as translator were conducted in Yolmo. I usually spoke to Mheme in Nepali, both during our formal interviews and during my visits alone to his home.

5. H.A. Jäschke, *A Tibetan-English Dictionary* (Delhi: Motilal Banarsidass Publishers, 1995 [1881]), 138, 380.

6. Jäschke notes that *brag-cha* can also stand figuratively "for something insubstantial, shadowy, not existing," 380.

7. Robert Thurman, *The Tibetan Book of the Dead: Liberation Through Understanding in the Between* (New York: Thorsons, 1994), 185–86.

8. Thurman, 185-86.

9. Thurman, 111.

10. Thurman, 112, 114, 167.

11. Garma Chen-Chi Chang, *The Hundred Thousand Songs of Milarepa*, 2 vols. (Boulder and London: Shambala, 1977), 511.

12. See, for instance, Janet Gyatso, *Apparitions of the Self: The Secret Autobiographies of a Tibetan Visionary* (Princeton: Princeton University Press, 1997), 6, 103.

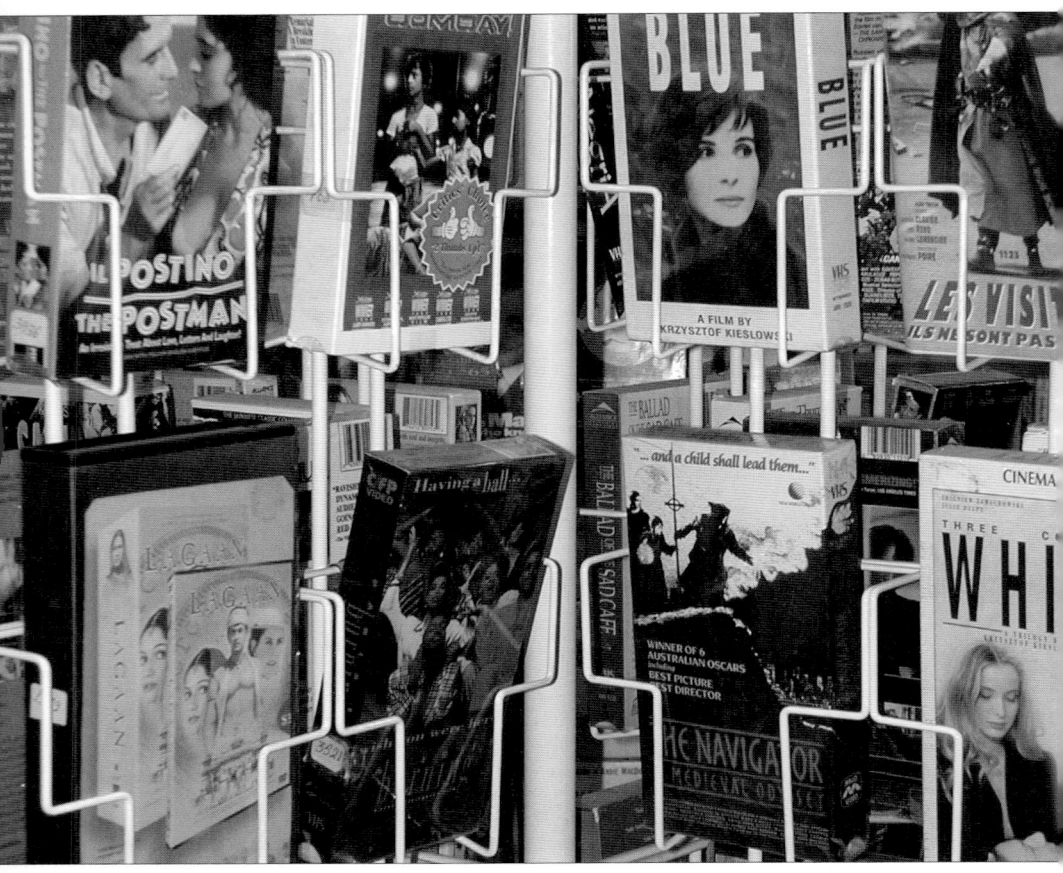

Don Simmons
2003

Aural Cultures: Artists' Pages and CD

Jim Drobnick

Sounds resonate in nearly every social activity – from symphonic concerts and ritual chants to cacophonous revelries and respectful silences. These acoustic situations do more than reflect cultural sensibility, they create it as a living presence. Engaging the body, experience, and the rhythm of relations, sound can merge individuals into larger collectivities. Yet not all sounds are culturally sanctioned. Embarrassing, neglected, or prohibited aural events are as revealing of cultural preoccupations as are mainstream musical trends. Other sonic phenomena bear a radical potential to disrupt conventions of listening and audio production. If the ways in which sound can manifest or transmit cultural values and identities are numerous, the converse is also valid; audioworks by artists and others can interrogate the politics of harmony, orchestrate asocial bodily and environmental noises, and construct alternative communities.

Complementing the essays in this book are a series of artworks and an accompanying CD that also negotiate the domains of art, sound, and culture. Artworks can be considered theory in condensed, experiential form, and the projects featured here provide a variety of ways in which imagery, language, and sound can dialectically interact. There are intimate connections between the artists' projects featured in the pages of the book and the soundtracks on the CD; the visual and the audible commingle and play off each other. Despite the diversity of the works, there are many points of similarity. Listening, as much as the production of sounds, is a cultural activity, one that changes with time, location, community, and intention. Sound is a preeminent means by which to expose as well as bridge cultural and geographical difference, especially when travelling and emigration are foregrounded. Strategies of plundering, mimicry, and translocation implicitly raise ethical issues that defy simple resolutions, yet effectively utilize the malleability of sound. And the number of works that employ collage, overlays, juxtapositions, and other means of fusing incongruous sonic materials point to sound's heterogeneous and endlessly recombinant potential.

A few of the artists' projects exist purely in the pages of the book.[1] Christian Marclay's *Snapshots* is an ongoing series emerging from the artist's travels in New York and cities around the world since the 1980s. His camera captures evocations of music in serendipitous encounters with pedestrians, sidewalk accumulations, architectural details, store signage, and other banal features in the urban landscape. In these photos, sonic references permeate the activities and spaces of everyday life, often in humorous or incongruous ways. Potential instruments abound, musical motifs erupt almost anywhere, and sound materializes in a compelling variety of forms. Elevated decibel levels are unavoidable in the contemporary metropolis – indeed, are one of its defining characteristics – and the acoustic situations Marclay photographs during his flâneries demonstrate the capacity of the visual, built environment to incorporate its own density of musical (and noisome) elements.

By titling his piece *Silence* (2001/03), Daniel Olson could be referring to John Cage or providing a wry antithesis to the projects featured elsewhere in *Aural Cultures*. The blank pages and singular line of text, however, direct attention away from a formal or theoretical notion of silence to one that is implicated in the exercise of power and the enjoyment of personal liberty. The text, heard in countless American detective shows and cop films, is from the Miranda warning that must be read to suspects as they are taken into custody, advising them of their constitutional rights. Olson's choice of micrographic

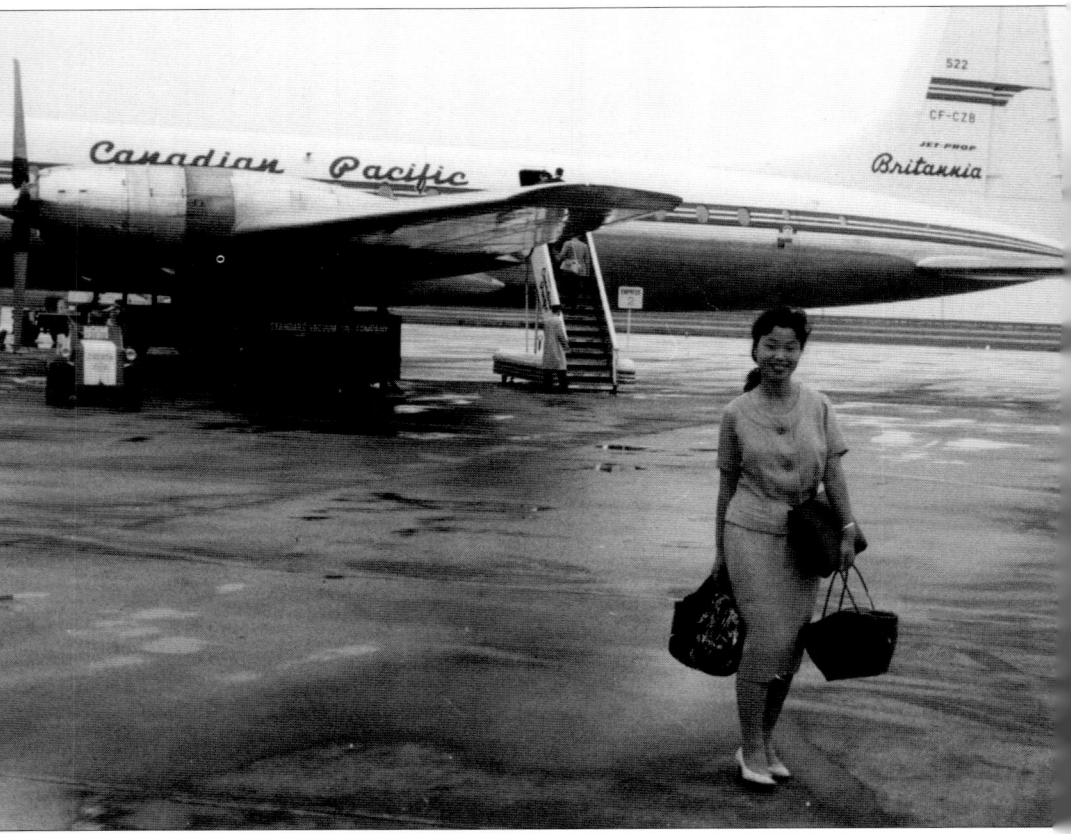

Claude deForest
Yoshiko deForest boarding plane at Haneda Airport, Tokyo, August 25, 1960
Silver gelatin print
Courtesy Kevin Ei-ichi deForest

type makes the words seem barely present, the equivalent of a whisper; yet the real-life context in which this sentence is usually voiced can induce grave, life-transforming consequences. Beyond protecting oneself against self-incrimination, silence may be allied with other rights that are less well-defined though often earnestly championed: freedom from advertising come-ons, relief from noise pollution, or the ability to shut out propagandistic messages. Olson's bookwork poses silence as an open-ended problematic – one in which the rights of the individual and the power of the state engender continual debate.

Via Caruso, by Raymond Gervais, examines the crossing of sensorial divisions that occurred in an actual meeting of two unique individuals: opera's preeminent vocalist, Enrico Caruso, and Helen Keller, the intrepid champion for the deaf and mute. Their coming together for a brief historical moment creates for the artist a particularly intriguing conundrum in which the voice and the body, listening and sensation, redefine each other. For Keller, hearing is a sense that extends beyond the ear and into the fingers and hand; for Caruso, the expressivity of his singing is conveyed solely by the throbbing of his throat. In both cases, sound and its appreciation are dislocated from the organs they are typically associated with, the mouth and ear, and dispersed to the sensitivity of the entire body.

Martin Kersels accentuates the bodily consciousness that is involved in acts of hearing and sound production. In several of his works, sound is intimately connected to the corporeal, especially as a force that can be both the cause and effect of intense emotional reactions. Yelling and anger are prominent in *Loud House* (1998). The artist's footfalls, shown on a rooftop monitor, send a clamorous thunder through a four-metre-high corrugated metal shed, filling the gallery space with an overwhelming din. *Objects of the Dealer* (1995/2002) focuses on the aggravating qualities of sound as trip-switches activate a cacophony of electronic beeps and buzzes whenever a piece of office equipment is used. The fate of the furniture in *Tumble Room* (2000) is even more devastating. Situated inside a revolving, sixteen-foot-diameter ring, the objects noisily disintegrate into unidentifiable rubble. *Brown Sound Kit* (1994) is perhaps the work with the most notorious implications. Originally designed by Nazi scientists and used as a technique to control student protesters by the French military in 1968, the apparatus emits low-frequency sound waves intended to affect the body's internal organs and induce incontinence.[2] Kersels thankfully displays his home-made version of it unplugged, but it nevertheless resonates with the capacity of the state to weaponize sound and exploit the body's vulnerabilities.

On the CD are fifteen audio works by thirteen artists. Su-Mei Tse's *Echo* (2003) positions musical conventions against the sonic features of the landscape. A video projection shows the artist playing a cello, poised on the edge of a canyon, to an expanse of encircling Alpine mountains. Blurring the distinctions between echoes, yodelling traditions, and call-and-response song patterns, the simple melodic phrase and its gentle answering resonates as a contemplation on culture's relationship to its terrain. With her back facing the viewer, and her figure overwhelmed by the idyllic mountainscape, Tse enacts a contemporary version of the sublime. Yet the rhythmic sounds of the cello and its soothing replies by the scenery posit a more sympathetic, even collaborative relationship between human and natural domains. This is especially apparent at points in the soundtrack where the echo answers differently, performing beyond its presumed subservient role to enact its own sense of identity and agency.

The three excerpts of audio projects by Santiago Sierra featured here are sonic readymades that operate on the principle of physical and conceptual transposition. In *Two Maraca Players* (2002), the artist hired a pair of blind men to perform in an art gallery, giving them a better wage than they would have earned begging on the streets of Mexico City. The ethical conflict raised here effectively disturbs the ideology of artistic autonomy, as viewers are confronted with the economic underpinnings of "pure" aesthetic experience. The transitional moment of New Year's Eve, recorded in Culiacán, the capital of Sinaloa state in Mexico, is the setting for *Shots* (2003). Amidst a background of music and playing children, the celebration includes bursts from handguns, rifles, and other assault weapons. When faint, the crackling noises sound like fireworks or distant thunder, but when the guns click and recoil next to the microphone, not to mention when

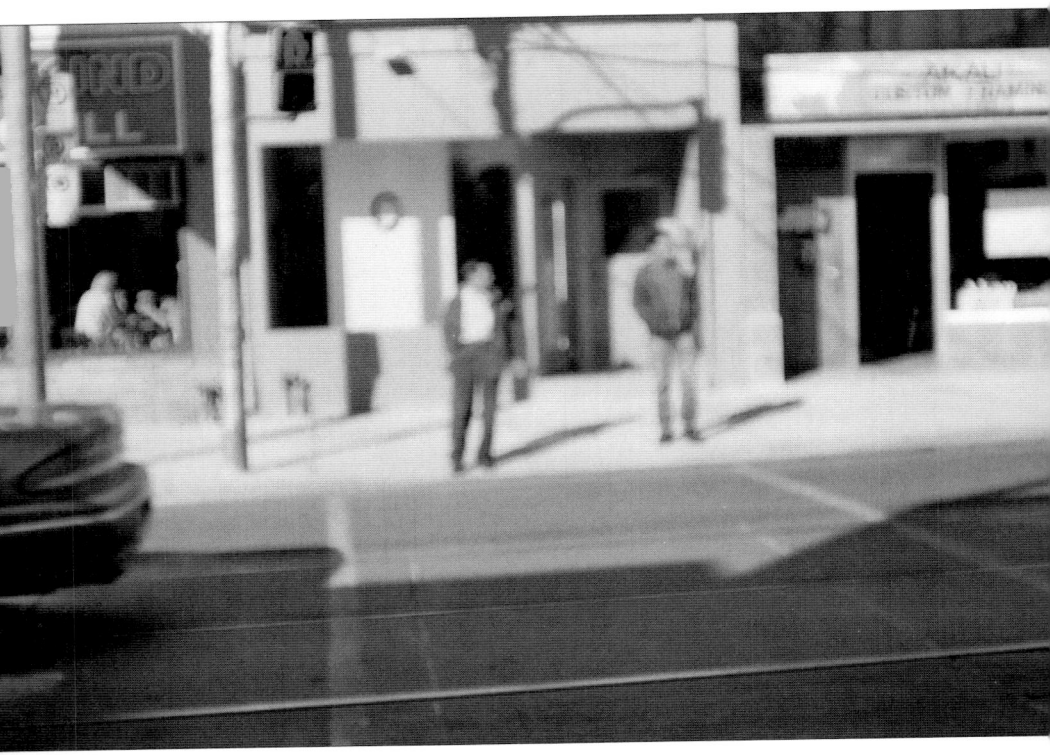

Eimer Birkbeck
2003

car alarms are set off and ambulance sirens wail, the sounds of celebration are disturbingly indistinguishable from war. *The Displacement of a Cacerolada* (2002) relocates the clamorous protests (*caceroladas*) of demonstrating Argentinians to the origins of their distress – Western capitals that set injurious global monetary policies. Furious at the peso's devaluation and resultant bank closures, citizens raucously banged on pots, pans, and the banks' corrugated metal facades. Sierra recorded some of these actions, burned them onto several thousand CDs, and then made the dissonance available for broadcast in cities such as New York, London, and Geneva, thus potentially disturbing the peace of financiers typically inattentive to the adverse consequences of their directives.[3] His installation, *Space Closed by Corrugated Metal* (2002), enclosed the Lisson Gallery and likewise implicitly invited Londoners to activate the noise potential of the barrier and to affiliate themselves with Argentinians both politically and sonically.

Lewis Kaye's *Echo Before, Between, and After* (2003) inverts the practice of listening by attending to the reverberations of the audience instead of the virtuosity of performers. Musical events, besides being occasions for sonorous experiences, are also social occasions where individuals connect, bond, and form a community. "Echo" in Kaye's title refers to a concert by the Echo Women's Choir, and "before, between, and after" pertains to his taping of the audience during their gathering, intermission, and exit. What is usually considered background commotion becomes an immersive ocean of sound as the murmurings, laughter, applause, announcements, and shuffling create an ambient composition with multiple affective registers.

The soundtrack from Shirin Neshat's video installation *Soliloquy* (1999) presents a cross-cultural meditation on exilic experience and identity. Composed and arranged by Sussan Deyhim, it features Koranic recitations, choruses of Kurdish men and children, Tibetan ritual music, Catholic chants, haunting cellos, and shortwave radio conversations from Syria and Turkey, as well as Deyhim's own sublime vocalizations. *Soliloquy* reflects the postmodern dilemma of conflicting cultural allegiances, and the challenges inherent in resolving the profound complexities that accrue when individuals migrate. The photographs and the soundtrack reveal some of the unexpected sonorities that emerge as global expanses, religious differences, and cultural variations are brought into tension. Given the extreme polarization and apparent incompatibility of East and West, Christianity and Islam, throughout history and especially in recent times, *Soliloquy* brings a focus upon the personal in the negotiation of these greater collectivities and hints at the emotional and spiritual depths of such a task.

Susan Hiller's juxtaposition of babble and personal narrative conveys testimonies that exist on the edge of believability. *Excerpts from the Witness Archive* (2000/03) is a collage of confessional stories about UFO encounters and inexplicable phenomena. Drawn from the Internet and constituting her audio installation *Witness*, these voices describe incidents that may generate incredulity on a singular basis, but when taken as a whole compel a more sympathetic response. The dreamlike visions sampled here, from Russia, England, Africa, Brazil, China, and Saudi Arabia, emerge from and recede into babble.[4] The excerpts hint at a community of individuals dispersed around the globe who, although varying greatly in cultural background and belief systems, have become linked through the similarity of their uncanny experiences.

The ability of cinematic soundtracks to evoke affect and exercise control over the mood of the audience figures prominently in Don Simmons's *Falling Apart/Briser* (2003). Culling samples from more than a dozen international films made in Europe, Asia, South America, Africa, Australia, and northern Canada, as well as Hollywood, the collage is an inventory of heightened emotional states that are often unconsciously incorporated into our psyche. The *briser* or "breaking" in the title refers to what the artist calls the nostalgia of a beautiful breakdown, and is especially evident in the snippets of untranslated dialogue conveying sadness, loss, isolation, angst, and mental unrest. The representation of sentiment in the media is often compromised by gender stereotyping (sobbings heard throughout self-consciously reprise the formula "woman = feeling"), yet the piece also offers listeners the chance to discern subtle cultural variations in the registering and expressing of emotions.

In Claire Savoie's *Mon cœur* (2000), a knock on a door initiates a series of acoustically vivid domestic activities. Iconic household sounds – lighting a match, opening a drawer, shuffling cards, sharpening a knife, blowing bubbles – link together to sketch a hyperactive, absurdist narrative. Some noises hint at a romantic encounter (the popping cork popping and clink of glasses), but overall the crashes, jingles, clattering, and buzzes render into an accelerated, comedic form the incongruous events of a day. As a chaotic inventory of sounds, *Mon cœur* challenges listeners to configure a cogent rationale; as a sonic *tranche de vie*, it eavesdrops on an apartment's interior and the discordant quirks of everyday life.

In Kim Sooja's *A Letter From New York* (2001), sounds from opposite ends of the global and emotional spectrum merge and reverberate. The sirens and horns of fire engines, ambulances, and police cars clearly signal a crisis, but when mixed with the whoosh of jetliner engines, a connection to the calamitous events of 2001 is unmistakable. Intervening into this state of emergency is the potential for serenity and calm transcendence. The trance-inducing chanting of Tibetan monks gradually intensifies, eventually overcoming the wails and swooping planes. The healing affects of the chant, however, are not solely a unilateral response to New York's catastrophe; Tibet suffers its own crisis, and the sirens reflexively render it an insistent presence in Western consciousness. Two other audio installations by the artist incorporate chanting. *Mandala* (2002) is a radiantly-hued jukebox outfitted with mirrored tesserae and plastic ornamentation. Its glistening circular form recalls the tail-finned cars and sock hops of 1950s America, but its soundtrack by Tibetan monks defies the expectation of popular tunes. Seemingly built to facilitate mandala contemplation for Westerners obsessed with flashy materialism and escapist entertainment, it also provides a sacred antidote. Mirrors are also integral to *A Mirror Woman* (2002), in which brightly coloured Korean bedcovers, hung like laundry, multiply in the reflections to surround the viewer. The chants, wafting through the space along with a gentle breeze, create an ambiance where sleeping, dreaming, and meditation are at once everyday acts and transcendental practices.

Ann Hamilton's *speaking the hand's pace* (2003) focuses upon the cultural practices of education – in particular, the learning of spelling and writing evident in pioneer-era copybooks. Visiting the Society for the Preservation of New England Antiquities, the artist was impressed by the multitude of copybooks still extant in their collection and the untold hours of labour the handwriting rehearsals represented. Collaborating with an expert calligrapher who describes and demonstrates the precise strokes of the methodical techniques instilled into generations of early American students, Hamilton's work revisits what is nearly, in the electronic age, an archaic form of language production and communication. The acts of listening, vocalizing, writing, and reading are fused as the calligrapher's softly-spoken directions are echoed and, one imagines, gestured by the rest of the group. The tender, communal affect evident in the audio contrasts strikingly with

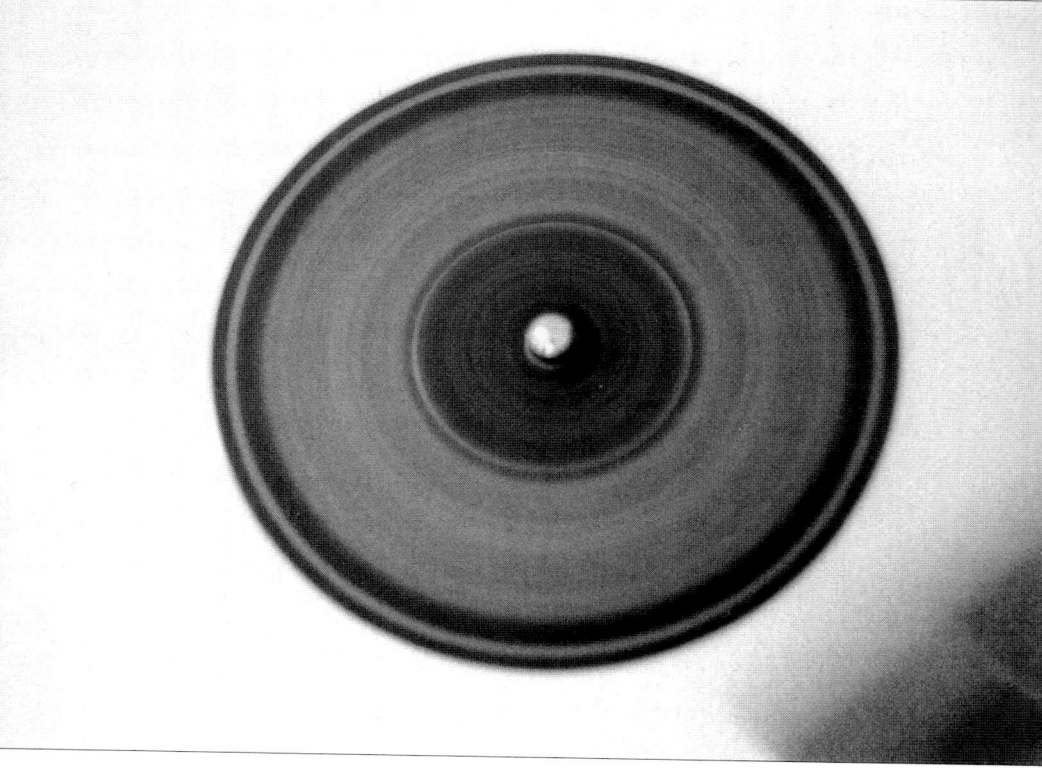

Dave Dyment
Photo of turntable playing The Beatles' *A Day in the Life* with the shutter left open for the length of the song
2003

the strict discipline usually associated with nineteenth-century pedagogy, and the skillful lettering hints at language's intimate connection to the body, physical training, and artistic appreciation.

Kevin Ei-ichi deForest's *Mom Dub* (2003) originates in his newlywed mother's journey from her birthplace, Japan, to a new home in Canada in 1960. Her narrative recounts the physical stress of the voyage and the mixed emotions triggered by the dislocation. Dubbed onto the instrumental version of a Japanese hit from that era, her at times inaudible story finds a sonic correlative, for the song too crossed the Pacific, eventually appearing on the American charts. DeForest's adoption of a reggae musical strategy merges the popular with the personal, juxtaposing the alienation of travel against the pleasures of a hit song.

The three versions of *Call to Art* (2001) included here, by Komar and Melamid in collaboration with composer William McClelland, polyphonically render the word "art" in an assortment of languages by a twenty-one person choir. Extending an otherwise succinct word into reverent, mellifluous invitations, the calls echo the appeals to prayer that exist in many faiths, such as muezzins summoning Muslim believers from minarets or church bells announcing Christian liturgies. The artists draw upon the history of sacred aspirations channelled through aesthetic media and irreverently propose that art serve as the next true religion. Avoiding any particular ecumenical or sectarian adherence, the sonorous harmonies of the calls engage with art's legendary salvific and therapeutic powers – those abilities to heal, inspire, and transform.[5]

Lacrimosa (2003), by Eimer Birkbeck, sonically documents three months of travelling through the streets, markets, and diverse neighborhoods of Toronto. Her audible map records the multiple, overlapping soundscapes of the urban environment as people work, play, shop, relax, eat, commute, play music, chat, and otherwise engage in a multitude of daily activities. Life in the city is experienced as an aural kaleidoscope with unpredictable superimpositions and cultural cross-fertilizations. The combination of rumbling trains, crackling footsteps, fragmented conversations, poignant melodies, and quotidian events is here intensified and made into a resonant portrait of a dynamic metropolis.

The final track, Dave Dyment's *24 Hours (A Day in the Life)* (2003), takes the title of the Beatles classic literally. Electronically stretching each second 284 times, the song is slowed down to last an entire day. The approximately five minutes of sound here, representing a moment from the concluding orchestral crescendo, matches the song's original length but the computer processing has thinned out its melody to an unrecognizable, monotonous drone. Just as the *Sgt. Pepper's* album crystallized an era of innovative rock, drugs, and "expanded experience," Dyment subjects this pop culture landmark to a conceptually rigorous temporal expansion of its own. As much as the original song collapsed and relativized notions of time and space, giving an epic sense to the protagonist's daily routine, *24 Hours (A Day in the Life)* reduces it back to the everyday mundane – an electronic hum nearly indistinguishable from a domestic appliance or office machine.

NOTES

1. My comments below on the artists' work incorporate ideas from my conversations and correspondence with them over the course of this project.

2. Jennifer Fisher, "Relational Sense: Toward a Haptic Aesthetic," *Parachute* 87 (July, August, September 1997): 9.

3. I am grateful to Cuauhtémoc Medina, the curator of the exhibition in which this work first appeared, for generously facilitating its inclusion here. For more information, see Medina's exhibition guide text, *20 Million Mexicans Can't Be Wrong* (London: South London Gallery, 2002), 2–3. The three audio works excerpted here, along with a fourth, have been released in conjunction with the publication *Santiago Sierra*, ed. Rosa Martinez (n.p.: Ministerio de Asuntos Exteriores, Dirección General de Relaciones Culturales y Científicas, 2003).

4. The original installation featured stories in over thirty languages, alluding to the difficulty of communication in the biblical Tower of Babel. See Susan Hiller, *Witness* (London: Artangel, 2000), and the interview with Hiller at < http://www.abc.net.au/arts/visual/stories/s597706.htm > .

5. *Call to Art* was originally intended to be broadcast from abandoned bell towers. Regarding its exhibition, see Jim Drobnick and Jennifer Fisher, *Museopathy* (Kingston: Agnes Etherington Art Centre/DisplayCult, 2002), 40-43.

NOTES ON CONTRIBUTORS

Philip Auslander is Professor in the School of Literature, Communication, and Culture at the Georgia Institute of Technology, where he teaches Performance Studies and Cultural Studies. His books include *Presence and Resistance: Postmodernism and Cultural Politics in Contemporary American Performance* (1992) and *Liveness: Performance in a Mediatized Culture* (1999).

Robert Bean is an artist, writer, and Associate Professor at the Nova Scotia College of Art and Design. Based in Dartmouth, Nova Scotia, his work has been exhibited and published in Canada, Europe, and New Zealand. He is represented by YHZ Gallery (Halifax).

Eimer Birkbeck is a U.K. photographer, filmmaker, sound, and installation artist. Recent screenings and exhibitions of her work have been held at Dundee Contemporary Arts (Scotland), Gallery Omote-sando (Tokyo), and the Manchester International Short Film Festival.

Jodi Brooks is a Senior Lecturer in the School of Theatre, Film, and Dance, University of New South Wales, Sydney, where she teaches film studies. Her essays have appeared in journals such as *Screen, Art & Text, Screening the Past*, and *Senses of Cinema*, and in a number of edited collections.

Gabor Csepregi is Professor of Philosophy and Vice-President at the Dominican College of Philosophy and Theology. He has written extensively on philosophical anthropology and the philosophy of art. He recently edited a book entitled *Sagesse du corps* (2001). He is Editor-in-Chief of the journal *Science et Esprit*.

Kevin Ei-ichi deForest lives and works in Montreal. He has exhibited in Canada, Europe, and the United States, and recently held a residency at Hallwalls Contemporary Arts Center (Buffalo). He earned degrees from Concordia University and the Rijksakademie van Beeldende Kunsten. His practice also includes critical writing (*Kyozon*, Kamloops Art Gallery) and curating ("Heterosexy," Galerie B-312).

Robert Desjarlais is Assistant Professor of Anthropology at Sarah Lawrence College. He is the author of *Body and Emotion: The Aesthetics of Illness and Healing in the Nepal Himalaya* (1992), *Shelter Blues: Sanity and Selfhood Among the Homeless* (1997), and *Sensory Biographies: Lives and Deaths Among Nepal's Yolmo Buddhists* (2003). He is currently researching processes of dying and death among Yolmo people in Nepal.

Jim Drobnick teaches in the MFA Program at Concordia University and is Senior Editor at *Parachute* art magazine. He has published on performance art, video, dance, and interdisciplinary practices in catalogues and anthologies such as *Crime and Ornament* (2002), *Foodculture* (2000), and journals such as *Performance Research, High Performance*, and *Angelaki*.

Dave Dyment is an artist and writer living in Toronto. His sound performances include a work with twelve turntables for the 7a*11d Performance Art Festival, a twenty-minute live feedback broadcast over CKLN radio, and a live duet with Lee Ranaldo of Sonic Youth. He also records pop music with his long-time collaborator John-Joe Kavanagh.

Daniel Fisher is a Ph.D. candidate in New York University's Department of Anthropology and Program in Culture and Media. During 2004 he will be living in Australia's Northern Territory and Queensland, conducting ethnographic field research on contemporary Aboriginal expressive practices and media. His past work includes a short-form documentary on Brooklyn's Hungry March Band and ethnographic radio research in Andean Peru and Bolivia.

Jennifer Fisher teaches in the Department of Art History and Communication Studies at McGill University. She has held research affiliations at New York University, Cornell University and the National Gallery of Canada. Her writings have appeared in catalogues and anthologies such as *Foodculture* (2000), *Naming a Practice* (1996), and journals such as *Art Journal, Border/Lines, Parachute*, and *Fuse*.

Wes Folkerth is Assistant Professor of English at McGill University and the author of *The Sound of Shakespeare* (2002).

Raymond Gervais is a multidisciplinary artist who has exhibited in Canada, Europe, and the United States. His work has been included in exhibitions such as "Okanada," "Aurora Borealis," and "Broken Music," and the Musée d'art de Joliette organized a retrospective entitled "The Musician's Gaze" in 1999. He has also written extensively on experimental music, jazz, and art, and contributed to radio programs.

Ann Hamilton's site-responsive work incorporates performance, installation, an intense focus on materiality and, increasingly, sound. Based in Columbus, Ohio, she has exhibited at the Venice Biennale, the Carnegie Museum of Art, the Musée d'art contemporain de Montréal, the Musée d'Art Contemporain de Lyon, the Akira Ikeda Gallery, Japan, the Irish Museum of Modern Art, and the Wanås Foundation in Sweden. She is represented by Sean Kelly Gallery (New York).

Susan Hiller's art practice innovatively occupies a wide range of media, from drawing to installation to video. She has participated in such watershed exhibitions as "Inside the Visible" (1996), "Now/Here" (1996), "Out of Actions" (1998), "The Museum as Muse" (1999), and "Live in Your Head" (2000). Her publications include *Thinking About Art* (1996), *After the Freud Museum* (1996), and *Witness* (2000). She is based in London, U.K. and is represented by Gagosian Gallery (New York).

Charles Hirschkind is Assistant Professor of Anthropology at the University of California, Berkeley. His work focuses on the intersections of religious practice, rhetorical traditions, media technologies, and emergent forms of political community in the urban Middle East and North America.

Mary Horlock is a Curator of Contemporary Art at Tate Britain. She curated the Turner Prize exhibition for several years, and currently programs the ArtNow project space. She has curated numerous exhibitions, including solo shows of Anya Gallaccio and Wolfgang Tillmans. She recently completed a monograph on Julian Opie.

David Howes is Professor of Anthropology at Concordia University. He is the co-author (with Constance Classen and Anthony Synnott) of *Aroma: The Cultural History of Smell* (1994), and the editor of *The Varieties of Sensory Experience* (1991) and *Cross-Cultural Consumption: Global Markets, Local Realities* (1996). His most recent book is *Sensual Relations: Engaging the Senses in Culture and Social Theory* (2003).

Lewis Kaye has been involved in sound construction and electronic performance since the late 1980s. Based in Toronto, he designs sound for all sorts of media, including radio, theatre, video installation, and live performance. Sonic collaborations include the live technofunk of PROJECT (with Prasad Bidaye) and real-time sound control for Neoist provocateur Istvan Kantor's Machine Sex Action Group.

Martin Kersels lives and works in Los Angeles. He is one of the founding members of the performance collaborative SHRIMPS and has worked in audio, installation, video, and photography. Recent exhibitions include "Yankee Remix" at Mass MOCA and "L.A. Post Cool" at the San Jose Museum of Art. He teaches at the California Institute of the Arts. He is represented by Deitch Projects (New York).

Kim Sooja is an artist based in New York. Specializing in video, installation, and performance, her work has been exhibited internationally and featured in numerous solo and group shows, such as the Whitney Biennial (2002), "Cities on the Move" (1997–2000), "Traditions/Tensions" (1996), and biennials in Kwangju, São Paulo, Sydney, Istanbul, Lyon, and Venice. She is represented by Peter Blum Gallery (New York and Los Angeles), The Project (New York), and Art & Public (Geneva).

Georgina Kleege is the author of a novel, *Home for the Summer* (1989), and a collection of personal essays about blindness, *Sight Unseen* (1999). She has taught creative writing, literature, and disability studies at the University of Oklahoma and Ohio State University, and is now based in the English Department at the University of California, Berkeley.

A choreographer, director, performer, and scholar, Kanta Kochhar-Lindgren is Assistant Professor of Performance Studies in the Interdisciplinary Arts and Sciences Program at the University of Washington at Bothell. She is currently writing about performance and disability, South Asian diasporic performance, and creativity. Her performance work includes community-based projects on stories about the land and a solo work on performing deafness.

Vitaly Komar and Alexander Melamid are celebrated for the initiation of the SOTS art movement, the Soviet version of Conceptual and Pop Art. They immigrated to the U.S. in 1978 and are currently based in New York. Their work is internationally acclaimed and represented in museum collections worldwide. Publications on their work include Carter Ratcliff, *Komar & Melamid* (1988) and JoAnn Wypijewski, *Painting by Numbers* (1998). William McClelland's compositions have been performed throughout the U.S. and he has performed and produced recordings on the New World and Albany record labels. He has collaborated with Komar and Melamid since 1996.

Richard Leppert is the Samuel Russell Distinguished Professor of Humanities and Morse Alumni Distinguished Teaching Professor at the University of Minnesota. His most recent books include *Art and the Committed Eye* (1996), *The Sight of Sound* (1993), *Music and Image* (1988), and *Music and Society* (co-ed. Susan McClary). In 2002 he published an edition of selected *Essays on Music* by Theodor Adorno. He is currently at work on a book called *Musical Extremes: The Dialectics of Virtuosity*.

A visual artist and experimental music performer, Christian Marclay has utilized a variety of media to explore the connections between sound, art, and its social context. Based in New York, he has performed and shown his work throughout North America, Europe, and Japan. Recent projects include a retrospective at the UCLA Hammer Museum and an exhibition at the Philadelphia Museum of Art. He is represented by Paula Cooper Gallery (New York).

Andra McCartney teaches Sound in Media in the Department of Communication Studies at Concordia University. She creates multimedia soundscapes, websites, CD-ROMs, tapeworks, and performances that evoke the sonic and sociopolitical resonance of places. Her sound projects have been produced by the Canadian Electroacoustic Community (Montreal), Terra Nova (MIT), Musicworks (Toronto), Artemisia Gallery (Chicago), the Canadian Society for Independent Radio Production (Ottawa), and Entartete Kunst (London, ON).

Christof Migone is a multidisciplinary artist and writer. His writings have appeared in journals such as *Musicworks*, *Semiotext(e)*, *Cahiers Folie Culture*, *The Drama Review*, *Angelaki*, and *XCP: Cross-Cultural Poetics*, and the anthologies *Radio Rethink* (1994) and *Site of Sound* (1999). He is the co-editor (with Brandon LaBelle) of *Writing Aloud: The Sonics of Language* (2001).

Shirin Neshat's work in photography, film, and video centres upon the vast cultural differences between her current residence in New York and her nation of birth, Iran. She has been featured in numerous catalogues and exhibitions worldwide, including Documenta (2002), the Carnegie International (1999), and biennials in Venice, Lyon, Kwangju, Johannesburg, Istanbul, and Sydney. She is represented by Barbara Gladstone Gallery (New York).

Daniel Olson is an artist living in Montreal. His work is documented in the catalogue *Small World* (2000), and has been shown at the Art Gallery of Ontario, The Power Plant, Oakville Galleries, Mercer Union, and exhibitions in Europe, South America, and Asia. He is represented by Robert Birch Gallery (Toronto) and Galerie Christiane Chassay (Montreal).

Claire Savoie is a Montreal-based artist working in installation, audio, and video. Her work centres on phenomena that hover on the edge of immateriality. She has shown throughout Canada, as well as in Spain, France, and Sweden, and has appeared recently in the exhibitions "Vital Signs," "Le Ludique," "La Manifestation internationale d'art de Québec," and "Espèces d'espace." She is Professor of Sculpture at the École des arts visuel et médiatiques, Université du Québec à Montréal.

Peter L. Schmunk is Associate Professor of Art History at Wofford College. His current research focuses on the influence of music on the theory and practice of painting during the nineteenth century. He has published essays on the musical interests of Corot and Van Gogh and is editor of *The Arts Entwined: Music and Painting in the Nineteenth Century* (2000).

Santiago Sierra is an artist based in Mexico City. His performances and installations have been featured internationally at venues such as Ikon Gallery, Kunst-Werke, Deitch Projects, P.S.1, Museo Rufino Tamayo, the Irish Museum of Modern Art, Deichtorhallen, and the Museo Nacional Centro de Arte Reina Sofia. He represented Spain at the 2003 Venice Biennale. He is represented by Lisson Gallery (London), Galerie Peter Kilchmann (Zurich), and Galeria Enrique Guerrero (Mexico City).

Don Simmons is a conceptual artist whose works take the form of robotics, electronics, audio, installation, and performance. He has exhibited across Canada and teaches at the Alberta College of Art and Design in the Media Arts and Digital Technologies Department.

Sherry Simon teaches in the Département d'études françaises at Concordia University. She is the author of *Le Trafic des langues* (1994), *Gender in Translation* (1996), and *L'hybridité culturelle* (1999), and the editor of *Culture in Transit* (1995) and (with Paul St-Pierre) *Changing the Terms: Translating in the Post-Colonial Era* (2000). Currently in preparation is *Crossing Town: Montreal in Translation*.

Trained in both music and the visual arts, Su-Mei Tse works in video, photography, sound, and sculpture. Her installation at the 2003 Venice Biennale, *Air Conditioned*, won the Leone d'oro Prize for Best National Pavilion for Luxembourg. She lives and works between Luxembourg and Paris. She is represented by Tim Van Laere Gallery (Antwerp) and beaumontpublic (Luxembourg).

CREDITS

Aural Cultures CD: Curated by Jim Drobnick. Mastering by Paul Dolden. Label image from Susan Hiller's *Witness* (2000); detail of installation view, courtesy the artist. Label design by Associés libres, Montreal. Reproduction services by Duplium Corporation.

Eimer Birkbeck, *Lacrimosa* (2003). Production support: Riccardo Iacono. The artist appreciates support from the Scottish Arts Council and gives special thanks to Christina Battle, Luminous Alexi Manis, Michele Stanley, Roberto Ariganello, Greg Boa, Sebastjan Henrickson, Rachelle Potvin, and Nathan Moles. Produced in conjunction with the Aural Cultures residency at Charles Street Video. Courtesy the artist.

Kevin Ei-ichi deForest, *Mom Dub* (2003). Narration by Yoshiko deForest, Kevin deForest on bass and guitar, Paul Litherland on drums. The artist thanks Paul Litherland and Nelson Henricks for technical assistance. Produced in conjunction with the Aural Cultures residency at Charles Street Video. Courtesy the artist.

Dave Dyment, *24 Hours (A Day in the Life)* (2003). Produced in conjunction with the Aural Cultures residency at Charles Street Video. Courtesy the artist.

Raymond Gervais, *Via Caruso* (1998). Installation view. Photo: E. Eymard. Courtesy the artist.

Ann Hamilton, *speaking the hand's pace* (2003). Sandy Mundy, calligrapher and lead voice. Other voices by Sandy Mundy, Ann Hamilton, Kristine Miller Helm, Kate Joranson, Nikhil Chopra, Madhavi Gore, John Flemming, Emile Flemming. Recording by Maggie Moore. Video stills and audio courtesy the artist and Sean Kelly Gallery, New York.

Susan Hiller, *Excerpts from the Witness Archive* (2000/03). Sound material selected from the audio installation *Witness* (2000). Mixed by Adad Hannah and Jim Drobnick. Audio and images for *Witness*, *Monument*, *Belshazzar's Feast*, and *Psi Girls* courtesy the artist.

Lewis Kaye, *Echo Before, Between, and After* (2003). The artist thanks Mike Whitla for assistance in the source recordings, and Becca Whitla and the vibrant community surrounding the Echo Women's Choir for the opportunity to record their concert on December 7, 2002. Produced in conjunction with the Aural Cultures residency at Charles Street Video. Courtesy the artist.

Martin Kersels, images of *Loud House*, *Brown Sound Kit*, *Objects of the Dealer*, and *Tumble Room* courtesy the artist, ACME, Los Angeles, and Deitch Projects, New York.

Kim Sooja, *A Letter From New York* (2001). © Kim Sooja and Sonic City. Courtesy the artist. View of *A Mirror Woman* courtesy Peter Blum, New York. View of *Mandala* photographed by Blaise Adilon, courtesy Musée d'art contemporain de Lyon.

Komar and Melamid, with William McClelland, *Call to Art* (2001). Performed by the William Appling Singers, New York City, and published by Nattering Nabob Music/BMI, © Komar and Melamid/William McClelland. Courtesy the artists.

Christian Marclay, *Snapshots* (Ongoing series). Courtesy the artist and Paula Cooper Gallery, New York.

Shirin Neshat, *Soliloquy* (1999). Audio portion from 16mm film transferred to video. Vocals, music, and sound design by Sussan Deyhim. © Shirin Neshat and Sussan Deyhim. Courtesy the artist and Barbara Gladstone Gallery, New York. *Soliloquy* production stills photographed by Larry Barns. © Shirin Neshat. Audio and images courtesy the artist and Barbara Gladstone Gallery, New York.

Daniel Olson, *Silence* (2001/03). Courtesy the artist.

Claire Savoie, *Mon coeur* (2000). The artist thanks Pierre Castonguay for technical assistance. Courtesy the artist.

Santiago Sierra, *The Displacement of a Cacerolada* (2002). Excerpt from CD produced by the artist for the exhibition "20 Million Mexicans Can't Be Wrong," at South London Gallery, curated by Cuauhtémoc Medina. Courtesy the artist and Cuauhtémoc Medina. Excerpts from *Shots* (2002/03) and *Two Maraca Players* (2002) courtesy the artist and Galeria Enrique Guerrero, Mexico City. Installation view of *Space Closed by Corrugated Metal* courtesy Lisson Gallery, London.

Don Simmons, *Falling Apart/Briser* (2003). The artist gratefully acknowledges the support of the Canada Council for the Arts, the Alberta College of Art and Design, and EMMEDIA, Calgary. Special thanks to Rod (Stu) Stuart, Tania Sures, Mikiki, Bruce Barber, and Donna Akrey. Produced in conjunction with the Aural Cultures residency at Charles Street Video. Courtesy the artist.

Su-Mei Tse, *Echo* (2003). Excerpt of soundtrack from video projection. The artist thanks Pleix for their collaboration and Fondation Musée d'Art Moderne Grand-Duc Jean (MUDAM). © Su-Mei Tse. Courtesy the artist. Still from video projection courtesy the artist and MUDAM.

Essays in *Aural Cultures* that have appeared elsewhere include: Philip Auslander's "Looking at Records" first appeared in TDR 45:1 (T169) (spring 2001), by permission of MIT Press; Jodi Brooks' essay is a revised version of an article originally titled "'Worrying the Note': Mapping Time in the Gangsta Film," *Screen* 42:4 (winter 2001): 363–381, by permission of Oxford University Press; Robert Desjarlais' text is excerpted from his article of the same name in *Cultural Anthropology* 15:2 (summer 2000): 260–293, by permission of the American Anthropological Association, and also appears in a different form in his *Sensory Biographies: Lives and Deaths among Nepal's Yolmo Buddhists* (Philadelphia: University of Pennsylvania Press, 2003); Jennifer Fisher's essay was published in *Parachute* 94 (April/May/June 1999): 24–31, by permission; Charles Hirschkind's text is excerpted from his article of the same name in *Cultural Anthropology* 16:1 (February 2001): 3–34, by permission of the American Anthropological Association; Mary Horlock's dialogue with Susan Hiller is an expanded and revised version of "An Interview with Susan Hiller" that appeared in Swedish in *Paletten* 245–246, 4/5 (2001): 22–27, by permission; David Howes' essay is excerpted from *Sensual Relations: Engaging the Senses in Culture and Social Theory* (Ann Arbor: University of Michigan Press, 2003), by permission; Georgina Kleege's text is from her book *Sight Unseen* (New Haven: Yale University Press, 1999), by permission; and Richard Leppert's essay is from the anthology *Le Concert et Son Public*, edited by Hans-Erich Boedeker, Patrice Veit, and Michael Werner (Paris: Editions de la Maison des sciences d'homme, 2003), 459–85.

YYZ Books

Susan Kealey: Ordinary
Marvel
Edited by Jennifer Rudder

Why Stoics Box:
Essays on Art and Society
Jeanne Randolph
Edited by Bruce Grenville

Crime and Ornament:
The Arts and Popular
Culture in the Shadow
of Adolph Loos
Edited by Melony Ward
and Bernie Miller

Money, Value, Art:
State Funding, Free
Markets, Big Pictures
Edited by Andrew J.
Paterson and Sally McKay

Plague Years: A Life in
Underground Movies
Mike Hoolboom

Practice Practise Praxis: Serial
Repetition, Organizational
Behaviour, and Strategic
Action in Architecture
Edited by Scott Sørli

Lux: A Decade of Artists'
Film and Video
Edited by Tom Taylor and
Steve Reinke

Foodculture: Tasting
Identities and Geographies
in Art
Edited by Barbara Fischer

Material Matters:
The Art and Culture of
Contemporary Textiles
Edited by Ingrid Bachmann
and Ruth Scheuing

Symbolization and Its
Discontents
Jeanne Randolph

By the Skin of Their
Tongues: Artist Video Scripts
Edited by Steve Reinke and
Nelson Henricks

Theory Rules: Art as
Theory/Theory and Art
Edited by Jody Berland,
Will Straw, and David Tomas

Mirror Machine: Video and
Identity
Edited by Janine Marchessault

Decalog: YYZ 1979–1989
Edited by Barbara Fischer

Struggles with the Image:
Essays in Art Criticism
Philip Monk

Psychoanalysis &
Synchronized Swimming
Jeanne Randolph

For more information visit:
www.yyzartistsoutlet.org

Walter Phillips Gallery Editions

Obsession, Compulsion,
Collection: On Objects,
Display Culture and
Interpretation
Edited by Anthony Kiendl
(forthcoming)

Beyond the Box: Diverging
Curatorial Practices
Edited by Melanie Townsend

The Edge of Everything:
Curating for the Future
Edited by Catherine
Thomas

Arousing Sensation:
A Case Study of Controversy
Surrounding Art and the
Erotic
Edited by Sylvie Gilbert

Private Investigators:
Undercover in Public Space
Essays by Kathryn Walter
and Kyo Maclear

When Pain Strikes
Edited by Bill Burns, Cathy
Busby, and Kim Sawchuk

Naming a Practice:
Curatorial Strategies for the
Future
Edited by Peter White

Questions of Community:
Artists, Audiences, Coalitions
Edited by Daina Augaitis,
Lorne Falke, Sylvie Gilbert,
and Mary Anne Moser

Queues, Rendezvous, Riots:
Questioning the Public in
Art and Architecture
Edited by George Baird and
Mark Lewis

Radio Rethink: Art, Sound
and Transmission
Edited by Daina Augaitis
and Dan Lander

Territories of Difference
Edited by Renee Baert

Frame of Mind: Viewpoints
on Photography in Contem-
porary Canadian Art
Edited by Daina Augaitis

For more information visit:
www.banffcentre.ca/press/
default.asp